STRANGE
BUT TRUE

STRANGE BUT TRUE

Mysteries, Scandals, Crimes,
Exploits and Disasters that
Shocked the World

BLITZ EDITIONS

Copyright © Bookmart Ltd 1992
This book created for Bookmart by Amazon Publishing Ltd

This edition reprinted 1994
Published by Blitz Editions
an imprint of Bookmart Ltd
Registered Number 2372865
Trading as Bookmart Ltd
Desford Road
Enderby
Leicester LE9 5AD

ISBN 1 85605 105 6

Thanks to the Hulton Picture Company and
Mary Evans Picture Library for sourcing pictures.

Printed in the Slovak republic
50868/2

Contents

Strange But True

It is often said that fact is stranger than fiction,
and this book is a graphic and sometimes chilling reminder of just how true
that can be.

The strories in STRANGE BUT TRUE describe a world about us
full of the most extraordinary and unpredictable phenomena. Stories that
prove there is no limit to what people are capable of - no depths to which they
cannot sink, no heights to which thcy cannot risc. Storics describing strange
myths and legends that continue to defy all rational explanation.
Stories to demonstrate that tragedy and disaster can strike from out of the
bluest skies without rhyme or reason,
that happiness can be wrecked in a moment and certainties broken into a
thousand pieces.

STRANGE BUT TRUE is a feast of the bizarre, the horrific,
the scandalous and the unthinkable. Whether it is the mysteries of UFOs or
the tragic secrets of Rock Hudson, whether the disaster of the Space Shuttle
Challenger or the macabre murders of Charles Manson, whether the puzzle of
Tutankhamun's curse or riddle of the Bermuda Triangle,
we see time and again that nothing is as strange,
as unpredictable and as unfathomable as life itself.

MISTAKES
AND
DISASTERS

THE TITANIC
Voyage to Disaster

They dined and danced under the glittering chandeliers ... and then they drowned in the icy North Atlantic. A single iceberg had destroyed for ever the myth of the unsinkable Titanic

She was built as the greatest ship of this or any age. Bigger, mightier, stronger, she was named *Titanic*, and she was unsinkable. The RMS *Titanic* went down on her maiden voyage in 1912, with the loss of over 1500 lives. So arrogant were the builders and operators of the gigantic vessel that they proclaimed: 'God himself could not sink this ship.' God didn't have to - all it took was a mammoth iceberg that buckled and ripped the double-steel, compartmented hull, causing the ice cold waters of the North Atlantic to flood in and sink her in just a matter of hours.

As the band played 'Nearer My God to Thee' and the ship slid below the icy, black waters, her passing seemed to mirror that of the golden age before World War I. Tom Shales, a Washington writer, said: 'The ship was not only a ship, but a time capsule, and it could be

Above: *First Officer Wilde who was on the bridge of the White Star liner when it sank beneath the waves with the loss of all but 705 of its 2227 passengers.*

Opposite: *The 46,000-ton* **Titanic** *is towed from her berth for sea trials prior to her disastrous maiden voyage in April 1912. She cost £4 million - about £100 million by today's value.*

Left: *Bruce Ismay, managing director of the White Star Line, leaves the Customs House in Southampton.*

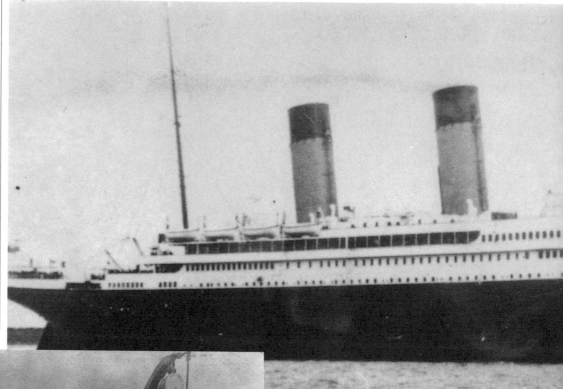

Right: *Four towering funnels indicate the astonishing 900-ft length of the ill-fated giant of the high seas. Her height was the equivalent of an eleven-storey building.*

Below: *Some of the twenty lifeboats on the* **Titanic.** *Many more lives could have been saved if the liner had been equipped with more of them.*

said she took the glittery, self-indulgent golden age with her to the grave.'

But the simple, inescapable fact of the *Titanic* tragedy is that it need never have happened if the White Star Line, her owners, had equipped her with enough lifeboats. They were left off in the utter belief she could not sink.

The *Titanic* began life as the largest moving object on earth in the drawing offices of the great Harland and Wolff shipyards in Belfast, Northern Ireland; she was conceived at a time when trans-Atlantic liner traffic was at its peak between Britain and Europe and the New World. It was to be built for luxury and speed, but not for safety.

Nevertheless, the engineers had come up with a 'revolutionary' design which would keep the ship afloat no matter what maritime accident befell it. The design was a series of watertight compartments, sixteen in all, running the length of the hull. The bulkheads separating them were also supposedly stronger and more efficient than those in use on any other ship, naval or merchant.

The makers boasted that up to two compartments could be flooded without the ship listing seriously. Not only the finest engineers, but the finest shipwrights, carpenters, tradesmen and designers were employed to make her the most luxurious vessel afloat. Everything about her was breathtaking and superlative. She was 900 feet long with four funnels, each 22 feet in diameter. From top to bottom she was the height of an eleven-storey building, and she weighed 46,000 tons. The rudder was as tall as a large mansion; the engines could produce 50,000 horsepower to move the ship at 23 knots; and there was enough electricity to power a small town.

For the first-class passengers there was unparalleled luxury. There was the first swimming pool aboard a ship - a great novelty - and a special crane which loaded and unloaded cars so the mobile millionaire could take his luxury limousine with him on a voyage. They could avail themselves of Arabian-style Turkish baths, a gym, a squash court, a lounge modelled after a room at Versailles, a Parisian cafe and a palm court.

There were sumptuous suites and cabins for 735 first-class passengers and cabins for a further 1650 passengers in second and third classes.

'The Millionaire's Special' had the first-ever swimming pool on board a ship

---

The White Star Line was proud to hype the *Titanic* as the greatest ship ever. Her passenger list for the maiden voyage from Southampton to New York read like a veritable *Who's Who* of the rich and famous of the day: there was the financier Benjamin Guggenheim, for whom the famous art museum was named in New York in a gesture to his philanthropy; Isador Straus, part owner of Macy's department store, the American painter Francis Millet and the man who built the Brooklyn Bridge.

The *Titanic* had cost £4 million to construct - equivalent today to £100 million - and she steamed under British and American flags from Southampton on her maiden voyage on 10 April 1912. On her decks were twenty lifeboats - four more than required under British Board of Trade regulations, but still woefully few for the passengers on board. Sixteen lifeboats, it was later calculated, would hold just one quarter of the passengers and crew aboard.

Survivors from the **Titanic** *wait to be recovered from the choppy waters of the icy North Atlantic. Few were as lucky. Those in the water died of extreme cold in two minutes.*

THE VOYAGE OF DOOM

Five days out at sea, the crew of the *Titanic* reported nothing extraordinary in the bitterly cold weather as the ship ploughed on towards the Grand Banks of Newfoundland. At night on the 14th the sea was glassy calm, but there had been sightings of icebergs in the area. They did not perturb Captain Smith, whose ship sliced through the starry night at 21.5 knots per hour.

Then, in the crow's nest, a lookout suddenly shouted at 11.40pm: 'Iceberg, right ahead!' and accompanied his shout with a warning bell that rang three times. Thirty seconds later the liner and the iceberg met in a collision that jolted the great ship, hurling ice on to the teak decks to the delight of first-class passengers who emerged moments later enthralled by the sight of the chunks of icecap littering them.

They did not know that the collision was, for the majority of them, their death knell. One of the survivors said later: 'So

Above: *American tycoon Isador Straus lost his life in the* **Titanic** *disaster. Part owner of Macy's department store, New York, he was just one of ten equally rich passengers aboard the so-called 'Millionaire's Special'.*

Above right: *Isador's wife Ida, who refused the offer of a place in a lifeboat and instead died in her husband's arms aboard the liner.*

the crash came and it sounded like this to me, like tearing a strip off a piece of calico, nothing more ... Later it grew in intensity ... as though someone had drawn a giant finger along the side of the ship.'

After the impact, first-class passengers laughed in delight at the shattered chunks of iceberg on the decks

The iceberg had risen some 90 feet out of the water and its massive submerged bulk had ripped a huge rent in the starboard section of the vessel, rupturing the watertight compartments in which so much faith had been placed. The behemoth was now taking on water at a phenomenal rate - 16,000 cubic feet of slate grey, cold Atlantic in the first forty minutes alone.

The first five compartments were completely flooded, with water slopping over into compartment 6, then compartment 7, and so on, filling them up one by one until the ship eventually sank.

On the bridge the unthinkable was slowly beginning to come home to Captain Smith, who at first could not believe his ears when his officers told him of the catastrophe taking place below. At almost exactly midnight he ordered the passengers to take to the boats while a message was flashed out that she was sinking.

Many human dramas occurred that have gone into legend; Ida Straus refused the offer of a place in a lifeboat and died in her beloved husband's arms as the liner sank beneath the waves. The chairman of the White Star Line showed no such courage and jumped into a lifeboat, thereafter forever condemned to live a life of disgrace.

Mining tycoon Guggenheim and his valet Victor Giglio dressed in evening clothes and prepared to meet their Maker like gentlemen. Ten millionaires died and valuables, including diamonds valued at £4 million, were consigned to the deep along with their owners.

Confusion reigned on the boat deck, not aided by the fact that the crewmen had never performed a proper boat drill during her sea trials. There were collapsible rafts as well as lifeboats but these were not assembled in time, or were stored in inaccessible places.

As the ship began to list dramatically distress rockets were fired into the darkness, the last faint hopes of a captain

Below: How the news was relayed on the streets of London. The 'unsinkable' ship had met an unthinkable fate.

Bottom: Survivors huddle pitifully on makeshift beds. They had been picked up by the Carpathia which steamed belatedly to the wreck site.

grasping for any salvation for his doomed passengers and crew. He didn't think anyone would see them - but people *did* - the crewmen aboard the passenger liner *California*, which was only nineteen miles away.

But due to incredible blunders the crew misread the distress flares as belonging to another vessel and sat in blissful ignorance in the icefield until way after five the next morning, long after the *Titanic* had slipped to her icy grave. It was later learned that the *California*'s skipper assumed that the rockets had been a false alarm.

The liner California saw the distress flares but interpreted them as a false alarm

---

The greatest tragedy on board that night befell the 670 immigrants in third class, or steerage, who were trapped below decks in doors kept locked by order of the US Immigration Department. By the time they had battered their way to the outside most of the lifeboats had slipped from their davits.

In two hours and thirty-five minutes the *Titanic* was almost at a 90-degree angle in the water, her lights twinkling and refracting on the water, casting an eerie, phosphorescent glow across the smooth sea.

Five minutes later she went under, creating a huge vortex on the surface that dragged down people and debris with it in a giant whirlpool. There was an agonizing hissing and massive air bubbles as the boilers exploded on the ship's slow descent through 13,000 feet of water.

The *Carpathia* was steaming now towards the wreck site and arrived an hour later to pick up the pitifully few survivors. Two thousand two hundred and twenty-seven people were on board the ship when it left Southampton; just 705 survived.

THE UNDERSEA GRAVE

For seventy-three years she lay undisturbed in her watery grave, a testimony to man's folly. The *Titanic*

Left: Shock and horror soon turned to outrage and sympathy...children put money in a collecting box outside London's Mansion House.

Opposite: A cross-section of the Titanic *shows how the iceberg tore through the hull between the foremast and the first funnel.*

Below: A silent throng watches as the Lord Mayor of London arrives at St Paul's Cathedral for the memorial service to the Titanic's *victims.*

became a byword for doomed ventures of heroism, cowardice, excitement and adventure. Historical societies were formed, as were survivors' associations and salvage merchants dreamed of raising her and her spoils within.

It was widely assumed that she would still be in one piece on the ocean floor when in July 1986 American oceanographer Dr Robert Ballard led an undersea team which found her. But, in the eerie, cold light, it was seen that she had broken up into three pieces - crushed by the water pressure on her descent.

In a 1600-metre debris field Ballard found the bow section, buckled under its own weight, embedded 600 metres from the stern section. In the middle was the collapsed remains of the *Titanic's* middle.

In the debris field itself are the artefacts of a lost age; an entire kitchen of copper implements, wine bottles with their corks still in them, coffee cups with the emblem of the White Star Line unfaded through the years, bathtubs, bedsprings, toilets, doorknobs, chandeliers, stoves and ceramic dolls heads that were once owned by little children who are now pensioners or long since dead.

One of the most poignant images his high-tech cameras captured was of a broken lifeboat davit, hanging limply on the edge of the ship, a silent testimony to a night that the world will never forget. A night, in fact, to remember.

KUWAIT OILFIELDS
A Dictator's Revenge

A power-hungry dictator behaving like a latter-day Hitler - but when Saddam Hussein's plans to occupy Kuwait were foiled he revenged himself on the world by unleashing environmental pollution of unimaginable magnitude

I t began as a power-play, a quest for real and imagined respect among the nations of the world who would view him as a modern-day liberator. It ended in total, utter and abject defeat, with 100,000 of his countrymen dead, his nation bombed into pre-industrial bleakness, his factories reduced to ashes and twisted steel.

The Iraqi dictator Saddam Hussein's

desert adventure was but a blip in history - an occupation of his neighbour Kuwait that lasted less than six months, followed by an air and ground war of less than six weeks which put paid to his grand vision as the Arab strong man seeking to find a place in the sun for all his people.

But there is no sun now on Iraq's

Above: *An Iraqi tank guards the entrance to Kuwait's Sheraton Hotel from where Europeans and Americans were rounded up.*

Opposite: *A sea of foul oil washes up on a Persian Gulf beach at the Kuwait-Saudi border. The oil had been released intentionally to hamper Desert Storm operations.*

Left: *On the first day of the invasion, 2 August 1990, Iraqi tanks stream into Kuwait City.*

Above: *Two oil-soaked cormorants on a Saudi beach near the Kuwaiti border. The birds can barely move, victims of the massive, deliberate slick measuring 8 miles by 30 miles.*

Above right: *An American marine surveys the oil-slick damage. He has turned away from a dead cormorant, suffocated by the black tide.*

horizon, or Kuwait's - it is blacked out in the stench and haze of six hundred burning oil wells.

It may be two years or more before the American and British fire-fighting teams have finally conquered each of the blown well-heads. By that time the damage to the planet may be beyond repair.

On the economic front, the Kuwaitis will have seen £100 billion worth of oil go up in smoke, and a further £25 billion worth lost in the desert sands. Nightly, on prime-time TV across the world, viewers have been given a glimpse of hell, where the fires obscure the sun at midday and young children cough their lungs out in the poisoned atmosphere. The orange fireballs roar like some mythical dragon, sending soot falling like snow across the desert wastes, blackening everything in its path.

The rain falls gooey black, mingling with the already polluted waters of the once-pristine Persian Gulf. The smoke-cloud cover makes the desert temperature 20 degrees cooler at midday and, depending on which way the wind blows, can blot out huge chunks of Kuwait City during the rush hours.

A NUCLEAR WINTER IN PROSPECT

As soon as Saddam's forces fanned out across the oilfields after his invasion of Kuwait in August 1990 the top priority for his sappers and engineers were the oil derricks in Burgan - the second largest oilfield in the world - Wafra, Sabriya, Umm Gudair, Ahmadi, Khasman, Bahra, Rugei, Raudhaitan, Mutriba and Minagish. The Russian explosive charges on the wellheads were proof positive of his plan to make good on his threat of destruction.

Darkness at noon was just one sinister result of Saddam's deliberate devastation of the Kuwaiti oilfields

---

Some wells were exploded during the air war - the blame being put on the bombs that were poured down on Iraqi positions by allied warplanes - and the rest were set off at twenty second intervals as the coalition's armoured spearheads smashed through the defences at breakneck speed.

The liberation of Kuwait thus took place under a black sky, in an atmosphere dangerous to breathe.

The well fires are sustained by the huge natural pressure from beneath the desert surface in the oil reservoir, pushing the oil to the surface at speeds of one thousand miles per hour.

Five hundred thousand tons of oil-related pollutants are spewed out daily by the oil well fires - ten times the amount emitted by all American industrial and power-generating plants combined. Toxic chemicals, including hydrogen sulphide, sulphur dioxide, carbon monoxide and hydrocarbons, are among the deadly particles trapped in the black, oily smoke.

HUMAN AND ECOLOGICAL VICTIMS

The smoke may yet trigger one of the deadliest scenarios in the environmental lexicon - a nuclear winter where the smoke rises into the atmosphere to cut off sunlight and air, turning parts of the earth into permafrost zones.

Above: *As allied forces continued to advance on Kuwait City in February 1991, Iraqi prisoners were led away from the desert in their thousands.*

Below: *Smoke and flames from burning Kuwaiti oil wells were visible for scores of miles around.*

At ground level, the burning oil wells threaten the delicate ecosystem of the desert itself. Although a desert may seem a lifeless place, it is in fact home to myriad species of insects, scorpions and snakes as well as to larger animals such as camels and gazelles. Micro-organisms form a crust on the desert floor in much the same way as coral forms under the sea. This crust catches the seeds of shrubs and prevents the sand from blowing away.

Now over 300 square miles of desert lies under oil - some of it inches deep, others vast lakes six feet and more in depth - the result of spewing gushers that did not ignite when the retreating Iraqis blew the wellheads.

It will be decades before the full ecological effects of these oil lakes can be evaluated, but in the short term they spell catastrophe for the desert's fragile infrastructure. Where the surface has not been flooded by oil it has been turned into sheets of glass, the result of searing 4000 degree temperatures.

The first victims of the smoke are people with respiratory problems. Asthma and bronchitis sufferers are already queuing up for aid in Kuwait and as far away as Bahrain, where the smog drifts when the wind blows in the wrong direction.

But far more worrying are the fears

about future generations. Because of the high volume of cancer-causing agents trapped in the smoke, doctors say babies could be born deformed, in much the same way that the escape of radiation at the Chernobyl power plant in the Soviet Union has triggered an appalling number of mutations in both human beings and animals.

FIGHTING THE FIRES

But that is a problem for the future. Currently firefighters from Texas, Britain and Belgium are battling the blazes at what seems at times like an agonizingly slow pace. Wearing nothing more hi-tech than cotton overalls, the £600 per day firefighters are slowly dousing the wells, using a combination of guts, brute force and wily know-how gleaned from tackling oil fires around the globe.

Under a constant barrage of water, they move towards the intense heat of the flames in cranes shielded with tin sheeting. Using either dynamite to blow out the flames or specially moulded steel to snuff them out, they then move in with a new set of valves called a Christmas Tree which they fit on to the pipe and gradually close to form a seal. One mistake and they will be blown sky-high.

Above: *Workmen dug fresh graves in Kuwait City's Raqqua cemetery as victims caught up in the fighting were discovered.*

Right: *The picture that told the world that the Gulf War was over. Thousands of Iraqi vehicles - private and military - had been blasted by allied forces.*

Red Adair, the Texan oil firefighter who bravely led his men against the inferno on the Piper Alpha oil rig disaster in the North Sea which claimed over a hundred lives, is awed by the spectacle of the burning wellheads. He said:

Each one in its own right would be a disaster. And we have hundreds of them to deal with. We have to improvise every step of the way - there is nothing cast in stone about how each one must be tackled. People who say we are not working fast enough don't know the power that we are dealing with. The job is as tough as hell and we are working seven days a week.

Even so, it could be two years before the fires are extinguished and the wellheads capped.

MARINE POLLUTION

No less of an environmental disaster has been created by Saddam and his forces in the Persian Gulf - again the target of the Iraqi dictator's unique brand of eco-terrorism. More than 460 million gallons of unrefined crude oil were leaked into the waters that are home to thousands of fish and seabirds and were once rich fishing grounds harvested by Arabs from several nations. Shrimp beds have been decimated, and the breeding grounds of rare marine life lost forever. The damage is truly incalculable.

The slick is still there, months after the end of the war. Thousands of seabirds and fish have died, the TV images of their bloated, pathetic bodies bobbing on oil-thick waves evoking more sympathy in Western nations than did the Iraqi dead on the road to Basra at the war's end.

Millions of gallons of oil have been skimmed from the Gulf already, but millions more have washed ashore to bake in the hot climate, forming a permanent tar pavement over beaches.

An estimated twenty thousand or more seabirds have died so far. The spring months are the worst, as forty-five different species of birds use the Gulf as a refuelling spot on the northward migration from Africa and Arabia to their summer breeding grounds in northern Europe, the sub-Arctic and beyond. Many of these sandpipers, plovers, redshanks and others will die in the fouled waters for years to come. One or two, like the red-necked phalarope, might even be lost altogether to their native breeding grounds.

A BLEAK FUTURE?

Dr Hassan Nasrallah, a climatologist, warns that the final consequences of the environmental disaster in Kuwait may not be understood for decades. He said:

We are talking about massive sources of pollution of a kind that have never been monitored before. The world has no experience of a conflagration of the kind which has engulfed Kuwait. Humankind has done this awful thing to the planet and humankind will have to see what permanent damage has been done.

Below: *Long after the fighting was over, the oil fields of Kuwait continued to burn, lighting up the skies and polluting the entire region.*

THE HINDENBURG
Flames in the Sky

The airship Hindenburg was built in the thirties as a symbol of Hitler's new Germany, and her safety procedures were second to none. So why did she explode in a blazing inferno in May 1937?

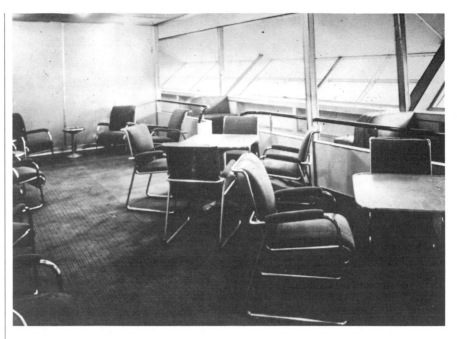

The *Hindenburg* was by far the most luxurious airship of all time, a floating palace dedicated to comfort, grandeur and efficiency as she ferried her wealthy clientele across the Atlantic.

She was so vast and so graceful, that she was to aviation what the once-mighty *Titanic* had been to shipping. And ironically, like the great liner which had sunk below the icy waters of the Atlantic Ocean twenty-five years earlier, the *Hindenburg*, too, was destined for disaster.

As she approached her dock at the Lakehurst naval station in New Jersey in May 1937, the great airship exploded into a fiery ball. Flames swept through the 198,000 cubic metres of highly inflammable hydrogen which filled the belly of the craft. In a scant thirty-two seconds the *Hindenburg*, more than twice the length of a football field, had been reduced to a charred skeleton of twisted metal. And in her death throes she had taken thirty-six people with her.

What happened? Was it an act of God, or was it sabotage? Even today, over half a century later, the answer remains as much a riddle as it did then.

HITLER'S FLAGSHIP

The tragic events of 6 May 1937 came just two years after the *Hindenburg* was completed, and less than twelve months after her first test flight. Symbolizing the

Above: *The promenade deck of the* **Hindenburg,** *literally the last word in air travel luxury in the 1930s.*

Opposite: *The huge bulk of the new airship fills its hangar. Her proud builders regarded her as the safest means of flight in the world.*

Below: *She was to the skies what the* **Titanic** *had been to the high seas. Both behemoths, however, were equally ill-fated.*

Above: *Proudly marked with the Nazis' swastika emblem, the tail of Hitler's flagship, the* **Hindenburg** *protrudes from its hangar.*

rise of the Third Reich, she was considered a national treasure, the largest, most expensive dirigible ever made. To the Fuehrer, Adolf Hitler, she was incontrovertible proof of the Aryan supremacy he so often bragged about.

To her builders, however, she was more than a showpiece of Nazi Germany. She was also the safest means of flight, fitted out with the most advanced security measures then available.

Regulations obliged both crew and passengers to hand over their matches and lighters before boarding

---

Indeed, safety measures were even more stringent than on other vessels. The crew wore anti-static overalls and shoes soled with hemp, and all those aboard - including passengers - had to hand over

their matches and lighters before they were allowed to board.

The airship's safety mechanisms were matched only by the grandeur of her many facilities, including quiet, comfortable state rooms.

The bar served the speciality of the ship, the LZ-129 Frosted Cocktail - gin with a dash of orange juice that took its name from the formal designation of the *Hindenburg*.

The meals were prepared by the finest chefs that Germany had to offer, and served on blue and gold porcelain. There was even a specially constructed, lightweight piano aboard for entertainment.

Most of the pampered passengers, however, preferred to spend their time relaxing in the observation room or cupola - a room enclosed by windows and attached to the craft's underbelly.

have been taken hold by a number of men in the field. The back motors of the ship are holding it just enough to keep it... it's burst into flame! This is terrible! The flames are 500 feet into the sky...

Then, choking back tears, he forced himself to continue: 'This is the worst thing I've ever witnessed. It is one of the worst catastrophes in the world. Oh, the humanity! All the passengers! I don't believe it!'

'It's a terrible crash,' he concluded. 'It's just lying there, a massive smoking

'A MASSIVE SMOKING WRECK'

Everything seemed to be going smoothly on 6 May 1937, as the giant craft passed so low over the Manhattan skyline that passengers waving from open windows in her vast silver belly came almost face to face with news photographers perched atop the Empire State Building.

But as the *Hindenburg* neared the Lakehurst naval station several hours late, after being buffeted by high winds on her eleventh transatlantic crossing, tragedy struck. Just seconds after her guide-ropes had been lowered for mooring and eventual landing, she exploded into a towering inferno above the stunned crowd which had gathered to greet the giant airship. The explosion was so loud that it could be heard fifteen miles away.

As the hydrogen in the Hindenburg's belly ignited, the explosion was heard fifteen miles away

---

Well-known radio reporter Herbert Morrison, on hand to describe the *Hindenburg*'s arrival in a broadcast to the American people, gave what is still considered to be the definitive description of the disaster.

As the huge airship neared, he began his report:

The ropes have been dropped and they

Above: *The* **Hindenburg** *was the largest - and most expensive - dirigible ever made.*

Right: *Forget sea travel ... this was the new way to span the globe in the optimistic Thirties.*

Below right: *The Hindenburg was a 'hotel' in the sky, with every comfort of a luxury liner.*

wreck.' Before their eyes, and those of other horrified witnesses, the *Hindenburg* was quickly consumed by the inferno, which fed itself on the vast hydrogen bags kept in its belly. Panicked passengers and crew jumped from the windows and doors to the ground below in a mad dash to escape the flames as the airship lurched and thrashed. The smell of burning flesh and the screams of the dying filled the night air. Meanwhile, as pandemonium was erupting all about him, Commander Max Pruss, a seasoned Zeppelin pilot, did his best to right the ship. He did not abandon the vessel until it crashed to the ground. Miraculously, Pruss and sixty-one other passengers and crew survived the disaster.

WHAT WENT WRONG?

What had turned the safest means of transportation yet known into a death trap? As reporters and concerned citizens scrambled for an answer, an official board of inquiry was set up to probe the disaster and try to pinpoint the cause of the fire.

At first the commission focused on the possibility of sabotage - not unlikely given the *Hindenburg*'s status as a showpiece of the hated Third Reich. Once sabotage had been ruled out, the commission considered numerous other possible causes, including leaking gas valves, static electricity and engine sparks. But nothing proved definitive.

Despite the outcry, however, the file on the *Hindenburg* disaster was closed. It would remain so until eight years later, after the end of World War II, when it finally emerged that the Nazis had wielded a strong influence over the official inquiry.

In fact, it become known that Hermann Goering, head of the Luftwaffe and once heir apparent to Hitler, had actually ordered the commission not to investigate the possibility of sabotage too thoroughly. The destruction of a Nazi symbol was embarrassment enough. Aryan pride could not take another blow by admitting that a saboteur had been responsible.

That possibility was raised again some thirty-five years later, when Michael

Right: *As it approached its mooring at Lakehurst naval station, an explosion of flames began to engulf the Hindenburg.*

Below: *'This is terrible,' announced radio commentator Herbert Morrison. 'The flames are 500 feet into the sky.'*

MacDonald Mooney claimed in his book that the disaster was no accident, but planned destruction by a young anti-Nazi saboteur. He identified the perpetrator as Erich Spehl, a twenty-five-year-old blond, blue-eyed airship rigger from the Black Forest, who perished in the flames.

He also alleged that both German and American officials agreed to the cover-up because they did not want to spark 'an international incident'. Although it can never be proved for certain that the *Hindenburg* was sabotaged and that Spehl was the misguided culprit, one thing can be stated beyond a doubt. The tragedy was the finale of an era when luxury was prized as greatly as speed.

Immediately after the crash, Germany halted all commercial Zeppelin services.

The *Hindenburg*'s sister ship, the LZ-130 or *Graf Zeppelin II*, was none the less completed - but Hitler's new-found antagonism towards airships soon led to the scrapping of all Zeppelins and ended the airship programme.

Eventually the *Graf Zeppelin II* was used to carry out spying missions against Britain. Interestingly, the *Hindenburg*, too, became part of the German war effort. The wreckage of the once-proud airship, which had peacefully plied the skies in quiet serenity, was shipped back to Germany - and recycled into war planes.

Below: *The* **Hindenburg's** *burnt-out remains. Miraculously 62 passengers and crew survived; 36 people perished.*

SEVESO
Cloud of Death

In July 1976 the little Italian town of Seveso was the victim of a terrible accident at the local chemical plant. A deadly cloud of poison gas was discharged into the atmosphere, and its effects may last for generations

Right: *Frightened, bewildered, the people of Seveso were evacuated after their town was contaminated in July 1976.*

Opposite: *Masked specialists worked day and night in an almost futile attempt to clean up the chemical plant.*

For years after 'it' happened, the ghost town of Seveso in Northern Italy still idled like some gigantic science-fiction movie set, shuttered behind a Berlin Wall of environmental quarantine panels. 'CONTAMINATED AREA - NO ADMITTANCE' read notices in five languages. Across the top of the panels

Below: *Animals and plants over many square miles were affected when a safety valve burst at the Seveso chemical factory...which then billowed out its poisonous cloud.*

and into the scarred area hung limp telephone cables attached to the sides of the humble houses within.

But the phones did not ring any more, for there was no one to answer them. The core of Seveso was a dead zone, snuffed out in one of mankind's worst chemical accidents. It would become known as the Italian Hiroshima.

It happened on 10 July 1976, when an explosion at the Swiss-owned Icmesa

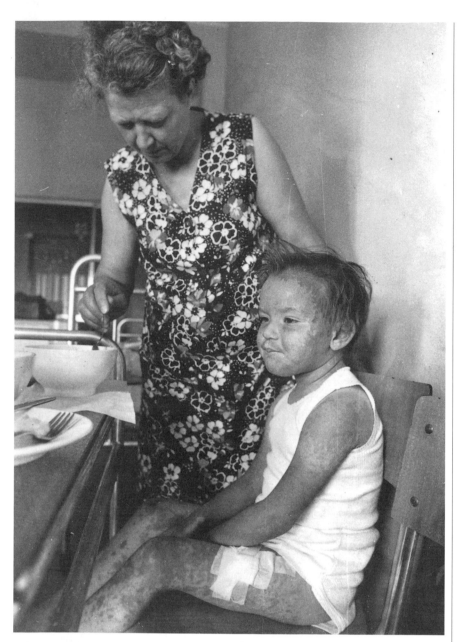

Above: *Little Alice Senno, aged four, was one of the many young victims of the poison gas cloud that escaped from the chemical plant near her home.*

supply of a major city would be enough to wipe out 8 million people; on that black summer day there was enough released in its concentrated form to wipe out 100 million. The long term effects upon the blighted land and the unborn babies of future generations have still to be assessed.

A STRANGE WHISTLING NOISE

The seventeen thousand residents of Seveso, a town nestling in the green foothills of the Po valley, still had plenty of countryside around them to offset the sprawling factories which fanned out from Milan.

At the plant, which employed many local people, Viro Romani, a technician, was just finishing his lunch. Since it was a Saturday there was no active production going on at the works, so only ten of the 160 employees were on duty.

The firm, a subsidiary of the massive Hoffman-La Roche pharmaceutical companies - one of the world's largest - used the trichlorophenol, or TCP, for the manufacture of hexachlorophene, the active ingredient in many soaps. Hexachlorophene had been banned in the USA but was still widely used in a number of other nations.

The plant's chemical reactor was closed that day, but as Viro Romani sipped his coffee in the canteen there was a loud bang followed by an eerie, piercing whistling. The men ran outside in time to witness the escape of the lethal dioxin, which spewed out at tremendous pressure from the safety valves on top of the apparatus.

Families preparing lunch were suddenly seized by fits of coughing as the cloud rolled over them

---

chemical plant discharged a thick white cloud of dioxin, one of the deadliest poisons known to man, over about six square miles of the small industrial suburb some thirteen miles from Milan. As the poison settled on homes and gardens in the following days thousands of pets died, crops were infected and hundreds of people developed nausea, blurred vision and a disfiguring disease known as chloracne.

As at Chernobyl, which came after it, human error unleashed on the unsuspecting innocents of Seveso a man-made disaster of epic proportions.

Dioxin is a by-product of trichlorophenol, used in germicides, deodorants and soaps. Four ounces in the water

Within minutes fine particles of the chemical were falling like snow while the air filled with the pungent smell of chlorine. As emergency taps were turned on to pour cold water inside the reactor the cloud rolled away gently over the Italian countryside on its ominous journey. Families sitting at cafes in the streets or making lunch in their homes

were suddenly stricken with fits of coughing and tears rolled down their cheeks. Later in the day, when the cloud had moved on, they complained of headaches and nausea, and a lingering, acrid smell like burned plastic hanging in the air.

WHY DID IT HAPPEN?

During the first twenty-four hours after the explosion the officials of the plant began their inquest into what had gone wrong. It seemed that the heat of the chemical reaction from the previous day's production had not cooled properly.

To deal with this potential problem, most companies have safety valves like the ones installed at the Seveso plant, and back them up with enormous dump tanks ready to absorb lethal poisons before they can be discharged into the atmosphere. But Seveso had no such dump tanks, and the safety valve not only failed at the crucial moment, but was located on the vent pipe leading to the roof. The result was the escape of the gas.

IMMEDIATE EFFECTS

It was only after the first three or four days that the full impact of what had happened began to hit home. By Wednesday the doctors' surgeries in Seveso were crammed with people - many of them children - suffering an abundance of ugly rashes and weeping boils, complaining of backache, sickness and blinding headaches.

Patients told the doctors that animals and birds in their gardens and vegetable plots had been dying suddenly. An old man saw three robins on his grass just keel over and die, as if the will to live had gone. Cats and dogs would walk down the street and drop dead. Tomato plants and maize fields seemed burned, the vegetation dry and crumbling, while in the pastures the stricken cattle began bleeding from their eyes and ears. Entire chicken roosts were destroyed, the pathetic carcasses rotting in the summer heat.

Doctors began to grow angry at the lack of information from factory bosses. News about it travelled slowly. There had been no huge explosion, no fire, to warrant the accident reaching the prime-time news broadcasts, so the company stayed silent.

It was on Friday, when a two-year-old baby was rushed into the local hospital, a mass of blisters and rashes, that the mayors of Seveso and nearby Meda pressed Icmesa officials for some answers. The company bosses worriedly said that the soil samples were being examined by boffins in Switzerland, but admitted that posters and warning notices about not eating local produce should be posted around town.

Overnight another eighteen children were taken to hospital and by now a state approaching panic was beginning to grip the innocent citizens of Seveso.

Birds were now no longer dropping in ones or twos from the sky, but in whole flocks. The animals seemed to be suffering more quickly than the humans, probably because they ate grass, drank rainwater and were generally closer to the fall-out of dioxin than were people. But the doctors, relying on information supplied by the company, were treating the patients as if they had been exposed to TCP - a mild irritant and a million times less toxic than dioxin.

THE TRUTH DISCOVERED

Bruno Ambrosi, a newsman working in Milan, had a university knowledge of chemistry and found out that dioxin was manufactured in TCP when the temperature of the chemical goes over 200 degrees.

That, he discovered chillingly, is exactly what had happened.

One paper he read about it said: 'It is the most potent small-molecule toxin known to man. Its effects dwarf those of arsenic and strychnine.' Dioxin attacked the liver and kidneys and it was also 'mutagenic' - it had the power to change the chromosomes in the body, leading to cancer and to birth defects in unborn children.

Ambrosi broke the story just as the Swiss scientists confirmed what he already knew to be true - that massive amounts of dioxin had escaped and leached into the soil and atmosphere, with catastrophic effects. Dioxin was insoluble in water, and once it penetrated a substance it could stay there for years.

STATE OF EMERGENCY

An emergency centre was set up in an elementary school, and local health workers were drafted in to run it. Eight days after the accident the Italian government declared a state of emergency.

Vittoria Rivolta, health minister in the province of Lombardy, began correlating the data on a huge map to try to chart where the cloud had gone and so

Below: *An Italian carabiniere feeds a cow. But like thousands of other farm creatures contaminated by the escaping poison, it had to be destroyed later.*

years thousands of tons of soil were removed and buried in concrete, while thousands of tons of plants and seventy thousand animal corpses were burned. Refugees were relocated in temporary accommodation, compensated for loss of produce and property, and promised new housing equal to that which they had abandoned.

Most of the 736 families evacuated were eventually returned to their homes, but 256 people were permanently locked out of the exclusion area in Zone A, where dioxin levels were the highest. An official report three years later by the Italian parliament damned the operators of the chemical plant. It said the plant was unsafe to begin with, and revealed that company officials waited twenty-seven hours after the accident before notifying even the most minor municipal official. The company went on to pay some £8 million pounds in compensation.

Miraculously, no humans have yet died. Some babies have been born with mutated insides, but it is not yet clear whether they have been the victims of dioxin. All but two of the 187 children stricken with chloracne recovered.

determine how far the dioxin had spread. On Saturday, 24 July there was a total evacuation from Zone A in the town, an area on Rivolta's map that suffered the most sickness among humans and the most deaths among animals. Two hundred families left the area, which was then cordoned off by police and caribinieri with six miles of barbed wire. Then the men, wearing protective suits, moved through the area killing every creature still left alive in it. At the end of the killing over fifty thousand animals had been slaughtered. There were a further ten thousand corpses from the effects of the dioxin poisoning.

FEARS FOR THE FUTURE

Dr Anne Walker, a dermatologist who had treated workers in previous dioxin accidents, said the full effects of the tragedy might not show up for two decades. Fear and uncertainty spread among the population.

As thousands upon thousands of tests were carried out on the local people, and they were graded into high-risk, middle-risk and low-risk categories, the Italian government authorized abortions in the region for fear of abnormal births adding to the disaster. Over a period of two

Above: *The disastrous effects of the poison cloud can clearly be seen on these leaves. The chemical had previously been used as a defoliant in Vietnam.*

Right: *Animals were generally affected more quickly than humans. Dogs and cats were collected in dustbin liners, as were birds which had fallen from the sky.*

CHERNOBYL
Nuclear Nightmare

Massive radiation readings in Sweden. Then days of Soviet silence about what had really happened. This was the worst disaster the nuclear power industry has ever known - Chernobyl

The first indication that something had gone wrong - terribly, irredeemably wrong - occurred at 9am on Monday, 28 April 1986, as boffins at the Forsmark nuclear power station, sixty miles from the Swedish capital of Stockholm, noticed disturbing signals bleeping on their ghost-green screens.

The signals were measures of radiation, and the horrified scientists feared a massive reactor leak at the power plant entrusted to their high-tech care. A careful and methodical check of all equipment and its monitoring gauges showed no leakage - and yet the sensors indicated that the air they were breathing was four times the ordained safe limit.

Geiger counters were hurriedly deployed for swift checks on all six hundred workers. The readings were haywire, showing that virtually every worker had been exposed to radiation way above safe limits.

Outside it was the same story - samples taken from soil and plant life showed extraordinarily high deposits of radioactive material. Sweden and much of Europe was being infected by a silent, unseen, unscented killer.

Sixty-seven-and-a-half hours earlier Lieutenant-Colonel Leonid Telyatnikov had been enjoying a few well-earned days off when the telephone rang at his home seventy-five miles outside Kiev in the Soviet Ukraine at 1.32am on 26 April. A breathless voice informed him that there had been an 'incident' at the Chernobyl nuclear power plant eighty miles from Kiev.

It was a bright, starlit night as Telyatnikov, leading his crew of twenty-eight firefighters, raced to the scene. A bright orange glow soon appeared on the horizon. 'I had no idea what had happened or what we were heading into,' recalled Telyatnikov. 'But as I approached the plant I could see debris on fire all around like sparklers.

'Then I noticed a bluish glow above the wreckage of reactor four and pockets of fire on surrounding buildings. It was absolutely silent and eerie.' Protected by no more than wellington boots and a hard hat, Telyatnikov, later honoured as a Hero of the Soviet Union, was confronting the worst disaster in thirty-two years of commercial nuclear power's history.

A WHOLE CONTINENT OF VICTIMS

The partial meltdown of the Chernobyl nuclear reactor caused a tragedy that continues to bring death, suffering and misery to this day. Untold thousands have died from tumours and cancer caused by the explosion. Human beings, cattle and other livestock, have given birth to nightmarish offspring, deformed and mutated by the effects of the radiation. The earth has been scarred forever, and

Opposite: *In the early hours of 26 April 1986, it became apparent that a dreadful disaster had occurred at the Chernobyl nuclear power plant near Kiev.*

Below: *By the time scientists had arrived to examine the damage, a cloud of nuclear poison was already drifting westwards towards Sweden.*

mankind left to ponder whether the benefits of nuclear energy are not outweighed by the spectre of such a disaster ever occurring again.

By the time the Forsmark scientists had discovered the presence of massive amounts of radiation in the atmosphere, strong winds were carrying it all over Europe. Light rain fell on the salt marshes of Brittany, making the milk in cows' udders toxic. Heavier rain poured down on to the Welsh hillsides, making the tender lamb forbidden flesh. Snow in Finland, Sweden and West Germany was infected too.

The Swedish scientists informed their government that they believed the source for this nuclear volcano, spewing its lethal residue into the skies, was the Soviet Union. But Communist Russia remained silent.

It was not until 9pm Moscow time that night when the Kremlin finally admitted that something had happened - but it gave no indication of the gravity of the mishap. A terse four-sentence statement was read on the evening news in Moscow.

Almost grudging in its admission, the statement said: 'An accident has taken place at the Chernobyl power station and one of the reactors was damaged. Measures are being taken to eliminate the consequences of the accident. Those affected by it are being given assistance. A government commission has been set up.' The announcer then picked up another sheet of paper and went on to read a story about a Soviet peace fund.

Moscow's first official announcement was a cover-up - a four-line statement on the nightly news

---

Western governments began to exert diplomatic pressure on the Soviet Union for details of exactly what had happened. But only men like Telyatnikov knew in those first few hours the enormity of the disaster. 'I realized it was not an ordinary situation as soon as I passed through the gate,' he said. 'There was just the noise of machines and the fire crackling. The firefighters knew what they had to do and proceeded quietly, on the run. The

Above: *Workers go about their duties in a reactor room of the Chernobyl plant. This picture was taken in 1982, four years before the disaster.*

radiation-measuring meters had frozen on their highest level. Thoughts of my family would flash through my mind and be gone. No one would discuss the radiation risk. The most frightening thought was that we wouldn't have enough strength to hold out until reserves came. About an hour after the fire began a group of fire-fighters with symptoms of radiation exposure were taken down from a rooftop close to the damaged reactor. When I approached five men to take up the position they rushed to the rooftop almost before I could get the words out of my mouth. They are all dead now, from radioactive poisoning.'

Telyatnikov too is one of what the

Ukrainians call 'the living dead'. He began vomiting even as he fought the flames and since then has battled cancer, like thousands of others.

The burning white-hot graphite core of the reactor blazed at 5000 degrees Fahrenheit - twice the temperature of molten steel - and thrust millions of cubic feet of radioactive gas into the atmosphere. Pictures taken by a CIA satellite four hundred miles above the earth were on President Ronald Reagan's desk forty-eight hours after the red alert was sounded by the Forsmark scientists. They showed a picture of hell that the embarrassed, technologically inept Soviets, refused to admit publicly.

In the immediate hours after the tragedy Per Olof Sjostedt, technical and scientific adviser at the Swedish embassy in Moscow, contacted officials of the Soviet nuclear energy programme armed with the information given to him via the Forsmark scientists. He was curtly told that there was no information to be had.

It took rising Soviet politician Boris Yeltsin to step forward several days later to lend gravity to his government's so far casual response to the disaster. He said: 'It is serious. Very serious. The cause apparently lies in human error. We are undertaking measures to make sure this doesn't happen again.'

The whole area within an eighteen-mile radius of Chernobyl was evacuated and declared an unfit zone, where cattle, drinking water and vegetation were all deemed unfit for consumption.

MELTDOWN

Nuclear physicists began to theorize about what had happened at the Chernobyl reactor and came up with a likely scenario. The reactor used uranium fuel rods to generate heat used to boil water into steam. The steam in turn powered turbine generators for power. Cooling water is essential in such a system to stop the fuel rods from super-heating, causing a meltdown or burn-up, in which the core virtually turns itself into a nuclear bomb.

It seems that the water circulation system to provide the cooling liquid had failed, causing the temperature in the reactor core to hit 5000 degrees. The uranium fuel rods melted and produced radioactive steam that reacted with the zirconium alloy cladding of the rods to produce explosive hydrogen gas.

Soviet officials proved reluctant to seek outside assistance while still trying to pretend that not much had happened. But a Soviet scientific officer attached to their embassy in Bonn did approach the West German nuclear power industry with a request for information on fighting graphite core fires. A similar request went out the same day to Swedish authorities, and Moscow invited Californian bone marrow expert Dr Robert Gale to provide medical aid to Chernobyl victims.

'Please tell the world to help us!' cried an anguished Russian voice picked up by a Dutch radio ham

---

Moscow tackled the blaze with an army of workers and soldiers - most of them now dead or suffering from the effects of prolonged exposure to such massive dosages of radiation. Helicopters carrying tons of wet sand and

Below: *Three months after the blast, clean-up crews hang chunks of graphite from a burnt-out nuclear reactor. Their 'protective' clothing failed to save many of them from cancer and death.*

lead flew over the site and dumped their loads directly on to the blazing reactor. Tons of the element boron, which absorbs neutrons, was also dumped on to the smouldering fires.

THE TERRIBLE AFTERMATH

By the end of the week the fire was out - but so was the radiation, incalculable amounts of it, spreading an ominous pall over Europe and the western half of the Soviet Union. On the ground, near to the site, the victims began dying of haemorrhages and brain seizures. They were often the lucky ones - the lingering deaths, the mutated stillborn babies, the cancer which racks heroes like fireman Telyatnikov, were yet to come.

In a bid to clean up some of the debris the Soviets dug a huge pit and filled it with shattered remnants of the reactor, twisted metal and broken concrete from the plant and clothes worn by disaster workers. Some 2 million cubic feet of concrete was mixed over the next six weeks and poured on to the reactor, sealing it forever.

As the rescuers struggled, President Reagan became angrier with Moscow, and said so in a nationwide radio address. He told America in his usual Saturday speech: 'The Soviets owe the world an explanation. A full accounting of what happened at Chernobyl and what is happening now is the least the world community has a right to expect.'

Nuclear experts declared the RBMK-1000 reactors at Chernobyl mighty but outdated machines. But most glaringly, said the experts, the Russians showed a distinct lack of care about safety by not building the reactor with a concrete outer structure that could have contained most of the fire and the subsequent radiation.

Ten times as much radiation escaped as at Hiroshima and Nagasaki

---

It is now known that over a hundred thousand people were evacuated from the region. Even the government newspaper *Izvestia* has admitted that as many as 3 million people are still living on irradiated land, selling as well as devouring their produce. After four years of bureaucratic book-cooking, health statistics show an increase in blood disorders, freak offspring and deformed plant life that is unlike anything else found on earth.

Dr Gale, who provided much of the medical expertise the Russians needed for bone marrow transplants on victims, predicts as many as 150,000 new cancer cases in the next ten years as a direct result of the Chernobyl fall-out. In Minsk alone the incidences of leukaemia have doubled in five years.

Due to the outdated technology and stagnant economy of the country, just a fraction of this number will be cured.

FEAR AND MISTRUST

Chernobyl's most lasting legacy will be the mistrust felt by the country's own citizens about a workers' paradise that condemned people to die with disinformation and disorganization.

Crude technology and disregard for safety were held to blame

As to blame for the tragedy, the Soviets were quick to find scapegoats. The former director of the plant, Viktor Bryukhanov, and the former chief engineer, Anatoly Dyatlov, in charge of doomed reactor number four, were both asleep when the cooling system failed and the reactor blew up at 1.23am. They were consequently jailed for dereliction of duty. Two others received three-year prison terms, and two more suspended sentences.

SICK IRONY

As a macabre postscript to the tragedy of Chernobyl, the Kiev authorities are offering to take death-wish tourists on a tour of the devastated nuclear power plant. Ever hungry for hard currency, the local tourist bureau apparatchiks are hoping to lure Westerners to the dead zone with advertising that promises fairground-type thrills:

*CHILL to the eerie dead city of Chernobyl as you walk through deserted

schools, farms and factories!

*GASP in awe at the tomb of the great melted reactor, now encased in tons of concrete!

*SWOON at the sight of the mutated farm animals born with horrifying defects as a result of the fall-out!

And as if to prove their social responsibility, the organizers behind this macabre voyeurism promise takers of the tour a full medical examination afterwards to check for radiation poisoning. Part of the tour - that will cost up to £200 for a single day - includes visits to the farms and homes where comrades have defied the Kremlin and returned to the land after the explosion.

It is highly unlikely that the land and buildings are completely free from radioactivity.

Some scientists believe that it could be up to a hundred years before the radiation levels have dropped sufficiently for it not to pose a potential health threat. Thirty-seven died in the reactor explosion and fire. But thousands more have died from radiation poisoning and cancers triggered by the fall-out. Scientist Dr David Abrahamovitz said: 'If tourists were to go there, say, after a rainfall, there would be more chance of a higher radiation level registering than if they went when it was dry because the water would release more toxins in the dry earth. It is not a visit that I would be queuing up to go on.'

Excursion officials say they will also take in the little town of Slavutich, a radiation workers' colony that is home to the people who monitor the dead zone and ensure that the radioactive pile is not leaking from its concrete tomb. The motto of the town is: 'Life is good - but too short!'

American writer Francis Clines said: 'The notion has the virtue of dark candour, of daring to think the outside world might like to at least leer, if not memorialize, an historic outrage upon one of the earth's humbler landscapes.'

Above: *It took years for the full horror of the Chernobyl disaster to be revealed. 'The problems will unfold well into the next century,' says Soviet scientist Igor Ignatchev.*

ZEEBRUGGE FERRY
Tragedy in the Channel

A short ferry crossing on a familiar stretch of water became a night of hell for crew and passengers. In March 1987 the Herald of Free Enterprise sank as she left port

Right: *As dawn broke over the Belgian port of Zeebrugge, the full scale of the tragedy of 6 March 1987 became apparent.*

Opposite: *The* Herald of Free Enterprise *set sail from Zeebrugge with her bow doors open. It was a recipe for an unparalleled tragedy in maritime history.*

As dawn broke over the Belgian port of Zeebrugge, the full scale of the tragedy of 6 March 1987 became apparent.

The English Channel is the world's busiest waterway. Each day the narrow sea lane separating Britain from continental Europe is negotiated by thousands of vessels of all shapes, sizes and nationalities. For holidaymakers the ferries which ply between the British, French, Belgian and Dutch ports are regarded as little more than lumbering omnibuses, making the journey with such regularity and such apparent ease that it is often forgotten that the Channel is the graveyard of countless ships, lost in waters that are dangerous and cold.

Weather has undoubtedly played a great part in claiming the lives of stricken vessels. But so too has human error. And it was an appalling chain of human errors - what an official inquiry would later brand forever as 'the disease of sloppiness' - which struck the *Herald of*

Free Enterprise as she steamed for Dover from the Belgian port of Zeebrugge on 6 March 1987.

Due to that 'disease of sloppiness', the bow doors of the Townsend Thoresen car ferry were left open as she steamed into the night. Water poured in, unstoppably, flooding the car decks before tilting the ship to a list that was irreversible. She rolled on to her side, saved from sinking only by a shallow sandbank, and in the confusion and chaos that followed 193 people lost their lives.

The agony of that night has been played over and over again in the minds of those who survived, those who were the rescuers, those who saw it on TV, and those who were left to judge the men who caused it.

'IT'S DEFINITELY GOING OVER'

The *Herald of Free Enterprise* was a 7951-ton ferry, 132 metres long and part of the Blue Riband fleet operated by Townsend which crossed the Channel in record times. Time, it was later to be learned, was a critical operating factor with Townsend bosses. On the highly competitive Channel routes, turnaround and speed at sea were of the essence if Townsend was to stay ahead of rival shipping lines.

When she steamed out of Zeebrugge that night Captain David Lewry was at the helm. An experienced skipper and a long-time employee of Townsend Thoresen, Captain Lewry was on the

Below: *Passengers had no time to don lifejackets as the ferry rolled on its side, hurling them into the freezing waters in pitch darkness.*

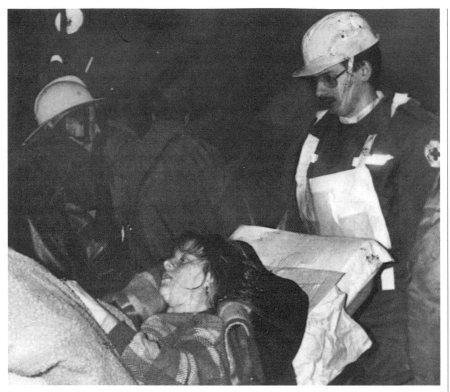

Above: The ferry lurched like a giant whale, throwing passengers across decks, shops, lounges, bars and restaurants. The injured were carried out shocked and disorientated.

looked back at it, it looked like something out of the Second World War that was hit with torpedoes.'

A lorry driver looked back and thought the stricken ship looked as if she had been hit by torpedoes

---

bridge as the *Herald* pulled away from pier 12 at five minutes past six.

Four hundred and thirty-six passengers were on board that night, many of them on the deck watching the twinkling lights of Zeebrugge recede in the distance. In her belly were nearly forty trucks and over eighty cars. For a vessel that could comfortably accommodate a thousand people she was, with her eighty crewmen on top of the passenger complement, marginally over half full.

Barely twenty minutes later the crowded bar, restaurant, duty-free shop, lounges and decks were turned into a maelstrom of nightmare panic as the ship violently listed and then lurched like a giant whale on to her side. It was the start of a night of hell.

As the vessel listed over many passengers were simply sucked out of the windows through sheer force. Larry O'Brian, a lorry driver from Ireland, was sitting in the ship's restaurant when he suddenly saw plates and china fly from the tables. He said: 'In forty-five seconds the boat was on its side and half-filled with water. People were sucked out through portholes like you see in those movies about air disasters. They didn't have a chance. And the boat - well, when I was being taken off it and I

Many of the people on board were day trippers taking advantage of an offer from Britain's biggest popular newspaper, the *Sun,* to sail cheaply, on a day return ticket costing £1. One of them, Andrew Simmons, 30, of Bushey, near Watford, recalled: 'We were trapped for twenty or thirty minutes after the boat went over. Within a minute it went from being upright to on its side with water gushing in down the stairs and corridors. I and my friend helped a little girl, who was only two or three years old, climb up with her father above the water. We were only rescued when people smashed the windows from outside and hauled us out to safety.'

THE HEROES

Many individual acts of heroism were performed that night, not least among them that of Londoner Andrew Parker. In the pitch dark, with a cold black sea rising, carrying with it the wreckage of furniture, old bottles, discarded lifejackets and fuel oil, this brave man turned himself into a human ladder bridging a gap over the water, thus allowing 120 people to clamber over him to safety. He would later be awarded the George Medal for bravery. To this day the nightmare of what happened haunts him and he suffers from post-traumatic stress disorder.

When one man offered himself as a human ladder, more than a hundred people scrambled over him to safety

---

Another hero was Lieutenant Guido Couwenbergh a Belgian Navy frogman one of the first on the scene. Singlehandedly he saved forty people from drowning. He received the Queen's Gallantry Medal.

Couwenbergh and his colleagues

arrived in naval helicopters whose rotors whined noisily above the screams of the trapped and dying below. For them, it was a race against time.

As with the passengers who died in the stricken *Titanic* seventy-five years before them, the cold sea threatened to claim even the strongest swimmer with hypothermia in minutes. One teenager, Nicola Simpson, from Hertfordshire, was clinically dead with a body temperature 25 degrees below normal after she was rescued by Belgian civilian diver Piet Lagast. She was even certified dead on arrival at a Belgian hospital, but thanks to sterling efforts by doctors and nurses who worked throughout the night to raise her temperature, she survived.

Nicola and eight others were trapped behind a sheet of thick glass in the ship that Lagast shattered with his diver's knife - almost severing his hand in the process. He too was a recipient of the Queen's Gallantry Medal.

Massive sodium arc lights were brought to play on the corpse of the doomed vessel as wire reports clattered into TV and newspaper offices around the world. Anguished relatives at Dover docks who besieged the Townsend Thoresen offices attacked pressmen who descended there to cover the worst tragedy in British maritime history in years.

The water was so cold that hospital staff laboured for hours to bring one young girl back from clinical death

---

The Royal Navy was on hand to help in the shape of HMS *Glasgow* and HMS *Diomede,* assisting helicopters from naval squadrons based at Culdrose as they hovered over the living and the dead in the sea. A pilot was later to say: 'I could see black shapes bobbing in the water, arms splayed out like jellyfish and I knew they were the dead.'

THE DOORS THAT NO ONE CLOSED

Daylight brought the real tragedy of Zeebrugge home to the world. Stabilized by tugs, the hulk rested in shallow water on a sandbar with the sea

Below: *A floating crane comes alongside the* **Herald of Free Enterprise.** *Only when righted was the full horror inside revealed.*

Left: *The first articulated truck is lifted from the vehicle deck of the capsized ferry. Many of the dead and injured were lorry drivers.*

Below: *It looked like a wreckers' yard. But these were the cars and trucks of passengers trapped within the freezing, black, waterlogged hulk of the channel ferry.*

coming roughly halfway up her hull. At the front of the ship, plain for all to see and obviously the cause of the disaster, were the cargo deck doors wide open. It was apparent in those hours after the accident that there was an awful lot of explaining to do on someone's behalf.

The captain, David Lewry, as master of his ship, ultimately takes the blame. But the public inquiry which followed proved that the *Herald of Free Enterprise*'s demise rested on far more than one man's shoulders.

It exposed a management system that was out of touch with the day-to-day operations of its fleet and crewmen who were negligent in their duties.

In July 1987, after a twenty-nine-day inquiry, Mr Justice Sheen, who chaired the investigation, concluded that: 'From top to bottom the body was infected by the disease of sloppiness.' Four men, including Captain Lewry, were singled out for making the fatal mistakes which

had led to the tragedy. The others were: Senior Master John Kirby, Assistant Boatswain Mark Stanley and Chief Officer Leslie Sabel. Mr Justice Sheen stated plainly what the cause of the accident was.

'The *Herald* sank because she went to sea with her inner and outer bow doors open.' But he went on to say: 'A full investigation into the circumstances of the disaster leads inexorably to the conclusion that the underlying or cardinal faults lay higher up the company.'

It was learned that Mark Stanley, in charge of closing the doors before the ship put to sea, had been asleep at the time. He only woke up as he was thrown from his bunk when the ship keeled over. Leslie Sabel was criticized because he did not check that the doors were shut before sailing. Various captains in the past had expressed concern about the practice of setting sail with the bow doors open to Townsend management in memos. At least one of them expressed the opinion that indicator lights were needed on the bridge to show whether or not bow doors had been closed. The inquiry said that this idea deserved 'serious consideration' - consideration that it had previously not received.

The indirect blame for the tragedy was laid firmly at the feet of sloppy management

---

He went on to say that Captain Lewry ultimately had to carry the burden of responsibility. 'Captain Lewry took the *Herald* to sea with the bow doors fully open. It follows that Captain Lewry must accept personal responsibility for the loss of his ship.' In mitigation it had to be borne in mind, said the judge, that the skipper was working to the same system that existed on other company ships, and that there were no standing orders to close the bow and stern doors.

And he was scathing in his criticism of Townsend's bosses for 'staggering complacency', which led to a 'malaise' which infected it.

After the inquiry, an inquest at Dover ruled that the passengers were the victims of unlawful killing. Charges were later brought against both crewmen and

management, but were later dropped. The memory of what had happened was to be punishment enough.

THE LEGACY

The legacy of the *Herald* disaster was a change in ships' operating procedures. Under maritime law it would be an offence for a vessel to set sail again in a similar fashion.

For the survivors there are only bitter memories left: of loved ones, including Nicola Simpson's mother, who were lost; for crewmen, who saw twelve of their shipmates go down; for Captain Lewry, who in the immediate aftermath of the accident wished he were dead.

The battered and scarred hull of the ship was finally taken apart in a scrapyard in Taiwan.

Above: *Giant floating cranes had to be brought in to raise the* **Herald of Free Enterprise.** *Her battered hulk was later taken apart in a scrapyard in Taiwan.*

ABERFAN SCHOOL
Disaster in the Valleys

The people of coal-mining areas are used to tragedy. But the little village of Aberfan in South Wales was visited by one more terrible than anyone could have imagined when a slagheap engulfed the school and took its children

The story of Wales is written in tragedy. The dark valleys have been witness to much suffering: hardship on the land, poverty in the homes, danger and death in the mines. Above it all, its people have remained strong and proud, descendants of hardy tribes who cherished their Welsh heritage despite its often uncompromising face.

But there is not a man or woman alive who could have foreseen that the greatest tragedy ever to strike Wales would occur in the village of Aberfan - the victim of the mountain that moved to claim the lives of a generation of children. In every sense they were the victims of the

Above: *The close-knit community toiled day and night to recover bodies from their black tomb.*

Opposite: *At 7.30am on 21 October 1966 the mountain of sludge known as Tip No. 7 began to slide towards the village of Aberfan.*

Below: *One of the victims is carried to an ambulance from the buried school.*

pits as much as their fathers and grandfathers - smothered by the very spoil that they had gouged from the earth in order to earn a living.

Aberfan bears the scars of the tragedy to this day, and it is not a village that one can easily feel comfortable in.

The tragedy began at precisely 7.30am on 21 October 1966. Tip no. 7, in National Coal Board parlance, sat like a black cancer on the side of Merthyr Mountain, 500 ft up in the mists and light rain that began to fall as the town stirred for another day. It had rained for weeks, the water acting like a loosening agent on the foul-smelling muck which besmirched the side of the mountain.

At that moment the black slurry began to move, its enormous weight shifting with all the creaks and groans of the beginning of a giant slide. Some 100,000 tons of rocks and mud, hewn by miners from the pits below and around, suddenly began its inexorable journey to the unsuspecting community below.

Little Paul Davies was one of the scabby-kneed kids of Aberfan who was in the Pantglas infants' and junior school at the foot of the mountain - one of a cluster of buildings that included a row of cottages and a farm. Five-year-old Paul loved drawing, and was sketching even as the unstoppable slurry was gathering momentum, moving faster and faster for its appointment with catastrophe. He drew clockfaces, all of them saying 9.25. One picture showed a mountain of sludge

Above: Rescue workers dig among the rubble after the rain-soaked coal tip avalanched onto the infants' school.

Right: Prince Philip, Duke of Edinburgh, rushed to the scene to talk to rescue workers and comfort relatives of the dead.

sliding onto his school while a plane marked 'National Coal Board' dropped bombs on to the mountain.

At 9.25am the moving mountain hit Pantglas infants' school. Later, when they pulled little Paul's smothered body from underneath the school clock, it was stuck at 9.25.

The tide of sludge had hit with the force of a hurricane, smothering, smashing, crushing everything in its path.

Survivors recall hearing the screech of dragged gravel and breaking rocks reaching a crescendo shortly before it broke over the village below.

THE TERRIBLE DEATH TOLL

The Rev. Kenneth Hayes remembers those split seconds with awful clarity. It is a moment in time that will never leave him. He rounded the corner of a street to see a mound of slurry climbing up the outside of the school building before the sheer weight behind it pushed it through on its lethal mission. His nine-year-old son Dyfig was among those it claimed.

'The slurry just overwhelmed the school,' he said. 'I saw the last of the living being taken out and the first of the dead. I knew I had lost my boy, although his body was not found until the following day. That was when the enormity of it all dawned on us. Whole families had been wiped out. I buried five from one house that Thursday.'

Phillip Thomas remembers crying as the stones crushed his hands, and calling out desperately for his 'mam'. He had left the school on an errand with another boy, and so was out of the classroom when the wall of mud smashed into it. He recalled:

I was buried immediately and found myself crying. Then all I remember was men digging me out, and muddy water was pouring, pouring all over me. Robert, the boy on the errand, was found two days later - dead. My right hand was crushed so badly I lost three fingers. My leg was injured, my pelvis fractured, my hair gone. I had bleeding internally and externally and they said I would have bled to death if the mud hadn't caked on me, forming a skin. The force of the mud was such that it smashed my spleen, which had to be removed, and ripped off an ear, which had to be sewn back on.

One boy would have bled to death if the mud had not formed a protective cake over his injuries

---

Susan Maybank, nearly eight years old, was sitting in her classroom. Her teacher glanced out of the window just as he saw the merciless black monster

about to engulf the school, and shouted a warning for her and her classmates to dive under their desks.

Seconds later, as the children - some of them believing they were playing an exciting new game - were on all fours, the slurry smashed through the walls as if they were paper. The teacher died instantly, and Susan remembers being engulfed by the cold blackness.

She has no idea how long she was underground - all she remembers was pushing her fingers through the muck to form an air-hole and waving them around. The small army of men - pensioners, off-duty miners, policemen, firemen, builders, doctors, solicitors, bakers and cooks that had descended on the school to begin frantically clawing at the rubble with their bare hands rescued her. In the slime were her best friends, entombed forever.

Eye-witnesses to the tragedy will never forget the scene of the sweating, wet-eyed men, their limbs trembling with rage and fury, their hands bleeding.

Elizabeth Jones was trapped for several hours with the dead body of another child jammed up against her. Now aged thirty-one, she believes she

Above: *Bereaved families weep at the communal grave where eighty tiny coffins were laid to rest side by side.*

Right: *A shocked world reacted immediately to the disaster by sending thousands of consoling letters containing hard-earned cash and cheques for the Aberfan Disaster Fund.*

escaped because she left a classroom to take her dinner money along to the school office when it happened.

'I only remember being engulfed in masonry and sludge,' she said.

I was trapped in the school corridor for a long time with the body of a little boy beneath me and by the side of me. When they pulled me out I was still holding my shilling dinner money. I am sure that saved me and I still keep it as a lucky coin.

Another souvenir is the plaster cast which my leg was in for months afterwards. Most of my memories have mercifully faded - when your mind luckily begins to think of other things. But I received severe internal injuries in the slide and as a result will never be able to have children.

All day and into the night the frantic struggle for survivors went on. Lord Snowdon and the ashen-faced Secretary of State for Wales, George Thomas, arrived to see the pathetic bodies of the children being plucked one by one from the black sea.

Later the agony was too much even for hardened journalists to bear as the children's pathetic corpses were laid in the Morriah Chapel for their agonized parents to come and identify them. An anguished keening rose into the skies above Aberfan that day: 'Why us, oh Lord, why us?'

By nightfall the generators hummed as the sodium arc lamps threw their light on the shattered school and surrounding buildings. Still the remains of tip no. 7 continued to yield casualties up from its smothering clutches.

Bryn Carpenter was in hospital the morning of the slide, recovering from a pit accident himself. He was rushed to the scene and found a sight more terrifying than anything he had ever witnessed below ground. He said:

We believed our ten-year-old Desmond was buried in there. When they told us of an unidentified ten-year-old in hospital our spirits lifted, but it turned out to be someone else.

Later that night they found Desmond's body. We were by no means alone in our grief. In my street alone we lost fourteen. Two houses lost two children each. And time doesn't heal - there is always something there to trigger grief again.

One of the lucky ones was Pat Lewis, whose eldest sister Sharon was killed in the slime that she managed to escape from. Just a week shy of her ninth birthday, she saw the wall splitting behind the teacher as he stood up to call the names on the morning register. Her shouted warning enabled him to get many of the children outside, and she was saved.

Below: *Homes too were destroyed as the killer coal slagheap swept past the infants' school and engulfed part of the village.*

Her mother, Sheila, scooped her in her arms as she arrived home - apologizing because her coat was still in the school. Sheila, a trained nurse, went back with her to the school and climbed in through a broken window. She recalled:

Inside were about twenty children who had been swept forward by the fast-approaching tip as it bulldozed the building. They were the ones who could be helped, though one of those children walked out of the ruins, seemingly all right, then collapsed and died.

I laid the survivors on blankets in the school yard and turned the infants' classroom into a first aid post. I worked the whole day but nobody came out alive after 11am. It was the most horrifying day, but your senses sharpen at times like that and so I can remember it all clearly.

I knew I couldn't go and identify Sharon's body. My poor husband had to go and do it. He came back from the chapel at about 5am on Saturday and

Above: *A touching tribute to the eighty children who perished. This giant Cross of Aberfan was made out of wreaths and flowers on a hillside overlooking the cemetery.*

Left: *Villagers openly wept as they witnessed bodies being brought out of the rubble and mud that was once a village school.*

said he recognized her. She had been found with the rest of the class and the teacher. I was sitting on a stool by the fire and I remember I slid back against the wall and made a terrible noise for I don't know how long.

Body after tiny body was laid in the chapel, their eyes and mouths filled with coal slurry that parents angrily cleaned out so their loved ones could rest with dignity. Throughout the night the parents came, and Aberfan was plunged into the post-shock trauma of a town that had suffered and lost on a tremendous scale. The final tally of dead was 144. Of the 116 schoolchildren, most of them were under the age of ten.

Afterwards, of course, bureaucrats moved in for the biggest government inquiry ever held. It lasted five months, and heard evidence from 136 witnesses.

Controversially the Coal Board chairman Alfred Robens, later Lord Robens, stayed away - although he attended later as the community felt painfully snubbed by his absence.

Due to goodness knows what rules of accounting, the government paid out £500 to each family that had lost a child. A further £5000 went to each family from a special fund patronized by the Queen, Prince Philip and Prince Charles.

THE TRAGEDY THAT SHOULD NEVER HAVE HAPPENED

There was only one verdict - that it could have all been prevented.

It emerged that there was no national safety policy for tips like Aberfan. The Coal Board was held to be legally liable for what had happened when it emerged that mandarins in the industry had ignored warnings about the dangerous state of the Aberfan tip since as far back as 1960.

Warnings about the state of the tip at Aberfan had been ignored for the previous six years.

Lord Robens had to live with the memory of what had happened to Aberfan, with the knowledge that it need never have occurred. In 1986, when newspapers around the world ran a retrospective on the tragedy to mark its twentieth anniversary, he said:

The one question I constantly turn over in my mind is how it could have been prevented. There were thousands of pit heaps all over the country and they all came within the local pit authority's guidelines. It is awful that it takes something like that to make sure every safety regulation is double-checked and brought into practice.

When I think of all I did during my time with the Coal Board it diminishes to nothing when I think of the Aberfan disaster. It is a terrible thing which will always haunt me.

On the bleak hillside above Aberfan stands one of the most poignant sights in Britain - row upon row of children's gravestones, the victims of the moving mountain that claimed them that day.

MI5 SPY RING
A Web of Deception

The sensational defection of Burgess and Maclean in 1951 triggered the exposure of a web of espionage and double dealing. For decades Englishmen in high places had been spying for the Russians

It was in the unlikely surroundings of Cambridge University that the twentieth century's most dangerous spy ring was spawned. In the 1930s as ex-public schoolboys punted down the River Cam, they formed the idea that Communism provided a better life and a stronger way to fight Fascism.

A former Russian envoy to London had started the recruitment ball rolling. Maxim Litvinov theorized that these undergraduates, already on the lower rungs of the Establishment ladder, would never have their loyalty doubted. So the Russian net was cast.

And within just a few years it hauled in a group of Cambridge students. Guy Burgess, Donald Maclean, Anthony Blunt and Kim Philby were to cause untold damage to Britain. Many died because of their treachery. Yet none of the spies was ever brought to justice.

In the thirties many undergraduates turned to Communism as a way of rejecting Fascism

It was Blunt who led the way to Cambridge and to Trinity College, which was to have the dubious distinction of being the breeding ground for each of the traitors. The son of a vicar, brilliant and a homosexual, he arrived at Trinity in 1928. He was a gifted student in mathematics, languages and art, and after he graduated he became a teaching Fellow.

Above: *Anthony Blunt's shame as a Soviet spy went unrevealed for years. He continued in his post as adviser to the Queen on her fabulous art collection.*

Opposite: *Kim Philby holds a press conference after he was wrongly cleared of being the 'Third Man' in the Burgess-Maclean affair.*

Right: *Foreign office intelligence chief Donald Maclean in a conference with the then British Ambassador to Washington, Sir John Balfour.*

Harold Philby - nicknamed Kim - arrived in 1929. And a year later they were joined by old Etonian Guy Francis de Moncy Burgess, an eccentric homosexual with a large capacity for alcohol and indiscreet gossip. Donald Maclean, the son of a religious Liberal cabinet minister, arrived in 1931.

Many Trinity College students became Communists. But for most it was a passing phase. For these four it became their life's work.

After university Maclean went to the Foreign Office. One of his interviewers,

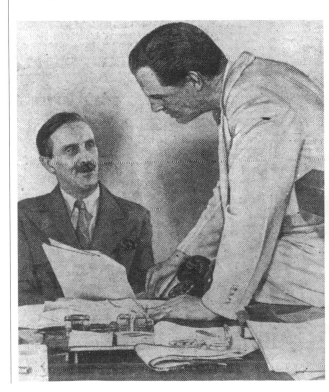

he later said, asked him: 'We understand that you held strong Communist views while you were at Cambridge. Do you still hold those views?'

'I decided to brazen it out. "Yes," I said "I did have such views - and I haven't entirely shaken them off." They must have liked my honesty.'

After Trinity, Burgess talked his way into a job with Tory MP Jack Macnamara. Burgess had already visited Russia and had met spy chiefs to arrange his contacts in London. He and Blunt became the organizers of the spy ring.

He was making contacts all the time and as war approached he became a secret courier carrying messages to European leaders. All the information he gained he was passing back to his Soviet spymasters. But at the same time he was feeding tip-offs to British Intelligence. His devious hard work paid off. In January 1939 MI6 offered him a staff job.

After Cambridge Philby went to Vienna, where he helped Communists to escape from the Nazis. He reappeared in London with a wife – a Soviet spy – and began to cultivate a right-wing image. In 1937 he went to Spain to cover the Civil War for the *Times* as a reporter. It was a useful cover to feed back information to the Russians, who were supporting the Republicans.

WAR WORK

In 1939 Blunt applied for a five-week military intelligence course. His Marxist past caught up with him, and he was returned to his unit as a 'security risk'.

But he wasn't downhearted by his first failure to infiltrate the security services. He joined the Army's Intelligence Corps and was evacuated from Dunkirk. And then, via the 'old boy' network, he was recruited by MI5.

Philby's chance to infiltrate the Secret Services came with a surprise phone call in June 1940 from the War Office. He was offered a job in Section D, in a new department formed to cause subversive chaos in Europe. His interviewers for the job included one Guy Burgess! And he soon progressed into MI6.

The job of MI5 was to protect security at home, while MI6 was in charge of

Right: *Donald Maclean in characteristic pose. This was the elegant Englishman who traded life in the West for a mundane existence behind the Iron Curtain.*

Opposite: *'Fourth Man' Anthony Blunt with the three defectors from British intelligence in the fifties and sixties - Guy Burgess, Donald Maclean and Kim Philby.*

Below: *A gardener tends the grounds of Maclean's house in Tatsfield, Kent, while the hunt goes on for the missing diplomat.*

intelligence-gathering abroad. Already Guy Burgess was hard at work for his Russian bosses.

Soviet Embassy cipher clerks were working full-time to encode the mass of material for transmission to Moscow.

Philby started by sending lists of agents, codenames and wavelengths from the central archives of the Secret Intelligence Services.

And from inside MI5 Blunt made sure that Russian atom spies Dr Klaus Fuchs and Dr Alan Nunn May could continue their work on the atom bomb – despite their obvious Communist leanings.

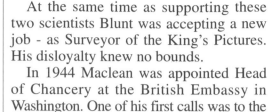

Above: *Maclean sent telegrams from Paris in 1951. To his mother he said: 'Am quite all right.' To his wife he said: 'Don't stop loving me.'*

Left: *Guy Burgess's mother, Mrs Jack Bassett in 1956.*

Below: *Guy Burgess (left)* with **Daily Express** *man Terence Lancaster in Moscow in 1957.*

At the same time as supporting these two scientists Blunt was accepting a new job - as Surveyor of the King's Pictures. His disloyalty knew no bounds.

In 1944 Maclean was appointed Head of Chancery at the British Embassy in Washington. One of his first calls was to the Soviet Consulate to meet his new controller.

He would have a lot of information to give him. Memos between Roosevelt and Churchill outlining war plans and post-war policy crossed his desk. And then after World War II Maclean was made secretary of the committee that dealt as the clearing house for atomic bomb information between the Western allies.

Meanwhile Philby had been promoted to a plum job too. He was made head of Section Nine, the department controlling espionage against Russia. It meant that Russia was warned of every planned spying mission against them.

RUMOURS AND DANGERS

The sheer bulk of information that the four were providing meant that suspicions were bound to be aroused. It was the Americans who first asked: why do the Russians know everything we're doing, before we've done it?

There was one specific case that threatened to uncover Philby. In August 1945 the Secret Service received a message that KGB man Konstantin Volkov wanted to defect to Britain with his wife. In return he promised to reveal the name of three British spies working for the Soviets in the Foreign Office and the Secret Service. Luckily for Philby, he was given the case to handle personally.

When a Russian defector offered to unmask British moles, it was Philby who was put in charge of the case!

When Philby arrived in Turkey, where he was supposed to meet the Russian, Volkov did not appear. He was next seen in Moscow – with a bullet in the back of his head. Years later the cynical Philby explained: 'It was either Volkov's head or mine.' And despite US suspicions, he got away with it.

After the war Burgess entered the

Foreign Office and became personal assistant to Hector MacNeil, the Labour government's deputy Foreign Secretary.

But the strain was telling on Burgess and Maclean and they were turning to drink. Maclean was sent to Cairo. But it didn't stop his boozing. After a drunken rampage, during which he snatched a nightwatchman's gun and then broke his leg, he was sent back to Britain.

By 1950 Burgess was in a terrible state. An official report on him stated: 'The sooner we get rid of this appalling man the better for all of us.' Wherever he went, he engaged in drinking bouts and fights. He launched vicious attacks on British policy. Still in August 1950 he was posted to Washington as first secretary. There he joined Philby, who had been appointed MI6's liaison man with the CIA.

But the noose around the spy ring's neck was tightening. Philby had already warned Burgess that British security was closing in on Foreign Office suspects.

In Washington he took Burgess under his wing - and under his roof. It was his last chance, the Foreign Office had decided. But both Burgess and Philby were still passing useful information to the Russians in Washington.

ESCAPE TO THE EAST

By 1951 Philby knew, because of his privileged position, that Maclean was close to being exposed. What he did not know was that the Americans had also targeted him and Burgess.

Maclean had to be warned, and had to escape. If he was captured he was bound to talk - he had become a nervous wreck. Philby nominated Burgess as messenger, but he could not return to Britain without an official reason. He contrived a series of embarrassing incidents, so the Ambassador had to order him home.

It was Blunt who discovered from his MI5 contacts the exact time when 'Homer' - the mole's codename - was to be picked up. On 25 May 1951 Foreign Secretary Herbert Morrison signed the paper ordering Maclean's interrogation.

Burgess knew within minutes and contacted Maclean. On the pretext of taking a holiday, they boarded a ferry to

Above: *Donald Maclean's wife Melinda arrives back from France with her family after the disappearance of her husband.*

Left: *The Maclean family car was found eight days after his disappearance, in a Lausanne garage.*

France that night. Neither was to be seen in Britain again. Their next public appearance was in 1956, when they were paraded in Moscow as heroes of the Communist struggle.

Why Burgess joined Maclean in his flight has never been revealed. He probably panicked. Their hurried flight left the remaining two Cambridge spies to face the music.

THE CHARMED LIFE OF A TRAITOR

It took a matter of hours for the authorities to link Philby with Burgess and Maclean's sudden disappearance. He was summoned back to London by MI6 chief Sir Stewart Menzies. Somehow Philby brazened it out, putting the blame

At Cambridge we had both been communists. We abandoned our political activities not because we disagreed with the Marxist analysis of the world situation, in which we still all find ourselves, but because we thought, wrongly it is now clear to us, that in the public service we could do more to put these ideas into practical effect than elsewhere.

It is probably our action in necessarily giving up political activities by entering the public service that, falsely analysed, led the Foreign Office to say through its spokesman that it "believed" we had been Soviet agents at Cambridge. The Foreign Office can of course "believe" anything it wishes. The important point however is that on this question we know, and it does not. We neither of us have ever been communist agents.

So far the ground was common for us both. The details of our subsequent careers were completely different and had therefore better be dealt with separately.

As regards Maclean, he worked in London and in Paris, Washington and Cairo as a regular member of the Foreign Service

Above: *The signed thousand-word statement of Burgess and Maclean. In it they say: 'Neither of us have ever been Communist agents.'*

fairly and squarely on the now absent Burgess. Philby was allowed to resign and take a £4000 golden handshake.

In his wake he left chaos. Ten intelligence service officials were forced to resign - not for being moles, but for failing to prevent spying.

In 1955 the government published the long-awaited White Paper on the disappearance of Burgess and Maclean. It was a whitewash. One MP described it as 'an insult to the intelligence of the country'.

But the most dangerous moment came for Philby when MP Marcus Lipton tabled a parliamentary question. The MP, primed by MI5, asked Tory Prime Minister Sir Anthony Eden: 'Have you made up your mind to cover up at all costs the dubious third man activities of Harold Philby?'

In 1955 Philby was named as the Third Man. Despite government warnings, MI6 continued to use him as an agent

---

For the first time Philby had been named as the so-called Third Man. And because the question was covered by parliamentary privilege the press could report it without running the risk of libel.

Foreign Secretary Harold Macmillan answered the question and told the House the conclusions of the Foreign Service's investigations:

I have no reason to conclude that Mr

Right: *Mrs Philby and a journalist in Beirut. She had reported her husband's disappearance but then heard that he had fled to Moscow.*

Philby has at any time betrayed the interests of this country, or to identify him with the so-called 'Third Man', if indeed there was one....

Philby was cock-a-hoop and held a press conference to celebrate. 'I have never been a Communist,' he lied.

MI6 took all this as a cue to use Philby as an agent again, when he was in the Middle East as a reporter for the *Observer* newspaper. There he began to feed the Soviets information again.

THE NET CLOSES

But Philby could not escape the truth for ever. MI5 still insisted that Philby was a mole, and final proof came with the sudden defection of Russian KGB man Anatoli Golitsin. He identified Philby as the Third Man beyond doubt.

In January 1963 agent Nicholas Elliott, an old friend of Philby's, flew to confront him with the new evidence.

'You took me in for years,' he said. 'Now I'll get the truth out of you even if I have to drag it out. I once looked up to you, Kim. God, how I despise you now.'

The Attorney-General, Sir John Hobson, had agreed that the spy could be offered immunity from prosecution - in exchange for a full confession.

He revealed how he had been recruited and trained, and detailed his work as a double agent. But he refused to name his contacts and to sign a written confession.

As Elliott returned to England for further instructions, Philby fled. In July the Supreme Soviet granted Philby's request for political asylum. Not only that, they gave him Russian citizenship and a job in the KGB as well!

THE MOLE AT THE PALACE

His escape left only the aesthetic intellectual Anthony Blunt still in place. Blunt had worked closely with Burgess, and now he feared that he would blurt out the truth from the safety of Moscow - to where Blunt had refused to flee.

By the time that Blunt faced William Skardon, the ace interrogator, he had already been questioned eleven times. This time though, he was faced with harder evidence. After being offered immunity, and after pouring himself a stiff drink, he then poured out his entire confession.

But astonishingly, despite his confession, the spy was allowed to keep his job as Surveyor of the Queen's Pictures and often met her in the course of his duties.

It was not until fourteen years later that Premier Margaret Thatcher was forced to act when the truth was uncovered by author Andrew Boyle. She announced: 'In April 1964, Sir Anthony Blunt admitted to the security authorities that he had passed information regularly to the Russians when he was a member of the Security Services...'

Minutes later Buckingham Palace announced that Blunt had been stripped of his knighthood.

The Queen was informed that her art advisor was a self-confessed spy

---

The so-called Mole at the Palace was finally exposed. He died disgraced seven years later, unloved save by his long-term homosexual partner, John Gaskin. At his funeral Blunt's brother Christopher said 'Anthony bitterly regretted that he got it wrong. But he was not ashamed. He was on the tiger and could not get off.' Burgess had died earlier, in 1963, homesick and an alcoholic. Maclean died in the same month as Blunt. Philby continued working for the KGB until the very end.

He swore that the only things he missed about Britain were the cricket scores and marmalade. But in 1982 a Russian freighter was spotted moored off the Sussex coast. On the bridge with a pair of binoculars was a stooped figure. It was Philby, taking a last longing look.

He died in Moscow in May 1988 and was given a full military send-off in Moscow's Kuntsevo cemetery.

Above: *Kim Philby with his mother in November 1955.*

Below: *Anthony Blunt addresses a press conference in London in 1980. He tried to fudge the accusations that he was the long-sought 'Fourth Man' in Britain's worst espionage ring.*

TENERIFE
Take-off to Tragedy

On a foggy day in 1977 two jumbos were diverted to a small, single-runway airport in the Canaries. As a result nearly six hundred people died in the worst airline disaster the world has ever known

Pan American pilot Victor Grubbs carefully taxied his fully loaded 747 along the runway at Los Rodeos airport, waiting for the all-clear for take-off. But as he steered the giant craft down the runway, he could scarcely believe what he saw through the cockpit window. Some 350 yards away he saw the lights of another 747, owned by the Dutch airline KLM, emerge from the fog.

At first, both Captain Grubbs and his flight crew thought the other plane was parked, but as the lights drew brighter it became terrifyingly clear that the Dutch jumbo was heading straight for them at 160 mph.

'We are still on the runway!' Grubbs screamed to the air traffic controllers in the tower. 'What's he doing? He'll kill us all!' His co-pilot, Robert Bragg, yelled for him to 'Get off! Get off!'

Desperately, Captain Grubbs swerved sharply to the left, heading for the grassy shoulder just off the runway. Tragically, he was a few seconds too late, as the KLM liner crashed broadside into the Pan Am clipper. Within seconds, the airstrip became a mass of tangled metal,

Above: *The arid peaks whose height causes the thick fogs that so often blank out Tenerife's airspace.*

Opposite: *The tailplane of the Pan Am jumbo jet after the worst air disaster in history.*

Below: *Tenerife is a sunny haunt for holidaymakers and the business heart of the Canary Islands.*

exploding fuel tanks and burning flesh.

It was 27 March 1977 - a day that saw the death of 583 Dutch and American citizens in the worst aviation disaster that had ever taken place.

BITTER IRONY

The tragedy was filled with the most bitter of ironies: neither plane had even intended stopping at Los Rodeos, a second-rate airport that was never considered among the safest in the region. But a terrorist bomb had exploded at their original destination, the more modern facility at Las Palmas some 70 miles away, and for safety's sake both aircraft had been rerouted to Tenerife.

That day had begun in a mood of innocent good humour. The Dutch airliner was carrying 283 holidaymakers, eager to begin their Easter break on Las Palmas.

The Pan Am clipper was carrying 380 passengers to a rendezvous with the cruise ship *Golden Odyssey*.

The disaster would never have happened if Las Palmas airport had not been closed due to a terrorist bomb

---

The re-routing seemed no more than a minor inconvenience, and both jumbos landed without incident. Captain Grubbs taxied his clipper, Victor, up to the terminal building and parked it alongside another 747, the Rhine, skippered by Captain Jacob Louis Veldhuyzen van Zanten, KLM's chief jumbo instructor.

Once the Rhine had been refuelled, Captain Veldhuyzen van Zanten asked for flight clearance. According to aviation officials, at Los Rodeos a plane would normally taxi its way to the south-east corner of the field for take-off, but because of the emergency at Las Palmas that route was now crowded by other diverted planes. So the tower instructed the KLM plane to taxi up the runway itself, and at the end Veldhuyzen van Zanten made a 180-degree turn and prepared for take-off.

At the same time, the tower instructed Grubbs too to taxi up the runway, but told him to turn off by the third exit on his left, thus leaving the airstrip free for the

KLM jumbo. A few minutes later, controllers asked him if he had made the turn. When Grubbs replied that he hadn't, they told him: 'Do it, and advise when the runway is clear.'

But as the clipper continued up the runway, shrouded in mist and therefore invisible both to the Dutch plane and to the tower, the KLM crew made its last transmission to the tower: 'KLM....We are now ready on [or 'at' - the exact wording was garbled] take-off.'

Grubbs's worst nightmare was happening. The KLM was hurtling out of the fog at 160 mph, and heading straight for him. Frantically he radioed the tower

that he was still on the runway, then swore angrily as he desperately gunned his engines and jerked his plane to the left. As he did so, Veldhuyzen van Zanten urgently tried to take his plane into the air. Its nose lifted but the tail remained on the runway, digging an ugly, gaping trench.

IMPACT

It smashed into the Pan Am jumbo in the forward part of the second-class section, while its right wing slashed through the bubble atop the cockpit, slicing off the roof. The Pan Am clipper, cut in half and already on fire, toppled to the side of the runway.

Above: *The burnt-out skeleton of the tail section of Pan Am's jumbo jet on the runway of Santa Cruz airport.*

A split second later, the Dutch plane slammed back to the ground, skidded around backwards and screeched to a halt about 300 yards away. In an instant, it exploded into a ball of flames, the inferno gorging itself on its just-filled fuel tanks. Everyone on board was killed. The impact was so hard and the explosive fire so hot that aluminium and steel parts on both planes were vaporized.

Back on board the American plane, there was pandemonium. Debris seemed to be falling from everywhere, and the flames were quickly spreading. Terrified and dazed, those who could scrambled to get out. Many were already dead, and

*Above: **The passengers who packed the Dutch and American jumbos had dreamed of lazing on sun-drenched beaches fanned by Atlantic breezes.***

others were too stunned to move.

Inside the twisted wreck, heroic thirty-three-year-old businessman Edgar Ridout tried to organize an evacuation.

Some of the Pan Am passengers were in such shock that they just stood there as if nothing had happened

---

The brave businessman helped one of the stewardesses inflate a life raft so that passengers could jump onto it as they leaped from the plane.

HEROES AND SURVIVORS

There were many heroes that day. As burning debris and red-hot metal continued to shower the immediate area, melting the runway, Jack Daniel helped his wife and daughter to safety, then disappeared. His frightened wife began frantically asking if anyone had seen a man in a white suit. Someone answered that he had heard a woman screaming for help, and that a man in a white suit had raced back to help. Then there was another explosion, and both had disappeared.

Meanwhile, as the tragedy continued to unfold, doctors and nurses at the nearby La Candelaria Hospital began dealing with the wounded. Most of them had rushed to the hospital as word spread of the crash, and they worked gallantly under the most difficult conditions.

There were not enough beds for all the dying and the injured, so orderlies laid them on the floor while nurses scampered about handing out painkillers and sedatives and doctors began the task of stripping away burned skin.

Other survivors who had less serious injuries were huddled in the airport terminal. Blankets and painkillers were handed out to the stunned passengers, some of whom had had the clothes burned off their backs. Each of them spoke of their escape as miraculous. 'I felt someone was watching over me,' said Theresa Brusco. 'It was like we had a guardian angel around us.'

WHAT WENT WRONG?

By this stage, scores of soldiers and police were combing through the gutted wreckage of both planes, engaged in the grisly task of sorting out bodies.

What had gone wrong? A horde of aviation experts from the United States, Holland and Spain quickly descended on Los Rodeos to find out, and at first suspicion fell on the air traffic controllers. It had been rumoured that they did not speak very good English - the language of international air traffic control - and that the two pilots might have been confused.

But that was quickly dispelled when investigators interviewed the three men who had been in the tower at the time of the crash. They all spoke 'textbook' English, and had followed take-off procedures to the letter.

The probe then targeted the captains, Grubbs and Veldhuyzen van Zanten.

At first, Dutch experts challenged the American flyer's conduct over the question of runway exits. There were four such exits along the runway, marked C-1 to C-4. KLM officials argued that Grubbs had been ordered to turn off at C-3 and that, had he done so, the catastrophe would never have occurred.

But Pan Am countered by claiming that their pilot had merely been told to

take 'the third exit' on the left. Pan Am executive William Waltrip asserted that C-1 was 'inactive', and that C-3 would have required an extremely difficult turn of 150 degrees. Therefore, the Americans maintained, the logical 'third exit' was C-4 - the one Grubbs never reached.

Moreover, argued the Americans, no matter where the clipper was supposed to be, Veldhuyzen van Zanten should never have taken off without clearance from the tower. The head of the Dutch investigation team had shocked his countrymen when he stated that he had found no clearance for the KLM take-off on the tower's nine-minute audio tape.

Top: *A memorial service for the victims of the disaster was conducted at Schiphol Airport, Amsterdam. On the runway were 232 coffins decked with flowers.*

Above: *Mourners leave the memorial service at Schiphol Airport.*

THE VERDICT

It took an exhaustive, eighteen-month investigation before the Spanish government would release its findings.

The tragic verdict of the investigation was that Captain Veldhuyzen van Zanten had decided to start his take-off run without clearance, and that had been 'the fundamental cause'.

The report recalled that the weather was dismal that day, with low-scudding clouds and fog that sharply reduced visibility. But that on its own couldn't account for the Dutchman's strange and inexplicable decision.

How could a veteran pilot like Veldhuyzen van Zanten have made such an incredible mistake? It seems that, harried by an already lengthy delay on Tenerife and the erratic weather conditions, he may have rushed his take-off to avoid violating a KLM rule against crew overtime.

The radio 'whistle' could have beeped out some essential communications. And imprecise language used by both the tower and the KLM crew may have confused matters still further.

In the end, to those who died, it didn't matter...because just seconds later, the world's worst-ever aviation disaster occurred.

CHALLENGER
A Shattered Dream

In January 1986 a fireball of horror erupted into the sunny Florida skies. After twenty-five successful missions the Challenger space shuttle had blown up, killing all aboard her. What went wrong? And why were the warnings ignored?

The morning of 28 January 1986 began like many others for the skilled team of NASA scientists and engineers at Cape Canaveral, as they checked and rechecked the Space Shuttle *Challenger* in preparation for what they thought would be another routine mission in space for the reusable craft.

The seven astronauts - including Christa McAuliffe, who was to be the first civilian in space - were given last-minute briefings and instructions. And around the massive base, thousands of excited spectators and media representatives had gathered to await the spectacular launch.

None could have known that within seconds of that spectacular lift-off, the unthinkable would happen. The *Challenger* would explode in a fiery orange-and-white ball, killing all the crew members aboard and derailing the American space programme for almost three years.

In one tragic instant, the world's complacency towards manned space flight would evaporate forever nine miles up in the blue skies over Florida.

One spectator's scream was heard and repeated around the world: 'Oh, my God! What's happened?'

Opposite: *A moment of hope as* **Challenger** *takes to the skies. Within seconds came disaster.*

Below: *The* **Challenger's** *astronauts line up for the photo album before take-off from Cape Canaveral on 28 January 1986.*

PRELUDE TO TRAGEDY

The story of *Challenger*'s fateful trip to oblivion began the previous night, as temperatures in the normally temperate Florida winter plunged to an unseasonable 27 degrees.

A spectator screamed: 'Oh, my God! What's happened?' Her agonized cry was heard by millions on TV worldwide

---

Early the next morning, NASA's so-called 'ice team' went to work, inspecting the shuttle for any signs of potentially dangerous build-ups of ice which could break away on lift-off and harm the *Challenger*'s heat-shield tiles.

It would later emerge that an engineer working with the Rockwell company in California, who had been watching the inspection on closed circuit television, called mission control to urge a delay because of the ice.

The gathered masses who stood cheering the astronauts as they walked to the *Challenger*, veteran of nine previous flights, knew nothing of the frantic warning which had come from three thousand miles away. Nor did the crew.

Once on board, they began their detailed checks of all systems with the aid of the craft's main computer.

Everything seemed right for the mission which included the deployment of a $100 million communications satellite into space and several on-board experiments. The astronauts were to measure the spectrum of Halley's comet; to sample radiation within the spacecraft at various points; and to examine the effects of weightlessness on the development of twelve chicken embryos.

From three thousand miles away came the unheeded advice to delay the launch because of the cold weather

---

At T minus seven minutes and thirty seconds the walkway was finally pulled away from the billion-dollar shuttle and its three huge engines.

The external tank stood more than ten storeys high and carried more than half a

Above: *The space shuttle lifts off from launch pad 39B. The orbiter craft carried the doomed crew of seven.*

million gallons of liquid oxygen and liquid hydrogen. The two booster rockets were packed with more than one million pounds of solid fuel.

The public address system continued: 'T minus forty-five seconds and counting,' as those in the huge crowd talked excitedly among themselves.

On board, Commander Dick Scobee and Pilot Michael Smith were strapped into the flight deck. Directly behind them were Judith Resnik, an electrical engineer, and Ronald McNair, a physicist. On the mid-deck below were Ellison Onizuka, an aerospace engineer,

Gregory Jarvis, an electrical engineer, and Christa McAuliffe.

With six seconds to go, the main engine was started. The roar was deafening.

'Four...three...two...one...and lift-off. Lift-off of the twenty-fifth space shuttle mission. And it has cleared the tower.' The spectators began to cheer wildly for the spectacular rise to the heavens.

Among those who watched the *Challenger*'s graceful ascent, its white plume of smoke shining brilliantly behind, were McAuliffe's family and eighteen of her third-grade class who had travelled some fifteen hundred miles from Concord, New Hampshire to see their teacher make history.

Sixteen seconds after launch the huge craft turned gracefully on its back as the main fuel tank and the two booster rockets assumed the course for leaving the earth's atmosphere. Mission control pronounced that all three engines were running smoothly.

'*Challenger*, go with throttle up,' said mission control exactly fifty-two seconds after launch. 'Roger, go with throttle up,' Scobee radioed back.

Three seconds later, NASA's long-range television cameras picked up an appallingly unfamiliar sight.

Television viewers could see what those below could not. A tiny but distinct orange glow flashed near the middle of the shuttle, between its underside and the external tank.

A split second later, the unthinkable nightmare happened. The *Challenger* was momentarily engulfed in flames, then disintegrated.

Unaware of the explosion, the official announcer continued his narration while the incredulous spectators watched in horror

---

Spectators felt an unspeakable horror as the hideous Y-shaped cloud spewed above them.

Incredibly, back at mission control in Houston, the official announcer had not been watching the TV monitor. Instead, he had his eyes glued on the programmed flight data displayed in front of him, and reported what should have been the readings from *Challenger*.

'One minute, fifteen seconds. Velocity 2900 feet per second. Altitude nine nautical miles. Downrange distance seven nautical miles.' To the stunned millions watching on television, the narration was surreal.

Suddenly, he stopped. A minute later he announced: 'We have a report from the flight dynamics officer that the vehicle has exploded. The flight director confirms that.'

In Washington, President Ronald Reagan was working in the Oval Office when suddenly his top aides burst in.

'There's been a serious incident with the space shuttle,' said Vice President George Bush. Patrick Buchanan, the White House Communications Director, was much more blunt: 'Sir, the shuttle has exploded.'

Reagan, like the rest of America, was stunned. It was his decision that the first private citizen in space should be a schoolteacher. McAuliffe had been selected from more than eleven thousand hopeful applicants.

Below: *The view from Kennedy Space Center as* **Challenger** *explodes within moments of its launch.*

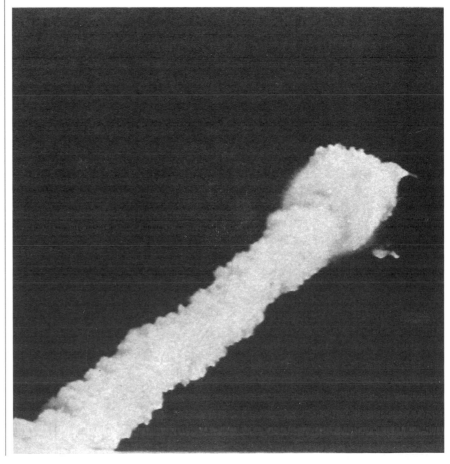

A few hours later he would try to soothe a grieving nation with a poignant speech in which he said that the seven pioneers had 'left the surly bonds of earth to touch the face of God'.

Then, addressing the nation's schoolchildren Reagan added: 'I know it's hard to understand that sometimes painful things like this happen. It's all part of the process of exploration...and expanding man's horizons.'

GRIEF AND SORROW

Americans were shaken. Their scientists and astronauts had soared into space fifty-five times over the past quarter of a century, and their safe return had come to be taken for granted. An age when almost anyone, given a few months' training, could go along for a safe ride seemed at hand. McAuliffe, a vivacious high school teacher, was to be the standard bearer of that new era. Tragically, the era lasted just seventy-three seconds.

'They have left the surly bonds of earth to touch the face of God,' said President Reagan in a moving speech

---

After undergoing rigorous training for three months, the teacher was ready for her fantastic voyage. Her task was to conduct two fifteen-minute classes in space as millions of schoolchildren watched via closed circuit television. She would explain the functioning of the shuttle and the benefits of space travel.

She never got the chance to do what she loved best, which was to teach. Nowhere was the tragedy felt more than in Concord, where fellow teachers and pupils had gathered inside the school auditorium to watch what they had presumed to be their colleague and friend's moment of triumph.

Throughout the town, the thirty thousand residents were engulfed by sorrow as the news quickly spread. 'People froze in their tracks,' said one local. 'It was like part of the family has been killed.'

American music was played on Soviet state-run radio, and officials in Moscw announced they were naming craters on Venus in honour of the two female crew members, McAuliffe and Resnik.

In Vatican City, Pope John Paul II asked an audience of thousands to pray for the American astronauts, saying that the tragedy had 'provoked deep sorrow in my soul'. British Premier Margaret Thatcher sadly observed that 'New knowledge sometimes demands sacrifices of the bravest and the best.'

And Senator John Glenn, the first American to orbit the earth, recalled: 'The first group of us always knew there would be a day like this. We're dealing with speeds and powers and complexities we've never dealt with before.'

Across the United States, communities reacted in their own ways to the news. In Los Angeles, the Olympic torch atop the Coliseum was relit. New York City's Empire State Building was darkened. And along the Florida coast an estimated twenty-two thousand people pointed torches at the sky.

THE INVESTIGATION

As the nation grieved, back at Cape Canaveral the US Coast Guard and NASA crews had already began the grim task of searching for the wreckage of *Challenger*.

They had to wait almost sixty minutes after the explosion before starting the search, because of debris still raining from the sky. Their search covered some six thousand square miles of the Atlantic.

Despite the power of the blast, searchers began finding surprisingly large parts of the wreckage scattered on the ocean floor, including a 25 ft long section of the *Challenger*'s fuselage.

As for the astronauts themselves, it was only after extensive prodding that NASA admitted that the crew had not perished instantly, as initially claimed. They survived the explosion and probably lived until their cabin hit the surface of the ocean.

Once the wreckage had been gathered, NASA investigators began the arduous task of finding out what had gone wrong. It was a three-pronged probe. First, there was the film to study from eighty NASA cameras and ninety belonging to news organizations. There were also the billions of computer signals sent between the doomed craft and its earthbound control centres. And lastly, there were the actual remains of the *Challenger.*

There was speculation that ice, which had formed on the launch pad the night before the lift-off, had damaged the craft - as the engineer at Rockwell had feared.

Also suspected was that the external fuel tank's insulation had been damaged during a minor accident a few days earlier, when a derrick arm supposedly scraped the tank. But NASA insisted the derrick had touched not the tank, but only part of the launch-pad equipment.

Speculation soon centred on the possibility of a failure in either the main tank or one of the two booster rockets. Experts noted that either could have caused the violent explosion. Another possibility was that a seam in the main tank had ruptured.

In closed meetings, a specially constituted panel began to grill top NASA officials as well as engineers from Morton Thiokol, the company that makes the solid fuel boosters suspected of triggering the disaster. What they uncovered stunned the commissioners.

The engineers had adamantly opposed the launch because of the icy weather at Cape Canaveral.

Robert Sieck, the shuttle manager at the Kennedy Space Center, and Gene Thomas, the launch director for *Challenger* at Kennedy, testified that they had never before heard that Thiokol engineers had objected to the launch.

Gradually, most rocket experts agreed that at least one of the two synthetic rubber O-rings that were meant to seal the joint between the booster's four segments had begun to burn. About 1/4 in thick, and some 37 feet in circumference, the O-rings are designed to keep the rocket's exhaust gases from escaping through any gaps in the joints.

The evening before the launch, Thiokol engineers and NASA officials met to discuss the potential problems. The engineers were unanimous in asking for the *Challenger* launch to be delayed.

They were worried that the O-rings might lose some of their elasticity, and hence their ability to sit tightly in their grooves around the rockets, when their

temperature fell below 50 degrees. That evening the temperature was 30 degrees.

Eventually, however, Morton Thiokol senior vice-president Jerald Mason declared that 'We have to make a management decision.' He and three other Thiokol vice-presidents, approved the launch.

But Allan McDonald, director of Thiokol's engineers after 'heated exchanges' with NASA officials, refused to sign an official approval to proceed. 'I argued before, and I argued after,' he told reporters.

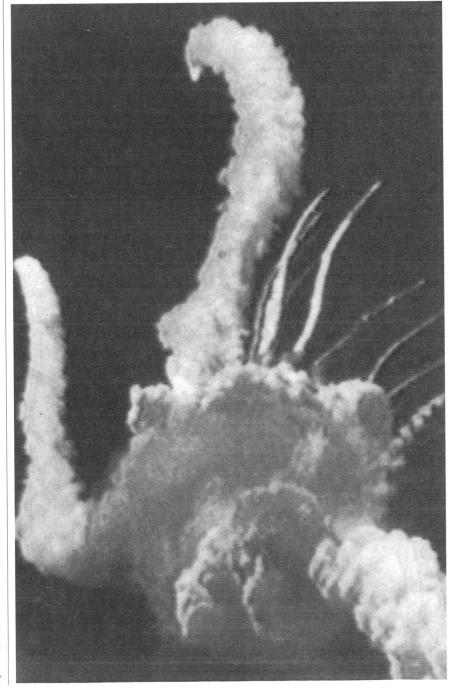

Below: *Plumes of smoke follow segments of the space shuttle which hurtled rocket debris to earth in several directions.*

NASA, it seemed, was not interested in 'fears', but instead demanded proof that the launch would be unsafe. At one point, a NASA official supposedly asked the engineers: 'My God, when do you want me to launch, next April?' Finally NASA over-ruled the engineers.

NASA, it seems, was not interested in fears of an unsafe launch - only in proof. Tragically, they got it

---

Incredibly, on the morning of the actual launch NASA missed another chance to abort the launch. Icicles had formed on the huge tower that supports the craft on the launch pad and Space Agency officials - concerned that ice breaking off might damage the heat shield tiles - sent in the 'ice teams' to inspect the pad three times.

Information in one of the reports about abnormal 'cold spots' on the right booster rocket was somehow missed. That meant that its O-rings were subjected to far greater cold than on any previous flight.

THE FINDINGS

At a public hearing of the Senate Subcommittee on Science, Technology and Space, Senator Ernest Hollings said of the disaster: 'At this particular juncture it seems like an avoidable accident rather than an unavoidable one.'

Later, he would charge that it was becoming 'apparent that NASA made a political decision to go ahead with [the] launch...despite strong objections.'

It was later revealed that since at least 1980 NASA had recognized that the seals between the booster sections were cause for concern.

On the first twelve shuttle flights, in four instances the O-rings had been partly burned away. Afterwards, the Space Agency began using a new type of putty to protect the joint - with the result that erosion of O-rings then occurred even more frequently.

Despite all the evidence NASA's top engineers and managers judged that this flaw was not serious enough to halt or delay shuttle flights.

The safety panel concluded that the tragedy had been caused by the 'failure of the pressure seal in the aft-field joint of the right solid-rocket motor', but noted that 'there was a serious flaw in the decision-making process'.

The panel was reluctant to assign personal blame for the tragedy, but instead outlined recommendations to ensure that such a disaster never happened again.

Its 285-page report to President Reagan urged that the shuttle's booster joints be entirely redesigned rather than just modified and that all the shuttle's critical parts be reviewed.

In addition, NASA had been eager to get the Challenger into orbit because of a series of earlier postponements to the original launch date three days before, on Saturday 25 January. First there was a dust storm at the emergency landing site in Senegal. Then, at Cape Canaveral, it rained, which could damage the heat-resistant tiles on the spacecraft. And on Monday, first a stuck bolt on an exterior-hatch handle, then 35mph winds delayed the launch until the next morning.

But the commission did not lay the blame entirely at NASA's feet. It also noted that the numbers of flights it had proposed had never been adequately funded by Washington, and that its budget had been so heavily slashed that even spare parts were running low.

AFTERMATH

Four days later, on the Friday, America held its final farewell for the Seven. Under grey skies at the Johnson Space Center near Houston, where they had trained, some six thousand NASA employees, congressmen and relatives gathered to hear President Reagan.

The sacrifice of your loved ones has stirred the soul of our nation, and, through the pain, our hearts have been opened to a profound truth: the future is not free...

Dick, Mike, Judy, El, Ron, Greg and Christa, your families and your country mourn your passing. We bid you goodbye, but we will never forget you.

The American people certainly would not let NASA forget them. The Space

Agency, once a source of national pride, was subjected to lengthy overhauls and reviews determined to ensure, as far as modern technology and human errors would allow, that there would never again be a disaster like the *Challenger*.

The entire shuttle programme was also revamped and many changes made to the existing fleet. On 29 September 1988 there was a collective sigh of relief at the dramatically successful flight of the space shuttle *Discovery*, which marked America's return to manned space flight after a thirty-two-month break.

Not surprisingly, given their woes in the wake of the *Challenger* disaster, NASA officials treated the *Discovery* mission as if it were the test flight of a brand-new vehicle. Engineers estimated that four times as much work went into the new design as had gone into the original development in the mid-1970s.

The main engines located at the tail of the shuttle had been plagued by problems from the beginning, and during the enforced hiatus NASA made thirty-five changes to them.

The razzmatazz of the space shuttle should be put aside, urged the panel, in favour of more sensible scientific projects

---

NASA's engineers made 210 changes to the design of the orbiter itself and another 100 modifications to its highly sophisticated computer software.

But in the ensuing three years the shuttle programme was plagued by major and minor problems, putting increased pressure on the workload. In 1991 a panel concluded in a report to the White House that NASA should focus on new goals in the wake of budget cuts, the recession and its own ineptitude.

The report strongly suggested that the Agency should not spend funds buying another after the *Endeavor* joined the current fleet of three later that year. It concluded that another tragic and disastrous shuttle accident was highly probable by the end of the century.

Other points raised were putting research and development ahead of splashy TV space extravaganzas, and not risking astronauts when robots can do the same job. NASA was told to cut costs and get back to more scientific missions.

The shuttle has been plagued by glitches in the early 1990s - everything from computer failures to clogged toilets. And the entire fleet was once grounded for five months by a dangerous fuel leak.

Still, experts say that the shuttle will play an integral part in the construction of the space station Freedom – the first step in America's plan to put a man on Mars before the year 2015.

Below: *Horror is frozen on the faces of watchers in the VIP area at Kennedy Space Center as the craft explodes 72 seconds after ignition.*

EXXON VALDEZ
Oil Spill Catastrophe

On 24 March 1989 the clear waters of Prince William Sound in Alaska became hideously polluted as the supertanker Exxon Valdez hit a reef. Ten million gallons of stinking black crude escaped after the accident that arrogant oil barons had said could never happen

Alaskan Eskimos are steeped in the traditions and beliefs of their forefathers. One of their deities is Sedna, goddess of the sea, a powerful ruler who deserved much homage to keep the ocean's harvest of seals and fish - the Eskimo lifeblood - well nurtured. The goddess is fabled for her distaste for man and his 'filth'.

THE CAPTAIN WITH A DRINK PROBLEM

Environmental agencies and government legislation had gone to great lengths - far more than in other American states - to keep the straits, lakes and seaways fresh and beautiful. But in 1989 Sedna suffered the most heinous blow ever delivered by a mortal against a god when a ship called the *Exxon Valdez* ran aground in one of the most unpolluted stretches of water in the world.

The goddess's distaste was justified - man had committed one of the world's worst acts of pollution, spewing millions of gallons of crude oil into the sparkling, clear waters.

The 'big spill', as the locals now call it, occurred at precisely four minutes past midnight on 24 March 1989 when Captain Joseph Hazelwood, master of the supertanker *Exxon Valdez*, was absent from the bridge.

At forty-two, Captain Hazelwood, was

Above: *The tanker* Exxon San Francisco *is pushed by tugs up against the stricken* Valdez *as work begins to salvage the oil remaining aboard her.*

Opposite: *Snow-peaked mountains dwarf the* Exxon Valdez.

Left: *The* **Exxon Valdez** *spewed 10 million gallons of oil into the sea when it ran aground on a reef in Prince William Sound.*

at the peak of his career with Exxon and earned around £100,000 a year as one of its star captains. He had wealth, responsibility, respect...and a drinking problem which would lead the ship to tragedy on that chill, starlit night.

The discovery of oil in the remote state of Alaska in 1968 had been a boon to the locals, whose only other sources of income were fishing, hunting and tourism. The oil revenues had reduced state taxes, and there were good wages to be earned as the black gold continued to flow into the bellies of the supertankers.

But with oil came a change in the bucolic way of life that the locals had enjoyed cheek-by-jowl with the native Eskimos for centuries. As well as the ever-present risk of an accident, the tough world of oilmen and sailors had stripped the area of its innocent charm for ever.

The current boom in communities like Valdez, on Prince William Sound, was the result of years of bickering and bitter argument about how best to move the oil three thousand miles and more to the thirsty markets awaiting it. The companies drilling for it had examined many different options, including building a pipeline through Canada to California and the Mid-West.

Captains of the US oil industry, though, were not best pleased with the prospect of moving American resources across foreign territory. In the end the trans-Alaska companies and the federal government settled on a pipeline that brought the oil down to Valdez from the permafrost fields further north.

The Valdez pipeline is a magnificent feat of engineering running for nearly eight hundred miles across the Arctic wilderness

---

That 789-mile pipeline is one of the most remarkable engineering feats in history - 101,850 sections of 48-in diameter steel pipe going through rivers and lakes and across Arctic ranges.

Once loaded on board ships like the *Exxon Valdez* it was transported to Texan or Californian ports for refining.

In the early evening of 23 March the *Exxon Valdez* was loading up with 1.26 million barrels of oil.

Captain Hazelwood, the third mate Gregory Cousins and Robert Kagan, the helmsman, were the only crewmen to leave the ship. Against all rules that forbade drinking at sea - and an Exxon regulation which prohibited the consumption of alcohol for at least four hours before a journey was started - Hazelwood and the two others went to sink some beers at the Pipeline Club. Later, eye-witnesses would report that they had seen him drink at least four beers. Hazelwood's employers knew about his previous drinking bouts and had once sent him to a drying-out clinic.

James Shiminski, an Exxon chief mate, said: 'He had a reputation for both partying ashore and on board the ship.'

In 1984 Hazelwood was convicted for drunken driving after a car crash.

A year later he underwent a twenty-eight-day stay in an alcohol addiction clinic not far from his home on Long Island, New York.

THE FATEFUL JOURNEY BEGINS

Within an hour of his latest drinking session Hazelwood and his party had returned to the dockside ready to board the vessel for sailing.

At 9.10pm he was on the bridge of the *Exxon Valdez* as she slipped her moorings for Long Beach, California, where a substantial refinery complex would process her cargo.

William Murphy was the harbour pilot who was obliged by law to navigate the ship for the two hours it took to weave through the shallow sea lane littered with jagged rocks. Later he would tell investigators that he smelled alcohol on the skipper's breath that night but that his demeanour did not indicate that he was intoxicated.

The ship, bigger than three football pitches end to end, lumbered off into the still, freezing night an hour before her scheduled sailing time. In the bowels of the ship engines capable of producing over 35,000 horsepower pushed her on her way.

Shortly after 11.30pm, only minutes after the pilot Murphy had left the bridge and returned home on a harbour launch, Hazelwood radioed the local coastguard and said he was altering the course of the ship from the outward, ice-infested channel to the inbound, ice-free channel.

At approximately 11.50pm Hazelwood turned over the bridge, and therefore control of the ship, to the third mate, Cousins. The second mate, Lloyd

Below: *The* **Valdez** *caused an environmental disaster ecologists had been warning about for 15 years - and which oil companies said was 'impossible'.*

LeCaine, was in a deep sleep.

Regulations stated that it was LeCaine who should have assumed the responsibility. However, maritime experts have since concurred it was a rule more often broken than observed by many skippers.

The coastguard had to give permission for the turn into the inbound channel - which it did - but shortly afterwards lost radar contact with the ship. Hazelwood had told Cousins to make a right turn back into the outbound channel when the vessel reached a navigational point near Busby Island, three miles north of a jagged underwater outcrop of rock called Bligh Reef.

The captain was just fifteen feet away from the bridge, completing paperwork in his cabin, when disaster struck. The *Exxon Valdez* was more than a mile from where she should have been.

One reason could have been that helmsman Robert Kagan, feeling that the ship was turning too sharply back towards the outbound channel, used a counter-rudder manoeuvre to slow the swing. Such a measure was logged in the ship's course recorder, a kind of maritime 'black box'.

Captain Hazlewood heard the groaning of tortured steel beneath him

---

Cousins repeated the order for a hard-right rudder, and then Captain Hazelwood felt the groaning and twisting of steel underneath him and knew that something had gone terribly, terribly wrong. Then came the phone call from Cousins: 'We are in trouble!'

Hazelwood bolted to the bridge and knew instantly from the lack of motion that the ship had grounded on the reef and was hanging precariously like a gigantic see-saw. His first job was to make sure it didn't slip off the reef, which could cause her either to keel over or to break her back. Hazelwood was in for the longest night of his life.

Beneath his 987-ft-long ship were huge rents in her steel hull, some fifteen feet long. Eight of the fifteen cargo holds were ruptured, and in time some 240,000 barrels of oil, forty-two gallons in each,

would be released into the sound with catastrophic effect.

Despite some question marks over Hazelwood's sobriety or otherwise, investigators would later say he showed excellent seamanship in his efforts at damage limitation. By adjusting the engine power he was able to keep the vessel firmly pressed up against the reef and stable.

Once the *Exxon Valdez* had run aground she was picked up again by the coastguard radar. In what seems to have been a case of bureaucratic bungling, the coastguards did not board the stricken ship until three hours later.

THE BUNGLED CLEAN-UP

Daylight brought with it full realization of the environmental horror that had occurred. Already the carcasses of sea otters and birds had begun to be seen on the outer reaches of the spill.

First the coastguards lost touch with the ship on their radar, then it took them three hours to reach her after she grounded

---

The scene was the environmental disaster that protesters had been warning of for years. But two years before the disaster the consortium of powerful oil companies had said haughtily: 'It is highly unlikely that there will ever be a spill of any magnitude.'

The consortium further boasted that slick-fighting materials would be on hand within five hours to neutralize the effects of any spill.

But the first clean-up crews did not get to the spill site until ten hours afterwards, during which time the 10 million-plus gallons gurgling from the shattered hull of the *Exxon Valdez* continued unabated into the sound. And even then they were pitifully inadequately equipped to deal with a spillage of such major proportions.

They had been lulled into complacency even though their equipment had been proved taxed to the limit in dealing with a small spill of just 1500 barrels in January the same year. There were no

booms to contain the spreading slick and few skimmers, which swept the surface of the water collecting oil.

All the equipment to deal with the vast slick was inadequate or out of action

---

Below: One of the several oil cargo tanks aboard the 987-foot **Valdez.** *Workers removed 1600 tons of damaged steel from the ship's hull before putting her back in service.*

The slick was still spreading, but chemicals could not be used because the water was calm, which rendered them ineffective. The coastguard, which by law was supposed to have vessels on hand capable of dealing with a 'major' spill, had its minuscule fleet of ships two thousand miles away in San Francisco.

By Sunday, 26 March, winds had picked up across the sound and were whipping the surface oil into a 'mousse' - a frothy cream that defied attempts to skim it up. Attempts were made to burn it, also to no avail.

The oil had now formed the biggest slick in history – covering 900 square miles, fouling the inlets that are home to sea otters, the nesting shallows of dozens of bird species and the once-pristine beaches where seals suckled their young.

At the last count the body count was grim: 86,000 birds, among them 139 rare bald eagles, 984 sea otters, 25,000 fish, 200 seals and several dozen beavers were the victims. Millions of mussels, sea urchins and other forms of marine life were wiped out for ever. Thousands more sea otters are feared to be dead, their bodies weighted down with oil to sink for ever beneath the surface.

Some beaches had to be treated with detergent chemicals seven times

---

Some beaches had to be treated seven times with detergents and other chemicals. Environmental scientist Paul Willard said:

The spill happened in almost the worst place possible. The jagged coast of Prince William Sound is dotted with innumerable coves and inlets where the spilled oil collected and stayed for months, killing young fish that spawn in the shallows.

LAWSUITS

Exxon came under a barrage of criticism. Newspaper advertisements urged people not to buy Exxon products and their service stations were deserted, the result of national disgust at their seemingly cavalier treatment of the disaster.

Exxon's President, Frank Iarossi, countered with the pledge of a billion dollars for the clean-up. Exxon also made a commitment to compensate fishermen and others who had directly suffered because of the spill.

In apportioning blame for the big spill it has been all too easy merely to point the finger at Captain Hazelwood and his

love for a drink too many. He was fired almost immediately after the disaster. Exxon cited as their reason positive blood alcohol tests taken nine hours after the ship grounded. But subsequent inquiries have concluded that he acted honourably afterwards and with great skill, and that he may only have gone over the limit afterwards when he needed to steady his nerves.

The fatigue of his crew, as much as the combination of errors in navigation that night, may well have played a part in the grounding of the *Exxon Valdez*. There were just twenty crewmen working that night on board one of the biggest vessels afloat - a reduction of twenty-four from when Hazelwood had first sailed in her.

Also at fault were the coastguards who, had they not lost the ship on their radar, might well have been able to notify her that she was navigating into dangerous waters.

New, more stringent alcohol rules have been applied in the disaster's wake, and double-hulled vessels are replacing single-hulled ones operating in the sound. But for those who live there, and for the defiled goddess Sedna, it is all a matter of too little, too late.

Above: *Oil from the stricken tanker is pumped aboard its sister ship the* **Exxon Baton Rouge** *as clean-up efforts continued on the oil spill in Prince William Sound.*

SAN FRANCISCO
Rocked by Earthquakes

Perched astride the San Andreas Fault, San Francisco has suffered two horrific earthquakes this century. But the Big One, the one that will utterly destroy this beautiful city, is still to come - and that fate is inevitable

Tony Bennett left his heart in it, Al Jolson begged it to 'open up that Golden Gate', and a generation of hippies were urged to put flowers in their hair when they visited it.

San Francisco's splendid vistas and its old European-style houses and plazas, serviced by a quaint cable-car network from another age, combine to make the city by the bay one of the most splendid and 'livable' of all the great American metropolises. In art, culture and social tolerance - it is home to America's biggest gay community as well as the nation's most rapidly expanding Asian

Opposite: *The smouldering rubble of an apartment building in San Francisco's Marina district after the 1989 earthquake struck.*

Below: *The devastated main shopping centre, with famous Telegraph Hill in the background, in 1906.*

Bottom: *Crowds watch part of old San Francisco go up in smoke.*

and Japanese districts - San Francisco stands out.

Only one force - a massive, irresistible force - stands in the way of the Utopia which San Francisco has become for so many people. And that force is nature.

A CATASTROPHE BOUND TO HAPPEN

Twice this century - in 1906 and in 1989 - nature has flexed its considerable muscles to prove itself more powerful than the most reinforced of reinforced concrete, not to mention the strongest of tungsten steel.

But the two earthquakes which wrought havoc on San Francisco are only the precursors of the the ultimate Big

One - the one which will level this beautiful man-made monument. This is not a Nostradamus-type prediction; the city's location dictates that one day it will crumble, burn and disappear into great fissures, to linger only as a memory.

Imagine two badly stacked dinner plates with a delicate wineglass on top - the wineglass is San Francisco

---

The reason for the city's ultimate demise lies in a mammoth geological hiccup spawned in the days when the earth itself was formed. Called the San Andreas Fault, it is literally a 650-mile-long crack in the earth where the Pacific plate is slowly but surely sliding underneath the landmass of California, itself part of the North America plate.

Scientists say one way for the human mind to grasp what is happening is to put two dinner plates on top of one another and move them so they overlap at each side. Place a full wine glass on the top plate and move the bottom one. Slow movements will cause the wine to shake - more energetic ones to make it spill over the top. The most violent wrench of all will see the glass and contents topple, spill and smash. That is the fate that awaits San Francisco.

This is not to scaremonger - the Big One could come next year or in a thousand years' time. All that is certain is that it will eventually come.

REHEARSAL

The first massive quake to devastate San Francisco occurred on 18 April 1906. When the first shock waves were felt the natives of the gold rush town that grew into the West Coast's most thriving community were blasé about it. Tremors happened a lot there - still do, in fact - and it was not uncommon to feel a rumbling beneath your feet or to watch the table cruet dance before your eyes.

Indeed, on that fateful day, when the newspaper magnate William Randolph Hearst was awakened in his ornate New York apartment to be told that his beloved native San Francisco was being consumed by earthquake and fire, he

Above: *A 1906 photograph of the corner of South Market Street and Main Street.*

Right: *Helpers set up an open-air canteen amid the devastation of San Francisco.*

replied: 'Don't overplay it - they often have earthquakes over in California.'

The San Francisco earthquake was sadly everything, and more, that his minion had told him - the single most cataclysmic event of the age.

'Don't overplay it,' said William Randolph Hearst, when first informed of the 1906 quake

---

The quake is estimated to have registered 8.3 on the Richter scale, the yardstick for seismic measurements, although it was only an estimate as the measurement system had not been devised then. That force is greater than thirty nuclear underground blasts triggered simultaneously. Eight hundred people perished in the collapsing buildings and the chasms which opened up in the streets, or in the firestorm which swiftly consumed the wooden buildings in the aftermath of the vibrations.

Mary Monti, now ninety-four, recalled the events of that grim day.

It knocked me out of bed. The walls of the house we lived in shook and then cracked - great spider's web cracks as the plaster crumbled with the force. We ran into the street and the surface of the road was boiling and rolling. My mother grabbed us kids and we got out of town on a cart, into the hills. Everywhere there was fire. Suddenly a new fire would start up as gas mains got ruptured or kerosene was spilled.

She was one of three hundred thousand people made homeless by the devastating natural disaster which destroyed close to twenty-nine thousand buildings.

On Telegraph Hill Italian families tried to douse the flames with ten thousand gallons of wine

---

The quake had destroyed water lines as well as gas pipes, so firemen could not tackle the blazes. On Telegraph Hill, one of the more celebrated promontories in the city, Italian immigrant families wasted ten thousand gallons of wine which they poured on to the flames.

Packs of looters roamed the streets, robbing shattered stores and stealing from the dead who lined the gutters. And from the few remaining lampstands hung those robbers who were caught by tearful and vengeful citizens.

The author, Jack London, wrote a moving account of the disaster for Collier's weekly magazine:*San Francisco is gone!...On Wednesday morning at a quarter past five came the earthquake. A minute later the flames were leaping upward. In a dozen different quarters south of Market Street, in the working class ghetto, and in the factories, fire started. There was no opposing the flames. There was no organization, no communication...all the shrewd contrivances and safeguards of man had been thrown out of gear by thirty seconds twitching of the earth's crust.*

By the time the fires burned out more than 75 per cent of San Francisco was destroyed, four hundred city blocks in ruins. It provoked scientists and government to pour money into researching the massive fault and what could be done to predict the next quake.

EARTHQUAKE TECHNOLOGY

At the time of the earthquake, geologists had only a sketchy understanding of the processes that combine to move and shake the earth. They realized that the disaster was linked to the San Andreas Fault, and that the land to the west of the faultline was edging northwards.

A geologist from Pennsylvania, Harry Fielding Reid, observing twisted fence posts and shattered roadways, found that there had been a ground lurch of as much as 21 feet during the quake.

More importantly, he recognized that the great blocks of earth on either side of the faultline had been under tremendous strain long before the earthquake happened. Tremendous friction had caused two faces of the fault to stick until

Below: *A rare, early photograph of one of the pioneers who founded San Francisco in 1849.*

Above: *A dramatic photograph of San Francisco's ruined skyline after the earthquake and ensuing fire storm swept the city in 1906.*

the accumulating forces were at last released with a massive snap.

In the 1970s scientists recognized that different sections along the San Andreas Fault were moving at different rates, causing strain to build up in some areas more than others. From Point Arena to San Juan Bautista, a small town south of San Francisco, and from Parkfield down to the Mexican border, the fault is stuck.

When the tremendous force has built up and the fault moves - then the next earthquake is born. California quake expert William Bakun says:

First and foremost we want to learn the earthquake generation process. Then we want to learn how to predict them in areas where they are a hazard.

Sadly, it is still not an exact science, although the colleges and universities of California lead the world in earthquake technology. Another quake expert, David Langston, said:

All we can do is to keep on trying to predict and hope we improve sufficiently to give the population a fair warning when a huge quake is on its way and not be accused of crying wolf.

Following hard on those studies, in 1980 the Federal Emergency Management Agency worked out a scenario that earthquakes would strike at both San Francisco and Los Angeles. Their findings were grim, with death predictions topping fifty thousand in the San Francisco quake and property damage at over \$20 million. The worst case scenario says that in the quake's wake will be a wasteland of fires and looting, with possible disease rife in the breakdown of law and order.

In 1989 a TV-age disaster dramatically set the scene for what will one day befall the city on a much larger scale.

FURTHER WARNING

In the words of housewife Annette Henry, who was in one of the city's main thoroughfares when it struck, here is what the great quake of October 1989 felt like: 'It was as if God just clapped his hands. The ground was like a wave underneath a surfboard, and the cars on the highway were jumping up and down like in a Disney movie. Every time we have an earthquake in California we giggle, we're cool, we're blasé about it. This time was different. I was just hanging on thinking, it's not so funny any more. I thought we were having the Big One.'

***

'The cars on the highway were jumping up and down like a Disney movie'

***

Rocks in the San Andreas Fault couldn't stand the pressure any longer and 58,000-foot-thick blocks of the earth's crust heaved violently. Pressure waves, travelling at five miles per second, raced from the quake's epicentre,

south-east of San Francisco through the bedrock under the Santa Cruz Mountains.

It hit San Francisco during the evening rush hour of Tuesday, 17 October and within fifteen seconds had reduced many buildings to rubble, had destroyed a section of the Bay Bridge, collapsed over a mile of elevated highway, and left the historic Marina district engulfed by fire.

Thanks to global TV coverage of the World Series baseball game between the Oakland A's and San Francisco Giants, viewers as far away as London witnessed the first shocks as the Candlestick Park stadium visibly swayed and huge cracks appeared in the concrete walls.

Most of the hundred deaths from the earthquake occurred when a mile-long section of Interstate 880, an elevated freeway, collapsed on to the lower roadway. Dozens of people were trapped in their cars that were concertinaed together by tons of reinforced concrete.

'It just sandwiched in,' said Henry Reniera, manager for emergency services for Oakland.

It is like a war zone out there. The upper deck fell like a hammer blow on to the lower deck, showering motorists below with rubble and cars. Trapped victims beneath tons of debris have been frantically honking their horns and we are rushing in massive amounts of lifting equipment and hydraulic jacks in a bid to get to them. It is an eerie sound, muffled horns that slowly fade as the car batteries run flat and you know that humans are trapped in there.

The most moving rescue of the entire disaster occurred in the rubble beneath the collapsed Nimitz Freeway section. Patrick Wallace, a paper mill worker, was one of the first on the scene to the sandwiched cars and heard the terrified screams of children trapped in a red car. Together with other rescuers he was able to help free an eight-year-old girl, Cathy Berumen, but her six-year-old brother Julio was trapped - pinned in the wreckage by the body of his dead mother.

Risking his life from further aftershocks, Dr Dan Allen crawled through a three-foot gap to give sedatives to Julio until another doctor, a childcare specialist, could climb up a fire truck's ladders.

Dr Thomas Betts said: 'Nothing could have prepared me for what I saw there. The boy was in shock. He would just cry and run his hands over his mother's face.'

After two hours of frantic work the medical team were no nearer to getting Julio free. His right leg was crushed beyond repair and they needed to get him out for immediate treatment. The boy was put under sedation while a chainsaw was deployed to cut his mother in half before his own leg was amputated.

As fires blazed through the night, glass popped from the twisted skyscrapers built without earthquake specifications and the sirens wailed eerily across the city, the politicians and planners did have some

cause for comfort. Initial reports proved
that the destruction was intensely
localized, concentrated in older structures
that had not been upgraded to withstand
earthquakes. The collapsed highway
section, which claimed most lives, was
itself thirty years old.

Experts concurred that the strict
Californian building code - instituted after
the 1906 disaster in a bid to minimize
damage in future quakes and updated in
the late eighties to incorporate the lessons
learned from the 1971 San Fernando and
1985 Mexico City quakes - played a large
part in minimizing the damage.

But there is no denying the inevit-
ability of the scale of disaster if a new
quake hits the 8.3 Richter scale reading
of the 1906 one. A study made by the
National Oceanic and Atmospheric
Administration after the quake concluded
that forty times as much energy would be
released as in the 1989 one, resulting in
thousands upon thousands of deaths.

San Franciscans are still clearing up the
mess of the quake, a process which will

*Above: **San Francisco's
elegant, wooden houses burn
after the 1989 quake.***

*Below: **This scene of
devastation was once a six-
lane highway. It was reduced
to twisted metal and
shattered concrete.***

take the best part of ten years to complete.
They are proud of having come through,
and flaunt their fatalistic attitude to
nature's aggression. The columnist for the
San Francisco Chronicle, Herb Caen,
summed up the city by the bay when he
wrote in the days after the quake: 'We live
with earthquakes and we live on a fault and
we live dangerously. And it's exciting.'

CRIMES
AND
CRIMINALS

LORD LUCAN
The Vanishing Peer

What happened to Lord Lucan? On a November night in 1974, the gambler earl murdered his children's nanny, attacked his wife – and has never been seen again

The door of the crowded saloon bar of the Plumbers Arms burst open and an hysterical, bloodstained woman stumbled in. 'Help me,' she sobbed. 'Help me. I have just escaped from a murderer. My children...my children. He's in the house.

'He's murdered the nanny.'

The distraught woman was too upset to reveal much more. Barman Arthur Whitehouse sat her down while his wife dabbed a wet towel at the deep gash on her face. The woman was wearing a rain-sodden dress and no shoes.

They called an ambulance and she was taken to the St George's Hospital while police went to her home nearby. It was a five-storey Georgian house, 46 Lower Belgrave Street in Belgravia, one of the most exclusive streets in London. For this was no ordinary victim of crime. The sobbing woman was Veronica, wife of the heir to one of the most aristocratic families in England. Her husband, by now on the run, was Richard John Bingham - better known as Lord Lucan.

'Help me. I have just escaped from a murderer...He's murdered the nanny'

When two policemen forced their way into Lady Lucan's house it was largely in darkness. Sergeant Donald Baker flashed his torch down the hallway and noticed bloodstains on the wall at the far end.

He and his colleague warily ascended a flight of stairs leading to a half-landing. In the dim light they noticed a pool of blood next to a door leading to the

Above: *Lady Lucan's doctor visits her palatial Belgravia home, 46 Lower Belgrave Street, where the attack took place.*

Left: *Lady Lucan leaves home to attend the inquest into the death of her children's nanny.*

Opposite: *Lord Richard John Bingham (later to inherit the title Lord Lucan) marries army major's daughter Veronica Duncan on 28 November 1963.*

breakfast room. Two or three bloodied footprints were evident. They continued to the second floor. Peering into one of the bedrooms, the officers noticed a bloodstained towel lying on a double bed.

Climbing further stairs, they found the sole remaining occupants of the house - a little boy and girl asleep in their nursery. Yet another door revealed an older child, Lady Frances Lucan, staring wide-eyed, and dressed in her pyjamas.

The last part of the house they visited was the basement. There the policemen found a large canvas mailbag containing the body of the children's nanny. She was twenty-nine-year-old Sandra Rivett, mother of a young child, and like Lady Lucan separated from her husband. She had been brutally battered to death.

Of the Seventh Lord Lucan there was no sign. Apart from one brief encounter that night, he was never seen again.

LADY LUCAN TELLS HER TALE

Meanwhile, in her hospital bed, Lady Lucan was telling her version of events of the night of 7 November 1974. Talking painfully through the bruising on her face and the lacerations to her scalp, she recalled how the evening had started. She had been sitting quietly at home with her children. Also at home was the nanny, Sandra. She had originally been given the evening off. Instead, at the last minute, she decided to stay in the house.

She couldn't recognize the figure, but she knew the voice of her attacker - it was that of her estranged husband

---

At around nine o'clock Sandra popped her head round the door of Lady Lucan's room and offered to make a cup of tea. Over twenty minutes later, when the nanny had not returned, Lady Lucan decided to find out what was wrong.

She walked down to the basement kitchen and saw in front of her the shadowy figure of a man crouched over a shapeless form on the floor. It was the body of Sandra Rivett and the intruder was trying to bundle her lifeless form into a canvas mailbag. Lady Lucan screamed out. She stopped only when the

Above: *Divers search for Lord Lucan's body in Newhaven harbour, close to where his car was found after his drive from London.*

Right: *Police dogs used at Newhaven in the hunt for Lucan, the peer who vanished without trace, sight – or scent.*

man turned his attention to her, beating her badly around the face and head.

She could not recognize the figure in the dim light but she told police officers afterwards that the voice she heard was that of her estranged husband. Yet, curiously, as Lady Lucan lay trembling moments later on her bed, it was her husband who was at her side trying to comfort her.

HUNTING THE RUNAWAY LORD

A huge manhunt was immediately launched. Police first checked his rented flat, a short walk away at 72a Elizabeth Street. The earl's Mercedes car was parked outside. Inside a suit, spectacles, a wallet and keys were neatly laid out on the bed. Police also found his passport.

The first police checks were completed within two hours. But by then Lord Lucan was 50 miles away - steering a borrowed Ford Corsair into the drive of the house of friends, Ian and Susan Maxwell Scott, at Uckfield, Sussex. It was then that he told his side of the story.

He said he had been walking past the family home en route to his own flat to change for dinner. Through the blinds of the basement window he spotted what appeared to be a man attacking his wife.

Through the blinds Lucan said he saw a man attacking his wife: 'I let myself in...and dashed down to protect her'

He said: 'I let myself in with my own key and dashed down to protect her. But I slipped on a pool of blood and the attacker ran off. My wife was hysterical and accused me of being the attacker.'

One other person who heard from Lucan that night - his mother, the Dowager Countess of Lucan. He telephoned her and told her there had been a 'terrible catastrophe' at the family home. He reported that his wife had been hurt and the nanny injured. He asked his mother to collect the children.

There was one further call to the Dowager Lady Lucan. It came just after midnight as she stood with a police officer by her side. Lucan again asked about his children and was asked by his mother: 'Look, the police are here - do you want to speak to them?' Her son told her: 'I will ring them in the morning, and I will ring you too.' Then he rang off.

The eldest child, Lady Frances, was also questioned. She said she had been watching television with her mother when nanny Sandra popped in to offer to make them tea. When this failed to arrive, her mother went down to look for the nanny and shortly afterwards Frances heard a scream. Her mother reappeared with blood on her face, followed into the bedroom by her father.

BATTLING IN THE BASEMENT

The following day, a more lucid Lady Lucan sat up in her hospital bed. She said that she had found the kitchen in darkness and called out Sandra's name. Hearing a sound behind her she turned but was struck on the head with a heavy instrument. She claimed that her attacker tried to force his fingers down her throat and into her eyes. He only let go when she grabbed his private parts. She then calmed her husband and went with him upstairs. When he left their bedroom, she had raced out and raised the alarm.

The weapon used in the attack had been recovered early in the hunt. It was a length of lead piping wrapped in hospital sticking plaster. It was found covered in blood beside some broken crockery. The debris revealed how the terrifed Sandra had dropped the cups and saucers when she was attacked in the darkness.

Above: *Lady Lucan arrives at Westminster Coroner's Court following her husband's disappearance.*

Left: *Roger Rivett, estranged husband of murdered nanny Sandra, arrives for the inquest on his wife.*

Two policemen who were to pursue the Lucan case for years afterwards - Detective Superintendent Roy Ranson, head of the local CID, and his deputy Detective Inspector David Gerring - launched a nationwide hunt.

They found the weapon - a length of lead piping covered in Sandra's blood

---

All ports and airports were alerted. But the alarm was futile. For the day after the murder, Lord Lucan's borrowed car was abandoned at Newhaven in Sussex. In it was part of the lead pipe used to batter Sandra Rivett to death.

Police also began a check of the fugitive peer's friends in Britain. They suspected that rich and aristocratic associates might be hiding him. But the more they dug into the lifestyle of the Lucans, the greater the mystery.

Below: *Lord Lucan's mother, the Dowager Countess, whom her son telephoned while on the run.*

A FAILED MARRIAGE

Pert, blonde Veronica Duncan had married Lord Bingham on 28 November 1963. Veronica, twenty-six, was an Army major's daughter who had done some modelling. Her husband, then Lord Bingham, was socially her 'superior'. Educated at Eton, he had served in the Coldstream Guards and worked in the City. But in 1960 he became a professional gambler. Less than a year after their marriage, Lucan's father died and he inherited his title and land.

Bankruptcy loomed, and Lucan blamed his wife for all his troubles

---

The marriage lasted only 10 years, however. The couple separated in 1974 at a time when Lord Lucan was spending all afternoon and every evening in the gambling clubs of London's West End. He fought for the custody of his children but lost. He even resorted to snatching two of them while they were out with their nanny. He was forced by a court to return them. He spied on Lady Lucan, and tried to commit her to a mental institution. Meanwhile, his gambling debts mounted. Bankruptcy loomed. He blamed his wife for all his troubles.

Yet on the evening of the murder, he did not seem to be acting abnormally. He left his flat in the morning to buy a book on Greek shipping tycoons and then went to lunch at the Clermont Club. Later, he met a friend before returning to the Clermont at about 8.45pm. He booked dinner for four at 10.30. The friends arrived but Lucan didn't.

The next person to see the fugitive peer was Susan Maxwell Scott. That night her husband was staying in London and she was alone at their grand home, Grants Hill House, Uckfield, Sussex. Lucan arrived at around midnight and awoke her. Susan Maxwell Scott told Ranson that Lord Lucan was somewhat dishevelled. She gave him a scotch as he told her his version of the night's horrific events. He made a phone call to his mother and he wrote some letters. He then left at about 1.15am saying that he was 'going back' to London.

WHAT HAPPENED TO 'LUCKY LUKE'?

The letters were sent to another friend, Bill Shand Kydd. One, headed 'financial matters', referred to a sale of family silver. In the other, Lucan wrote: 'The most ghastly circumstances arose tonight ... when I interrupted the fight at Lower Belgrave Street and a man left. Veronica accused me of having hired him...

'Veronica has demonstrated a hatred for me in the past,' Lucan wrote to a friend

---

'The circumstantial evidence is strong in that Veronica will say that it is all my doing and I will lie doggo for a while, but I am only concerned about the children. If you could manage it I would like them to live with you. Veronica has demonstrated a hatred for me in the past and would do anything to see me accused. For George and Frances to go through life knowing their father had been in the dock accused of attempted murder would be too much for them...'

Both letters were signed 'Lucky'.

The two letters were the last word in the hunt for the vanishing lord. It was a search that spread abroad with reports of sightings in Australia, North America and southern Africa.

A year after his disappearance, a coroner's inquest investigated Sandra Rivett's death. Its finding was Murder. And, unusually in British law, Lord Lucan was named as the murderer.

Left: *Lady Lucan and her husband split up in 1974, largely because of his lifestyle around the gambling clubs of London.*

Below: *Lady Lucan's marriage lasted only ten years. She was left with the custody of their son and two daughters.*

So what happened to Richard John Bingham, Seventh Earl of Lucan, Baron Bingham of Castlebar, Baron Bingham of Melcombe, baronet of Nova Scotia, known to his family as John, to his friends as Johnny or Luke, and to his gaming table associates as 'Lucky'?

Although both of them since retired from Scotland Yard, the two policemen who led the search expressed strong yet differing views about the fate of their quarry. David Gerring believes: 'Lucan is still in hiding somewhere and he is the only man who knows the full story. He is a lord and he is still a gentleman and he is still gambling on the odds that no one will ever find him.' Roy Ranson maintains: 'Lucan killed the nanny by mistake, thinking he could dispose of his wife and get custody of the children he loved. When he realized his error, he killed himself in some remote spot like a lord and gentleman.'

ADOLF EICHMANN
Nazi War Criminal

Adolf Eichmann left school at fifteen without qualifications. Looking for a purpose in life, he joined the infant Nazi party and found it: the extermination of 6 million Jews in the death camps of wartime Europe

The Holocaust stands as the most monumental crime in history - the systematic extermination of 6 million Jews and the murders of a further 6 million Russians, Poles, gypsies, homosexuals and other 'inferiors' who threatened Adolf Hitler's warped vision of a racially pure world dominated by his cruel stormtroopers.

The vanquished races died at the hands of unspeakably evil men - drunken Lithuanian quislings in the conquered eastern territories who machine-gunned their victims into lime pits; brutish *Volksdeutsche* [ethnic Germans] from Poland and Czechoslovakia who dropped the gas into the chambers of Auschwitz

Above: *Bullet-proof glass is used in the making of the 'cabin' in which Eichmann would face trial.*

Opposite: *Adolf Eichmann was the ice-cold officer who put his leader Hitler's maniacal holocaust into effect.*

Below: *Eichmann, in sweater and carpet slippers, writes his memoirs in his Israeli jail cell.*

and Treblinka; Berlin bullies who murdered their enemies in the cellars of the Gestapo HQ on Prinz-Albrechtstrasse.

Wherever they came from and however they killed, they shared equal blame for the suffering they inflicted on mankind during Hitler's twelve years in power.

No physical blood ever stained his hands, but it took a hideously warped mind to plan the systematic murder of millions

It is one thing to be responsible for individual death. Many concentration camp guards and other SS thugs argued at their war crimes trials that they were 'only obeying orders', and that to resist would have meant putting their own necks on the chopping block. Others offered no defence and gloried in their persecution of the defenceless.

THE EVIL MIND OF A MEDIOCRITY

But it took a mind of unfathomable coldness, of deeply twisted logic devoid of human emotions like love and kindness, to pluck the entire, maniacal Holocaust theory out of the Nazis' perverted philosophy and put it into practice. Such a mind belonged to Adolf Eichmann.

Eichmann shares a place in hell with the truly evil criminals who have scorched history. For although his

Right: *Banks of television monitors arrayed for the trial of Eichmann which began on 11 March 1961.*

uniform was never spattered with an innocent's blood, although he never pulled a trigger in anger, it is accurate to say that he was the biggest mass murderer of them all.

Eichmann made the trains run on time to the infernos of the death camps. He organized the round-ups, the timetables for the 'Final solution to the Jewish Question', and garnered the manpower and hardware necessary to make the whole diabolical scheme possible. At war's end he was the top fugitive Nazi.

Born in 1902 in Solingen, Germany, he grew up in Austria when his father's job as an accountant took him to Linz. Karl Eichmann ran a loveless home which nurtured respect for thrift and order.

As a teenager Adolf did poorly at school and preferred to spend his time daydreaming, talking with the men who had served in the Kaiser's army at the front in World War I, drinking in their tales of glory and sharing their disgust that the politicians, not the soldiers, had lost Germany the war. As Nazism began to thrive in both Germany and Austria he

Below: *Israeli official picture of Eichmann before he was brought into court in Jerusalem before 750 people, mostly members of the world's press.*

drifted towards the flags and the rhetoric which blamed an international Jewish conspiracy for the defeat.

By the age of twenty Eichmann was employed as a travelling salesman for an oil company. But increasingly he saw his destiny interwoven with the shadow of Hitler's swastika, and on 1 April 1932 he joined the Austrian Nazi party.

THE YOUNG NAZI CONVERT

As the depression throughout Europe and the world worsened in the thirties he left his job to travel to Dachau, twelve miles from Munich, to train at an SS barracks near the infamous concentration camp.

During Eichmann's SS training he had crawled over barbed wire and broken glass - he claimed it made him immune to pain

---

There he was put through gruelling training that left him with permanent scars on his elbows and knees - the legacy of forced crawls over barbed wire and broken glass. 'In that year I rid myself of all susceptibility to pain,' he would later boast. With his training completed Eichmann volunteered for the *Sicherheitsdienst* or SD, the security

branch of the SS, and was entrusted in 1935 by its head, Heinrich Himmler, to create a 'Jewish Museum'.

The title was a euphemism for a bureau whose sole task was to collect data on Jewish business and property holdings in Germany and Austria.

Eichmann, the unexemplary student at school, proved himself an astonishingly quick learner when it came to the mortal enemy of the Reich. He plunged into the customs, religion and habits of the Jewish race, quickly establishing himself as an expert in the field.

A TASTE OF POWER

In 1938, with the non-violent annexation of Austria by Germany, came Adolf Eichmann's first taste of absolute power. He was placed in charge of the Office for Jewish Emigration in Vienna.

Using duplicity and brutality in equal measure, he brought terror to the cultured Jewish population of the old imperial capital. Rabbis were dragged from their homes and their heads shaved. Synagogues were razed, businesses looted and homes ransacked.

The victims were stripped of everything they possessed, given a passport bearing the letter 'J' for *Jude* [Jew] and told they had two weeks to find a foreign country to take them in. Failure to do so meant a one-way ticket to a concentration camp.

In Vienna the accountant's son developed a passion for the high life. He lived in the magnificent town house once owned by a member of the Rothschild banking dynasty. He dined at the best restaurants, drank his fill of the splendid vintages arrayed in the Rothschilds' ten thousand-bottle cellar and took a mistress to provide amusement away from his wife of three years.

By 1939 he was under the direct control of Reinhard Heydrich - Hangman Heydrich as he was later known - and was promoted to captain.

Heydrich was charged with selecting hardened SS men for the great tasks which lay ahead in 'cleansing' Europe of her Jews and other undesirables. He saw, after the brilliant success of Eichmann in making Vienna *Judenfrei* or Jew free,

that he had indeed chosen an admirable sorcerer's apprentice. When he recommended him to Himmler for promotion, Heydrich wrote that Eichmann 'should direct the entire Jewish emigration question'. Eichmann created his own file for it.

He called it the Final Solution.

THE KILLING FACTORIES

When war came later in the year and Poland was over-run, the atrocities began. Poland had an enormous Jewish population and the first extermination centres were set up there.

These were not to be concentration camps. The new centres were factories created for the specific purpose of killing human beings by the hundred thousand.

Under a new department headed by Eichmann called ID IV - but known within the SS ranks simply as the Eichmann Authority - he ordered the construction of ghettoes in major Polish cities like Warsaw and Lodz where the Jews were penned up. He planned for

Below: Israel was so determined to make a show trial of the Eichmann hearings that they even ran classes for teleprinter operators. The trial's result was a foregone conclusion.

In his office in Berlin Eichmann pressed for more efficient killing methods so that every part of a body - hair, gold teeth, body fat - could be utilized after death. He pushed for the use of Zyklon B gas in the chambers at Auschwitz - colossal rooms masquerading as bathhouses that could 'process' ten thousand human beings every day - and he neatly tabulated the numbers of the dead alongside figures of looted wealth. He also kept count on how many bars of soap were made from the rendered fat of the victims.

THE OBSESSIVE JEW-HUNTER

In 1942, at a villa formerly owned by a prominent Jewish family in the pleasant Berlin suburb of Wannsee, the Nazis made their full and final pact with the devil. Eichmann was there for the conference. There was only one subject on the agenda: 'The final solution of the Jewish question in Europe.'

Right to the end, Eichmann the Nazi zealot remained fiercely proud of what his extermination programme had achieved

---

Above: *Behind bars in an Israeli prison, Eichmann is given a pre-trial medical examination by a police doctor.*

disease and hunger to take its toll among them so that valuable Reich ammunition would not be wasted.

Eichmann authorized experiments with mobile gas vans - Jews were crammed into sealed trucks and killed by the carbon monoxide gas from the engine exhaust - and he drew up the plans for Auschwitz-Birkenau, in the south, to become the Armageddon for Jews.

Eichmann kept records of how many bars of soap were made from the rendered down fat of concentration camp victims

---

In 1941, when Hitler launched his invasion of the Soviet Union, Eichmann was a lieutenant colonel and the great plains of Russia were to become his personal killing fields for the inferior races. The gas vans had proved themselves to be ineffective and the mass shootings of Jews and Slavs across Russia were time-consuming, costly and traumatic - even for hardened SS men.

The Third Reich was embarking on the biggest single crusade of mass murder in history. To uproot Jews from all over Europe, bring them to death factories and kill them without arousing the suspicion of the victims or the neutral countries took masterful planning. Eichmann travelled endlessly throughout Europe, commandeering trains that were needed for the war effort to carry more and more 'enemies of the Reich' to the gas chambers and the ovens.

Not since medieval warlords ruled Europe has such evil power been vested in one man. More pragmatic SS men argued that the extermination of the Jews was secondary to winning the war. Not to Eichmann. He relentlessly continued to press for more freight trucks to transport his victims, more manpower to staff the camps, more gas for the chambers.

In 1944, with the Allies snapping at the gates of Germany, he set off for Hungary where, by dint of the nation's status as a

German ally, its eight hundred thousand Jews had remained largely free from persecution. Eichmann took this as a personal affront and arrived in Budapest to organize their departure to the death camps. Between mid-May and July 437,000 Jews were sent off on trains to be executed. It was, he said, one of the more gratifying moments in his life.

The unique characteristic of Eichmann was that he believed wholeheartedly in the righteousness of his mission. He saw himself as a subservient disciple of the religion of Nazism who, like a member of a monastic order, deprived himself in his zeal to complete his mission.

By this time the heady grandeur of his earlier times in Vienna, when he had swanned around the city in Rothschild's limousine terrifying hapless rabbis, had evaporated. Instead he was gaunt, tired and thinner - but his eyes burned with the fire of the zealot. He despised those who tried to cover up what had been done in the name of National Socialism.

But the end he refused to see was coming. Allied saturation bombing cut most major rail junctions in Europe, the death camps in Poland had been liberated or destroyed.

In October 1944 he left Budapest on a forced march with hundreds of thousands of civilians as hostages. As he made his way back to a burning, beleaguered Berlin he was able to report to Himmler that, by his reckoning, 4 million Jews had died in the death camps and a further 2 million had been executed by the *Einsatzgruppen* - execution squads - which roamed Russia.

He was a contented man in that so much had been achieved, but concerned that much of his work was left undone. He had, as one historian remarked of him, drenched his soul in blood.

THE HUNTER HUNTED

In the chaos of the final days of the Reich, Eichmann escaped. In April 1945 he made his way with a band of fellow fanatics to the Austrian Tyrol where he hoped to forge a 'Werewolf' unit - a guerrilla group committed to fighting the occupying Allies.

But almost immediately after entering

Below: *Flanked by police in the bullet-proof glass cabin, Adolf Eichmann faces his accusers. On 1 December 1961 he was sentenced to death.*

the mountains his comrades ordered him to leave. His reputation had preceded him and, loyal Germans though they were, they did not want to be tarred with the same brush. So he wandered down a lonely mountain path with some ammunition and light provisions and set out to lose himself in the chaos engulfing his homeland.

Everywhere there was a price on his head. A ten-man commando unit was formed from death camp survivors in Poland with the specific task of bringing him to justice. With his adjutant, Rudolf Jaenisch, Eichmann made his way through Bavaria wearing the uniform of a Luftwaffe corporal.

Loyal Nazis wanting to fight on after the surrender turned Eichmann away because of his monstrous reputation

---

He was captured twice by American troops. The first time he escaped to Munich, after being put in charge of the holding camp's motor pool, and upon recapture claimed he was a lieutenant in the Waffen [fighting] SS.

At the Oberdachstetten camp in Silesia he led a relatively untroubled existence. But then he heard reports coming through from the war crimes tribunal being assembled in Nuremberg - reports which were laced with the words 'Eichmann', 'monster' and 'mass murder'.

Realizing it was only a matter of time before his true identity was revealed, he set about making plans for a third escape. In January 1946 he got away while working in a road-mending gang. He found his way to the town of Celle where, using the alias Otto Heniger, he lived for four years as a lumberjack.

He knew that he could not stay in Germany: by 1950 the name Eichmann and the extermination of the Jews were inseparable. With the aid of Odessa - the Nazi network of former SS men - he obtained a set of false papers and headed for South America where he vanished, protected by old comrades. Vera Eichmann and their two sons arrived on false papers in Argentina in 1952.

There was no remorse for what had been done during the madness of the Third Reich. He told Dutch Nazi journalist Willem Sassen, in tape-recorded interviews: 'I have to conclude in my own defence that I was neither a murderer nor a mass murderer. I carried out with a clear conscience and faithful heart the duty imposed upon me. I was always a good German, I am today a good German, and I shall always be a good German!'

NEMESIS

In 1957 a blind Jew living in a Buenos Aires suburb, had his curiousity aroused about a man called Ricardo Klement. His daughter had been seeing a young man who called himself Nicholas Eichmann and he stupidly boasted to her that his father's real name was not Ricardo Klement but Adolf Eichmann. It meant nothing to her, but to her old father it meant everything.

Soon the intelligence was in the hands of Isser Harel - founding father of Mossad, the Israeli secret service. Equipped with this scant information he sought permission from David Ben-Gurion, the fledgling state's leader, to mount a mission to bring Eichmann to Israel and to justice.

A hand-picked team of Mossad agents arrived in Buenos Aires in 1958, but the house at 4621 Chacabuco Street was deserted. The Klement family had left there just two months earlier.

It was not until December 1959 that it was picked up again when a Mossad agent discovered that Nicholas Eichmann worked in a motorcycle repair shop in the city. He trailed him to the dismal suburb of San Fernando.

A surveillance team was quickly assembled to stake out the home of Ricardo Klement. For many days the team watched the balding, bespectacled clerk at the local Mercedes Benz plant return home, but they were uncertain it was him.

It wasn't until he appeared on 24 March 1960 clutching a bouquet of flowers that the team were satisfied they had him. A quick check in the Eichmann dossier confirmed that it was his wife's birthday and, like any dutiful husband, he was congratulating her with flowers.

At 8pm on 11 May Adolf Eichmann was snatched by avenging angels of the Mossad. But there was no gratuitous violence on the agents' part. Their prey was bundled into the back seat of a car, covered with a blanket and driven to a safe house.

There his armpit was checked for the tell-tale SS number which every member of the elite had tattooed on him. It was missing, in its place a crude scar.

But there was no pretence on Ricardo Klement's part. He looked calmly at his captors and said in perfect German: *'Ich bin Adolf Eichmann'* - I am Adolf Eichmann.

Ten days later he was aboard an El Al jet bound for Israel. He had been drugged and smuggled out of the country dressed in a pilot's uniform. By the time the aircraft touched down in Israel, Ben-Gurion had already announced to the Knesset that he was under arrest and would be tried in Israel for war crimes.

If the world expected a fanged monster in the dock, it was sadly disappointed. It was only the banality of evil that was exemplified in the bald, shrivelled man in the glass-covered stand. He was dressed in a sober suit and looked like a faceless commuter late home from the office.

In his trial, which lasted from 11 April to 14 August 1961, there was no repentance, no hatred, and no bitterness; save that he did not understand why the Jewish people hated him, because he had merely obeyed orders - and surely that was a trait worthy of admiration in any man? Justification for the Holocaust belonged to somebody else.

On 1 December that year he was sentenced to death, and on 31 May 1962 he rejected an appeal by a Protestant minister that he repent as he was led into the death chamber. Refusing a hood as he mounted the scaffold at Ramle Prison, he said: 'Long live Germany. Long live Argentina. Long live Austria. These are the countries with which I have been most closely associated and I shall not forget them. I greet my wife, family and friends. I had to obey the rules of war and my flag. I am ready.'

His remains were cremated and scattered at sea. No prayers of any kind were said for him.

Above: *A neatly suited Eichmann makes a point during his trial, while Judge Moishe Landau wearily rests his face in his hands.*

TED BUNDY
The All-American Killer

'Hi, I'm Ted,' was how a good-looking all-American boy used to introduce himself to women. But he said goodbye in a grotesque ritual of sexual violence - for Theodore Bundy was the worst serial killer the world has ever known

With drop-dead looks and whirlpool eyes, Theodore Bundy was a woman's dream. Three innocent words - 'Hi, I'm Ted' - were his opening lines to his conquests, the blondes, brunettes and redheads who fell under his spell. Handsome, charming, energetic - Bundy attracted women like a magnet pulling paperclips from a box.

But those three little words were also the death sentence for maybe as many as fifty women - for he was the worst - the very worst - serial killer that America and the world have ever known. Using his good looks and charm, he roamed the towns and cities of the USA for four long years like some nomadic angel of death.

His victims died in a sexual frenzy of such intensity that he was alternately labelled the Werewolf, the Vampire and the Ripper slayer. He killed and killed and killed again before he was finally trapped by that most mundane of police methods, the routine check.

His victims died so horribly that Ted Bundy was compared with the werewolves and vampires of horror movies

One of his favourite tricks was a fake plaster cast. He would slip it on, pretend to be lifting a heavy piece of equipment or changing a tyre on his car, and wait for a sympathetic female to offer help. 'Hi, I'm Ted.' The phrase would drip from his lips and the prey was hooked.

Ted Bundy finally 'fried' in Florida's electric chair in 1989, and no tears were shed for him. In fact a local DJ told listeners near the state jail: 'Turn down your coffee makers, folks, because they're gonna need all the juice they can get there today!'

Opposite: *Theodore Bundy in the drab garb of a prisoner - a far cry from the debonair charmer who attracted women like a magnet.*

Below: *Three of Bundy's victims in police files: (from left) Laura Aime, Debbie Kent and Melissa Smith.*

Bundy left behind an astonishing legacy of evil that puts him at the very top of the serial killer tree.

Bundy was a skilful liar, and his psychotic hatred of women began some time during his unhappy childhood. As a teenager he devoured hard-core pornography - which he later blamed for 'triggering the demons' that sent him on the killing spree.

THE BACKGROUND OF A SERIAL KILLER

He was born in a home for unmarried mothers in Burlington, Vermont to nineteen-year-old Louise Cowell, and for the first four years of his life was raised in a modest flat nearby. Later, on the promise of a better job, Louise flew with her son the 3000 miles across America to Seattle. Here she married Johnnie Bundy, a cook at the Madigan Army Hospital on the outskirts of the city. Bundy adopted Ted as his own son, and the couple subsequently had four more children.

Bundy blamed the pornography he had devoured as a teenager for turning him into a violent killer

---

Stamped in the all-American mould, Bundy was a Boy Scout who started the day with a paper round and had a small lawn-mowing business at weekends. He also won a place on the high school track athletics team. His girlfriends then, and later during his years as a law student in Washington, say they were attracted by his looks - but in bed he was sadistic, acting out bondage fantasies.

From high school he entered the University of Puget Sound in Seattle. Later he switched to Washington - where he dropped out in 1967, preferring instead to enrol for a non-degree course in Chinese at Stanford University. His butterfly mind was incapable of studying for long and he dropped out of that course too, heading back west to spend the winter working at odd jobs.

The following year in Seattle he became a volunteer worker for a Republican election campaign before setting off in 1969 to Philadelphia.

Above: *Bundy in his many guises: in 1975 top left; 1976 top right; 1977 middle left and right; 1978 bottom left and right.*

The nationwide flitting is important in the story of Ted Bundy. It gave him a sense of how vast America was and how easy it would be for a criminal to become lost in it.

In a twist of irony, in 1971 he became a counsellor at a rape crisis centre in Seattle. Someone who remembers Bundy from those times is Ann Rule, a real-life sleuth who has chronicled American criminal history in best-selling books.

In the early seventies she worked on the crisis hot-line with Bundy. She says:

When people ask me about Ted I wish I could show them this person that I knew who was everything you would expect a fine, twenty-two-year-old guy would be. He was active in politics, wonderful on the phone, handsome, witty, charming.

I was a friend of Ted Bundy's and I did not expect him to be a serial killer. Never. When I last saw his face before he was executed I saw this same kind of self-deprecating look, the duck of the head, the look that said: 'You can believe this guy.'

Though attracted by his looks, early girlfriends didn't always fall for his sado-masochistic activities in bed

---

Bundy wrote a pamphlet on rape which, with hindsight, was a piece of self analysis: 'A number of rape offenders do not seem to be sick people but individuals who believe they can exert their will over others with impunity.'

THE MURDERS BEGIN

The madness began in 1974 when Ted Bundy was 28 years old.

On 31 January, Lynda Ann Healy, a twenty-one-year-old law student at the University of Washington State, in Seattle, set her alarm for 7am. She had to make a report on skiing conditions for a local radio station and didn't want to be late. Two hours after the designated time the alarm clock was still ringing when her roommate walked in to find her gone, with a one-inch bloodstain on the pillow.

Six weeks later on 12 March Donna Manson walked from her dormitory and headed across the Evergreen State College Campus to a student faculty music recital - and was never seen again.

On 17 April Susan Rancourt, eighteen, left a discussion at the university campus to walk to a cinema 400 yards away. She too vanished as did Roberta Parks, twenty-two, on 6 May, Brenda Ball, twenty-two, on 6 June, and Georgina Hawkins, eighteen, on 16 June.

On 14 July a young man with his arm in a sling was among a crowd of forty thousand sun worshippers lured to the water at Lake Sammamish State Park just

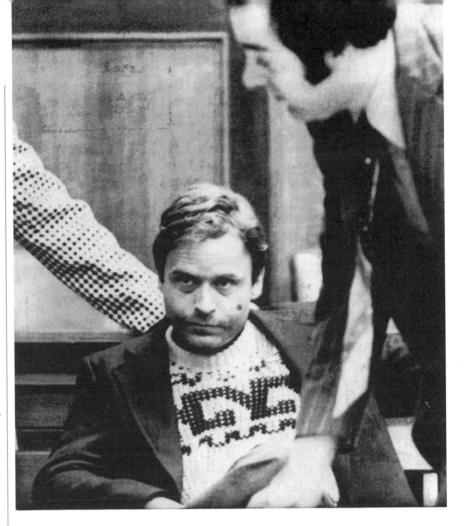

outside Seattle. Janice Orr was sunbathing when he came up to her and said: 'Would you help me put my sailboat on top of my car?' Janice, twenty-three, pushed her bicycle to where his car was. She became victim number seven.

That same afternoon, Denise Naslund went with a group of friends to a sparkling brook that fed into the lake. At 4pm she got out of the water to go to a public lavatory.

Carol DaRonch was called the luckiest teenager in America when she narrowly escaped being victim number twelve

---

Two months later a team of grouse beaters found the remains of both girls scattered under a line of trees. The corpses were stripped of all jewellery and clothes, and they had died in a sexual frenzy of some intensity.

When detectives began investigations they found a number of women who had been approached on that day by a dishy looking man with his arm in a sling. He told them all: 'Hi - I'm Ted.'

Above: *Ted Bundy sits in court in Pensacola, Florida, before his arraignment. He had twice previously escaped from custody.*

Above: *Bundy chats amiably with the press as he leaves the courthouse at Tallahassee, Florida, where he conducted his own defence against murder charges.*

officer. Carol managed to roll out of the vehicle as it slowed down in traffic, then fought Bundy on the pavement as he tried to beat her with an iron bar. She was finally rescued by an elderly couple.

The slaughter spread from Utah to Colorado. Bundy claimed the lives of four women between 17 January and April 1975. His blood lust seemed limitless, and to detectives trying to solve the killings - now in three states - Ted Bundy was the worst nightmare: a methodical killer who travelled. With no fixed abode, he could be anyone.

A lucky break for lawmen came in the early hours of 16 August when Utah Highway Patrolman Robert Hayward was sitting in his parked car near his home. With only twenty minutes left on his shift, he was biding his time until 3am when he heard over the radio that two of his deputies were chasing suspected vandals in his town of Granger.

Hayward cranked his vehicle into life and set off to rendezvous with the pursuing officers. But *en route* he saw a VW pull away from the kerbside in front of him, at speed with no lights on. He gave chase to the car.

Although Bundy's VW contained what looked like burglar's or rapist's equipment, he was only booked for a minor traffic offence

---

After twelve blocks Ted Bundy stopped and climbed out to meet Officer Hayward who had drawn his gun. Inside the car the policeman discovered handcuffs, a crowbar, a ski mask and a nylon stocking that Bundy described as 'just some junk'. Amazingly, Bundy was merely booked for failing to stop for a police officer and released on bail.

It wasn't until later, when Utah patrol officers liaised with the murder hunt detectives, that Carol DaRonch's testimony was discovered to match the description of Bundy.

Bundy was arrested the next day in his apartment at 565 First Avenue, Salt Lake City, and charged with possessing tools for burglary. Meanwhile DaRonch identified Bundy from pictures on his driving licence and said the vehicle in

THE SLAUGHTER SPREADS

On 30 August Bundy left his job at the state's Office of Emergency Services to enrol at the University of Utah law school in Salt Lake City. Two months later the killings had begun in Utah.

Melissa Smith, eighteen - raped and murdered on 18 October. On 31 October - Laura Aime, seventeen, battered and strangled. Debra Kent, also seventeen, died on 8 November. Debra was his second choice that night - Carol DaRonch, eighteen, had a miraculous escape from his VW camper when he handcuffed her after posing as a police

which she had been snatched resembled his. Bundy was out on bail, but the net seemed to be drawing in when two days later, after DaRonch had identified him in a line-up, he was charged with kidnap.

In a further twist, Officer Hayward was the brother of police Captain Bob Hayward, the officer in charge of the DaRonch kidnapping case and the murders of three other women.

A Utah prosecuting attorney later declared that Bundy changed his appearance as often as he did his underpants

---

When Bob spoke to Peter about Bundy a distant alarm bell rang in his brother's mind. In November 1974 a former fiancée of Bundy's, a girl called Liz Kloepfer, had called Peter twice from Seattle, urging him to consider Bundy a suspect in the Utah murders. Hayward

had made routine checks but saw no reason to go any further.

Luck was with Bundy. There was not, at this stage, a shred of solid evidence to tie him into the killings in either state. He was bailed on the charge of a single kidnap and possessing burglary tools.

Women who claimed they had seen him at the lakeside on the day that Orr and Naslund died said they were sure that that man was not Ted Bundy. 'That is because we later found out he changed his appearance ... as often as I changed my shorts,' said Utah prosecutor David Yocum later.

FREE TO KILL AGAIN

Bundy's trial for kidnapping began on 23 February 1976, and he waived his right to a jury trial. He got fifteen years when the trial, after lengthy legal appeals and wrangles, finished in December - but served no time in Utah. Instead he was

Above: Bundy sits with defence attorney Margaret Good as he hears the jury return a verdict of first-degree murder.

Above: *Theodore Bundy photographed after his death in the electric chair was finally scheduled. The serial killer's amazing luck had run out.*

Moving quickly upstairs, he entered her room and beat twenty-one-year-old Margaret to death, then strangled her with her own tights before taking great bites out of her buttocks. He moved across the hallway and despatched Lisa Levy, twenty, in the same foul manner.

He beat two others - Karen Chandler and Kathy Kleiner - to the verge of death before fleeing the scene. Both girls were scarred for life and now wear heavy make-up to hide the deep indentations he made on their faces.

On 8 February he killed his youngest-known victim, a ten-year-old girl, Kimberly Leach, in Lake City, Florida, and left her body in a pig-sty.

BUNDY'S LUCK RUNS OUT

The following week luck ran out for Bundy on 15 February when Patrolman David Lee of the Pensacola Police Department became suspicious of a Volkswagen that drove out of a restaurant car park at 3am. A hurried computer check showed that it had been stolen.

It was for the murder of a little girl of ten that Bundy was finally brought to book

---

After pulling the car over the man identified himself as Ken Misner, attacked the officer and made a run for it. He was tackled, clubbed unconscious, and when he came around told Lee: 'I wish you would have killed me.' Misner was just one of twenty-one identities that Bundy had assumed.

The case against Bundy was assembled painstakingly slowly, but instead of trying to pin dozens of crimes on him he was charged with the single murder of schoolgirl Kimberley. Strong forensic evidence linking him to the killing gave police their best chance of finally nailing him. That evidence came in the form of bite marks that corresponded to his teeth and the marks on her little body.

At his trial Bundy received messages of support, even proposals of marriage, from women who could not believe that so handsome a man could be responsible for such heinous crimes.

He lived in the shadow of the electric

extradited to Colorado to stand trial for the murder of a twenty-year-old student called Carolyn Campbell. On 30 December, using a stack of books and some deft manoeuvring, he escaped through the roof of the Colorado Springs jail, stole a police car and was gone.

On 15 January 1977 came one of his most infamous nights of violence. Armed with a heavy wooden club, he slipped into the Chi Omega sorority house, a female dormitory at the University of Florida in the state capital, Tallahassee. The girls there had just returned from their Christmas holidays.

Diana Cossin had most of the girls in her large room where they sat around swapping gossip into the early hours. Diana, a survivor of that terrible night, said: 'I noticed Margaret Bowman walking past and I said something like: "How are you, Margaret?" And she said: "Life couldn't be better." It was the last time I saw her alive.' When the lights went out, Bundy went in.

chair for eight years after his conviction for Kimberley's murder and protested his innocence up to the end.

But when Bundy saw there was no way out he broke down and confessed to his grisly catalogue of death - nearly forty murders which, he said, 'I deserve to die for.' Even now police suspect he was still holding out on more crimes.

Sometimes Bundy would fly into a city, then select a victim at random and kill her before flying out again

---

His confession included murders of girls in Idaho, California, Michigan, Pennsylvania and Vermont. Some were committed as 'day trips' when Bundy would jet into a city, select his victim, kill her and then fly out again.

After ten years on death row, he was finally executed at Starke Prison in Florida in February 1989. Religious broadcaster James Dobson spent the final night with Bundy in his cell. Bundy refused his condemned man's last meal, and wept openly as he told Dobson of his perverted crusade of death. Dobson said:

He said society had a right to be protected from him. He said that after he killed the first woman he went through a period of great distress for six months. He was extremely guilty, he didn't believe he could have done something like that. That gradually subsided and that sexual frenzy which he would go through occurred again and he killed another woman to sate it. Each time became a little easier to cope with and he did that so many times that he got to the point where he could not feel any more.

Below: *The body of Ted Bundy is wheeled to the medical examiner's office following his execution at Gainesville, Florida, on 24 January 1989.*

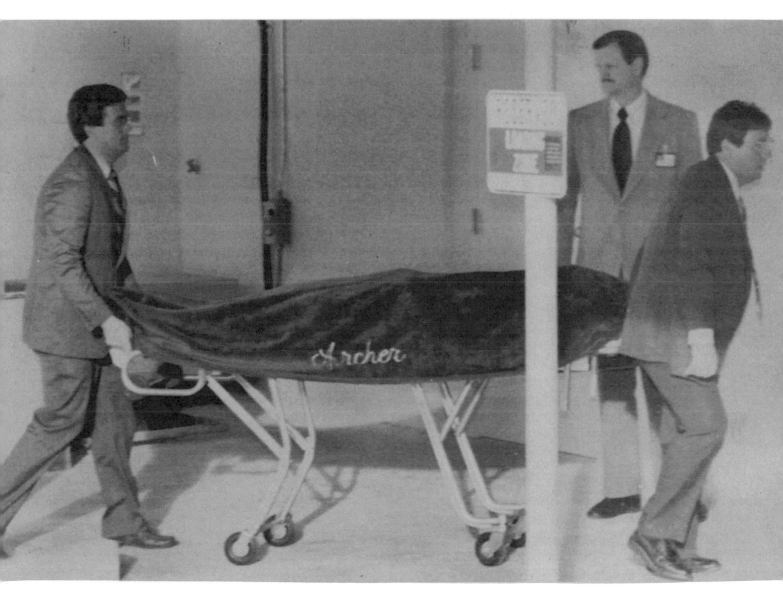

DAVID BERKOWITZ
The Story of Son of Sam

Who was the baby-faced psychotic who stalked the streets of New York in search of innocent young victims? For twelve months 'Son of Sam' held the city in a deadly grip of terror

By day David Berkowitz was a seemingly innocent post office worker, a pudgy, cherubic-faced loner who lived quietly in his tiny suburban apartment.

But by night he was a fiend, the madman whose unearthly alter ego, Son of Sam, would become the most terrifying and mysterious serial killer ever to stalk New York City. For more than twelve months, beginning in July 1976, the curly-haired killer went gunning for attractive victims whose only 'crimes' were their innocence and youth.

Initially dubbed 'the .44-calibre killer' because of the weapon he used in his attacks, Berkowitz killed six of his victims and severely wounded seven others during his reign of terror.

'I love to hunt,' ran Berkowitz's gruesome note. 'Prowling the streets looking for fair game - tasty meat.'

Five of those who died were dark-haired women, sparking a stampede on blonde wigs as frightened women sought to protect themselves. For at the height of the widespread panic the police were helpless to stop the carnage. Moreover, the random nature of the crimes, coupled with the apparent lack of motive, frustrated their efforts - despite the largest manhunt in New York's history.

But what terrified the city almost as much were the bizarre, twisted letters that the twenty-four-year-old Berkowitz sent

to police and to a newspaper columnist at the peak of his rampage. He taunted the city's efforts to track him down, warning that 'I'll be back', and boasting: 'I love to hunt. Prowling the streets looking for fair game - tasty meat.'

A TWISTED MIND

By July 1977 New York was, according to a newspaper account of the time, 'exploding', a city under siege from an unknown terror.

On the surface, the evil that would later be known as Son of Sam began

Above: *Police sketches of the killer labelled 'Son of Sam' who brought terror to the streets of New York.*

Opposite: *Drama student Valentina Suriani with her boyfriend Alexander Esau. Both were to fall victim to one of David Berkowitz's murderous frenzies in April 1977.*

Left: *Deputy Sheriff Craig Glassman displays two threatening letters he received from his neighbour Berkowitz. Glassman noticed similarities between his letters and those 'Son of Sam' sent to newspapers.*

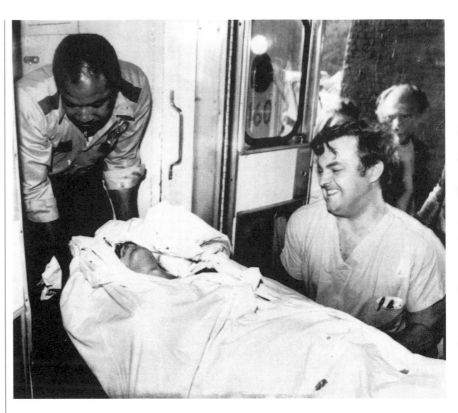

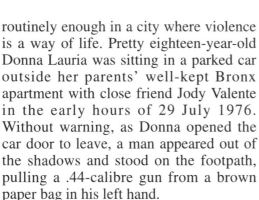

routinely enough in a city where violence is a way of life. Pretty eighteen-year-old Donna Lauria was sitting in a parked car outside her parents' well-kept Bronx apartment with close friend Jody Valente in the early hours of 29 July 1976. Without warning, as Donna opened the car door to leave, a man appeared out of the shadows and stood on the footpath, pulling a .44-calibre gun from a brown paper bag in his left hand.

He crouched, held the gun with both hands and fired three shots, killing the youngster and wounding her friend.

Police were baffled by the senseless killing, but on the streets of New York it was hardly cause for headlines. Within a few days Donna Lauria's name had faded from the newspapers.

THE SERIAL KILLINGS TAKE OFF

For no one could have foreseen that many months later the incident would come back to haunt an entire city.

The unknown assailant would not strike again until 23 October but, luckily for his two helpless victims, this time his aim was off as he fired at a parked car in Flushing, in the borough of Queens.

Carl Denaro, a twenty-year-old who was due to enlist in the US Air Force the

Above left: *Twenty-year-old Stacy Moskowitz, sixth victim of 'Son of Sam', pictured in bed at her Brooklyn home.*

Above: *The critically injured body of Robert Violane after he was attacked by 'Son of Sam' while sitting with his girlfriend Stacy Moskowitz in a Brooklyn lovers' lane.*

following week, was critically wounded by a bullet to the head, but survived. His companion, Rosemary Keenan, eighteen, and the daughter of a police detective, thankfully escaped unhurt.

The overworked New York Police Department failed to notice significant similarities between the first two incidents

---

Again, police ballistic tests showed that the gunman had used a .44-calibre pistol, but it was too early for the alarm bells to ring at Police Headquarters. New York in the 1970s averaged about thirty killings a week, and an overworked police force failed to notice the similarities between the two incidents: the type of gun, the fact that the victims were young and shot while in parked cars, and that the killer struck late at night or early in the morning.

Two more young women were shot and seriously wounded - one was to spend the rest of her life in a wheelchair - when the mysterious gunman surfaced again on 27 November. It wasn't until the faceless force behind the .44 killed his second victim two months later - twenty-six-year-old secretary Christine Freund -

that police finally realized there might be a connection behind the attacks.

The death of Virginia Voskerichian, a Bulgarian-born émigré, in March, made them certain. A madman was on the prowl. Worried city officials immediately organized a .44 Killer Task Force. But even after checking out literally hundreds of leads, police still had neither suspect nor motive.

THE BIRTH OF SON OF SAM

All that changed with the next attack, on 17 April 1977, which left acting student Valentina Suriani and her boyfriend Alexander Esau dead. This time, not only did Berkowitz leave behind two broken bodies cut down in their prime, but also a haunting four-page letter - a missive which gave birth to Son of Sam.

In it, the twisted killer wrote that he was 'deeply hurt' about the descriptions in the press which characterized him as a woman-hater.

I am not. But I am a monster. I am the 'Son of Sam'. I am a little brat. Sam loves to drink blood. 'Go out and kill' commands Father Sam... I am on a different wave length than everybody else - programmed to kill. However, to stop me you must kill me. Attention all police: Shoot me first - shoot to kill or else. Keep out of my way or you will die!

Then, he warned: 'I'll be back! I'll be back!' before signing it, 'Yours in murder, Mr Monster'.

To panic citizens the twisted killer sent one of his sick letters to a newspaper, knowing it would be published

---

The authorities decided against publicizing the letter, though some parts of it were eventually leaked to local newspapers. On 30 May the killer, hoping to heighten the terror, changed his tactics. He wrote directly to Jimmy Breslin, a well-known columnist on the *New York Daily News*. This letter, even

Below: *Berkowitz is taken from Manhattan police headquarters to be charged with the slaying of six young people and the wounding of seven others.*

more nightmarish than the first one, was published in the following day's edition and sent the city into the fearful panic Son of Sam had craved.

It began:

Hello from the gutters of NYC, which are filled with dog manure, vomit, stale wine, urine and blood. Hello from the sewers of NYC which swallow up these delicacies when they are washed away by the sweeper trucks. Hello from the cracks in the sidewalks of NYC and from the ants that dwell in these cracks and feed on the dried blood of the dead that has seeped into these cracks.

The killer cautioned Breslin not to think he had finished his 'work'.

Mr Breslin, sir, don't think that because you haven't heard from [me] for a while that I went to sleep. No, rather, I am still here. Like a spirit roaming the night. Thirsty, hungry, seldom stopping to rest; anxious to please Sam... I love my work... Sam's a thirsty lad and he won't let me stop killing until he gets his fill of blood.

On the back of the envelope was written:

Blood and Family,
Darkness and Death,
Absolute Depravity,
.44

It was as though Son of Sam was writing from the very depths of hell.

On 25 June the gunman struck again, seriously wounding a young woman and her date in a parked car in Queens.

New York was in panic, and as the police seemed powerless, vigilante groups sprang up. In one incident a Brooklyn burglar was caught carrying a large-calibre gun, and a mob slung a noose from a lamp-post ready to lynch him. It took a dozen policemen to free the man from his irate captors.

In the days after the attack, from the seedy bars of the Bronx to the élite business clubs of Manhattan a terrified populace turned its attention to the calendar. Would Son of Sam 'celebrate' the black anniversary of his first attack on 29 July 1976?

Since the police seemed powerless, trigger-happy vigilante groups sprang up all over the terrified city

---

Berkowitz may have been a brute but he was not a fool. He was well aware that every available policeman throughout the metropolitan area would be on the lookout that night. So he let the date pass without incident - but his lust for blood couldn't be suppressed for long.

In fact he chose the very next night to commemorate his evil, killing Stacy Moskowitz and critically injuring her date, Robert Violante, as they sat in a parked car in Brooklyn.

New York exploded in fear and violence, as more vigilante gangs began attacking people they believed were the elusive Son of Sam. And yet the days of Berkowitz's reign of terror were fast coming to a close - thanks to a stroke of good fortune and a bizarre coincidence.

WHO WAS DAVID BERKOWITZ?

But just who was this unknown madman who, just days later, would be making the front page coast to coast? He was born illegitimate in Brooklyn, New York, on 1 June 1953, and raised by adoptive parents Nathan and Pearl Berkowitz. They were a hard-working, blue-collar couple who saw to it that David led as

Below: A bearded Berkowitz calls a press conference at Attica prison, New York State, minutes before a judge refused to rule him competent to handle his own defence.

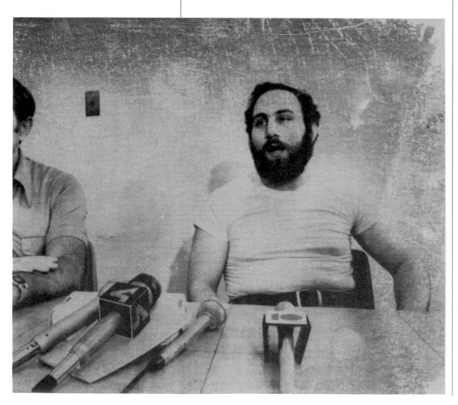

fundamentalist Christianity. Indeed, so complete was the change that Berkowitz often tried to convert fellow soldiers and residents of Louisville, Kentucky where he was stationed for a time.

While he was in the Army Berkowitz got hooked on fundamentalist Christianity

---

On his return to New York, in the late spring of 1974 Berkowitz was hired as a security guard and moved into a small apartment in his native Bronx. It was shortly after his return to civilian life that the events began to unfold which would eventually help turn the tubby, religious Berkowitz into the madness of Son of Sam. First his father, from whom he had been estranged for some time, left New York for retirement in Florida. Next, in his search to find his real mother he discovered that he was illegitimate.

These events left Berkowitz a brooding drifter. By February 1976, five months before he began the slaughter, he moved from his Bronx home to nearby New Rochelle. But after two months, he abruptly changed addresses, to Yonkers, 25 miles north of the city. Eventually he joined the US Postal Service.

THE FATAL MISTAKE

He was still sorting mail ten days after the Moskowitz murder, when the police department in Yonkers received a call from a Detective James Justus at the 10th Precinct in Brooklyn.

Justus, a veteran member of the NYPD, had been telephoning owners of cars which had been given parking tickets near the Moskowitz death scene. It was a boring, routine part of police work, but Justus was an experienced cop, and knew it had to be done.

His repeated telephone calls to the owner of a 1970 four-door Galaxie, cream-coloured with a black vinyl roof - which had been ticketed just thirty minutes before the most recent murder - went unanswered. So he decided to ask the Yonkers police force to notify the man, one David Berkowitz, and ask him to call the 10th Precinct.

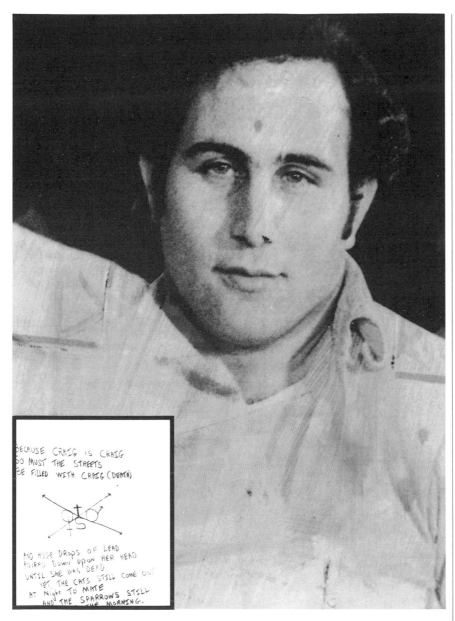

normal a childhood as possible. He was of above-average intelligence at school, popular with his classmates and baseball team-mates - though acquaintances would later reveal that his love life was virtually non-existent.

But when he was fourteen, his adoptive mother succumbed to cancer, a tragedy from which the troubled teenager would never fully recover.

By the time he was eighteen, David, who had long liked uniforms, decided to join the Army, much to the chagrin of his recently remarried father. But Berkowitz was insistent, and in June 1971 enlisted. He stayed in the Army, for three years.

His service was unremarkable, except for a few minor disciplinary charges and his apparent conversion from Judaism to

Above: *A posed prison photograph of 'Son of Sam' David Berkowitz.*

Inset: *A note found by police in Berkowitz's car when they arrested him outside his apartment in Yonkers, New York, in October 1977.*

Above: *A police officer displays a .44-calibre Charter Arms Bulldog revolver, found fully loaded in Berkowitz's apartment.*

After locating his apartment building on Pine Street they spotted his vehicle parked about thirty yards down the quiet street. They went over to investigate.

Through the window they noticed a rifle butt protruding from a duffel bag. They decided to probe more fully.

In the glove box was an envelope addressed to Timothy Dowd, a deputy inspector who was leading the task force. Zigo opened it and read the enclosed letter, which Berkowitz had intended leaving at the side of his next victim.

It promised more attacks - including a planned massacre at a posh nightclub on the eastern tip of Long Island. The police had found their Son of Sam.

Fifteen police gun barrels were aimed at him, but Berkowitz merely smiled and said, 'What took you so long?'

Zigo called for back-up units while legal experts began organizing a warrant to search the apartment. But there was no need for such formalities that night, because just before 10pm, the night stalker himself, dressed in jeans, brown boots and a short-sleeved white shirt, appeared out of the doorway of the building. He was carrying a brown paper bag, which the police would discover contained a .44-calibre gun.

Not realizing that his days as Son of Sam were about to end Berkowitz sauntered casually to his car, so confident in his own evil power that he didn't even bother to look around. He got in, turned the ignition...and looked up to see the barrels of fifteen guns levelled at him.

'Police! Don't move!' the officers screamed.

Berkowitz smiled that eerie smile. 'Okay,' he said softly. 'You've got me. What took you so long?'

ARREST OF A SATANIST

Those present at the scene would later recall how he met his fate with icy detachment. Following the arrest, Berkowitz was ferried back to Manhattan police headquarters.

Word of Son of Sam's capture had already been leaked to the media, and

Justus spoke to switchboard operator Wheat Carr - an incredible coincidence given her family's association with Berkowitz which later came to light - and explained the problem. When he mentioned Berkowitz's name, Justus was amazed at her response.

'He is the guy that I think is responsible,' she told him. Carr went on to describe bizarre incidents involving Berkowitz, including claims that he had shot her dog with a .44-calibre gun and had been sending threatening notes to her father, whose name was - Sam.

A casual conversation with a switchboard operator gave Detective Justus astounding information about the killer's identity

---

Justus immediately reported all this to his superiors. And yet they weren't particularly excited because they had been receiving worthless tips about thousands of suspected 'Sons of Sam'. Still, they realized Berkowitz had to be interviewed. So the following day Detectives Ed Zigo and John Longo were sent up to Yonkers.

they were on the scene at One Police Plaza when the convoy arrived. But instead of seeing a chained, wild-eyed beast they saw David Berkowitz, smiling and looking as dangerous as a lamb.

Nevertheless, behind that vacuous smile lurked a madman. Six hours after his arrest, the interrogation began...and even veteran law enforcement authorities were stunned by the twisted mind that sat before them. Sam, Berkowitz told them, was the person responsible for the crimes because he kept ordering them.

'Who is Sam?' asked Ronald Aiello, head of the homicide bureau at the Brooklyn District Attorney's office.

'My master.' In fact, the police later discovered, the killer was referring to his neighbour Sam Carr - whose barking dog had bothered him.

'Do you want to tell me how you got those orders?'

'Yes, he told me through his dog, as he usually docs. It's not really a dog. It just looks like a dog. It's not. He just gave me an idea where to go. When I got the word, I didn't know who I would go out to kill - but I would know when I saw the right people.'

Berkowitz was grilled for almost two hours, confessing to all the crimes.

During his stay at the Kings County Hospital for psychiatric evaluation, Berkowitz answered a letter smuggled in from Steve Dunleavy, a columnist on the *New York Post*. His reply spoke of Sam as 'one of the devils of Satan...a force beyond the wildest imaginations of people. He is not human.'

'When I killed,' he ranted, 'I really saved many lives... People want my blood but they don't want to listen to what I have to say. There are other Sons out there - God help the world.'

According to one psychiatrist, killing a woman was the only way that Berkowitz could achieve sexual gratification

---

It was in part the declaration that 'other' depraved killers like him were loose in the world that has led some private investigators, writers and even law enforcement officials to suspect that Berkowitz had not acted alone, that he was part of some demonic cult.

Still, at his subsequent trial he admitted all guilt, and the only psychiatrist to judge Berkowitz sane after his arrest, Dr David Abrahamsen, says Son of Sam was driven to kill by a deep fear of women, not by Satanic influences.

'He could not approach a woman as a man would do and have sex with her or date,' Abrahamscn told an interviewer. 'That was not for him. I think he developed a great deal of contempt for women. He's very, very dangerous.'

Below: *Four victims of the 'Son of Sam' killer: (from left) Valentina Suriani, Christine Freund, Virginia Voskerichian and Stacy Moskowitz.*

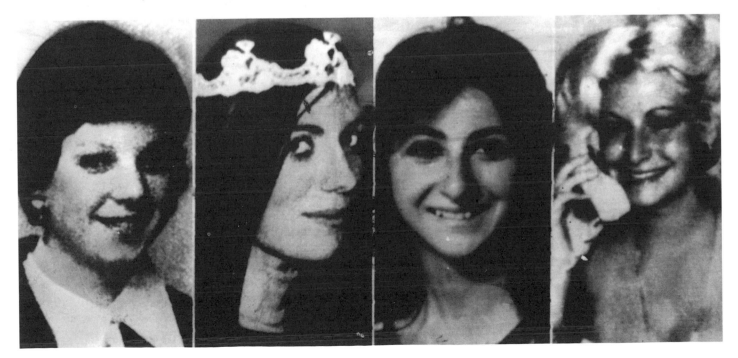

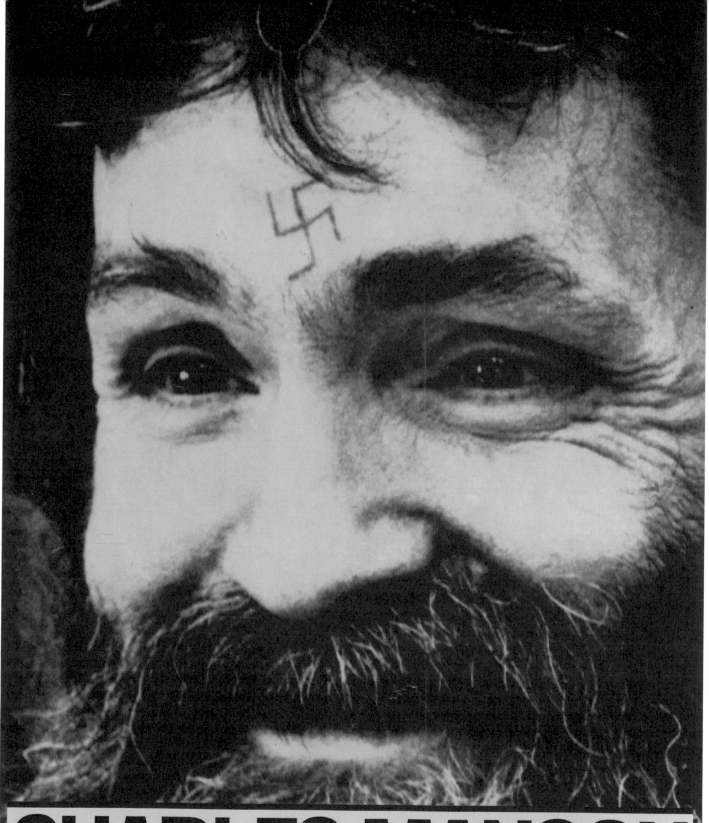

CHARLES MANSON
Hollywood Murderer

Even in the drug-crazed, hippie seventies this was a mass murder that shook America. The perverted, maniacal cult leader Charles Manson and his disciples were responsible for two days of evil that went beyond society's worst nightmares

In August 1970, on an old movie ranch not far from the sprawling, sun-baked city of Los Angeles, a motley group of hippie drop-outs, bikers and petty criminals sat amid the ramshackle, decaying buildings listening to the eerie words of a small, bearded man whom many of them considered a prophet.

It was time, he quietly told them, for Helter Skelter, the beginning of his visionary race war between black and white that would cleanse the earth for all time and pave the way for his reign as master of an entire planet.

With that macabre declaration Charles Manson, pimp, thief and failed musician, unleashed on the world a terror that even today continues to haunt and horrify.

AN ORGY OF BLOOD-LETTING

By the time the twisted, two-day orgy of blood-letting was over, seven people, including the beautiful young actress Sharon Tate, who was more than eight months pregnant with her first child, had been savagely butchered - their blood used to scrawl bizarre, taunting messages on the walls and doors of their homes.

No money had been stolen, despite the obvious wealth of all the victims. And there was no revenge motive - only the senseless slaughter of seven human beings whose sole 'crime' had apparently been that they were successful. The crimes would become known around the world as the Tate-LaBianca murders.

For several weeks investigators came up empty-handed despite checking thousands of leads and tips. The bizarre discovery was to come only after five painstaking months of futile search.

Above: *An early picture of Charles Manson with his beard shaved and hair cut.*

Left: *Scruffy, bearded Manson walks to the Los Angeles court room where he is to stand trial for the murder of Sharon Tate and six others.*

Opposite: *Gloating, mad Manson, his beard now greying, wears a swastika on his forehead as he faces a parole board in San Quentin prison.*

Above: Sharon Tate, butchered at her Benedict Canyon home on the night of 9 August 1969, along with four others.

Above right: Scene of slaughter in the living room of Sharon Tate's home in Los Angeles. Bodies were found in front of the couch and outside the house.

The big break came quite by accident. The police arrested a suspect in another, seemingly unrelated, murder.

Susan Atkins, a veteran of countless acid trips whose flower child innocence masked what even Manson described as 'the most perverted imagination' in the so-called Family, was picked up in connection with the murder of drug dealer Gary Hinman ten days before Tate and the others were massacred.

It was as if Manson had let loose a pack of demons from hell into the heart of Hollywood

---

While awaiting arraignment, Atkins began to brag to fellow inmates about her role in the Tate-LaBianca murders. She claimed she had even tasted the pregnant actress's blood, and spoke reverently of the 'Family' leader - a living god who had the power to make his followers do anything he wished.

Atkins was gloating as her tale of terror unfolded, especially when it came to the death of the actress herself.

'It felt so good the first time I stabbed her, and when she screamed at me it did something to me...and I stabbed her again. I just kept stabbing her until she stopped screaming. It was like a sexual release. Especially when you see the blood. It's better than a climax.'

Two of those privy to the disclosures tipped off the police who, by a stroke of pure coincidence, had already rounded up the cult members charging them with unrelated arson and car theft charges.

'It was like a sexual release. Especially when you see the blood. It's better than a climax,' boasted Susan Atkins

---

Days later, in a bid to play down her role in the killings, Atkins told her tale to the *Los Angeles Times*, deliberately omitting her previous confession. Within hours the story had been flashed around the world - and Manson was the most talked about criminal in the annals of American law enforcement.

ORIGINS OF A CULT LEADER

Charles Manson was born the illegitimate son of a cold, uncaring prostitute in Cincinnati, Ohio in 1935. The young Charlie, who never knew his real father,

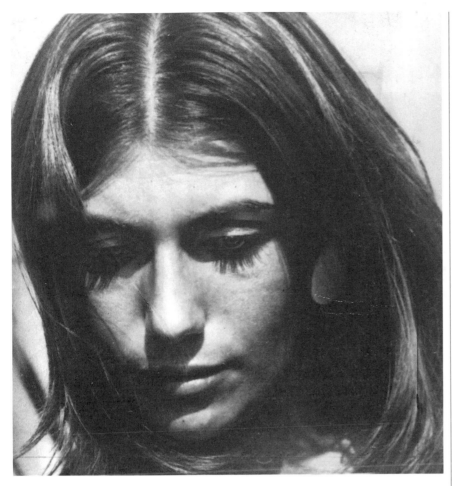

frequent visits, but in 1957 the visits stopped - Rosalie had found real love with another man.

Manson was paroled the following year, but continued to be constantly in trouble with the law. In between his many prison terms he found time to remarry and sire a second son.

Just before his parole hearing, seventeen-year-old Manson held a razor blade to another boy's throat while he raped him

---

It was now 1964, and Manson, like many young Americans, became infatuated with the Beatles. But unlike the millions of other fans of the Fab Four, Charlie's obsession with the band turned into fanaticism.

In 1967, Manson, now thirty-two, was finally released. He asked the authorities if he could stay in jail. But they refused, so he drifted to San Francisco. Here he fell in with the simple flower children of Haight-Ashbury. Armed with little more than a guitar and the clothes on his back, Manson had finally found his niche - a wolf among lambs.

AMONG THE DROP-OUTS

The shaggy folk singer with a street-wise philosophy was an instant hit with the drop-outs and drug addicts of the area, a messianic Pied Piper. He, in turn, found something he had always craved - a sense of belonging and an attentive, easily manipulated audience.

By 1969 Manson and his followers, mainly adoring young women who had abandoned their middle-class roots, drifted south. Eventually they moved to the old Spahn Ranch outside Los Angeles, where they established the beginnings of 'The Family'. Soon afterwards other disillusioned youngsters were joining the ragtag group.

Together they would smoke marijuana, drop acid and dance naked under the stars of the Californian desert, all the while eagerly listening to Charlie's ramblings - a complex fusion of the Beatles, the Bible and his own twisted bitterness towards the society that had spurned him.

spent his most formative years bouncing between several foster homes.

The rebellious youngster had little inclination for school, and his transition from child to teenager was marked by petty criminal enterprises and stints in various corrective institutions.

On 9 March 1951 he was sentenced to the National Training School for Boys in Washington, DC. But just before he was due for a parole hearing, in February the following year, he held a razor blade to another boy's throat while he raped him. This incident got him transferred to the Federal Reformatory in Virginia. He remained there until May 1954.

Even though his sexual experiences had until this point been homosexually oriented, shortly after his parole he met a seventeen-year-old waitress, Rosalie Jean Willis, and married her. He and his pregnant bride travelled to California, but Manson could never reform - he stole the car they used for the trip, and was sentenced to three years' jail.

He was still incarcerated when Charles Manson Jr was born. Rosalie made

Above: Susan Atkins, one of Manson's 'love slaves', who faced trial alongside her evil Svengali. She said of Sharon Tate: 'It felt so good the first time I stabbed her.'

Charlie, as witnesses would later recount, announced it was time for Helter Skelter. Soon the race war would begin. According to his twisted mind the blacks would emerge victorious, destroying the white race forever - everyone, that is, except for him and his motley band.

Manson and his disciples would take drugs and dance naked together at their commune in the Californian desert

---

Then, he asserted, the blacks would turn to the Family - which by this time would have grown to 144,000 (Charlie's 'Chosen People', which he got from the biblical reference to the twelve tribes of Israel, each numbering twelve thousand).

Manson had grandiose dreams and believed he would come to rule the entire planet. According to Greg Jakobson, a talent scout who knew him, Manson also believed 'the Beatles were spokesmen'.

'They were speaking to Charlie, through their songs, letting him know from across the ocean that this is what was going to go down,' said Jakobson.

It was the bizarre 'Revolution 9' that Manson spoke of most. 'It was the Beatles' way of telling people what was going to happen,' said Jakobson ... 'it directly paralleled the Bible's Revelation 9.' The biblical reference was to the battle of Armageddon, and in Charlie's mind, it was a call to the black man that it was time for Helter Skelter. But the blacks, he believed, needed 'help' in

Above: *Victims of the Manson cult raid: (from left) Voytek Frykowski, Sharon Tate, Steven Parent, Jay Sebring and Abigail Folger.*

Below: *Manson leaves the court after asking to be allowed to conduct his own defence.*

starting the race war. That's where he and the Family would fit in. They would strike at the heart of the white Establishment, leaving behind 'clues' that indicated a murderous rampage by a gang of radical blacks. Helter Skelter would get a kick start.

THE HORROR OF HELTER SKELTER

And so, in the pre-dawn hours of 9 August 1969, Manson despatched four black-clad Family members, three of whom were women: Susan 'Sadie' Atkins, a former church choir singer; Patricia Krenwinkel, a one-time office secretary; and Linda Kasabian, who would later prove instrumental in the prosecution's case. The lone male was

Charles 'Tex' Watson, who had been a star athlete back in his Texan high school.

Together the four 'Angels of Death' drove into the prestigious Benedict Canyon section of Los Angeles and made a brief stop on top of a hill with a view of 10050 Cielo Drive, the mansion which Sharon Tate and her film director husband Roman Polanski were renting. There, Watson cut the telephone wires, before proceeding to the estate.

They scaled the fence and crept down the drive to the house. They crept inside and the slaughter began.

Tate, just twenty-six, was later found butchered along with three friends and a caretaker's guest. She had been stabbed sixteen times. Her foetus, a boy due any day, died along with her.

The other victims were similarly massacred. As Watson clubbed and stabbed Voytek Frykowski, a Polish film director, he whispered: 'I am the devil, come to do the devil's work.' Steven Parcnt, the eighteen-year-old guest of the caretaker, was stabbed four times; Jay Sebring, Hollywood's premier hair stylist, was shot and stabbed. Abigail Folger, a coffee heiress, was stabbed on the front lawn as she tried to flee.

'I am the devil, come to do the devil's work,' whispered 'Tex' Watson as he clubbed and stabbed one victim to death

---

Before the marauders left, they used the blood of their victims to scrawl 'Pig' on the front door of the mansion.

But even as Los Angeles reeled in shock, Manson was planning his next murderous move. This time he himself would lead the attacks.

The very next night, he and three disciples broke into the home of Leno and Rosemary LaBianca, owners of a small supermarket chain. He personally tied the victims up, then left them to await a slow, agonizing death at the hands of his devil children - Watson, Krenwinkel and pretty Leslie Van Houten, a former college beauty queen.

According to the gruesome testimony which would come out at the trial months later, the three maniacs carved away at their helpless victims with knives and forks they had found in the kitchen. Krenwinkel carved the word 'war' in the stomach of the dead Leno LaBianca, and left a fork protruding from his stomach.

At first the police did not link these killings to the Tate murders. Quantities of cocaine and marijuana had been found in and around the Polanski mansion, and the authorities had speculated that the murders could have been the result of a drug deal gone horribly wrong.

Yet the police's single-minded belief in the drug motive made them ignore a vital clue. Soon after the slaughter on Cielo Drive two detectives working on another murder case, that of Gary Hinman, told their superiors that at the death scene, just as had occurred in the Tate killings, the murderers had scrawled on the wall a message, 'political piggy', using the victim's own blood. They further explained that they had arrested a

Below: Manson arrives at the Los Angeles court - wearing a purple velvet shirt and gold corduroy trousers.

suspect, Bobby Beausoleil, who was part of a bizarre hippie clan in the desert headed by a guy named Charlie.

But the officials refused to believe there was a connection. It wasn't until Atkins began confiding in her cellmates that the truth became known.

A MADMAN ON TRIAL

When the real culprits were finally caught, Manson's tribe of slavishly devoted followers added a new dimension to an already bizarre case.

The rich and famous, it became known, had been slaughtered by children of privilege, who had left their comfortable middle-class homes for a life of drugs, sex and murder.

At the nine-month-long trial, it was Manson himself who addressed the underlying fear that his disciples had engendered. In a rambling one-hour statement, he sounded almost eloquent.

'These children who come at you with knives, they're your children,' he began.

I didn't teach them. You did. I just tried to help them stand up...Most of the people at the ranch that you call the Family were just people that you did not want...So I did the best I could and I took them up on my garbage dump and I told them this: that in love there is no wrong.

Above: *Shaven-headed Manson in the early days of his prison sentence.*

Below: *Manson is led away from court after being found guilty of first-degree murder on all seven counts.*

...I am only what lives inside each and every one of you...

I never went to school, so I never growed up to read and write so good, so I have stayed in jail and I have stayed stupid and I have stayed a child while I watched your world grow up, and then I look at the things that you do and I don't understand.

But then, as his eyes widened and his voice boomed, courtroom observers saw a glimpse of the madness, and the mesmerizing power over others, that was Manson:

Fascinated courtroom spectators observed how Manson's mesmerizing power would make others do his bidding unquestioningly

---

If I could, I would jerk this microphone off and beat your brains out with it, because that's what you deserve, that's what you deserve...Is it a conspiracy that the music is telling the youth to rise up against the Establishment?...The music speaks to you every day, but you are too deaf, dumb and blind to even listen to the music...There are many, many more, coming in the same direction. They are running in the streets - and they are coming right at you!

Indeed, during the trial Manson's words appeared to be coming true. He was considered a heroic martyr by many disillusioned teens and counter-culture revolutionaries, and the underground press praised him as an 'innocent man' fighting the oppressive establishment.

SOCIETY'S VERDICT

On Monday, 29 March 1971, after what was then the longest criminal trial in American history, the jury returned guilty verdicts on all counts against Manson and his robotic disciples of death.

Three weeks later, Judge Charles Older sentenced the defendants to death. But the sentences were commuted to life imprisonment in 1972, when California's death penalty was outlawed.

Today Charlie is just as frightening as ever. At fifty-six he still gets stacks of mail from troubled youngsters. He spends his days strumming his guitar or making model scorpions out of whatever is available in his solitary confinement at a maximum-security prison in California.

He has even written about himself in a book called *Manson, In His Own Words*, co-authored by a former prison cell mate and published in 1988.

As for the followers who carried out the killings to 'fulfil' his prophecy, all of them are still in prison. However, unlike Charlie, they appear to have changed their demonic ways. Susan Atkins, now forty-three, is a married, born-again Christian. Leslie Van Houten, forty, has obtained a college degree in literature and psychology.

The third woman convicted for the murders is Patricia Krenwinkel, now forty-three. In November 1989 her parole appeal was denied.

'I want you to know that I've got everything in the world,' Manson wrote from jail in 1988. 'At my will, I walk your streets, and am there among you'

'Tex' Watson, now a forty-six-year-old born-again Christian, is serving his life sentence in the California Men's Colony in San Luis Obispo. He has become a member of the prison chaplain's staff. He is married, and has three children.

Linda Kasabian, who was the star witness at the trial and was granted immunity from prosecution, is now forty-two. She lives in rural New Hampshire, raising her four children.

Manson himself professes not to care about his slim prospects of ever walking free: 'I want you to know,' he wrote from his jail cell in 1988, 'that I've got everything in the world, and beyond, right here. At my will, I walk your streets, and am out there among you.'

Left: *Susan Atkins arriving in court for the hearing wearing a long cotton dress.*

Below: *Charles Manson, by now showing every sign of madness, during a prison interview with a reporter at San Quentin.*

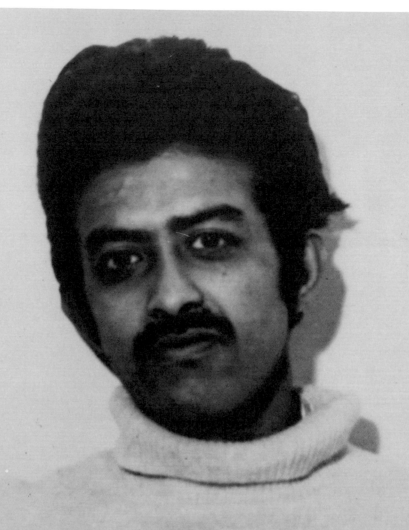

HOSEIN BROTHERS
Muriel McKay's Murder

A middle-aged suburban housewife is kidnapped - and for her newspaper husband the tabloid headlines of his working day become a dreadful nightmare reality. But to this day only her kidnappers know what grisly fate really befell Muriel McKay

The world of Muriel McKay was one of genteel, suburban luxury, far removed from the cut-and-thrust life of her husband Alick. As number two to newspaper tycoon Rupert Murdoch and deputy chairman of the mass circulation *News of the World*, he was in daily contact with stories of crime and vice.

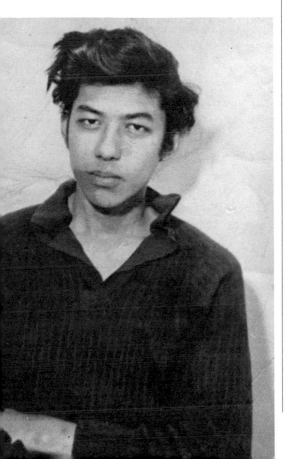

Mrs McKay, however, saw her husband off to work in the morning and was happy to spend her day looking after their expensive home in Wimbledon, South London, a stone's throw away from the All England tennis club.

It was a cosy, comfortable world for the forty-eight-year-old housewife... a world that on the night of 29 December 1969 she was to leave for ever.

KIDNAP IN SUBURBIA

Alick McKay returned home to St Mary House in the tree-lined Arthur Road at 8pm and knew immediately that something was wrong. The front door was unlocked, which worried him since he and Muriel had taken the utmost care after a burglary some months before.

As he stepped through the door he saw a tin of sticking plaster, a ball of string and a meat cleaver

As he stepped into the hall, he found his wife's handbag open on the floor, its contents strewn on the staircase. On a table was a tin of plasters, a ball of thick string and a menacing-looking meat

Above: *The genteel, suburban home from which Mrs Muriel McKay was abducted on the evening of 29 December 1969.*

Opposite: *Arthur Hosein was nicknamed by villagers 'King Hosein' because of his boasts that he would one day become a millionaire.*

Left: *Nizamodeen Hosein who, with his brother, trailed Rupert Murdoch's Rolls Royce - to the wrong house.*

Left: *A meat cleaver found by police at the Hosein brothers' farmhouse.*

cleaver. Alick yelled out his wife's name, grabbed the cleaver and dashed upstairs. There was no sign of Muriel. The distraught husband raced to a neighbour's house and called the police.

Hours later, as the officers swarmed over the house taking fingerprints, Alick received a phone call.

Caller: *This is Mafia Group Three. We are from America, Mafia M Three. We have your wife.*

Alick: *You have my wife?*

Caller: *You will need a million pounds by Wednesday.*

Alick: *What are you talking about? I don't understand.*

Caller: *Mafia. Do you understand?*

Alick: *Yes, I have heard of them.*

Caller: *We have your wife. It will cost you one million pounds.*

'Please co-operate', ran the anguished message, 'for I cannot keep going ... What have I done to deserve this?'

Alick: *This is ridiculous. I haven't anything like a million.*

Caller: *You had better get it. You have friends. Get it from them. We tried to get Rupert Murdoch's wife. We couldn't get her, so we took yours instead.*

Alick: *Rupert Murdoch?*

Caller: *You have a million by Wednesday or we will kill her. Understand?*

Alick: *What do I do?*

Caller: *All you have to do is wait for the contact. You will get the instructions.*

Have the money or you won't have a wife. We will contact you again.

The line went dead and police were unable to trace the call.

At 8 the next morning the postman arrived with a letter. Inside, on a piece of cheap blue paper was a message in Muriel's handwriting.

It read: *Please do something to get me home. I am blindfolded and cold. Please co-operate for I cannot keep going. I think of you constantly and the family and friends. What have I done to deserve this treatment? Love, Muriel.*

A CLAIRVOYANT IGNORED

Over the next few days Alick heard nothing more from his wife or her kidnappers. But a Dutch clairvoyant,

Below: *'Have you seen this woman?' The poster that went up around Britain after Mrs McKay's disappearance.*

METROPOLITAN POLICE

HAVE YOU SEEN THIS WOMAN?

Missing from her home at Wimbledon since evening of 29th December, 1969.

Height 5ft. 9in., medium build, dark brown hair, brownish green eyes, dark complexion, Australian accent.

Wearing black cashmere reversible coat, fawn coloured wool on reverse side, no button. Green jersey suit. Cream patent shoes, square toes, 1¼in. heel, yellow metal chain across instep.

IF YOU HAVE SEEN Mrs. McKay since 5 p.m. on 29th December, 1969, please inform Wimbledon Police Station at 01-946 1113, or your nearest Police Station.

Printed by the Receiver for the Metropolitan Police District, New Scotland Yard, S.W.1

...thing Alick — I am deteriorating in health &
...it please cooperate
...use writing I'm blindfolded & cold —

...se keep the Police out of this and cooperate
...The Gang giving Code No. M3 when telephoning
The earlier you get money
you. quicker I may come home or
...will not see me again. Darling. Can you
...et quickly Please.
...ease Keep Police out of this. if

Alick Darling — If I could only be home
I can't believe this thing happened to me
Tonight I Thank X See you
But it seems hopeless This is all I can say
at the moment.
You betrayed me by going
to Police
The M3 Gang not co operating with

Love Muriel

Gerard Croiset, who had accurately pinpointed the graves of the child victims in the Moors Murders case, claimed that Muriel was being held on the borders of Essex and Hertfordshire, some forty miles north of London. Police ignored his guidance - to their cost.

It was not until 20 January that the thirty-strong team of detectives assigned to the case got their first breakthrough. It was another letter from Muriel, posted in Wood Green, north London:

I am deteriorating in health and spirit. Please co-operate. Excuse handwriting, I am blindfolded and cold. Please keep the police out of this and co-operate with the gang giving Code M3 when telephoning you. The earlier you get the money, the quicker I may get home or you will not see me again. Darling can you act quickly? Please, please keep the police out of this if you want to see me. Muriel.

The villagers of Stocking Pelham called West Indian tailor Arthur 'King Hosein' because of his grandiose ideas

---

The following day there were three phone calls from the kidnappers issuing instructions on where to leave the ransom money. Alick demanded proof that his wife was still alive; the gang sent a package containing three pieces of material from Muriel's green wool outfit and a snip of leather from her shoes.

From a stamp on the package, forensic experts managed to get one thumbprint. It was later a crucial piece of evidence.

The ransom was to be handed over in two payments of £500,000. Alick gave police £300 in used notes, but the rest of the 'money' would consist of cut-up newspapers. There were two or three attempts at a handover, but they failed.

Finally, Friday, February 5 was the date demanded by Muriel's captors. The cash was to be dropped near Bishop's Stortford in Hertfordshire. Police staked out the area. But no one picked up the bait. The waiting officers, however, did spot a Volvo saloon cruising the area. The registration number ' XGO 994G ' had been noted at an earlier failed handover attempt. A check revealed the car belonged to a man called Arthur Hosein.

He was a West-Indian born tailor who aspired to be accepted in English middle-class society.

In 1967 he and his German wife Else had bought Rooks Farm in the village of Stocking Pelham, just a few miles from Bishop's Stortford. And within months Arthur's younger brother Nizamodeen had moved in with them. Villagers called

Above: *Mrs Elsa Hosein, German-born wife of Arthur, on her way to the Old Bailey to see her husband stand trial.*

day dawned on 6 February, twenty detectives swooped on Rooks Farm. When Else answered the door they told her that they were investigating a cache of stolen jewellery.

The police were impressed by Arthur's calm manner. 'I earn a lot of money,' he told them. 'I do not deal in stolen goods. You may search where you like.'

But when they began the search they soon knew they were on the right track. First an officer emerged from a bedroom with scraps of blue notepaper identical to the kind used in the ransom notes.

Then they discovered a writing pad on which could be made out the indentation of words written in Muriel's handwriting. The officers also unearthed a sawn-off shotgun which had recently been fired.

Was Muriel McKay's dismembered body put into the pigswill at Rooks Farm?

What they did not find was any trace of Mrs McKay herself - alive or dead.

But there was one discovery that morning which was to lead to the most gruesome theory. Traces of bone were found in a fireplace, and a billhook which had been used to slaughter animals.

Arthur Hosein said he had borrowed it from a farmer to 'cut up a calf'. He added, chillingly: 'We fed it to the dogs and put the bones and head in with the rubbish which we fed to the pigs.'

The brothers had recently sold several pigs but police were unable to trace them. If they had been, they might have confirmed their theory: that Muriel McKay had been murdered and her dismembered body put into the pigswill.

CHARGED WITH MURDER

In any event, the police believed they had enough to charge the brothers with murder. The evidence included the thumbprint from the stamp on the package sent to Alick McKay which matched Arthur Hosein's. And experts also discovered Arthur's prints on a newspaper, which the kidnappers had dropped in the drive of the McKays' house on the night Muriel disappeared.

Arthur 'King Hosein' because of his assertion that he would become a millionaire. What they could not know was how he planned to realize his dream.

HOW THE PLAN WAS HATCHED

One night Arthur and his brother were watching TV when they saw Rupert Murdoch being interviewed. During the show, reference was made to Murdoch's wife Anna. Suddenly, Arthur had a plan.

He and Nizamodeen would find out where Anna Murdoch lived, abduct her and demand £1 million. The brothers did their homework, or so they thought, but made two errors. They got the addresses of Murdoch and McKay mixed up, and followed Murdoch's Rolls Royce, not realizing that Alick was using it while his boss was away.

All these facts were to emerge in court at the trial of the decade. Meanwhile, as

The brothers denied their guilt, however - and during police interrogation revealed very different characters.

Nizamodeen was almost child-like in his attitude to detectives. He once broke down sobbing on an officer's shoulder and cried: 'Oh my, what has Arthur done to me? What did Arthur say I was?'

Self-confident Arthur envisaged a film being made of the story - starring Richard Burton and Sammy Davis Jr

---

Arthur was a different kettle of fish altogether. He was articulate, and showed astonishing bravado. He even boasted that he would write a book about the case - the ensuing film would star Richard Burton as the officer in charge and Sammy Davis Jr as himself.

It was no use. At their trial at London's Old Bailey, Mr Justice Sebag Shaw jailed both brothers for life.

For months, police searched for the body of Muriel McKay. But the only people who know what happened to Mrs McKay are Arthur and Nizamodeen Hosein. And they have kept silent.

In a poignant postscript to the crime, Alick wrote in the *Sun* on the morning after the brothers were convicted:

One can accept death in the ordinary way...But in these circumstances, one is unable to accept the explanation of death without finding a body, although I am convinced Muriel is never coming home again. I must face this situation, of course, and face my life as best I can.

I suppose I do not want to know the brutal facts really, and yet I must always ask: How did she die? What happened to her? Where is her body?

Above: *Rook's Farm, Hertfordshire, where police searched for any sign of the remains of Mrs McKay.*

Below: *Dogs are employed in the search in the vicinity of Rook's Farm.*

LIZZIE BORDEN
The Mad Axe Killer?

It's one of the great unsolved cases in American criminal history. One sultry August day in 1892, did the browbeaten Sunday School teacher Lizzie Borden brutally axe to death the father and stepmother who made her life so miserable?

Lizzie Borden took an axe
And gave her mother forty whacks
When she saw what she had done
She gave her father forty-one

It was a children's rhyme which was chanted in every school playground across the United States. Its echoes would haunt Lizzie Borden until the day she died. Had she, in blind fury, battered her hated stepmother to death, then done the same to her puritanical father? A judge and jury decided that she hadn't, and she walked free from court a wealthy young woman.

But if Lizzie was innocent, who was the Fall River Axe Murderer? The case remains one of the classic unsolved crimes in American history.

AN UNLOVING CHILDHOOD

Lizzie Borden was born in 1860 at 92 Second Street, Fall River - a cotton town in Massachusetts. And her relationship with her father was sealed at her birth. He had her christened Elizabeth Andrew, because he had wanted a boy.

Lizzie's mother died two years later and her father, Andrew J. Borden, married Abby Durfee Gray, a plain, plump, shrewish woman of thirty-seven. Mr Borden was a wealthy man, a former undertaker who had amassed close to half a million dollars in property deals. But he

Above: *Lizzie's mother had been dead for only two years when her father, Andrew J. Borden, remarried.*

Left: *Mrs Abby Durfee Gray Borden, who became Lizzie's stepmother.*

Opposite: *Lizzie Borden, whose father had given her the middle name Andrew because he had wanted a boy, not a girl.*

was also a miser.

Despite their wealth, the Bordens lived in conditions worse than many of the town's mill workers. Andrew Borden spent nothing on the shabby house in Second Street, even less on his children Lizzie and her elder sister Emma.

As Lizzie grew up she at first resented, then despised, her stepmother. She was

THIRD ST.

VIEW OF THE VICINITY OF THE MURDERS.

I. Borden house.
II. Borden barn.
III. The well.
IV. Fence with barbed wire on top.
V. Side entrance.
VI. Churchill residence.

VII. Dr. Bowen's house.
VIII. Dr. Chagnon's house.
IX. Kelley house.
X. Yard from which officers watched the Borden house.
XI. Kelley's barn.
XII. Pear orchard.

Above: *Second Street with the Borden home marked with the figure 'I'. Lizzie's father spent no money on their shabby home.*

convinced that the only reason she had married her father was to get her hands on his money. Lizzie refused to sit down for meals with her and always addressed her as Mrs Borden. Lizzie was plain, with curly red hair, quiet and introspective. She was an ardent churchgoer and her spare time was spent fishing, sewing - or just brooding at her bedroom window.

Despite the wealth he had accrued Andrew Borden was a miser, and his family lived in miserable conditions

---

It was in these unhappy surroundings that Lizzie Borden spent the first thirty-two years of her life. Then, on 4 August 1892, a single act of horrific violence destroyed the Borden household for ever.

THE DEED IS DONE

The little town of Fall River was in the grip of a severe heatwave. Lizzie's sister Emma could stand it no longer and moved out to the country to stay with friends at Fairhaven, twenty miles away.

Lizzie herself had been ill with food poisoning, and she had been brooding over two incidents which lately had made

her even more bitter. The first was when she discovered that her miserly father was going to spend some of his hoarded wealth - on her stepmother's sister.

Lizzie had flown into a furious rage and ransacked her stepmother's bedroom, taking some cheap items of jewellery. She claimed the house had been burgled, but it did not take long for her father to realize that Lizzie was the culprit.

The second incident had occurred in May when intruders broke into outhouses at the bottom of the Bordens' garden. Mr Borden's reaction was bizarre. He was convinced they had been after Lizzie's pet pigeons, so he took an axe to the birds and chopped their heads off.

Convinced that the intruders had been after Lizzie's pet pigeons, her father inexplicably chopped all their heads off

---

It was in this brooding frame of mind that Lizzie awoke on that fateful August morning. The family routine began as usual. After breakfast Mr Borden set off to check on his businesses. John Morse, his first wife's brother who was staying a few days, left to visit relatives. Mrs Borden began tidying and the servant, a good-natured Irishwoman, Bridget Sullivan, was cleaning the windows.

Just after 9.30am Mrs Borden was hunched on all fours cleaning the stairs leading to the spare bedroom. She was struck on the head and the body by nineteen blows from an axe. The first blow would have killed her instantly.

At 11am Mr Borden arrived back at the home, sweating from the heat. Lizzie made a fuss of him and left him dozing in the living room while she went into the kitchen to chat to Bridget. The maid then went upstairs to rest from the heat.

Ten minutes later she heard wild screams from Lizzie Borden. 'Come down, come down!' she yelled. 'Father's dead. Someone came in and killed him.' Bridget raced downstairs to find Lizzie guarding the living room door. She refused to let the maid enter, but ordered her to fetch Dr Bowen, the family doctor.

After a delay, the doctor arrived and examined the mutilated body of Mr Borden. He had been killed in exactly the

Above: *The murder house, 92 Second Street, photographed in the late autumn of 1892.*

Left: *Lizzie, it was revealed, had bought a bottle of prussic acid and a bottle of cyanide from the town's pharmacy.*

same way as his wife. There were ten blows to his head, aimed mainly at his nose and eyes. Blood was splattered over the walls, the settee and carpet.

As Dr Bowen pulled a sheet over the corpse neighbours arrived at the house. One, Mrs Adelaide Churchill, did her best to comfort Lizzie, but was struck by the fact that Lizzie showed no emotion. At the time she put this down to shock.

Mrs Churchill then asked Lizzie where her stepmother was, to which she replied: 'I'm sure I don't know, for she had a note to visit someone who is sick. But I don't know that perhaps she isn't killed also, for I thought I heard her coming in.' Mrs Churchill and Bridget took some minutes to find Mrs Borden's body, lying in a pool of blood on the stairs.

THE SUSPECTS LINE UP

At first, suspicion fell on John Morse, whose behaviour when he returned to the house had puzzled the crowd outside. He had been seen to slow down as he approached. Then, instead of going straight to the front door, he went round the back and picked some fruit from a tree. Police also thought he was a little too quick with his alibi. But when they checked it out it stood up well enough.

Detectives were convinced that the murders had to be the work of someone in the household. They soon eliminated Bridget Sullivan. She had no motive to commit such horrific killings: she was not mentioned in Andrew Borden's will, and there was no ready cash in the house.

That left Lizzie Borden. Her behaviour after the murders had been curious, to say the least. When Bridget had asked her where she was when her father was attacked, Lizzie replied that she had been out in the yard. But she told Mrs Churchill that she had been in the barn getting a piece of iron. When questioned by detectives she said that she was in the barn and had eaten three pears while she was there. Police combed the barn, but could find no trace of pear cores.

Lizzie said she had not seen the body of her stepmother as she came downstairs to greet her father. A neighbour told the police that the night before the murders Lizzie had told her that her father had enemies and that she feared for his life. But the detectives found no motive for murder among his business rivals.

It was also discovered that the day before the murders Lizzie had bought a bottle of prussic acid - cyanide - from the town pharmacy. She offered no explanation for this strange purchase.

THE AXE-WOMAN ON TRIAL

In the weeks following the murders almost every newspaper in the USA tried and convicted Lizzie Borden. After all, it was a great story - spinster daughter takes bloody revenge on tyrannical father and wicked stepmother.

Detectives investigating the case tended to agree with the newspapers. Secretly they had drawn up a warrant for Lizzie's arrest, but they wanted to wait until after the inquest before it was served. They believed that Lizzie might give evidence at the inquest which would damn her.

The police were not disappointed. Lizzie Borden stood in the witness box and duly put her foot in it. She incriminated herself by stating that she had not been upstairs when her father had arrived home. It meant, of course, that she was trying to wriggle out of the awkward question of why she had passed her stepmother's body on the stairs without seeing it.

'I thought I was on the stairs but now I know I was in the kitchen,' she told the inquest. And she added confidently: 'Looking back on this dreadful event has made me recall things much more clearly.' After the inquest, Elizabeth Andrew Borden was charged with the first degree murder of Andrew J. Borden and Abby Borden, née Gray.

But by the time the case came to court the following June, small town America had rounded on the press for its shabby treatment of Lizzie. The God-fearing, clean-living daughter of a heartless father was now an object of public sympathy. In a complete turnaround, ordinary folk had decided that quiet Sunday School teacher Lizzie should not be standing trial for such a diabolical crime. Quite simply, she was innocent.

The police had a wealth of circumstantial evidence but hoped that Lizzie would give herself away at the inquest

---

Lizzie, meanwhile, had hit the jackpot with her choice of lawyer, George Robinson, a former Governor of Massachusetts. While in office he had appointed one of the three trial judges to the bench. At a pre-trial hearing this judge, at Robinson's request, decided to disallow any prosecution statements about the prussic acid episode. Lizzie's trip to the pharmacy was never mentioned in open court.

The trial lasted ten days, and as it progressed the prosecution's case began to look decidedly frayed around the edges. Lizzie helped her own cause by fainting in the dock, which brought a wave of sympathy from the jury.

COURTROOM BRILLIANCE

Robinson was brilliant throughout. He convinced the jury that the state had been callous in allowing such a put-upon, saintly girl to stand trial for a crime she could not possibly have had the heart or the stomach to commit. He finished his case for the defence by asking the jury: 'To find her guilty, you must believe she is a fiend. Gentlemen, does she look it?'

By the time of the trial public opinion had swung in favour of the God-fearing daughter of a heartless big businessman

---

The jury decided that she didn't, and pronounced her not guilty. Lizzie Borden stepped down from the dock and, to cheers from the public gallery, walked from the court a free woman.

And a rich woman too. She inherited most of her father's wealth, a sum beyond her dreams while he was alive. Despite the cruel chants of the children, Lizzie had no qualms about staying in Fall River, although she could not face living in the house which had brought her so much unhappiness. She soon moved to a house in a wealthy suburb.

Bridget Sullivan soon sailed back to Ireland, taking with her, it was said, a large amount of money generously donated to her by Lizzie out of her father's will.

For a while there were rumours that Lizzie and Bridget had hatched a plot together to rid themselves of the cruel old miser and his peevish wife. But the case was never reopened by the police. They appeared to be quite satisfied that they had arrested the true culprit, and that justice had run its course. The real killer, they were convinced, had been freed by a jury of twelve good men and true. The mad axe murderer of Fall River never struck again.

Lizzie settled into her new house with her sister Emma, but according to neighbours they soon began arguing and Emma moved out. Lizzie Borden died a lonely spinster in 1927 at the age of sixty-seven, taking the secret of that hot August morning with her to the grave.

Today, the Axe Murders of Fall River still spark controversy. There exists in America a Friends of Lizzie Borden Society who regularly protest her innocence. But there are as many who are convinced that on that hot August day the downtrodden daughter of Andrew J. Borden finally snapped and wreaked her terrible revenge on those who had made her life a misery.

Left: *Lizzie and her lawyer, former Massachusetts Governor George Robinson, during the trial.*

Below: *The court house at New Bedford where Lizzie's ten-day trial took place.*

OSCAR SLATER
Victim of Prejudice

Sherlock Holmes's creator had a mind as brilliant as that of his fictional detective - without it, the stories could never have been written. On one occasion Conan Doyle turned his powers of perception and deduction to a bizarre crime in the real world

More than a century after Sir Arthur Conan Doyle's gifted pen gave birth to Sherlock Holmes, the crime fighter and violin virtuoso remains fiction's greatest detective mind.

His enduring qualities of deductive reasoning, an eye for the minute and a skilled, analytical brain served him well throughout the amazing adventures he shared with his ever-loyal companion, Dr Watson. None of those who followed - not Poirot, Maigret or Ellery Queen - could equal him.

Almost from the very first appearance of Holmes, the public closely identified the author with his creation. From all over the world, letters poured in to Conan Doyle's home asking for his help.

Sir Arthur rarely accepted the implied challenge. There were a few exceptions, however, when the great writer felt a sense of outrage that justice had not been served and fair play thrown to the wind.

One concerned George Edalji, a vicar's son who happened to be a Hindu. Edalji was accused of a series of horrible animal mutilations around his village of Great

Above: *Scene of the crime - the dining room of 15 Queen's Terrace, a cushion by the fireplace showing the position of the body.*

Left: *An early picture of Miss Marion Gilchrist who was brutally murdered four days before Christmas in 1908.*

Opposite: *Oscar Slater strolls through London's Hyde Park shortly after his release.*

Far left: *Oscar Slater in 1908, the year he was accused of bludgeoning Miss Gilchrist to death.*

Above: *The hushed High Court in Edinburgh as Oscar Slater goes on trial.*

Above right: *Lord Guthrie, the High Court Judge who presided at Slater's trial. Slater was sentenced to death, but two days before he was due to be hanged his sentence was changed to life imprisonment.*

Wyrley in Staffordshire. Although he was of impeccable character and an established lawyer, the police, motivated by racism, got a conviction. Edalji was sentenced to seven years' hard labour.

Unfortunately Sir Arthur did not become aware of the young man's plight until three years later, in 1906. But within weeks he had gathered enough evidence to prove Edalji's innocence, and published his findings in the *Daily Telegraph* in January 1907.

Race hatred in the English Midlands sent a young Hindu lawyer to prison for crimes he had not committed

---

The articles had the desired effect. A commission was ordered to investigate Conan Doyle's claims, and Edalji was promptly released.

'He came to my wedding reception,' Sir Arthur recorded, 'and there was no guest whom I was prouder to see.'

THE CASE OF OSCAR SLATER

The second exception came soon afterwards - a series of events which Dr Watson might have recorded as 'The Case of the Ungrateful Dog'.

Like many of the Holmes stories it involved the bizarre, the fantastic and murder. In the end Conan Doyle's dogged investigation freed an innocent man,

Oscar Slater, from a wrongful life sentence with hard labour.

The story began just four days before Christmas, on 21 December 1908, with the brutal murder of Miss Marion Gilchrist. A reclusive, elderly spinster, she was found bludgeoned to death in her home at 15 Queen's Terrace, West Princes Street, Glasgow.

At first Conan Doyle was reluctant to get involved. But, as he later explained in his autobiography, 'when I glanced at the facts I saw...that this unhappy man had in all probability no more to do with the murder for which he had been condemned than I had.'

The eighty-two-year-old Miss Gilchrist seemed an unlikely victim for murder. She was a virtual hermit, and her only real pipeline to the outside world was her young maidservant, Helen Lambie.

On the night of the murder, Helen, twenty-one, left her mistress's residence to buy an evening paper. She would be gone less than ten minutes.

Miss Gilchrist, who had long been ill at ease with the noise and uncertainties of the world outside, made sure the locks of her double doors were securely fastened. Because of her advanced age, the lonely spinster had installed a latch on the outer door which could be opened by a long piece of string attached between it and her upstairs flat.

Returning with the newspaper, Helen found a frantic young man named Arthur

Adams outside Miss Gilchrist's door. Adams, a neighbour from a flat below, explained that he had heard a noise coming from inside the apartment, followed by a heavy thud. When he yelled out to Miss Gilchrist and got no answer, he came upstairs.

Helen unlocked the door with her key. Just as they were about to enter, a man appeared from inside. He approached as if about to strike up a conversation, then he suddenly brushed past them and fled.

Startled by the strange encounter, the servant and the neighbour cautiously entered the flat...and recoiled in horror as they found the body of Miss Gilchrist, her head brutally beaten and covered with a rug, sprawled out in the dining room in front of the fireplace.

The elderly spinster lay sprawled on a rug, battered to death - yet her valuable jewellery had hardly been touched

---

Despite her valuable jewellery collection, which was estimated to be worth more than £3000, all that was missing was a crescent-shaped diamond brooch worth some £50. However, a box of papers had been broken open and the contents strewn about, as if someone had been frantically searching for something.

Although Adams and Helen had both seen the man at close range, they were in some disagreement over his actual appearance. However, one thing later became clear: neither of the descriptions fitted that of Oscar Slater.

Adams immediately ran out to fetch a policeman, while Helen raced to the home of Mrs Margaret Birrell, Miss Gilchrist's niece. The maid blurted out that she had recognized the killer. But strangely Mrs Birrell rebuked her.

PREJUDICE CLAIMS A VICTIM

As word of the vicious killing spread, there was an immediate public outcry and the police were quickly put under intense pressure to make an arrest. Slater, a German-born Jew, was apprehended solely because he had pawned a diamond brooch of similar value to the one stolen just before embarking for America on the liner *Lusitania* with his French mistress.

The New York authorities were notified, and Slater was promptly seized and returned to Glasgow. Here, however, it was discovered that not only had he owned the brooch in question for many years, but that he had pawned it three weeks before the killing!

And yet both the public and the police refused to yield. They wanted blood and Slater, whose morals were shown not to have been of the highest standards, remained the only suspect.

The police then found a box of tools in his possession, and claimed he had used a small hammer to kill the elderly spinster. Never mind that Slater had a clear alibi - because his mistress and maidservant were his witnesses it was not allowed. Even the description of the killer was amended to resemble Slater more closely.

Slater's alibi was disallowed because its witnesses were his mistress and his maidservant

---

And so, in one of the greatest miscarriages of British justice, the hapless Slater was duly convicted in the High Court and sentenced to death. Then, just two days before he was due to be hanged, his sentence was commuted to life imprisonment.

Above: *Helen Lambie, the maid of eighty-two-year-old Miss Gilchrist and virtually her only connection with the outside world.*

Below: *Queen's Terrace (on the right) is where Miss Gilchrist lived and died.*

Above: *The body of Miss Gilchrist was found battered and covered with a rug, sprawled in the dining room in front of the fireplace.*

CHAMPIONED BY CONAN DOYLE

Slater would have spent the rest of his days in confinement, if he had not been championed by an indignant Conan Doyle. After an investigation which would have done Holmes proud, the author outlined the reasons why Slater could not have been the murderer in a brilliant pamphlet, entitled *The Case of Oscar Slater.*

'The trouble ... with all police prosecutions,' Conan Doyle wrote, 'is that, having once got what they imagine to be their man, they are not very open to any line of investigation which might lead to other conclusions.'

First, the author punched holes in the official motive of robbery:

When he [the killer] *reached the bedroom and lit the gas, he did not at once seize the watch and rings which were lying openly exposed upon the dressing-table. He did not pick up a half-sovereign which was lying on the dining-room table. His attention was given to a wooden box, the lid of which he wrenched open. The papers in it were strewed on the ground. Were the papers his object, and the final abstraction of one diamond brooch a mere blind?*

And yet, if it was indeed a robbery, ... it is very instructive to note his knowledge of their [the jewels'] *location, and also its limitations. Why did he go straight into the spare bedroom where the jewels were actually kept? The same question may be asked with equal force if we consider that he was after the papers. Why the spare bedroom?...Is not this remarkably suggestive? Does it not pre-suppose a previous acquaintance with the inside of the flat and the ways of its owner?*

But as Conan Doyle cleverly observed, there were limits to the intruder's knowledge. 'If it were the jewels he was after, he knew what room they were in, but not in what part of the room.'

Moreover, he suggested:

How did the murderer get in if Lambie is correct in thinking that she shut the doors? I cannot get away from the conclusion that he had duplicate keys. In that case all becomes comprehensible, for the old lady - whose faculties were quite normal - would hear the lock go and would not be alarmed, thinking that Lambie had returned before her time. Thus, she would only know her danger when the murderer rushed into the room, and would have hardly time to rise, receive the first blow, and fall, as she was found, beside the chair upon which she had been sitting.

Conan Doyle revealed how the police had misinterpreted the evidence and jumped to a hasty but illogical conclusion

---

The only other possibilities, he claimed, were that the murderer was actually hiding inside the flat when Lambie left, 'of which there is no evidence whatsoever', or that the intruder was someone whom Miss Gilchrist knew and who was therefore let in.

Next, Sir Arthur went over the evidence taken from the scene of the crime, his gaze as perceptive as that of

Holmes. He correctly pointed out that no blood was found on the wooden box, despite the bloody nature of the murder.

It has never been explained why a rug was laid over the murdered woman. It is at least possible that he (i.e., the murderer) used the rug as a shield between him and his victim, while he battered her with his weapon. His clothes, if not his hands, would in this way be preserved.

DOGGED PERSEVERANCE

Despite his conclusive and logical analysis, and his stinging rebuke of the Scottish Lord Advocate, the pamphlet still failed to win Slater's release.

But Conan Doyle waged a relentless newspaper campaign, and eventually an official government inquiry into the case was set up. Nothing came of it. Slater languished in prison.

It was not until November 1927 - eighteen years after Slater's conviction - that Conan Doyle's unyielding efforts proved successful. Slater was released pending a retrial. In June the next year he was pardoned - he was never exonerated - and given £6000 compensation.

Conan Doyle believed that the real murderer was a prominent citizen protected by the police

---

But if Sir Arthur had expected to meet a grateful citizen when Slater was pardoned, he was in for a rude awakening. Incredibly, he refused to repay the money that the author had put up as bail for his release before the retrial.

'He is not a murderer,' the author told a reporter, 'but an ungrateful dog.'

A MYSTERY UNSOLVED

The key question, of course, was never answered. To this day, the identity of Miss Gilchrist's murderer remains a mystery forever lost to the past. Helen Lambie kept her silence about the man she said she had recognized coming from the flat, and many people later believed the killer was a public person with a reputation to safeguard.

Sir Arthur was certain that was the case. Although he never publicly revealed his suspicions, shortly before his death he said he believed he knew who the real killer was: 'A man who was protected by the police because he was a prominent citizen who desperately wanted something from the private papers of Miss Marion Gilchrist. He has gone unpunished, but it is more important to me that an innocent man is free.'

It was never established just what secrets those private papers contained. But one thing is certain: they contained something to prompt a man to murder a helpless elderly spinster.

*Left: **Oscar Slater in London in 1928, watching the pigeons outside St Paul's Cathedral.***

*Below: **Cleared of murder ... Slater and his wife beside a Scottish river.***

D. B. COOPER
The Mystery Skyjacker

Skyjackers are reviled by most responsible governments, and feared by aircrews and passengers. So how did a mysterious American hold a plane to ransom and then pass into legend as a folk hero?

Not many skyjackers become heroes - but that was the way it happened for one of America's most mysterious criminals, the legendary D.B. Cooper, who bailed out of a passenger plane with $200,000 in cold cash to become an overnight folk hero!

Adored by millions who continue to sing his praises even to this day, Cooper nevertheless threatened to blow out of the sky more than 150 innocent men, women and children if the authorities didn't come up with the money. But the swashbuckling nature of the crime - and the fact that in the end no one was ever hurt - captured America's attention and turned this mysterious little man into a modern-day version of Robin Hood.

It was the perfect crime - and no one knew what had happened to the perpetrator

---

Indeed, it was the perfect crime...and to this very day, more than twenty years later, no one is really certain what ever became of him. Did he die in his brazen leap into the night? Did he succumb to a fatal disease? Or is he still alive today, living off his ill-gotten swag?

No one is sure how the bizarre story ends, but everyone knows how it began, quietly enough, on Thanksgiving Day, 24 November 1971, at Portland airport in the state of Oregon.

As hundreds of travellers milled around the departure lounge eager to get to their families and friends for the American national holiday, no one gave the quiet little chap clutching a canvas bag a second glance. He sat patiently amid the boisterous holiday atmosphere, seemingly a person of little consequence behind his dark-tinted glasses.

Almost an hour went by, but finally the 150 passengers who were taking Northwest Airlines' one-hour flight to Seattle were paged to begin boarding.

SHORT WALK TO FAME

D.B. Cooper - the name he had used to purchase his ticket - stood up from his seat in the departure lounge and began the short walk to the waiting Boeing 727. Still clutching the canvas bag, the only luggage he had brought with him, he worked his way down the cabin until he found his aisle seat - which was, as he had requested, opposite the place where the stewardesses would sit for take-off and landing.

The stewardess thought the passenger wanted a drink. Instead he handed her a note: 'I have a bomb with me...'

For the next twenty-five minutes, as the plane roared through the sub-zero temperatures towards Seattle, the man continued to play the part of a holiday-maker. But then, about halfway through the 400 mile flight, he pressed the button above his seat to summon a stewardess.

Tina Mucklow responded, thinking the man probably wanted a cocktail or a blanket. But to her horror he handed her a note, short but exact in its dire warning: 'I have a bomb with me. If I don't get $200,000 I will blow us all to bits.'

Mucklow was stunned as she read and reread the note. Then, without taking his eyes off her, Cooper opened the bag just wide enough so that she would know that this was no bad joke or bluff.

She could clearly see the intricate maze of dynamite sticks, wires and a detonator.

Then he closed the bag, and watched the shaken stewardess walk as calmly as

Opposite: *After warming by an early-morning fire, FBI agents resume digging for more of the $200,000 ransom beside the Columbia River.*

she could to the flight deck. It wouldn't be long now, he must have thought.

As soon as Mucklow delivered the quiet man's threat to the startled cabin crew the pilot radioed Seattle ground control, explaining the nature of their emergency. He couldn't have known, but within minutes a crack team of FBI agents, police marksmen and even local units of the National Guard were being deployed at key points around the airport. The authorities believed they were in for a long night of negotiations.

All that everyone, including Cooper, could do now was wait. For the next thirty-five minutes the Northwest jet proceeded to Seattle.

WAITING AT SEATTLE

As the plane made its way to the tarmac the pilot made a brief announcement to the passengers, explaining that there would be a delay in disembarkation. No reason was given, and the passengers reacted with understandable dismay.

As his fellow travellers talked angrily among themselves of missed connections and spoiled dinners, Cooper got out of his seat and, with the canvas bag still clutched tightly to his body, walked calmly up to the flight deck to face the pilot and his two senior assistants.

'Now, gentlemen,' he said quietly, without rancour. 'Don't bother to look around.' For the next twenty minutes there was a tense stand-off, as Cooper explained first to the air control tower staff, and then to a senior police officer, that his demands were inviolate: $200,000 in used bills and four parachutes in exchange for the safe release of all his hostages.

It wasn't until the released hostages were safely inside the terminal that they realized a skyjacking had taken place

---

The authorities knew they had no choice. They could not gamble with the lives of so many innocent people, who could be blown to bits if a rescue attempt was staged. Reluctantly, they despatched two FBI agents towards the captive jet.

Disguised as airport maintenance men, they wheeled aboard a trolley, containing a sack sealed with wire. Cooper opened it and, to his glee, knew he had won - the money and parachutes were inside.

Keeping his word, he then allowed the passengers to leave the aircraft. Incredibly, it wasn't until they were safely inside the main terminal and confronted by hordes of waiting reporters that they learned they had been the victims of a skyjacking, and that a man had threatened to snuff out their lives.

THE PASSENGER VANISHES

Meanwhile, as the passengers reacted first with surprise, then with shock, at their near-miss, back on the plane Cooper was preparing to put phase two of his carefully conceived plan into action.

With the flight crew still at the mercy of his bomb, he demanded that the plane be refuelled and then ordered flight plans to Mexico.

During his conversations with air traffic staff and ground crews, Cooper displayed such a knowledge of planes and airport procedures that authorities knew they were dealing with a smart, calculating supercriminal.

Once his demands had been carried out, Cooper ordered Captain Bill Scott to take the plane back into the night sky, where it was tailed by an Air Force fighter jet. But the skyjacker was a cautious, quick-thinking man who had apparently calculated the various responses the authorities would make.

In his instructions to the pilot Cooper revealed an intimate knowledge of flying and aerodynamics

---

As a result, not long after they were airborne he ordered the flight crew to change course. He never intended flying to Mexico, and instead told Captain Scott to head south - using detailed flight instructions that revealed an intimate knowledge not only of flying but also of the complexities of aerodynamics.

'Fly with the flaps lowered, 15 per cent,' he ordered. 'Keep the landing gear down. Keep the speed below ninety metres per second. Open the rear door and do not climb above 7000 feet.'

Once Captain Scott had got over the slight shock of realizing his captor was no ordinary criminal, he did some mental calculation regarding Cooper's specific instructions and informed him that they would cut heavily into their fuel supply.

Cooper calmly informed the captain he could land in Reno, Nevada.

Before leaving the cabin, he ordered the flight crew to keep the steel bulkhead door - which separated the cabin from the rest of the Boeing - locked for the remainder of the journey. He also ordered Scott to activate, as soon as he had left the cabin, the system which would open the rear door of the plane.

The captain complied, and the plane was suddenly engulfed by the deafening rush of thin, cold air.

For the next four hours, Scott and his crew flew by Cooper's instructions towards their ultimate destination. It wasn't until they had safely landed in Reno that they realized their passenger had literally vanished into thin air.

Cooper, wearing only light clothing, had parachuted out into rugged country in sub-zero temperatures. Was this his fatal mistake?

Later, a detailed examination of the plane's black box recorder would indicate a slight but perceptible altitude increase at 8.13pm - thirty-two minutes after the take-off from Seattle. Under cover of darkness and clouds, which hid him from view of the tailing Air Force jet, Cooper had leaped into the night, his ill-gotten booty strapped to his waist.

On the surface, it appeared to be the perfect crime. Not only had Cooper made a daring escape, but he had outwitted the combined efforts of the police, the FBI and the United States Air Force!

But after checking the black box recordings, officials realized he had made one terrible mistake in an otherwise flawless plan. When Cooper jumped, the Boeing had been flying over the inhospitable terrain of south-western Washington State - a rugged landscape dotted by deeply wooded areas.

Above: *American newspapers reported in 1983 that Cooper was actually a Missouri conman. It was just one of many 'leads' that led exactly nowhere.*

Moreover, the temperature would have been below zero that night, and Cooper had been dressed only in lightweight clothes and shoes, a raincoat his sole protection against the bitter elements. Further, he had no food.

The odds against him surviving the leap were overwhelming.

The terrain was so hostile that ground searches quickly became bogged down, and the authorities were instead forced to rely on wave after wave of aerial searches in the two weeks after Cooper's incredible disappearing act. But even planes equipped with heat sensors turned

Above: *FBI agent Himmelsbach who was specially assigned to the Cooper case. Not even the FBI, however, were able to track down the phantom skyjacker.*

would be romantic, or heroic, or any of the other euphemisms that seem to attach themselves to situations of high risk. I don't blame people for hating me for what I've done, nor do I blame anybody for wanting me caught and punished, though this can never happen. I knew from the start I would not be caught. I have come and gone on several airline flights since and I'm not holed up in some obscure backwoods town. Neither am I a psychopath. I have never even received a parking ticket.

A FOLK HERO IS BORN

The letter caused a sensation. Cooper may not have considered himself a hero, but the public did.

Letters and phone calls poured into newspapers and radio stations across the country praising his slick escapade. T-shirts bearing his name became as trendy as those espousing 'Peace and Love'. And hundreds of young women pledged themselves to be his bride - that is, if he could ever be found.

But not everyone was enamoured with Cooper - a frustrated FBI reportedly held back from the public a psychiatric mental profile, fearing it would only bolster his swashbuckling image.

Moreover, not everyone was convinced that it was he who had written the letter. Many of the woodsmen who were at home in the hostile terrain over which Cooper had jumped openly labelled it as the work of a crafty con man.

When part of the rear door of a 727 was discovered, a 'Gold Rush' of excited treasure-seekers turned up

---

up empty, and people began to wonder if the high-flying thief would surface again.

Then, suddenly and without warning, three weeks after the skyjacking, a mysterious letter arrived at the offices of the *Los Angeles Times*.

'I am no modern-day Robin Hood,' the letter began. *Unfortunately, I have only fourteen months left to live. The hijacking was the fastest and most profitable way of gaining a few last grains of peace. I didn't rob Northwest because I thought it*

They believed that Cooper had been killed in the jump, or soon afterwards by the elements, and continued their hopeful treasure hunts across the wild landscape. So too did thousands of holidaymakers who went on 'Cooper's Loot' weekends - though they were attracted to the area more for the scenery and the barbecues than for any serious treasure-hunting.

As fortune-seekers - earnest and amateur - poured into the region where Cooper had gone down, the authorities continued their aerial reconnaissance for traces of the elusive skyjacker and his ill-gotten booty. They, too, doubted the validity of the *Times* letter, and believed he could not have survived the jump.

But all the searches came up empty and finally, twelve months after the skyjacking, the FBI publicly announced that they believed him to be dead. Four years later, on 24 November 1976, the Bureau officially closed its file on the Cooper case.

Under the statute of limitations, the only crime he could possibly be charged with by then was tax evasion - assuming, of course, that he was still alive.

That was the last time most people thought they would ever hear of the mysterious D.B. Cooper...and for several years they were correct.

But in 1979, a hunter stalking deer came across a tattered plastic sign which read: 'This hatch must remain firmly locked in flight.' It was the warning sign from a Boeing 727 rear door hatch. The discovery caused a sensation, and treasure-seekers by the thousands began to pour into the dense forests where the sign had been found.

COOPER'S LOOT

Despite their efforts, however, the missing loot remained undiscovered.

Then in 1980, a full nine years after Cooper's dramatic escapade, father and son Harold and Brian Ingram were walking along the muddy bank of the Columbia River north-west of Portland when the eight-year-old boy noticed a wad of old, sun-bleached $20 bills.

There was $6000 in all, which the authorities believed had been washed down the river from the higher terrain to the north.

When the money was handed over, officials checked the serial numbers against those of the bills given to Cooper. There could be no mistake - the money was part of Cooper's cache.

To many, the discovery proved beyond a shadow of a doubt that Cooper had indeed died in his daring parachute jump, and that his loot had been scattered to the four winds. The Ingrams' discovery sparked yet another bout of interest in

Cooper's Loot by locals and out-of-towners, who came pouring into the region once more in hope of suddenly striking it rich. But again they were foiled. No more money was ever found.

Then, in 1989, a skin-diver seeking clues to Cooper's fate found a small parachute in the Columbia River about a mile upstream from where the money had been located.

Despite the immediate frenzy the discovery caused - even after so many years had gone by - it was eventually determined that the parachute was not connected to the Cooper case.

With the parachute and the money weighing him down, did Cooper drown in the icy Columbia River?

Earl Cossey, the man who had helped pack the original chutes demanded by Cooper, said it bore no resemblance to those given to the skyjacker, and because of its small size he thought it might have been used for a flare. It could even, he felt, have been a child's toy.

The diver who found the parachute was working for Californian lawyer and former FBI agent Richard Tosaw, who has spent every Thanksgiving for the past ten years searching for Cooper's remains.

Tosaw, who wrote a book titled *D.B. Cooper, Dead or Alive*, says he believes the skyjacker drowned, and that his remains got caught up on one of the rows of pilings that extend into the river about every half-mile to prevent erosion.

'He didn't know where he was when he baled out,' said Tosaw. 'He hit the water with the parachute on his back and the money packs around his waist, and went down. He is still down there somewhere. So is the rest of the money, snagged on an old rock or stuck in the mud.'

Despite his annual searches, however, Tosaw, like hundreds of other treasure-seekers before him, has come up empty-handed each time. None the less he vows to continue the hunt.

D.B. Cooper's most elusive secret remains just as enigmatic as it did twenty years ago - and the chances are that it will never be solved.

WHITE MISCHIEF
Who killed Lord Erroll?

Cocaine, champagne and adultery were the hallmarks of the rich and pleasure-seeking Happy Valley set in 1940s Kenya. This was the background for a crime of passion committed by a jilted husband who saw his whole world crumbling

Not since the Romans frolicked with Bacchanalian abandon did a ruling caste indulge in such wanton displays of hedonistic pleasure. The white elite which lived in splendour among the breathtaking natural beauty of Kenya's White Highlands, a place nicknamed Happy Valley, abandoned themselves to pleasure in all its forms.

COCAINE, BOOZE AND SEX

They reached their zenith in what was then a British colony during the years of World War II. As their compatriots at home endured the privations of rationing and separation, the gilded set of Happy Valley partied at a feverish pitch.

Drunken, sexually depraved cocaine snorters, the Happy Valley residents cared little for the world's woes as long as their frivolous existences were not menaced by Hitler or the taxman.

Happy Valley's residents cared little for the world's woes so long as their own frivolous existences were not menaced

---

Near to the Wanjohi River, not far from the capital, Nairobi, the first white settlers in Kenya had been drawn to the magnificent White Highlands by the fertile soil which yielded high grade coffee and tobacco. But any frontier spirit

Above: *Sir Henry Delves Broughton was thirty years older than his English rose of a wife, Diana.*

Opposite: *Among the flowery 'bright young things' at Ascot racecourse in 1937 was Lady Diana Delves Broughton.*

that may have existed in Victorian times had been washed away by the expats who inhabited these beautiful hills during World War II. This 'little England' had become an enclave for laziness and lotus eaters whose idea of a tragedy was too little ice for their sundowners at the Muthaiga Country Club.

No one was more suited to this meaningless existence than Josslyn Hay, a philanderer and a rogue. Hay was the Earl of Erroll and High Constable of Scotland, but he forsook the rigours of the Scottish Highlands for those of Kenya. Expelled from Eton, cited in an English divorce court where the judge branded him 'a very bad blackguard',

Hay arrived in the cushiest of wartime foreign postings as British military secretary in Nairobi.

He had commented to a friend in England before his departure: 'Not much chance of catching a bomb there, what?'

Had it not been for a certain meeting, a certain knowing smile, it might well have been that Josslyn Hay would have sat out

Above: *Josslyn Hay, the Earl of Errol, who was murdered, undoubtedly because of his infidelities.*

Below: *The Muthaiga Country Club, where the Happy Valley set liked to meet, drink and flirt.*

the war and the rest of his idle life in Kenya. As it was he was murdered - undoubtedly for his philanderings.

But to this day his killer's identity remains a secret, although more than a few fingers have been pointed to the grave of Sir Henry Delves Broughton.

Sir Henry was the exact opposite of Josslyn Hay. True, he was aristocratic, privileged and drank too much. But he had two attributes alien to Hay - honour and a wife. The wife, Diana, was an English rose beauty who at twenty-six was thirty years younger than him.

Sir Henry - known to all his friends simply as Jock - was suffering financially in England, the legacy of bad business judgement and even worse judgement on the racecourses. Ancestral homes in England had been mortgaged and Kenya was seen as his last great chance to recoup a fortune by raising cattle.

But he still had sufficient funds to enjoy a splendid lifestyle in Happy Valley, and he felt certain that his young bride would appreciate the social whirl.

'I saw her eyes boring into me and I knew then I must have her'

Within weeks of his arriving in Africa Josslyn Hay met Diana for the first time, on 30 November 1940, at the Muthaiga Club. Hay would later say to friends: 'Never can I remember a woman having such an immediate impact on me. I saw

her eyes boring into me and I knew then I must have her. I walked over to her while Jock was at the bar and said: "Well, who is going to tell Jock, you or I?" '

Diana found his dangerous sensuality electrifying. Both of them were willing participants in the passion.

THE MISERABLE CUCKOLD

It was said that Hay derived as much pleasure from seeing cuckolded husbands squirm as he did from bedding his sexual conquests. Diana was no exception.

Hay began to flaunt her mercilessly in front of their friends, including of course Jock. He twirled her around the dance floor, their embrace lingering too long, their clinches too tight for anyone to mistake what was passing between them.

Poor Jock, muttered friends with some shreds of morals left. But the kindly old man bore his humiliation with British stiff upper lip stoicism.

In January 1941 he found a letter addressed to him at the club. It read: 'You seemed like a cat on hot bricks last night. What about the eternal triangle? What are you going to do about it?' Several days later, when Diana left for an 'all girls' swimming party, another note informed him that there were no girls on the outing. Just Josslyn Hay.

Hours after Jock received the last note, Diana returned from her trip and told her husband she was leaving him.

Desperate to keep his wife, Jock said he would tolerate Diana's affair if she kept up the pretence of marriage

---

It is a measure of the man that he told her then that he was willing to put up with the relationship provided she continued to live with him. He offered her a three-month cruise to Ceylon.

Diana declined the offer of the cruise, and two days later walked out on Jock with a £5000 set of pearls which he offered as an inducement to stay.

What this trauma did to the balance of Jock's mind has been the subject of

Above: *Happy Valley's dwellers enjoyed all that privilege and position could bring them. The dashing young Earl of Errol (in the back row, wearing a bow tie) was one of their leading lights.*

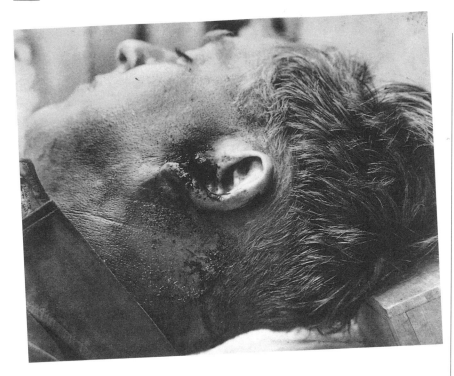

Above: *The Earl of Errol, who was shot in the head in the free-living paradise community known as the Happy Valley.*

gentility, even going so far as to inquire of Hay how the war was going. The tea party was followed by evening carousing, during which Jock raised his champagne glass at the Muthaiga Club and said: 'I wish them every happiness. May their union be blessed with an heir. To Diana and Joss.'

Less than three hours later Hay was dead in his car which had careened off the Nairobi-Ngong road. There were three neat bullet holes in his head.

THE MURDER

When the police later reconstructed the bizarre events of that night, they discovered that Jock had wheedled from him a promise that Diana could spend one last night under her husband's roof.

It transpired that Jock had staggered to bed, inebriated, at 2am and was sound asleep at 2.15 when Hay's American Buick purred through the wrought iron gates of his ranch and dropped Diana off.

It then left the road two and a half miles from Jock's mansion and plunged into a gravel pit. At 3am two labourers found Hay. Two hours later Jock was woken by police, who broke the news.

Jock, of course, was the chief suspect. He had both the motive and the means to commit murder. Within twenty-four hours the police had found near his home bullet casings that matched those found near the murder scene.

The Happy Valley set thought Diana was against her husband. Instead she hired a first-class lawyer for him

---

While his wife slept, Jock went into town to see the corpse of her lover. Then in the afternoon he piled numerous personal effects into a pyre and set them alight. Only one item remained, to be found two days later - a charred, bloodstained sock that led police to their conclusion: the cuckolded husband had killed his rival and burned the clothes splashed with the victim's blood.

The Nairobi CID had formulated a theory which went like this. Far from being sozzled on champagne, Jock had merely feigned inebriation. He had then

speculation ever since. His staff who served dinner for him that night reported that he seemed pensive. Perhaps he was plotting the next move in the tragedy - which came the next day.

On 21 January he called the local police to say that two revolvers - Smith and Wesson service-issue models - had been stolen by burglars who had broken into his study.

After making a statement to the police he visited a lawyer to see about getting a divorce, and then wrote a painful letter to a friend back in England. He said: 'It is a hopeless position...I think I will go to Ceylon. There is nothing for me in Kenya any longer.'

It was painful but true; as well as losing his wife, his cattle venture had fared badly, losing him £10,000 in the first few months.

At June Carberry's tea party the cuckolded Jock was charming to his rival Hay

---

Some of his friends rallied around poor old Jock. As Diana moved into Hay's home, Mrs June Carberry, who despised Jock's wife, invited him to a tea party to try to cheer him up.

Unfortunately, at the last moment Diana and Hay turned up too. Jock gave a command performance of civility and stolen out of the house and lain in wait on the lonely road for Hay to come by.

They lowered Josslyn Hay into the ground on 25 January, but it was not until 10 March that charges were laid against Jock. More surprising, however, was Diana's flight to South Africa, where she hired the eminent Johannesburg lawyer Harry Morris to defend her husband.

CIRCUMSTANTIAL EVIDENCE

Jock performed magnificently in court. Observers felt a groundswell of public gallery sympathy, as Morris laid bare the philandering, cocaine-taking antics of this gilded but tarnished set.

Jock walked free on 1 July 1941. Morris had sent the ammunition from the murder scene to ballistics experts in London, who ascertained that the bullets could not have come from a Smith and Wesson service-issue revolver.

Jock was free, but his life destroyed. His relationship with Diana survived long enough for her to share the cruise to Ceylon. But halfway through it Jock fell badly and hurt his back, and transferred

Right: *Sir Henry Delves Broughton and his wife Diana at Sandown Park racecourse in 1939.*

Below: *Sir Henry Delves Broughton and the first Lady Broughton (born Vera Boscawen) with their son Jock at Derby racecourse in 1928.*

to another steamer to take him to England. Diana continued on the voyage and then made her way back to Kenya.

Jock, with nothing left to live for, committed suicide in Liverpool in 1942.

One of the witnesses at his trial had been June Carberry. She testified that she too had been staying in his house the night the killing was committed, and swore that he was too drunk to do anything other than flop on to the bed.

Did Jock Broughton confess all to a sympathetic fifteen-year-old schoolgirl?

But now, aged sixty-five, her daughter Juanita has come forward with a startling claim - that Jock confessed all to her when she was a schoolgirl. She said: 'He told me: "I hate Happy Valley and its people." I felt a great loyalty to him and I don't think he was wicked or a criminal...I know he killed him.'

Perhaps in the end the only person who really knew what had happened was Diana. Was it possible that she sensed, one day, that she too would be discarded when Hay's fancy turned to another woman? Was it possible that she took his life to spare herself that dreadful day?

Maybe. But Diana died in 1987 and the secrets of those days died with her.

POLICE *THE ILLUSTRATED* NEWS
LAW COURTS AND WEEKLY RECORD

No. 1,284.   SATURDAY, SEPTEMBER 22, 1888.   Price One Penny.

"IS HE THE WHITECHAPEL MURDERER?"

READY FOR THE WHITECHAPEL FIEND. WOMEN SECRETLY ARMED.

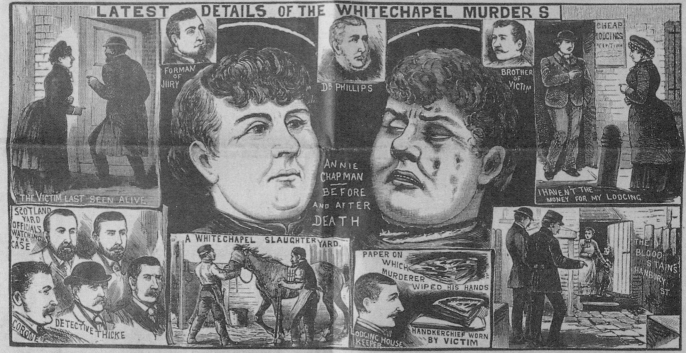

LATEST DETAILS OF THE WHITECHAPEL MURDERS

FORMAN OF JURY

DR PHILLIPS

BROTHER OF VICTIM

CHEAP LODGINGS

THE VICTIM LAST SEEN ALIVE

ANNIE CHAPMAN BEFORE AND AFTER DEATH

I HAVEN'T THE MONEY FOR MY LODGING

SCOTLAND YARD OFFICIALS WATCHING THE CASE

CORONER

DETECTIVE THICKE

A WHITECHAPEL SLAUGHTER YARD.

PAPER ON WHICH MURDERER WIPED HIS HANDS

LODGING HOUSE KEEPER

HANDKERCHIEF WORN BY VICTIM

THE BLOOD STAINS HANBURY ST.

JACK THE RIPPER
Monster of the East End

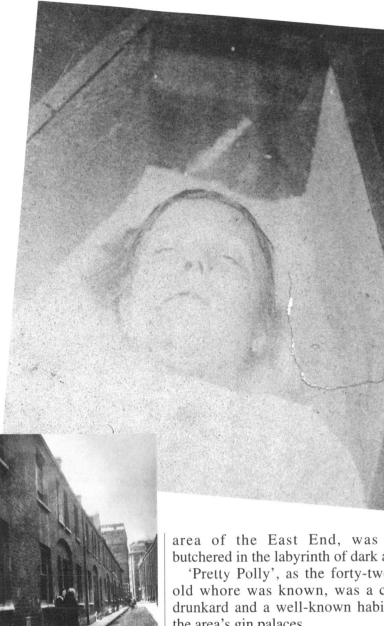

In 1888 London's East End saw a series of brutal murders of prostitutes which remain unsolved today. Was Jack the Ripper a maniacal surgeon? A Jewish ritual slaughterer? An insane member of the royal family?

In 1888 the British Empire was at its zenith. The lands ruled from faraway London spanned the globe, embracing peoples of every race, creed and colour.

But in the centre of this huge domain there was a place where the sun never shone. The East End of London was a disgrace to the empire and to civilized values. People lived there in poverty and squalor. Child deaths were double the national average. Prostitution and drunkenness, sexual abuse of minors, murders and muggings were all rife.

This was the sordid environment for a killer whose notoriety lives to this day. Jack the Ripper made the mean streets of the East End his killing ground.

His crimes were not that remarkable, given the catalogue of horror man has come to terms with in the twentieth century. He only murdered five women - admittedly in a gruesome manner.

But it is the question of identity, with all the lingering suspicions that Jack the Ripper may have been someone highly placed in British society, which has made the 'Monster of the East End' an immortal creature of intrigue.

THE FIRST VICTIM

Jack the Ripper may have gone down in history as an infamous murderer but his reign was in fact short. He first struck on 31 August 1888. Mary Ann Nichols, a prostitute who haunted the Whitechapel

*Top: **Mary Ann Nichols, a prostitute known as 'Pretty Polly', was the first victim of the horrific 'Monster of the East End'.***

*Above: **The street where the body of Mary Ann Nichols was found lying across the gutter.***

*Opposite: **A contemporary newspaper relates the Ripper story in a particularly lurid fashion.***

area of the East End, was found butchered in the labyrinth of dark alleys.

'Pretty Polly', as the forty-two-year-old whore was known, was a chronic drunkard and a well-known habituée of the area's gin palaces.

Fourpence provided a whore with a doss house bed for the night and a few swigs of cheap gin

---

Police believe she had approached a tall stranger with the time-honoured 'Looking for a good time, mister?' She would have requested fourpence for her services, enough for a doss house for the night and perhaps a few tumblers of gin.

By the time the man had dragged her into the shadows it was too late. A hand went round her throat, and in seconds she was cut from ear to ear.

'Only a madman could have done this!' said a police surgeon later. 'I have never seen so horrible a case. She was ripped about in a manner only a person

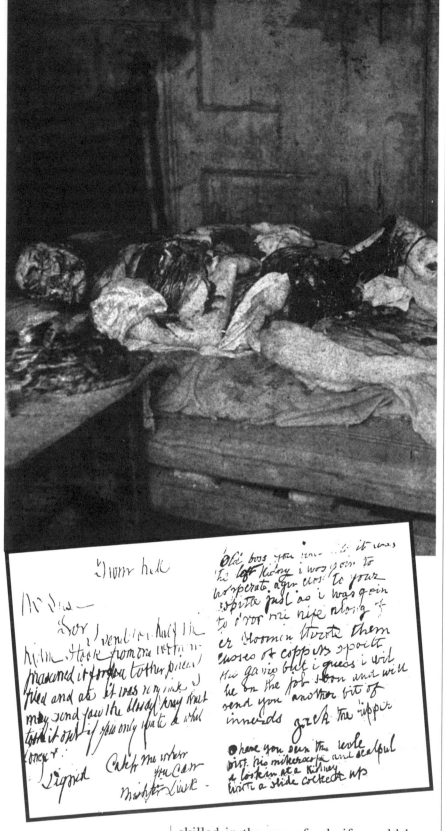

Although there was no obvious sign of rape, with this murder - as with the first - there was every indication that the killer had been motivated by some terrible sexual rage as he cut and slashed. The dissection of Dark Annie, with all her entrails laid next to the corpse, indicated a knowledge of anatomy or surgery not found in the the average sex killer.

GRUESOME SEQUEL

The second murder had an extraordinary sequel. On 28 September a mocking letter was sent to a Fleet Street news agency. It read:

I keep on hearing that the police have caught me. But they won't fix me yet. I am down on certain types of women and I won't stop ripping them until I do get buckled. Grand job, that last job was. I gave the lady no time to squeal. I love my work and want to start again. You will soon hear from me with my funny little game. I saved some of the proper stuff in a little ginger beer bottle after my last job to write with, but it went thick like glue and I can't use it. Red ink is fit enough I hope. Ha! Ha! Next time I shall clip the ears off and send them to the police, just for jolly.

It was signed: 'Jack the Ripper'.

The way the bodies were disembowelled indicated a knowledge of anatomy or surgery on the part of the murderer

---

A later letter, sent to the Whitechapel Vigilance Committee, was accompanied by half a kidney. The sender claimed it was from a murder victim - and that he had eaten the other half.

No one can be sure that the writer of this second letter was the same as the author of the first. But it is known that the Ripper removed some of the victims' organs. After expertly slitting their throats he would set about gruesome mutilations, slashing open faces and abdomens, ripping out intestines. Some he would arrange around the bodies, others he would take away.

The Ripper's third victim was Elizabeth Stride, nicknamed 'Long Liz' because of her height. On 30 September a

Top: *'Dark Annie' Chapman, already dying of tuberculosis, was disembowelled.*

Above: *One of the letters sent to the police - possibly from Jack the Ripper.*

skilled in the use of a knife could have achieved.' Yet despite the horror, murders in that deprived and depraved area of London were not uncommon, and the police were happy to put this one down to a single, frenzied attack...until one week later.

On 8 September 'Dark Annie' Chapman, a forty-seven-year-old prostitute dying of tuberculosis, was found butchered near Spitalfields market.

rag-and-bone cart driver alerted police to a suspicious bundle. They found the body of forty-four-year-old Liz near factory gates in Berner Street, Whitechapel.

Like the others, her throat had been cut from behind - but she had not suffered mutilation or sexual savagery. This led police to think that the Ripper had been disturbed in his grisly work. For on the same day they found victim number four a few streets away in Mitre Square.

THE SPATE OF BUTCHERY CONTINUES

Catherine Eddowes, in her forties, was disembowelled and her face practically hacked off. Her intestines were draped across her right shoulder and both her ears were missing.

By the time of the fourth murder, Ripper hysteria had gripped London. Women began arming themselves with knives and carrying whistles to attract the police. *The Illustrated London News* rather fancifully suggested that ladies should now carry pearl-handled pistols in case the Ripper was tempted to move up the social scale. One shop even advertised steel corsets. Lower down the social order, in Whitechapel itself, policemen took to dressing as prostitutes in an attempt to decoy and trap the killer.

In one rare moment of farce a constable was accosted by a journalist, also dressed in gaudy women's clothing, and asked: 'Are you one of us?' The policeman replied: 'Certainly not' - and arrested him.

Half a human kidney accompanied a letter signed 'Jack the Ripper' - the other half, said the sender, he had eaten

---

The Eddowes murder disturbed the police greatly. Her body was the worst mutilated of all the victims. From her corpse there was a trail of blood leading to a torn scrap of her apron in a doorway. And nearby on a wall was scrawled in chalk the message: 'The Jewes are not men to be blamed for nothing.'

Sir Charles Warren, head of the Metropolitan Police force, personally removed the message, and may thereby have destroyed vital evidence. He was

Below: *Mary Kelly, just twenty-five years of age, was grotesquely mutilated in her squalid home. The previous night she had been accosting strangers, asking for money.*

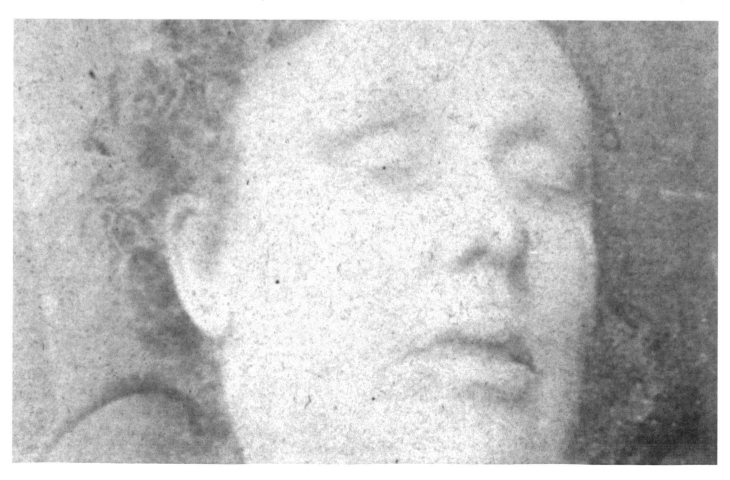

concerned that, with the influx to the East End of Jews from eastern Europe, the inscription could lead to savage reprisals.

RUMOURS AND SUSPECTS

The rumours about who the killer could be spread like wildfire. Some of the frightened wretches who lived in the area said it was a policeman on his beat.

Another suspect was a Russian-born doctor called Michael Ostrog, rumour having it that he had been sent by the tzarist secret police to stir up hatred against expatriate Jews.

Others said it was a mad surgeon. Blame even attached to Sir Charles Warren himself - a leading freemason who had supposedly removed the notice to protect a masonic killer.

The final death came on 9 November. The only difference this time was that the victim was a better class of prostitute; she had a room of her own.

Mary Kelly, twenty-five years old, was grotesquely mutilated in her rented home. This time the Ripper had been able to spend many hours at his grisly work.

On the morning of the 10th, her landlord Henry Bowers knocked on her door to collect unpaid rent. The previous evening the attractive blonde had been accosting strangers for cash. The last one she approached - tall, dark, with a moustache and deerstalker hat - was her killer. Later it was discovered that the woman had been three months pregnant.

Her death was to be the last. Yet, a century and more later, the puzzle of the Ripper's brief but bloody reign had still not been solved.

' there she was, all her entrails steaming hot. She had red and white stockings on'

In 1959, seventy one years after the killings, an old man recalled driving a cart down Hanbury Street on 7 September, 1888 and hearing the cry 'Murder!' He said: 'I jumped off, being a lad, and joined the crowd...and there she was, all her entrails steaming hot. She had red and white stockings on.' That was the second victim, Annie Chapman.

*Above: **Rumours were rife about who the Ripper could be. One eye-witness described Mary Kelly's last client (and therefore probably her killer) as tall, dark and with a moustache.***

One suspect who has continued to cause violent debate is Queen Victoria's grandson, Prince Albert Victor, Duke of Clarence. The finger of suspicion was pointed at him because he was said to be mad - and after the killings was supposedly incarcerated in a mental institution for fear of the scandal.

The Duke was the eldest son of the future Edward VII, and was said to be a bisexual who turned insane after catching syphilis. But police claimed he was either at Balmoral or Sandringham on the nights of the murders.

But perhaps the number one suspect is Montagu (some reports spell his name

Montague) John Druitt, whose body was found floating in the Thames a few weeks after the murder of Mary Kelly.

In their book *The Ripper Legacy*, authors Martin Howells and Keith Skinner say that Druitt, an impoverished barrister, was the man whom the police of the day reckoned to be the guilty party. Druitt's family, it was claimed, had a history of mental illness, and Druitt himself had been trained in medical skills as a young man.

JILL THE RIPPER?

Another author, William Stewart, suggested that Jack the Ripper was really Jill the Ripper, a midwife and illicit abortionist jailed as a prostitute who took a terrible revenge when released.

Top cop John Stalker, who retired in the late 1980s as Deputy Chief Constable of Greater Manchester, delved into the Ripper files and declared:

Was the Ripper Queen Victoria's grandson, turned mad by syphilis?

There is still not a shred of real evidence against anyone sufficient for a court of law. The truth is that Jack the Ripper was never in danger of capture. The police, I am certain, came nowhere near him. The Metropolitan Police of 1888 were dealing with something quite new - the first recognized series of sexual murders committed by a man who was a stranger to his victims. And a hundred years on, those are still the most difficult crimes to investigate.

And yet one man who has delved into the Ripper files more than anyone else believes firmly that a culprit for the murders was identified.

John Ross is an ex-policeman, now curator of the Metropolitan Police's so-called Black Museum at New Scotland Yard. Not a man noted for jumping to conclusions, he tells visitors to his grisly exhibition that Jack the Ripper was an immigrant named Kosminski, of whom little is known beyond his surname.

Mr Ross believes that all the on-the-spot police work at the time pointed to this suspect. And he is not alone.

In February 1894 a predecessor of Mr Ross with the same analytical mind, Sir Melville McNaughton, wrote a seven-page memorandum which was added to the Ripper file in an attempt to silence some of the wilder theories being postulated at the time.

Former top policeman John Stalker says Ripper-type cases are still the most difficult to solve

---

His notes read: 'Kosminski, a Polish Jew and resident in Whitechapel. This man became insane owing to many years' indulgences in solitary vices. He had a great hatred of women, especially of the prostitute class, and had strong homicidal tendencies. He was removed to a lunatic asylum around March 1889. There were many crimes connected with this man which made him a strong suspect.'

Below: *Millers Court, Dorset Street, in the East End of London - typical of the squalid spots where Jack the Ripper committed his grisly crimes.*

NAZI TREASURE
Division of the Spoils

A series of brutal murders, all of old people, in a small community. Not Agatha Christie, but the work of someone determined to keep an old wartime secret. It all stemmed from the Nazis' lust for riches...

Above: *Neuschwanstein Castle near the Swiss frontier where the US Seventh Army found a huge hoard of loot stolen by the Nazis from private collections.*

Right: *An American soldier examines an item of Goering's stolen art treasury.*

Opposite: *Invaluable paintings are removed from Neuschwanstein Castle.*

The ringing of the doorbell roused Salvatore Leonardi from his armchair in front of the television at ten o'clock on a Sunday night. It was unusually late for a friend to be calling. Something was clearly amiss. Why else would anyone walk up the dirt track to his home, perched on a hill overlooking the village of Bargagli in northern Italy?

Leonardi pushed himself out of his chair and walked to his back door. Opening it, he found himself staring into the barrels of a sawn-off shotgun.

It is unlikely that his eyes had time to focus on the face of his visitor, for both barrels were emptied before the door had swung fully back.

The killing was inexplicable to the police who descended on the village after the crime in September 1989, and no one in the small community seemed willing to enlighten them. Even Leonardi's widow could provide no clues to the murder of a silver-haired retired barber.

'My husband...was a calm man,' she said, 'who led a quiet life and enjoyed looking after his chickens and his rabbits. But my husband said many times recently that he would not live long.'

The mayor of Bargagli was unwilling to discuss the murder. He also said: 'I don't want to get involved. We don't discuss these deaths in this town.'

The reason for his remarks was that Leonardi was not the first villager to have been murdered by the night stalker who had become known as '*il mostro di Bargagli*' (the monster of Bargagli). The

assassin had claimed twenty-one victims - seventeen men and four women - and the only clue to his identity was his age. He must have been an old man...having first struck forty-four years earlier.

AMBUSHED BY THE PARTISANS

For it is in 1945 that the answer to the mystery lies. In February that year, three months before the liberation of Italy, a Nazi convoy carrying banknotes, gold, and possibly jewellery, paintings and other looted works of art, was ambushed

Above: *Hermann Goering planned to build a vast art gallery in Linz, to be named after himself and to be handed over to the Third Reich on his sixtieth birthday.*

Right: *As an art connoisseur and an ex-art student himself, Hitler (seen here with Prince Paul of Yugoslavia) knew the value of Europe's art treasures.*

by Bargagli partisans in the nearby Tecosa valley. The SS guards escorting the loot back to Germany were wiped out by machine-gun fire and the 'Treasure of the Tecosa' disappeared without trace.

Carmine Scotti, a policeman detailed to investigate the disappearance of the loot, was found days later horribly tortured and roasted alive on a spit. He was to be the first link in the chain of victims attributed to '*il mostro*'.

A local policeman ordered to investigate the disappearance of the treasure was found roasted alive on a spit

---

'*Il mostro*', whoever he or she may have been, was determined to ensure that the whereabouts of the treasure remained a secret. Within two months of Scotti's death there were eight more killings. In April 1945 four partisans, thought to be meeting to share out part of the treasure, were machine-gunned to death. Two days

later four more partisans perished, this time the victims of a bomb.

The villagers, it appeared, had fallen out over the spoils of war. But the murders quelled any dissent. Clearly '*il mostro*' had suppressed the opposition within the partisans' ranks, because during the next sixteen years peace prevailed in the village.

A few of the villagers had by then built new houses from apparently freshly generated wealth, but no one asked questions and police interest had petered out. It was not aroused again until 1961.

THE MONSTER RE-EMERGES

In December that year Giuseppe Musso, a seventy-two-year-old gravedigger and former Bargagli partisan, fell from a bridge into a ditch and fractured his skull. It was dismissed as an accident.

The death of Maria Balletto, sixty-four, at her home in the village in December 1969 was certainly no accident. The old lady, a former despatch rider for the partisans, had been bludgeoned to death.

The killings continued. In November 1972 Gerolamo Canobio, aged seventy-six, drank too much one night and shouted out that he was going to reveal the secret of the missing treasure. Hours later he was found dead, his skull smashed in with a rock.

A distinct pattern was emerging. All the victims were elderly and had fought with, or had strong links with, the partisans during World War II - the sort of people who might know the answer to the riddle of the missing Nazi loot.

The next to die was seventy-four-year-old Giulia Viacava, a former freedom fighter whose head was smashed in by a stone in March 1974. Two years later

Pietro Cevasco, aged fifty-four, was found hanged by his own belt from a tree.

Carlo Spallarosa, sixty-nine, met a still more horrific death in June 1978. He was decapitated when he 'fell' down a cliff.

Some villagers actually survived attacks but remained silent ever after. Francesco Fumera, seventy-five, was shot at close range with a sawn-off shotgun in 1980 but later insisted he had not seen his assailant.

In July 1983 the story took a bizarre new twist. It revolved around Anita de Magistris, the widow of the German officer who had led the ambushed convoy - and who had survived the attack.

In 1974 'the Baroness', as she became known, suddenly moved to a villa on the outskirts of Bargagli. Surely she had returned to try to trace the treasure.

As the years passed she became integrated into the community, a regular churchgoer who led the parish choir. But at least one villager was concerned by her continued presence. In July 1983 'the Baroness' was killed by a series of blows to her head with a heavy stick or club.

A woman magistrate, Maria Rosa d'Angelo, was drafted in to investigate the murders. One woman who appeared willing to help her was Emma Cevasco, aged seventy-seven. But shortly before she was due to give evidence she fell to her death from a second-floor window.

Fearful for their own lives, the villagers had been too scared to give evidence

---

D'Angelo concluded that the villagers had been immobilized by fear. 'This may explain the seeming indifference of the local population,' she said.

The silence that kept the village's treasure safe has done the same for secret hoards throughout Italy and beyond. For the story of Bargagli is just one small chapter in the mysterious saga of the Nazi fortunes - first looted, then left as the Germans retreated across Europe.

As the threat of conflict grew in the late thirties, Europe's moneyed classes, Jews and non-Jews alike, began to panic. How could they keep their homes and riches safe from the Nazis?

It didn't take the Nazis long to realize

that easy pickings were slipping through their fingers. Hitler ordered the formation of a shady organization - headed by his ruthless right-hand man Martin Bormann - called *Sonderauftrag Linz* (the 'Linz Special Mission'), which was in effect a legalized band of thugs and thieves.

The Fuehrer now ordered special vaults to be constructed to house the various fortunes. Once his armies moved west, the vaults were quickly filled as Bormann's human vultures extorted and stole. New treasure chambers were still under construction when the most valuable prize of all fell - art-rich Paris.

The race to loot the French capital was obscene. Hermann Goering, head of the Luftwaffe, built his own personal fortune by diverting trains of art treasures to his private estate at Karinhall, near Berlin.

Apart from the national heritage of France, the Nazis stole all they could lay their hands on in a spree of trans-European crime. More than half the national wealth

Above: *Rudolf Hess addresses a Nazi rally. Chiefly famous for his dramatic flight to Britain in 1941, Hess was also the nominal boss of Martin Bormann, one of Hitler's henchmen in the rounding-up of loot.*

Above: *Martin Bormann tried to bully Swiss bankers into handing over the accounts of clients whose money could go into the coffers of the Third Reich.*

of Belgium and Holland vanished. Polish and Czechoslovak bank vaults were stripped. In Russia, 50 trains a month returned to Germany with the contents of museums, art galleries and banks. By the time the tide of war had turned, the Nazis had plundered an estimated £15 billion worth of treasures - worth inestimably more at present values. But as Allied bombers ripped the heart out of German cities, the greedy Nazis realized that their loot was not safe.

Some of the ill-gotten bullion was hidden in salt mines near Alt Aussee in Austria. Diamonds were stored in a monastery in Czechoslovakia. Outside Füssen in Bavaria lay a treasure-store castle, Schloss Neuschwanstein. So much is known. But a great part of the hoard just vanished. Again, this can be put down to Teutonic efficiency. For the

defeated Nazis formed a new, secret organization with the title ODESSA.

ODESSA was set up with the aim of finding secure escape routes and fresh identities for the German war criminals. A fortune was spent. But there was still a greater fortune left over...

WHAT HAPPENED TO THE REST?

During the final assault on Berlin in May 1945, a bizarre bank raid took place as American forces raced their Soviet allies to reach the centre. The target was Berlin's Reichsbank - and its contents.

To this day nobody knows who got the bulk of the booty. But it is believed that, of the American share, £200 million in gold and securities went missing.

Intelligence services on both sides of the Iron Curtain believed that after the war about £50 billion of gold alone remained unaccounted for. Much of it may still be hidden in Europe.

In their flight, many of the Nazis found the sheer weight of their booty too heavy to transport. Billions of pounds' worth was dumped by the roadsides of Europe.

In 1983 workmen renovating the well of a monastery in northern Italy found the shaft blocked by heavy metal chests. When they were raised, they were found to contain 60 tons of gold, worth well over £500 million at the time.

An embarrassed Italian government admitted that their wartime allies had removed 120 tons of gold from Rome's central bank in 1944 and had loaded it on to trucks to take back to Germany.

How much actually reached the Fatherland no one knows. Some may have been stolen by the Germans, some abandoned. Some may have been ambushed by Italian partisans...

Which brings us back to Bargagli, and the string of grisly murders culminating in the shooting on his doorstep of poor old Salvatore Leonardi in September 1989. Whatever secret Nazi treasure he was protecting, it failed to protect him.

As one farm worker of Bargagli said in 1989: 'Some terrible things happened during the war and some terrible things are still going on. It's as simple as that.'

SCANDALS

IMELDA MARCOS
The Iron Butterfly

Rags-to-riches stories are not unusual. But the appallingly corrupt Imelda Marcos ruled the Filipino people with a rod of iron, ignoring their squalor and poverty while squandering the country's money on herself

To her few supporters Imelda Marcos was known as the mother of her country, a rags-to-riches beauty who overcame a limited education to fête and deal on equal terms with presidents, kings and popes.

But to her critics she was the violator of her country, a money-grabbing, despotic witch who indulged her every whim while her compatriots eked out a living in their ramshackle tin ghettos.

Imelda inspired great loyalty, but even greater hatred. As the wife of former Philippines President Ferdinand Marcos, and as his chief diplomat, executioner and loyalist, she has become a twentieth-century Marie Antoinette, despised and ridiculed as the Iron Butterfly.

Her greed, gluttony and selfishness knew no bounds. While her peasant 'worshippers' starved, her dog wore a

Above: *Imelda Marcos rouses her loyal followers with a song on her return to Manila in November 1991. Behind her is her son Ferdinand Marcos Junior.*

Opposite: *A military band plays for Imelda Marcos and a friend...she was demure, sophisticated, beautiful, adored and despised as the female despot of the Far East.*

Left: *President and Mrs Marcos on a state visit to Japan drink a toast to Prime Minister Eisaku Sato in Tokyo in 1966. Marcos was a war hero following his campaigns against the Japanese.*

diamond necklace. While her nation struggled to meet its foreign debts, she spent her country's treasury on everything from Bulgari baubles to pastel-coloured mink coats.

Her supporters starved, but her dog wore a diamond collar

Visitors to the Malacanang Palace - now a museum - know first-hand of her all-consuming greed. Under Imelda's former sumptuous bedroom is a 5000 sq ft basement, where visitors can gasp at the now infamous monument to corruption: 2700 pairs of shoes, 500 black brassieres, 1500 handbags, 35 large racks stacked with fur coats and 1200 designer gowns she wore but once.

During shopping trips to Paris, Rome or New York she stayed at the plushest hotels, where there was a standing order to provide her rooms with £500 worth of fresh flowers every day.

After partying with wealthy jet-setters she would then resume her journeys in a private twin-engined plane complete with built-in shower and gold bathroom fixtures. And through it all, she scoffed at the critics. 'The poor people want me to be their star,' she would sniff.

But these lavish spending sprees were

Above: *An idol in her own land, Mrs Marcos views a statue in Cairo museum during a visit to Egypt.*

Below: *President Marcos in 1971 at the time of yet another armed insurrection in the Philippines. Martial law cemented the power base of the Marcos dynasty.*

but a pittance compared with her major crimes. She reportedly stole - with the help of her husband - some $5 billion from the Philippine treasury.

SCALING THE SOCIAL LADDER

But her early days were spent in poverty, not luxury. Imelda Romualdez was a poor, barefoot child whose family lost almost all its valuable possessions when the Japanese occupied the Philippines in World War II. Those closest to her say it was her impoverished childhood that gave rise to her greed.

In spite of the poverty, however, the future first lady did have one thing going for her as a teenager. She was classically beautiful, a tall, wide-eyed 'Asian Angel'. Her stunning looks did not go unnoticed by the rising young senator Ferdinand Marcos, who quickly realized that his shrewdness and ambition, together with her charms, would make a politically irresistible combination.

He was right, and after their marriage in 1954 Imelda became a tireless campaign worker for him, often singing traditional Filipino folk songs to stir up the crowds before her husband addressed them. They were the most glamorous political duo the nation had seen.

But it was a hectic, grinding road to the Malacanang Palace. In later years Imelda would recall that the rigours of playing wife, mother, political aide and adviser became so much that she suffered a nervous breakdown. Marcos packed his wife off to New York for a break. Doctors there told her either to get used to the very public life of a politician's wife, or to leave him. She learned to handle it, then to embrace it.

Eventually the years of hard work and campaigning paid off. In 1965 Ferdinand Marcos was voted into the presidency. He and his wife would rule the country with an iron fist for the next twenty-one years.

At first, the Marcoses had to pay some regard to the Philippine constitution. But after eight years Ferdinand knew he could not run for a third term under the existing laws. So, on 21 September 1972, he declared martial law.

Irksome things like elections, due process of law and freedom of the press could now be done away with. But not the growing resentment of the people.

Just two months after the declaration of martial law, Imelda was officiating at an awards ceremony when one of the recipients suddenly lunged at her with a long, curved knife known as a *bolo*.

Imelda never threw away any article of clothing - to prevent it being seized for use in voodoo rituals against her

---

Her attacker was quickly killed by palace security guards, but not before he had badly slashed her on both arms. From that day on, Imelda would always wear a scarf at her throat in heed of a soothsayer's warning that it would ward off a beheading. And never again did she throw away any personal article of clothing, lest it be used in voodoo rites to unleash evil spirits against her.

CHIEF DIPLOMAT

Although martial law cemented the Marcoses' power base, Ferdinand rarely left the palace. Instead he relied increasingly on his socially adroit wife to handle overseas diplomatic missions.

These she frequently turned into mass buying sprees with her infamous 'Blue Ladies' - socialite supporters. They wore white *ternos* - the traditional native Filipino dress with butterfly sleeves - with 'Marcos blue' sashes. Together, Imelda and her 'ladies in waiting' would tour the world, buying and partying their way through the 1970s.

Whenever she departed or landed at the capital, the whole of Manila airport was frozen to other air traffic, while hundreds of native-costumed children, friends, cabinet ministers, wives and military leaders were forced to see her off, or welcome her home.

Visiting dignitaries were also afforded these garish displays - though one, in 1981, was a petty, tasteless joke at the expense of the Pope.

Years before, when Imelda was visiting Rome, she had been granted an audience with the Holy Father and insisted on wearing a white *terno*. Vatican protocol officials politely

Below: Imelda Marcos, dressed like royalty, goes shopping during a visit to London in 1970.

informed her that she must wear black, with long sleeves. Eventually Imelda was resigned to wearing black, but she never forgot the 'insult'. So when Pope John

Above: *President Marcos the world statesman, fêted by Western leaders while his police and soldiers quelled unrest at home with the threat of the gun. He took a model democracy to a total dictatorship.*

Left: *A garlanded President Ferdinand Marcos has a quiet word in the ear of UN Secretary - General Kurt Waldheim during an economic conference in Kenya in 1976.*

Paul II arrived in Manila, every one of the hundreds of 'Blue Ladies' was instructed to greet him bare-armed in white *ternos*.

The Pope wasn't the only VIP to bear the brunt of Imelda's vindictiveness. Years earlier, the Beatles had learned first hand of her brutishness. When the famed pop group were touring the Philippines in 1966 Mrs Marcos let it be known that she would like them to play for her at the Malacanang Palace.

The Fab Four sent back word that if she wanted to see them she could come to their stadium concert. The snub infuriated the egotistical Iron Butterfly, and on the day the band left Manila they

were attacked by some of her hired thugs.

The 'Blue Ladies' also helped Imelda in organizing the lavish parties she threw - including her own birthday bash every July. That 'national celebration' was often held at the beachside palace at Olot, which contained two Olympic-size swimming pools, an eighteen-hole golf course and three heliports.

One of her favorite pastimes at Olot was to serenade guests in her soprano voice - her 'repertoire' ranged from folk ballads to Western pop tunes. Sometimes even Ferdinand would join her, and together they would sing a love ballad.

After a perceived snub by the Beatles, Imelda had them beaten up at Manila airport

---

Visitors were also given mementoes of their stays - usually gems or gold. Underneath her palace Imelda had store rooms filled with such 'trinkets'.

A compulsive, obsessive shopper, Imelda would buy a dozen pairs of the same shoes if she liked them, and hundreds of the same blouse. In one trip, a 1983 jaunt through Rome, Copenhagen and New York, she splurged more than £3 million in just ninety days. The tab included everything from £2 million for a Michelangelo painting to £8000 pounds for bath towels!

And always she scoffed at suggestions that she and her husband were corrupt. 'They call me corrupt, frivolous,' she complained. 'I would not look like this if I am corrupt. Some ugliness would settle down on my system.'

SANDS FROM AUSTRALIA

But Imelda didn't have to travel, of course, to spend her spare change. While preparing to play hostess to European royals and dignitaries at the 1979 opening of the Marbella beach resort outside Manila, she noticed that the sand wasn't white enough. So she simply sent a plane to Australia for a load of sand of the correct colour.

According to those who knew her, Imelda's buying binges and ruthless quest for power started in 1969 - after she learned

her husband was having an affair with an American actress, Dovie Beams. She immediately sent the woman back to the USA. But Beams had secretly recorded her lovemaking sessions with the President.

On one buying binge she bought a Michelangelo painting and £8000 worth of bath towels

---

Copies of those tapes fell into the hands of the Marcoses' political enemies including Senator Ninoy Aquino, who often joked about their contents. That began Imelda's intense hatred of the senator, who was jailed in 1972.

Publicly humiliated by her husband's infidelity - and Beams's statements that Ferdinand thought Imelda frigid - she gave the President an ultimatum. She would not seek a divorce, and she would still campaign for him - but at a price. The price was that he would not interfere with her grandiose schemes to put the Philippines on the world map.

These extraordinary plans included the Manila Film Festival. It folded after just two years - but not before it had proved how callous Imelda could be. As construction on the huge building to house the festival fell behind schedule, corners were cut. Cement floors were not allowed to dry properly before the next phase of construction began. Inevitably, there was a disaster - a floor collapsed and killed up to 168 workers.

Relatives came to collect the bodies, but before they could claim them the order came down that not even a national tragedy could delay construction. The dead were covered by cement.

By 1975, the President had lost all control of his wife. She had him appoint her to top government positions, and flaunted her friendships with handsome jet-set cronies.

Imelda made a deal with the unfaithful President: she would still support him provided he let her lust for power and possessions go unchecked

---

But those who knew her believe the relationships were not of a sexual nature. The icy Imelda liked her men for public display, not private pleasures.

By 1979 she had become so powerful that she launched a cabinet shake-up, and

Above: *Mr and Mrs Marcos receive gifts on a state visit. Normally her presents were more beautiful than mere flowers. She once said: 'They call me corrupt. I would not look like this if I am corrupt.'*

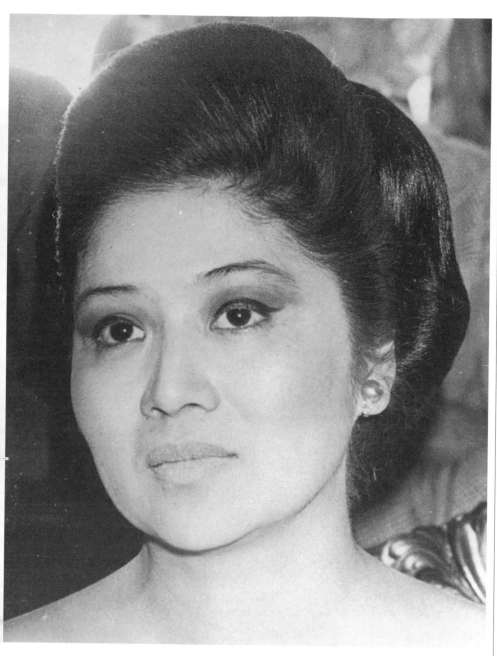

the presidential ministers became known as 'Imelda's Cabinet'. Family members and cronies were placed in senior positions, and profitable businesses were 'miraculously' transferred to those who pleased her.

Above: *Arrogant beyond belief, by 1975 the President had lost all control over his power-hungry wife. He appointed her to a high government office.*

In 1981 the President suspended martial law and put himself up for re-election - but all opposition was rapidly put down

---

But even Ferdinand realized that he and his wife could not maintain absolute power indefinitely under martial law. In 1981 he put himself up for re-election.

It came as no surprise to anyone when he was proclaimed the people's choice! The few opponents who challenged the dictatorial couple were quickly quashed.

Now, firmly cemented in power once again, the First Lady decided to do some real buying - this time expensive real estate in New York. She snapped up properties like designer dresses - the Herald Centre shopping complex, the prestigious Crown Building on plush Fifth Avenue, office complexes on Wall Street and Madison Avenue, homes in New Jersey and New York's Long Island.

As Ferdinand's health deteriorated, she meddled more and more in affairs of state. But events were developing which would make her manoeuvring worthless.

THE BEGINNING OF THE END

In August 1983 Ninoy Aquino, who had been in exile in the United States for several years, returned to the Philippines. As he stepped off the plane he was shot dead, the victim of a plot by one of the Marcoses' cronies.

The Marcos regime scrambled to control the damage, but it would never overcome the ensuing turmoil and cries for justice. The Aquino murder was the last straw for many who previously had been too scared or too ignorant to care.

Now there were daily demonstrations, the media grew bolder, workers went on strike and there were even cries for Ferdinand's impeachment.

But the President was by this time gravely ill from a series of ailments. Imelda knew their grip on the country was weakening, and she turned for reassurance to occultists and soothsayers.

With the Marcoses' grip on the country slipping fast, Imelda turned to occultists and soothsayers for reassurance

---

The regime was also coming under increasing pressure from the USA - long its staunchest and most generous ally. So in 1986, somehow believing he could ensure another four years in power, Ferdinand called a snap election.

But the years of brutality had finally caught up on the First Couple. Corazon

Aquino, the widow of Senator Aquino, was swept to power. On 15 February, despite evidence of nationwide rigging, Ferdinand declared himself the winner.

The Philippines plunged into near revolution, and Ferdinand and Imelda finally fled one night taking whatever booty they could.

EXILE...AND RETURN

Ferdinand, racked by illness, died in their Hawaiian exile less than three years later, leaving Imelda to face the complex array of court cases against her family for their two-decade orgy of greed and corruption.

But tracking down the millions in foreign banks and property holdings in New York, Rome and London and elsewhere may prove too difficult for even the most dedicated detectives.

American officials say they are not sure how much money she might be worth, but it could be as much as £7.5 billion. Whether any will eventually be returned to the people of the Philippines is impossible to say, but under a New York court ruling in 1990 Imelda was allowed to keep all her money and investments in America.

Incredibly, she believes she is being persecuted by ungrateful compatriots and that she and her husband 'worked hard to be the symbol of what each and every Filipino would like to fight and die for: freedom, justice, democracy and, above all, human dignity'.

In 1990 the former First Lady was allowed to return home - on condition that she would face tax charges.

Imelda still belives that during their rule she and Ferdinand stood for freedom, justice, democracy and human dignity

---

Astonishingly, she has ended up running for the presidency. 'Whatever the people want from me, I shall obey,' she had said before leaving for home. It seems that the people - by her reckoning at least - have called on her to put her name forward as a contender to succeed Corazon Aquino in the 1991 elections.

Below: *Part of Imelda Marcos's collection of shoes. She was a shopaholic. In just 90 days of a shopping spree through New York, Rome and Copenhagen she splurged more than £3 million.*

WATERGATE
A Presidential Scandal

When an alert security guard reported a break-in he unwittingly exposed a tale of immorality, subversion and political scandal. The break-in took place in Washington's exclusive Watergate complex, and its ultimate victim was President Nixon himself

It was a little after two o'clock on the morning of Saturday, 17 June 1972. Five men, dressed in dark business suits and wearing rubber surgical gloves, made their way quietly through the maze of blackened offices and corridors, their vast array of hi-tech equipment in tow.

Despite their obvious professionalism and knowledge of the layout, they could not have foreseen that an alert security guard would, at that moment, decide to make his rounds of the complex.

The arrest of five burglars would normally be an inside page story in the local paper. This time it would be headlines worldwide

Realizing there had been a break-in, the guard immediately called the Washington Police Department which sent a squad car to the scene. The five men, found cowering in one of the vacant offices, were arrested and held for arraignment.

Six hours later, the phone rang in reporter Bob Woodward's one-room apartment. The young ex-Naval officer fumbled for the phone, to hear the city editor at the *Washington Post* order him down to the courthouse.

Woodward wasn't impressed at first with his Saturday assignment - the arrest

Above: *'Freshmen' Congressmen line up after winning election to the US House of Representatives in 1947. Richard Nixon stands on the far right in the back row alongside John F. Kennedy.*

Opposite: *World War I hero Dwight D. Eisenhower's vice-presidential running mate Richard Nixon, during the 1952 election campaign.*

Right: *A stern-looking President Gerald Ford, Nixon's successor, in the Oval office with the veteran Secretary of State Henry Kissinger.*

of five burglars. Nevertheless, his interest peaked somewhat when told that the burglary had occurred at the headquarters of the Democrat National Committee.

And so began the most explosive story in American political history - a scandal that would climax with the fall of President Richard Milhouse Nixon.

After its course had run, the very name 'Watergate' would be synonymous with immorality, subversion and officially sanctioned crimes.

Above: *Republican candidate Richard Nixon was given a tumultuous reception in 1960 when he took the stage with President Eisenhower and Mr Cabot Lodge.*

THE RISE TO POWER

But Nixon's scandalous behaviour did not begin with Watergate. That was merely the culmination of a political life steeped in often shady conduct.

Curiously, the man who later wanted to hire union thugs to deal with anti-Vietnam activists began life as a Quaker, imbued with non-violent ideals. The second of five brothers, he was born on 9 January 1913 in the Californian town of Yorba Linda, where his father grew lemons. His parents were ordinary working people.

The man who sent thousands of young Americans to their deaths in Vietnam was actually born a Quaker

---

Although a shy, introverted youth, Nixon was nevertheless an excellent student. While he did well at all subjects, he preferred history and music. In a bid to overcome his inherent shyness he also took up public speaking, and became a leading member of college debating teams.

While working his way through Whittier College, a Quaker institution not far from where he was raised, he won a scholarship to the prestigious Duke University in North Carolina. In 1934, he entered law school there.

Three years later he emerged with his degree - third in his class - and joined a legal firm back in his home state of California. One of his outside activities was acting in an amateur theatre group, and it was there that he met pretty Pat Ryan, a red-haired typing teacher who would later become his wife.

Nixon became the aggressive mouthpiece of the 'Reds under the bed' paranoia that swept America after World War II

After the Japanese attack on Pearl Harbor on 7 December 1941 Nixon decided to do his part for the American war effort. So he moved to Washington, where he did legal work for the government. Later, despite his Quaker background, he was given a Navy commission as a lieutenant. He ended the war a lieutenant commander.

In 1946, on the urging of a banker friend, he decided to enter politics, running as a Republican in California's 12th congressional district.

The thirty-three-year-old Nixon won the seat easily, and within the next two years consolidated his position as a tough, no-nonsense politician.

In his second term in Congress he was

appointed to the controversial House of Un-American Activities Committee. Here his ruthlessness singled him out as the 'pit bull' of Congress, constantly badgering the American people with the deviousness of the Red mind.

His reputation as a Communist-hunter helped carry him to victory in the 1950 Senate race. He was now thirty-seven, and a veteran of Washington's wheeling-and-dealing machinations. Two years after becoming the youngest Republican senator he was selected by Dwight D. Eisenhower as his vice-presidential choice on the 1952 party ticket.

But in September Nixon's surging political life was almost cut down. He was nearly forced to quit the ticket after a New York newspaper accused him of secretly misusing £10,000 of campaign funds for his personal expenses.

Eisenhower told Nixon he would have to prove he was 'as clean as a hound's tooth' or face political exile

---

The outcry shook the Republican party, and Eisenhower told Nixon he would have to prove he was 'as clean as a hound's tooth' or face political exile.

On 23 September, the young senator appeared on national television, his wife at his side, to explain the alleged misconduct. His defence became known as the 'Checkers Speech'.

Nixon explained that the funds had been used entirely for political campaign purposes, and that he would never allow anything immoral or illegal to taint his career. Then he told his audience that although someone had given his children a dog - a cocker spaniel they named Checkers - he didn't believe he should take it away from them just because he was in the public eye.

He concluded the speech with a line that he would paraphrase more than twenty years later during Watergate: 'I don't believe I ought to quit, because I'm not a quitter.'

The American people believed in his innocence in overwhelming numbers, and he returned to what he did best - attacking his Democrat opponents. He claimed that the Democratic nominee for

Above: *President Nixon was received by Pope Paul VI in a special audience at the Vatican. His piety was questioned in 1952 when the press accused him of misusing £10,000 of election campaign funds.*

Left: *'Happy Birthday Mr President.' A king-sized birthday card from his White House staff is presented to Nixon by two secretaries on 9 January 1970.*

President, Adlai Stevenson, had given support to Alger Hiss. Hiss was a former State Department official whom Nixon had convicted as a Communist several years earlier.

The attacks duly paid off, and the Eisenhower-Nixon ticket steamrollered to a landslide victory.

AIMING AT THE WHITE HOUSE

With the retirement of Eisenhower, Nixon decided to aim for the top: the presidency. On his first attempt however, in 1960, he lost to the charismatic John F. Kennedy, and retired to California where he joined a law firm in Los Angeles.

But the power-hungry politician inside him would not stay idle long. Just eleven months after his narrow loss to Kennedy, he announced he would run for the governorship of California. This time he lost badly, and the wounded Nixon bitterly complained that the media had done him in with its 'biased' coverage. He solemnly announced he was quitting public life.

'You won't have Richard Nixon to kick around any more,' he stormed, and that was the last everyone thought they would hear of Richard Milhouse Nixon.

Two political failures in one year was too much for Nixon's pride, and he announced his retirement from public life

---

They were wrong. By 1968, six years after Nixon went into political 'retirement', America was a country at war with itself. The lengthy conflict in Vietnam had become a quagmire for the American military machine, and race riots were rocking the inner-city ghettos.

On top of that, President Johnson announced that he would not seek the Democratic Party's nomination for another term. This made the 1968 presidential race the most open in many years. That was enough incentive for Nixon. He quickly

Above: *Nixon the peacemaker. The President attends a conference in Moscow in 1972. His diplomatic efforts caused his popularity to soar.*

Below: *Edward Heath watches as Nixon shakes hands with the Queen at Chequers during his visit to Britain and Ireland in 1970.*

proved he could still be a vote-getter. With his running mate Spiro Agnew, the former Governor of Maryland, Nixon slipped into the White House with the slimmest of majorities - his margin of victory was 1/2 per cent.

The fifty-six-year-old Nixon had at last captured the highest office in the land. At the same time, the seeds of what would become known as Watergate were already being planted, thanks to his obsessive secrecy and distrust of anyone he feared might challenge his authority.

After winning the presidency with the slimmest of majorities, Nixon quickly turned it into a den of corruption

---

Although details would not surface until the early months of Nixon's second term, which began with a landslide victory in 1972, there were two major scandals brewing during his first four years. These were the Air Force bombing of Cambodia, and Watergate.

In 1970, as the Vietnam War dragged on, Nixon assured the American people that Cambodia's neutrality would be respected by the United States. Later, it was learned that the USA had carried out more than 3500 bombing sorties over Cambodia in 1969-70.

But this gruesome deception would later pale into insignificance once the full extent of Nixon's immorality - and that of 'all the President's men' - became known through Watergate.

THE WATERGATE AFFAIR

After the 1972 break-in and arraignment of the five burglars a massive cover-up operation began inside the White House. Thanks, however, to the dogged efforts of people like reporter Bob Woodward and his colleague Carl Bernstein, the world eventually learned the truth.

But as early as 1969 there was a hint of what was to come when John Mitchell, then Attorney-General, claimed that presidential powers permitted the use of wiretapping without court supervision.

A second clue - though no one outside the administration could have known - came in July 1970, when Nixon approved the intelligence community's plan to subvert his domestic opponents through break-ins and covert mail coverage.

There were, of course, many behind-the-scenes instances of Nixon's lust for power. As revealed in the White House tapes several years later, Nixon suggested using hired thugs from the Mafia-controlled Teamsters' Union to break up

Top: *Nixon on his inauguration day in January 1969 when he became 37th President of the United States...and the face of disgrace in 1974.*

Above: *Former White House aide John Dean testifies before the Senate committee investigating the Watergate scandal in Washington in 1973. The evidence increasingly damned the President.*

anti-war demonstrations. 'They've got guys who'll go in and knock their heads off,' was Nixon's gleeful comment.

And before the election he wanted the tax records of insufficiently loyal bureaucrats. When asked by his aides how they would obtain these details from inside the Internal Revenue Service building, Nixon replied: 'Goddamn it! Sneak in in the middle of the night.'

The President was so paranoid about plots against him that he set up a secret investigations unit known as the 'plumbers'

But the first real Watergate-related incident came in the wake of the release of the so-called Pentagon Papers in 1971.

Even though these documents, which were leaked to the *New York Times*, detailed the secret history of previous administrations' policies in Vietnam, Nixon was sure it was part of a plot against his own administration. To

safeguard against further releases he set up a secret special investigations unit.

The unit, known as the 'plumbers', included senior adviser John Ehrlichman, Egil Krough, Gordon Liddy, Howard Hunt and David Young. All would later gain infamy in the Watergate scandal.

One of Ehrlichman's first tasks was to draw up a 'Priority List' of twenty of the President's 'political enemies'. At the top of that list was Senator Edward Kennedy. The unit also discussed the possible killing of crusading newspaper columnist Jack Anderson and the sabotage of Democratic rallies.

Nixon and his aides had persuaded themselves that the US intelligence set-up was their own personal spy network

---

By the time the full extent of the Watergate scandal became known, the word 'Watergate' had long since meant more than an office break-in.

As the investigation neared its dramatic conclusions in 1974, the affair had brought down two Attorney-Generals, most of the senior White House staff and Vice President Agnew, who had abused his office to accept 'kickbacks'.

As if that were not enough, it was eventually uncovered that Nixon had

Above: *Thumbs up...but the road was all downhill in August 1974 as Richard Nixon, with son-in-law David Eisenhower, bids farewell to his White House staff.*

Above right: *Nixon hugs his daughter Julie in his private quarters at the White House after the heart-wrenching decision to resign as President of the United States.*

been telling bare-faced lies to the American people when he reassured them that he had no knowledge of the break-in.

WORTHY OF IMPEACHMENT

'I am not a crook,' he said during one televised speech. But the records and tapes indicated otherwise, and moves were mounting to have him impeached. In fact, the Justice Committee of the House of Representatives had already recommended impeachment.

Its report was a stinging indictment of a President who had run amok. It read that Richard Nixon 'has acted in a manner contrary to his trust as President and subversive of constitutional government...such conduct warrants impeachment and trial, and removal from office'. Despite those strong words Nixon still refused to yield his office, telling the nation: 'I have no intention whatever of ever walking away from the job that the American people elected me to do...'

However, the Watergate steamroller could not be stopped.

On 16 July 1973, White House aide Alexander Butterfield disclosed that since 1970 Nixon had secretly recorded all conversations and phone calls in his offices. Congress demanded that the tapes be handed over. But Nixon 'hunkered down', to use a favourite expression, and refused to yield the tapes, claiming 'executive privilege'.

Eventually, realizing he had no choice, Nixon offered to hand over summary transcripts of the tapes. Archibald Cox, the special prosecutor who had been appointed by the Justice Department to co-ordinate the Watergate probes, took issue with Nixon's partial compliance.

The tapes would eventually reveal him as a foul-mouthed vindictive man who had abused the trust of the American people

---

But by this time Nixon's gall knew no limits, and in the infamous 'Saturday Night Massacre' of 20 October Cox was fired by the President's hand-picked Attorney-General, Robert Bork.

It was clear to everyone, however, that Nixon was fighting a losing battle. The tapes would eventually reveal him to be a foul-mouthed, vindictive man.

By late February, the Watergate prosecution team had obtained guilty pleas to a variety of criminal enterprises from a host of former Nixon associates. In addition, irregularities were found in the President's tax returns. It was also disclosed that he had used about £10 million of government money to improve his homes in Florida and California.

By June 1974, Nixon had become a virtual prisoner inside the White House.

The next month, John Ehrlichman and other White House 'plumbers' were found guilty of conspiracy, and twelve days later the Supreme Court ruled unanimously that Nixon had no choice but to turn over sixty-four missing tapes.

THE END OF A PRESIDENT

The end came, finally, on 9 August. Knowing that he was now certain to be impeached by Congress, Nixon resigned the presidency in an emotional farewell address. Then he retreated to his home in California - a bitter, broken man.

Yet, thanks to that great healer, time, Richard Nixon is today considered by many to have been a first-rate world statesman. In effect, his renaissance began less than a month after his exit from Washington, when his hand-picked successor, Gerald Ford, pardoned him of all criminal doings while in office.

In the years since, Nixon has tried to play down the horrors of Watergate. He prefers to say that, in hindsight, he should have acted more quickly to defuse the situation. He recalled:

Looking back on what is still in my mind a complex and confusing mass of events, decisions, pressures and personalities, one thing I can see clearly now is that I was wrong in not acting more decisively and more forthrightly in dealing with Watergate... I know that many fair-minded people believe that my motivation and actions in the Watergate affair were intentionally self-serving and illegal. I now understand how my own mistakes and misjudgements have contributed to that belief...

Nixon, who was revealed as both liar and cheat for the entire world to see, still cannot bring himself to admit that it was he who was to blame.

Below: *In 1978 an older and wiser Richard Nixon visited Britain. He gave a welcoming smile to pressmen at London airport four years after he ceased to be US President.*

JEAN HARRIS
Scarsdale Diet Murderer

The Scarsdale Diet caused a sensation. But it was nothing compared with the story of its creator, Herman Tarnower. What turned a demure headmistress into his lover and then his murderer?

It ranks as one of the most sensational murder trials in contemporary American history and its outcome still leaves rancour and bitterness. When Jean Harris - spurned mistress of the famed Scarsdale Diet doctor Herman Tarnower - ended his cheating life with a gun, she unleashed a story of passion and jealousy that no fiction writer could ever have competed with. It was all there, a tabloid heaven of sex, intrigue, wealth, power, glamour, kinky games and murder.

What could have possessed a matronly, balanced woman in her fifties to plunge over the abyss into madness and kill a man hailed as a waistline messiah for millions of over-eaters? Did she intend to kill him or kill herself, as she told the jury at her trial? Does she deserve to languish in jail to this day?

In this case it was intent that was really on trial, for Jean Harris was a one-time killer who really ended her own love-lorn life when she shot Herman Tarnower.

THE VICTIM

Tarnower was born on 18 March 1910 in Brooklyn, New York, the son of a wealthy hat manufacturer. His early years were mirror images of the style he later came to enjoy so much. While many in impoverished Brooklyn lived hand-to-mouth existences, there were no such privations for the young Herman and his brothers and sisters.

He was bright and preferred to spend his adolescence reading the classics and

*Opposite: **Jean Harris the high-powered girls' school headmistress was also an anguished lover aching for the security of marriage.***

*Below: **The book that made Herman Tarnower's fortune The Scarsdale Diet,** published in 1979 told would-be slimmers how to lose weight without giving up the good life.*

science books rather than in pool halls or at the beach. By the time he was seventeen he was over six feet tall and had acquired the nickname 'Hi'.

College was a cakewalk for him. At Syracuse College in New York State he always achieved grade As. He went on to medical school, and in 1933 graduated with his medical degree.

It was the depths of the Depression and some colleagues of his father's had already ended their lives as their fortunes crumbled. Tarnower knew that the world always needed doctors. He enrolled as an intern at New York's Bellevue Hospital.

Popping pills down his patients' throats, however, was not the way he wanted to continue life for ever. Medicine offered challenges he wished to explore in research laboratories. In 1936 he was awarded the Bowens Fellowship which

LOSE UP TO 20 POUNDS IN 14 DAYS AND KEEP THEM OFF

THE COMPLETE SCARSDALE MEDICAL DIET PLUS Dr. TARNOWER'S LIFETIME KEEP-SLIM PROGRAM

For the first time - the total plan for the diet that's taking America by storm, explained in full by the noted doctor who created it.

Herman Tarnower, M.D. & Samm Sinclair Baker

allowed him to travel for two years to England and Holland. He became particularly interested in heart disease as pioneers began to trace direct links between diet and disease.

When he returned to America it wasn't to New York but to the wealthy suburb of Scarsdale. He became a cardiologist, breaking new ground in the study of the heart and, while he was at it, making money hand over fist.

The ambitious Tarnower knew the world would always need doctors, Depression or not

---

He was a charming man described by writer Jay Davis: 'He made no bones about the fact that he was a man of very demanding appetites for the better things in life - and that included high cuisine, high art, high society. It also...included the society of beautiful, compelling, and willing women.'

The entry of America into World War II saw Dr Tarnower posted to hospital service with the American Army. When the atomic bombs were dropped on Japan he was invited to be part of the medical team which went into the shattered cities of Hiroshima and Nagasaki.

In peacetime he returned to Scarsdale, where a post-war baby boom and new prosperity brought many young couples to the area. It was also crammed with stressed-out executives whose hearts were going into overload.

In 1975 Tarnower penned the outline of what would eventually be published in 1979 as *The Scarsdale Diet*, the regimen for foodies who wanted to shed pounds but did not want to give up the gourmet delicacies they relished so much.

His mistress of fourteen years, Jean Harris, thought it was a great idea.

THE ACCUSED

Jean Harris - born Jean Struven - was a child of the Depression, but she was cushioned from its worst effects by the comfortable surroundings of her thrifty parents. She was the daughter of a military officer and her childhood and adolescence were spent in Cleveland,

Ohio, where she excelled at the best girls' schools in the area. She was at university during the war years, and graduated in 1945 with a degree in economics. A friend who remembers her said: 'She was a totally in-control person. A fine, wonderful girl and a born leader.'

In May 1946 Jean married James Harris, the son of a Michigan banking family. Her first son was born in 1950, her second four years later. But as the children grew up and her husband prospered, something stirred in her. She took a daring trip to Moscow in 1958, but returned even more unhappy and restless than before. She was plunged into depression when she failed to get a top teaching post at the school in their suburb of Detroit. Her frustrations culminated in her divorce from Harris in October 1964.

Jean went on to further education, gaining a master's degree in education before landing herself the job of director of the middle school at a girls' academy in Philadelphia. Here she met Dr Tarnower, who escorted her to the theatre, to restaurants and to his bed.

A dull marriage combined with professional frustration turned Jean Harris into a restless free spirit

---

It wasn't until 1972 that she moved to Connecticut and became the chief administrator of an exclusive girls' establishment called the Thomas School.

THE MURDER

That two people as refined, single and responsible as Herman Tarnower and Jean Harris should drift into each other's lives seems no big surprise.

But there was a sword of Damocles hanging over the relationship in the form of Tarnower's utter abhorrence of marriage. Poor Jean thought she was the woman to change him. 'It was', said one observer, 'the one dark shadow in her otherwise sunny life. She so desperately wanted to marry him and he so desperately wanted to remain single.'

In July 1977 she moved to Virginia to take over as the headmistress of another exclusive all-girl academy, Madeira

Opposite: Dr Herman Tarnower, cardiologist and philanderer. 'He made no bones about the fact that he was a man of very demanding appetites,' wrote one acquaintance.

Above: *Jean Harris and her lawyer Bonnie Steingart leave Westchester County Court.*

School. But the relationship was slowly disintegrating as Jean became aware of her partner's more-than-passing interest in Lynne Tryforos, his medical assistant.

It was never disputed that Jean Harris killed Herman Tarnower - she admitted it herself. She drove, on 10 March 1980, five hours from her home in Virginia to Tarnower's Scarsdale mansion.

She entered the bedroom, saw negligées that were not hers, and then shot her lover

---

She planned to kill herself, she said, intending to see him one more time before pulling the trigger in front of his eyes. Armed with a Harrington and Richardson .32-calibre revolver, she arrived shortly before 10pm.

In his bedroom she saw negligées in the closet that did not belong to her.

She shot him.

She was standing outside in the pouring rain with a bunch of daisies in her hand when the police arrived an hour later to arrest her. Her lover, still alive, was gurgling incoherently in his death throes, four bullets in his head and body.

'What happened?' asked the cop.

'The doctor's been shot,' she replied.

'Where is he?'

'Upstairs.'

'Who did it?'

'I did.'

As the body was taken away past her she yelled at him: 'Who was at dinner tonight? Who did you have here?' He died on the way to hospital.

THE TRIAL

Only when the demure divorcee was arraigned on the charge of murdering Dr Tarnower did the world glean the full extent of her passions. She pleaded not gulity to murder - claiming she went there with every intention of ending her own life that night, and that Tarnower died in a struggle that he instigated.

On the stand she painted a picture of years of emotional abuse at the hands of Tarnower - how she cooked and kept house for him, even though she knew he was taking his younger assistant Lynne out to dinner. She told how Hi - his nickname had become her pet name for him - boasted: 'I don't need love any more' as she begged him to marry her.

She revised chapters of his book *The Scarsdale Diet*, which made him wealthy, as he philandered with Lynne. She said: 'When his relationships with other women began to rub off on my life in ugly, dirty ways, my personal struggle over integrity became increasingly complicated. Should I walk away without flinching or stay without flinching?'

Soon the headlines began appearing in the tabloid papers in New York: 'Was Jean a Killer or a tragic victim?'

Just before his death Tarnower cut his fourteen-year lover out of his will in favour of her younger rival Lynne

---

Evidence poured out that Tarnower had instructed his housekeeper to have two separate closets - one where he let Lynne store her sexy nighties, and another where Jean kept her things. He had treated her to exotic trips - Warsaw, Rome, Paris - but never one to the altar.

Then came the sensational 'Scarsdale Letter', a classic piece of poison penmanship. It mentioned that Tarnower had changed his will against her - again, a possible motive for murder. The letter, posted to Tarnower on the morning of the day that he died, was read to the court with electrifying effect:

I am distraught as I write this - your phone call to tell me that you preferred the company of a vicious, adulterous psychotic was topped by a call from the Dean of Students ten minutes later and has kept me awake for almost 36 hours...What I say will ramble but it will be the truth - and I have to do something besides shriek with pain...

Having just, not four weeks before, received a copy of your will with my name vigorously scratched out, and Lynne's name in your handwriting written in three places, leaving her a quarter of a million dollars and her children $25,000 apiece - and the boys and me nothing. It is the sort of thing I have almost grown accustomed to from Lynne... It isn't your style, but then Lynne has changed your

Below: *During her trial Jean Harris painted a vivid picture of years of emotional torture at the hands of cynical manipulator Tarnower. She was still sentenced to a minimum of fifteen years imprisonment.*

style. It is the culmination of 14 years of broken promises...

It didn't matter all that much, really - all I ever asked for was to be with you - and when I left you to know when we would see each other again so there would be something in life to look forward to. Now you are taking that away from me too and I am unable to cope...

To be jeered at, and called 'old and pathetic' made me seriously consider borrowing $5,000 and telling a doctor to make me young again - to do anything but not make me feel like discarded trash.

Medical testimony revealed that Jean Harris was on amphetamines for depression, and that she had been steadily increasing the dosages. And the greater part of the witnesses called to give evidence testified that her lover was cool, cynical, manipulating...almost a man who deserved to die.

THE VERDICT

The trial revealed a classic crime of passion - but jurors found it differently. Her lawyers persuaded her to plead to accidental manslaughter, saying that it was 'definite' she would be acquitted. On 28 February 1981 she was found guilty of murder, sentenced to a minimum of fifteen years imprisonment.

In 1981 a US court gave Harris a lengthy prison sentence for a classic *crime passionnel*

Many saw it - and still do - as a miscarriage of justice. She has suffered three heart attacks behind bars, and her family continue to press for a pardon. There has been a groundswell of support for her since the late 1980s as a result of a poignant book written by her of prison life and its crushing indignities.

Shana Alexander, who wrote a book about the affair, said: 'For me the bottom line...is that the question put to the jurors - what was Jean's intent that night? - is one that simply cannot be dealt with by the mechanisms of law. Because you cannot cut open a person's head and look inside.'

A ROYAL SCANDAL
Edward and Lillie

The prim morality of Victorian society tolerated the Prince of Wales's affairs when they were conducted discreetly. But it was scandalized when he made the beautiful Lillie Langtry his 'official' mistress and paraded openly in public with her

Right: *Top notch...His Royal Highness the Prince of Wales as a young man.*

Opposite: *Lillie Langtry... the prince's fatal attraction for the striking beauty began when he was introduced to her at a private supper in London in 1877.*

Below: *Lillie Le Breton (later Lillie Langtry) with her family in the Channel Isles in 1864. Lillie stands beside her father, the Dean of Jersey.*

H e became known as Edward the Caresser, a cheeky sobriquet for the monarch who cared little for public opinion and even less for those who tried to thwart his dalliances. Edward VII was

the last of the 'golden age' of monarchs before World War I came along to smash the old order for ever.

The Edwardian era that he gave his name to is remembered in nostalgic terms as a time of shooting parties, lawn tennis and croquet, an age altogether more relaxed than the decades of Victorian moral steadfastness. No wonder, for Edward was a well-known debaucher, a man given to gluttony and high living and possessed of a voracious sexual appetite which he satisfied in the bedrooms of his friends' wives as well as the bordellos of Europe.

Edward satisfied his voracious sexual appetite in the bedrooms of his friends' wives as well as the bordellos of Europe

---

It was the novelist Henry James who first dubbed him Edward the Caresser and indeed Bertie, as his friends and the masses referred to him, prided himself on his vast sexual experience.

His mother Queen Victoria, and stern father Prince Albert, made his early life miserable. There were regular beatings and lectures on the correct way for a member of the royal family to behave, and many latter-day psychologists have sought to explain away his insatiable appetite for sexual conquests as some sort of prolonged youthful rebellion.

But there was nothing youthful about the manner in which the Prince of Wales - his title before ascending the throne - set about enjoying his hedonistic lifestyle. He lived for life's pleasures - huge ten- and twelve-course meals, endless games of baccarat and days at the splendid racecourses of Europe, shooting parties, yachting, the theatre and, in between everything, his marathon bouts of sex.

He lost his virginity at the age of nineteen while serving with the British Army in Ireland. Some of his fellow officers smuggled an actress named Nellie Clifden into his bed at the Curragh camp. It was not to be the final whiff of scandal surrounding young Bertie.

His gambling and womanizing were to continue to land him in trouble. Twice Britain witnessed the scandal of his appearing in court - although as a witness, not as the accused.

Once was over a gambling feud, the second occasion when Lady Harriet Mordaunt insisted that her child, born blind, was a curse from God for her many adulterous relationships, including one with the Prince. He testified he was not the lady's lover, but speculation has remained rife to this day that he may have added perjury to his many other sins.

Below left: *The cigar-smoking Edward, Prince of Wales in 1869. He had not yet met the woman who was to change his life - and scandalize society.*

Below: *When the prince met Lillie he leaned over to tell her that no pictures did justice to her beauty. Within a week they were lovers.*

THE JERSEY LILY

In 1877, when he was thirty-six years old, his path crossed with that of a woman called Lillie Langtry and English society was never quite the same again. Although he - and many men of his aristocratic upbringing - indulged in mistresses, it was never the done thing to be seen to be parading them in public. They were kept for discreet dalliances and private dinners in clubs, well away from the glare of a disapproving, moralistic society.

What Edward did was to fly into the face of the English Establishment and flaunt his 'Jersey Lily' with abandon. For ten years his liaison with the showgirl scandalized Europe and the world, and it is said that in the House of Windsor to

Above: *A caricature of the Prince of Wales. He was a dandy who could not control his sexual adventures.*

Left: *King Edward VII... although married to Princess Alexandra of Denmark, he flaunted his 'Jersey Lily' to the world.*

this day there has never been total forgiveness for his wicked, wicked ways.

Although married to Princess Alexandra of Denmark - his father insisted upon the union after the disgrace over the Curragh incident - the Prince was so bored in his useless existence that he was led further and further astray.

Speculation has remained rife to this day that the Prince of Wales may have added perjury to his other sins

---

There were no stately duties for him - his mother had no intention of relinquishing the throne - and so his teeth sank into the pursuit of pleasure and never let go. His fatal attraction to Lillie Langtry began when he was introduced to her at a private supper thrown by his bachelor friend Sir Allen Young at his London home on 27 May 1877.

Lillie was a mysterious newcomer to the London social scene. Described as an actress, she had escaped from a stifling and puritanical existence which offered her no excitement and little hope. She was the only daughter of William Corbet le Breton, Dean of Jersey, in whose rectory she was born in 1853.

Perhaps it was her father's insatiable sexual appetite that made her the woman she was. Her father was known as the

'Dirty Dean' due to endless philandering. Indeed, he had to separate her from her first suitor when she was seventeen because the boy in question was one of his many illegitimate children!

Her only thought as she grew up was to escape her humdrum life and use her stunning looks to her own advantage - and stunning she was. She had a Grecian nose, flawless skin, large violet eyes, a perfect figure and hair that fell loosely in a cascade around her shoulders.

Lillie's clergyman father was known as the 'Dirty Dean' because of his endless capacity for womanizing

---

That alone was a shocking departure from the well-coiffed conventions of the period. One writer described her thus: 'She did not use whalebone corsets either. The result was a blend of classical goddess and earthy peasant girl, of the alabaster pedestal set amid the haystack.'

For Lillie, growing up with six brothers in the bucolic isolation of Jersey,

Top: *Bedchamber of a mistress. Lillie Langtry's boudoir around the year 1895.*

Above: *Fur-trimmed temptress Lillie Langtry so obsessed her royal escort that he turned her into his 'official' mistress.*

only her beauty seemed to offer a way out. She married Edward Langtry, the son of a prosperous Belfast shipowner who had come to live in Jersey with the sole intent of frittering away his father's money. He succumbed to her beauty and was whisked off to England as her hapless consort while she embarked on her quest for wealth and fame.

She had first come to the notice of London society two months before the supper party when, with her morose, dim-witted husband in tow, she had turned up at the home of a London socialite, Lady Sebright.

Whistler the artist was there, as were many prominent bright young things of the day. One of them, Frank Miles, saw the potential to turn Lillie into a 'PB' or professional beauty.

These were ladies of mostly genteel birth who were photographed in decent, though alluring, poses. Their portraits sold the length and breadth of Britain for the delectation of the lower classes. When Lillie was introduced to Bertie that first night - minus her husband - it was as the newest 'PB' on the circuit.

The situation with Lillie Langtry, however, soon proved itself to be a relationship that went far beyond his usual flings with the well-bred ladies of Europe. For Edward soon began to insist that the relationship was recognized in society by turning her into his 'official' mistress. He escorted her to major public events such as Ascot races and built a love-nest for her at Bournemouth where, at one stage, he spent virtually every weekend. He even kissed her fully on the lips in public in Maxim's, the most famous restaurant in Paris.

For two years English society was agog at this spectacular new turn of events in the upper classes. Where there was no invitation to country house parties for Mrs Langtry, Edward simply wrote her name on the RSVP slip and brought her along. He even introduced her to his wife and to Queen Victoria in her drawing room at Buckingham Palace, because she was curious to see the creature who had exerted such an influence on her son.

Princess Alexandra responded to her husband's admissions of infidelity by treating them as schoolboy pranks

---

THE START OF THE AFFAIR

During supper with the prince he leaned over to tell her that she was even lovelier in the flesh than she was on cardboard. Ever the keen aficionado of beautiful women, he told her that he had seen several pictures of her, but that none did real justice to her 'radiant beauty'. Within a week they were lovers.

By the time of their first tryst Edward was already father to three children. To Edward, Victorian moral attitudes smacked of hypocrisy and, flawed though he most certainly was, hypocrisy was the one trait he was not prepared to condone.

He was a devoted and conscientious parent to his children, and tried as best he could to redeem his infidelities to his wife by being surprisingly frank with her about mistresses.

Princess Alexandra responded by treating his dalliances as though they were the childish pranks of some uncontrollable schoolboy.

Above: *Edward VII in dandified checked spats rests his foot on a 'wild' bull that he has shot at Chillingham Castle in Northumberland.*

They travelled to Europe together, staying in the same suite at hotels in Paris and Monte Carlo. Cuckolded Ulsterman Edward Langtry could no longer take the humiliation and ran off to a future of debt and heavy drinking while his wife was paraded at the best restaurants as the most stunning woman of her age.

All went swimmingly for two years for the Prince and his showgirl - she still harboured ambitions to take to the stage - until she fell ill one night at his London home. Edward's wife summoned medical assistance, and she was packed off home while the doctor broke the news to Edward and his wife that she was pregnant.

Speculation and accusation have reverberated to this day that the child, a daughter born in secrecy in France and called Jeanne-Marie, was Bertie's baby.

But there was another rumour which has never been laid to rest - that Lillie, while indulging in the affair with Edward, had another lover, the young

Prince Louis of Battenberg. Royal gossip has it that for eighteen months both affairs ran in tandem, with Louis ever eager to share her bed when Bertie was elsewhere.

Whatever the truth, Lillie hid the identity of her daughter from the world and passed her off as her niece, telling the child that her natural father, Lillie's brother, had died while in India.

FROM BOUDOIR TO STAGE

Public interest in Lillie seemed to wane in the two years after the child's birth. By some bizarre social convention of the time she seemed to have angered those 'Professional Beauty' admirers by having a young child, and found herself frozen out on the edges of the circle she once thought herself to be an important part of.

The Prince continued to offer her his patronage and his boudoir, but even he was forced to distance himself from her somewhat. It is said that he actively encouraged and helped her to achieve the career she had always fancied for herself - the stage. She made her professional debut at the Haymarket Theatre on 15 December 1881 playing the role of Kate Hardcastle in *She Stoops to Conquer*.

The Prince of Wales, his wife and many figures from London society were there to see her performance and ensured enthusiastic applause and encores - a level of enthusiasm which was not, however, shared by the critics. Eva, one of the pre-eminent theatrical reviewers of the day, said caustically: 'She has small ability, no more than that of the respectable amateur,' while the satirical magazine *Punch* scalded her with: 'As a novice she should first master the art of acting.' Perhaps the *Times* best summed up the feelings of the day when it commented: 'At least the audience got their money's worth.'

The town of Vinegaroo, Texas, was so captivated by her that the local council voted to change its name to Langtry

---

Despite the critics' coolness the 'Jersey Lily', as she was soon dubbed, continued to bloom in her new career. Americans, enchanted by the royal scandal, flocked to England and became her greatest fans as her touring company took theatres all over Britain by storm.

Within the space of five years she became known as the toughest and most prestigious actress of her time. She visited New York in 1882 to rapturous applause and her wealth increased spectacularly. On the same visit she went to the Texas town of Vinegaroo, which was so taken by her that the town council voted to change its name permanently to Langtry.

European, American and domestic touring did little for the royal relationship, but Bertie seemed content to let his mistress have her head. He was as much impressed with material gain as he was with beautiful women, and when both were

Below: Resplendent in his state robes, the King of England looked the picture of Establishment respectability.

As with all his affairs the relationship began to wither, but she remained on close terms with him for the remainder of his life. He went on to bed a succession of new conquests - among them the French theatrical star Sarah Bernhardt, the 'Madonna' of her day - and she found solace in the arms of many wealthy society men. The Prime Minister, Gladstone, was rumoured to be among them.

In 1897 she married Hugo De Bathe, whom she had met two years previously. In 1907 her husband became a baronet and Lillie became Lady de Bathe.

The Jersey Lily lived until 1929. She had seen the 'golden age' and its manhood destroyed in the foulest war man had ever waged, and was heart-broken by the slaughter on the western front. She went into a decline after the war, claiming her heart was shattered at the loss of so many fine young men, and was buried in the same tiny churchyard as her father back on the island where she was born.

Her husband, the poor, cuckolded Ulsterman who had brought his magnetic wife to London, had died several years before in Chester lunatic asylum. He had been found wandering about Crewe railway station, dazed and with a serious cut to his head. He was carted away and incarcerated for claiming to be married to the great Lillie Langtry!

combined he found the mix irresistible.

In 1975 royal letters were unearthed that showed the depth of his feeling for her and how he always seemed to be prepared to put her career ahead of the romance they shared. On 5 September 1885, while on a visit to the Swedish royal family in Stockholm, he wrote, 'I am glad to hear you are in harness again and most sincerely wish you all the possible success in your tour though I fear you have very hard work before you. I am glad to have the list of towns in which you are to play. Since the 2nd I am the King's guest in Sweden. I told him I had heard from you and he particularly begged to be remembered to you and wish you success in your profession.'

In another letter he wrote of the sadness he felt at her leaving for a long American tour, but finished the note off with the words: 'Perhaps you are right to make hay while the sun shines.' Another, addressed to 'Ma Chère Amie', said: 'You are so busy...and so am I!'

Above: *Still striking in later life...Lillie Langtry as Lady de Bathe in 1928.*

Right: *Lillie takes a stroll in Hyde Park in 1911. As Edward's passion began to fade, she took on new lovers - including the great Liberal statesman Gladstone, according to one distinctly unlikely rumour.*

UNITY MITFORD
Hitler's English Rose

As the shadow of war loomed in the 1930s an upper-class English rose flirted with Nazism and became an Adolf Hitler 'groupie'. Her obsession ended in tragedy in a Munich park

Life at the crazy court of Adolf Hitler veered between the normal and the insane, from the spartan to the luxurious, and the people that the Fuehrer collected around him reflected the madness of those days like bevelled mirrors.

As well as the usual fawning circus of Nazi flunkeys, in the 1930s a woman entered the inner circle who had the same kind of mesmeric effect on him that he had upon others. Unity Valkyrie Freeman-Mitford was the spellbinder who earned the scorn of her own countrymen when she became a member of the elite clique who had Hitler's ear.

Nothing could have seemed a more absurd proposition. He was the working-class, embittered Austrian corporal who had seized power on a mandate of abolishing the old order in favour of his hypnotic National Socialism. She was to the manner born, a lady of high breeding, the daughter of a dazzling family of aristocrats who belonged to another age.

Together they formed what the French have long termed a *folie à deux* - the madness between two people. Electricity crackled between them as Unity preached to England that Hitler was the Messiah to be obeyed, not fought.

'I want everyone to know I am a Jew-hater,' she wrote to the Nazi paper *Der Sturmer*. 'England for the English! Out with the Jews! *Heil Hitler*!'

In a short time she had become an ever-increasing influence on the monster destined to lead the world into the most destructive war in history. And yet, seemingly as quickly as the spell was woven, it was broken. Hitler's invasion of Poland in 1939 plunged Unity back into an appalling reality - one that had been clouded, as it had been clouded for millions of decent Germans, by the image of the swastika.

Unity shot herself days after the war began and never recovered from the wounds, although it would take her another eight agonizing years to die. Her journey from gifted English rose to maniacal Fascist and back again was one of the the strangest stories to come from those turbulent times.

A FAMILY OF ECCENTRICS

It all began in August 1914, the start of World War I. But Unity's family was a throwback, a time-warped hybrid of Victorian and Edwardian morals and values that her father, Lord Redesdale, intended to preserve. He brought up Unity, her five sisters and one brother to respect the 'old order', even as it was dying in the shellholes and trenches of the Western Front.

The Mitford girls were a remarkable family. Diana went on to marry Sir Oswald Mosley, who founded the British Union of Fascists. Nancy became a writer – penning among other books *The*

Above: *Unity Valkyrie Freeman-Mitford made no bones about her anti-Semetic views.*

Opposite: *Three sisters at a friend's wedding in 1932... Unity Mitford (left) with Diana and Nancy.*

Below: *One of a literary family, Jessica Mitford shows her autobiography to husband Bob Treuhaft.*

Pursuit of Love – as did Jessica. Unity achieved infamy over fame, but none the less made her mark on the world.

She was brought up mostly at home at Swinbrook in Oxfordshire, where a series of governesses and her mother taught her privately. As a teenager she did the 'regular debutante thing', as she herself put it, and acquired a reputation as a partygoer and prankster. One of her favourite tricks was pulling out her pet rat 'Ratular' from her handbag at posh country house balls to stroke him in front of her horrified hosts!

Unity was addicted to practical jokes and would take her pet rat in her handbag to smart balls

---

Hers was a world without want or cares. As the industrialized nations of the world slumped into history's greatest depression, Unity could well have frittered away her life as a 'bright young thing'. Instead, in 1932 she changed

direction when she was hypnotized by the rise of Fascism.

Sir Oswald Mosley, with his legions of blackshirts, was the British attempt at Fascism, the fervent movement that had rooted itself in Germany and Italy and would soon flourish in Spain. For many, torn between the Communists of the Soviet Union and the crumbling *anciens regimes* of the West, Fascism seemed a viable, vibrant, promising new creed.

THE LURE OF THE BLACKSHIRTS

With her sister Diana, Unity thrust herself wholeheartedly into the party. In August 1933, as a member of the delegation of the British Union of Fascists, she attended the light-and-sound spectacular of the first Nuremberg Rally since Hitler had seized power.

Watching the searchlights arcing through the misty air, the blazing hand-held torches, the solid blocks of men marching to guttural songs, Unity's dreams were fuelled as never before.

Below: *Adolf Hitler and his mistress Eva Braun with their dogs at Berchtesgaden. Unity Mitford was a favoured visitor.*

She drank it all in and believed in the gospel of hate the Nazis were preaching.

Photographs of her at the time showed her with William Joyce, better known to a generation of English people as Lord Haw-Haw, the sycophantic Nazi lover who was later to die on Allied gallows for treason. She was also pictured with various Nazi bigwigs.

But only one man, holding hypnotic sway over the massed ranks before him, interested her. 'The first moment I saw Adolf Hitler, I knew there was no one else I would rather meet,' she said.

If England had been defeated in 1940, Unity would probably have been Hitler's PR in an office in Downing Street

---

Back in England, she became a celebrity. Hitler, with his toothbrush moustache and lopsided haircut, was still something of a joke, and the thought of a young woman as well connected as Unity Mitford being entranced by him was a source of endless gossip. One cartoon in the *News Chronicle* newspaper showed Unity hiding behind a strident Hitler with the caption: 'You can't criticize Unity with impunity. If you try to belittle 'er, you have to answer to Hitler!'

She was nineteen on her return, and imbued now with the full passion of National Socialism. She persuaded her doting father to send her to a German finishing school - the perfect place to arrange a meeting with the Fuehrer.

Armed with an English translation of

Above: *Street rabble rouser. Sir Oswald Mosley gives a fascist salute as he leads a march through London at the end of 1937.*

Below: *Lord and Lady Redesdale with daughter Unity and her German Embassy escort Dr Fitz-Randolph at an Anglo-German Fellowship concert at Christmas 1938.*

Mein Kampf - Hitler's new testament - she arrived at the school in Munich. Run by Baroness Laroche, the school was intended as an establishment 'to nourish the body and soul of young females in preparation for the life which awaits them outside these portals'. But Unity was not interested in any lessons or marquetry classes. 'It was her chance to lay siege to Hitler,' said biographer David Pryce-Jones, who penned an authoritative work on her.

It was with the persistence of the dizziest fan after a beloved pop star. Perhaps she should be regarded as the prototype groupie.

The Mitfords were in my opinion terribly sinister. I do believe it's people like that who sign the death warrant. They would say to their friends: 'Of course we'll shoot you, but you can have a darling little cigarette first.' They were part of that upper-class English group - from the Duke of Windsor down - who had the makings of an embryonic Fascist state...Our bacon was saved from them at the eleventh hour!

Once Unity was in Munich, she soon learned Hitler's favourite spots in the city. She calculated where the best places would be to effect an introduction to the great man and decided in the end on the Osteria Bavaria restaurant. No one ever had any idea when Hitler would drop in unannounced at the restaurant to eat

German noodles and drink - contrary to popular myth that he was completely teetotal - a little Rhine wine or beer mixed with water.

THE FATEFUL MEETING

Saturday, 9 February 1935, seems to be the date that destiny smiled on Unity. Relaxing there with party functionaries, Hitler saw the petite blonde and sent over a flunkey with an invitation that she should join him for lunch. Her friend, a woman known only as Mary, recorded in her diary: 'Hitler sent for Unity on Saturday and she had lunch at his table. Thrilled to death, of course!'

Unity had made it known to her and her other friends at the school that the boys who wooed them at tea dances held no interest for her. Politically - and, some would later suggest sexually - she only had eyes for Adolf Hitler.

Lienritte von Schirach, daughter of Nazi photographer Heinrich Hoffman, recalled how Hitler became increasingly fascinated with 'the English Lord's daughter'. She witnessed the way Unity wove herself, with her faltering German, into his inner circle, against the advice of people like Rudolf Hess, Hitler's deputy, who feared she might be a British spy.

Frau von Schirach said: *Hitler was caught up not only in her beauty, but also her social position... Hitler fell under her spell and refused to believe those who*

Above: *Fanatical about her politics, obsessive about her men... Unity had eyes only for Adolf Hitler.*

Below: *Unity Mitford arrives on a stretcher at Folkestone on her ignominious return to Britain.*

said she could be a spy. He preferred to trust his own instinctive understanding of people. He also used her to relay his ideas to Britain.

Unity moved out of the school and into a room at a Munich University students' hostel. She bought copies of *Der Sturmer*, which portrayed Jews as pigs and rats, and bedecked her dressing table with pictures of the Nazi hierarchy. She also immersed herself in the writings of Alfred Rosenberg, the Nazis' quack racial theorist.

The pin-ups on Unity's dressing table were not film stars but senior members of the Nazi party

---

On 26 May 1935 the British public learned just how brightly the torch she was carrying for Adolf Hitler burned. A *Sunday Express* correspondent interviewed her about her life in Germany. Sefton Delmer wrote: *Her eyes lit with enthusiasm as she spoke to me of Hitler. 'The hours I have spent in his company,' she said, 'are some of the most impressive in my life. The entire German nation is lucky to have such a great personality as its head.' As I left her in the students' home in which she has lived for the last year, she raised her arm in the Nazi salute and cried: 'Heil Hitler!'*

DESPISED IN EUROPE AND ENGLAND

By many Unity was seen as a naive young woman seeking to absolve her class guilt by riding on the coat-tails of Nazism. They claimed that she could not possibly know anything about the Nuremberg decrees which stripped Jews of their rights as citizens, nor of the camp at Dachau where political opponents were incarcerated and murdered.

But what, in many eyes, made Unity fascinated with Nazism is that she *did* know what was going on. She became a familiar face in Hitler's entourage, and in the summer of 1936 she addressed a huge crowd gathered on the Hesselberg Mountain near Nuremberg. There she espoused the full venom of the Nazis' twisted philosophy, saying that she thought Dachau was the best place for the

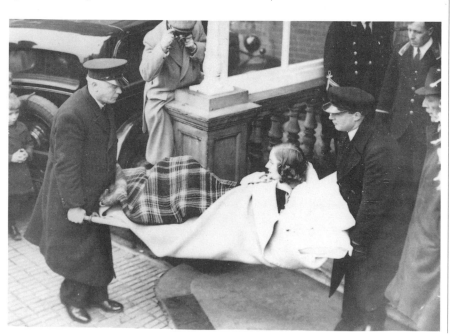

Jews and that only under Hitler could the 'lesser races' of the East be subdued.

In England there was no longer curiosity about Unity but derision and hatred. She had nailed her colours firmly to those of the crooked cross as Europe braced itself for the coming conflict.

At Fascist rallies in England Unity needed police protection to save her from the wrath of the crowds

---

Unity even had to be rescued by police when she returned to England to attend a Hyde Park Fascist rally, and the crowd of demonstrators opposed to them tried to hurl her into the Serpentine.

Unity was not without patriotism for her own country. She deeply loved England and justified her pro-Hitler sentiment by claiming it was the only political system that could save a fragmented Europe. 'I followed with despair the political developments surrounding relations between Britain and Germany,' cried Unity, torn between the love of two flags and two utterly different philosophies.

HITLER'S PROTEGEE

She returned to Germany. In 1936 Hitler took her to Bayreuth, one of the premier opera festivals of Europe and one that he had commandeered and turned into a showcase exhibition of German 'art'.

But after his rise to power art had very little to do with it, and the festival became instead a celebration of stirring Wagnerian music which embodied his concept of Germanic greatness.

Albert Speer, the one member of the inner circle who could be said to be a true intellectual, was convinced she was besotted with him, while he was spellbound by her. 'She was highly in love with him,' he declared. *It was hero worship of the highest order. I doubted if he ever did more than take her hand in his... She was the only woman whose opinions he listened to... In discussions over tea...she would always be willing to argue a point, to try to make him see something another way, and he would be tolerant and always willing to listen.*

Hitler had moved her into a gracious pension in Munich, and began sending an SS staff car over each afternoon to collect and deliver her to his own apartment for afternoon tea and the gooey cream cakes he relished so much.

She was even a privileged visitor to the Eagle's Nest, his mountain retreat high above Berchtesgaden, where he would hold long conversations with her. He used her as the divining rod for understanding British political thought and wanted Britain to use its Navy to patrol its imperial outposts - not to turn it against German shipping.

What Unity told Hitler at these cosy chats can only be guessed at. But by this time she had become such a committed Nazi, it can only be conjectured that she agreed with him and spurred him on.

Experts believe, however, that while she may have found herself falling in love with him, Hitler never wavered from his mistress Eva Braun, and it is thought

Below: *Unity is helped by her parents on her return to England, sick and in disgrace after her dalliance with the Nazis.*

Above: *Hitler acknowledges the adulation of the masses as he takes the salute on his fiftieth birthday with Mussolini and Goering.*

secretary to Hitler, was personally ordered by his master to arrange a selection for her to choose from. She eventually picked one with magnificent rococo ceilings and french windows that led on to a terrace.

THE FINAL TERRIBLE DECISION

Unity returned to England to collect English antiques to furnish her new apartment. But while she criss-crossed the Channel, Adolf Hitler was drawing up plans for the annihilation of Poland.

Unity had no idea that war was just around the corner. Up until then she had seen Hitler's moves against other sovereign states - Austria, Czecho-slovakia - as territorial rights. She could soothe her conscience with the balm of 'rightful possession', but an aggressive war which threatened the peace of the world was another matter.

Most people agree it is unlikely that the Fuehrer's relationship with his English admirer was ever a sexual one

---

Two days before the invasion of Poland on 1 September she pleaded with the British ambassador in Berlin to give an assurance that Britain would not be dragged into war. When no such assurance was forthcoming Unity was plunged into depression. She was now truly torn between two nations that she cared deeply for: she had to choose.

Two days later, when England found itself at war, Unity could take no more. She went to the Gauleiter of Munich, Adolf Wagner, and pushed into his hands a brown envelope. Wagner recalled: 'She wept, she could not speak. In the envelope was her Nazi party badge, a picture of Hitler and a letter to the Fuehrer in which she said she could no longer find a reason to live.'

In a grand, romantic-tragic gesture, she took a small calibre handgun with her to the English Garden, in the centre of Munich, put it to her temple and pulled the trigger. The bullet lodged in her brain - far enough in to be beyond the reach of surgeons, but not far enough to kill her.

She was found by park officials and

that the two women never met. Like Speer, biographers of Unity believe her infatuation never blossomed into a sexual relationship. Eva was intensely jealous of the prim Englishwoman, and once referred to her in a temper as 'that damned English Valkyrie'!

Every day Hitler sent a car to Unity's Munich apartment to collect her for afternoon tea

---

In the summer of 1939 Europe basked in a heatwave. Unity was back in Munich and had now been given an exquisite apartment in the Agnesstrasse, a fashionable address in the heart of the city. Martin Bormann, sinister personal

rushed to the university clinic where the best surgeons in Germany, on the orders of Hitler, endeavoured to save her. The Fuehrer was at her side within twenty-four hours. Aides said they had never seen their leader as shaken before.

He used German intelligence contacts in Switzerland to get a message through to her parents in England to tell them what had happened.

Hitler gaver orders to Germany's finest surgeons to save her life

---

There were tears in his eyes on the night of 8 November 1939, when he saw Unity for the last time in the hospital. She asked him then if she could be sent back to England. He agreed that it was the best course of events, but advised her to wait a little longer until she was stronger.

THE JOURNEY HOME

By the spring of 1940, shortly before he was to unleash his panzer blitzkrieg on France and the Low Countries, he ordered a first class railway carriage to be converted into a travelling hospital ward. One of his personal physicians accompanied Unity to Zurich, where an English doctor awaited her arrival. The journey continued through the south of France to one of the Channel ports, where Lord Redesdale waited to take his daughter back into the country that despised her.

'So ended the story of the remarkable relationship between a woman and Hitler,' said Frau von Schirach.

Above: *Released from detention at the end of the war, Sir Oswald and Lady Mosley hid at the Shaven Crown Inn, Oxfordshire.*

Below: *Sir Oswald Mosley whipping up support at the formation conference of his new Union Movement in the spring of 1948.*

A woman who, like few others in Hitler's circle, showed independence and enterprise. She had not fallen prey to the Fuehrer, like so many other women. As an Englishwoman of the aristocracy she was never subject to the rule that woman must be man's devoted servant; but she had fallen prey to his ideas and her own, so that she failed to notice for far too long where this man and his policies were actually leading.

Unity arrived at Folkestone amid a national furore, with an armed guard meeting her; there was a clamour for her internment. But she escaped detention and retreated to the family's Scottish island, Inchkenneth, for recuperation.

She lived in a kind of twilight zone throughout the war, finally succumbing to her injurites in 1948. Hitler continued to care deeply for her and for two years afterwards could not talk of the suicide attempt. When Munich came under Allied air assault later in the war he issued a decree to save her belongings.

Since her death her life has been studied in minute detail, many apologists for her pointing out that in the end the spell woven by Hitler was finally and irrevocably broken. But one story persists. It was after the Coventry firebombing, one of the worst during the blitz against Britain, which destroyed the cathedral and cost hundreds of lives. The story goes that Unity sat up in bed and said: 'Such a tragedy ... we lost twenty of our best bombers.'

Hardly the remark of a penitent.

KISS AND TELL
Dangerous Liaisons

The lure of a younger woman has broken many a marriage and destroyed many a career. Sometimes men even marry them - with equally dire consequences. When such scandal attaches to public figures there is no privacy and no mercy

Question: What do Bible-thumping evangelist Jimmy Swaggart, mega-tycoon Donald Trump and former aspiring US President Gary Hart have in common? Answer: They're all victims of bimbo-itis - that dread malady which has toppled titans and pummelled politicians almost since time began.

The malady has affected bishops, boxers and billionaires, and turned otherwise 'normal' men into love-sick sycophants who sometimes risked - and lost - all to carry on their relationships with younger women.

Hart lost his chance to become President. Actor Rob Lowe may have lost his career, and certainly his reputation. Donald Trump lost some $25 million thanks to his affair with Georgia peach Marla Maples. And TV preacher Jim Bakker lost his freedom.

Women it seems, still have the power to make or break their men.

THE GREASY POLE OF POLITICS

Unlike some of her 'peers', Donna Rice has eschewed the spotlight - save for one promotional stint for a jeans company - since her 1987 affair with Senator Hart ruined his chance to make the Oval Office. The leggy, blonde model is virtually in hiding these days, studying acting and performing with a small community theatre in northern Virginia.

'She wants to remain private,' said Tricia Erickson, who provided 'crisis management' when Rice hit the headlines. 'She's been doing volunteer work, helping the disabled and the terminally ill. She could have exploited her own situation - I had a couple of million dollars' worth of offers on my desk - but she chose to have her self-respect and dignity.'

And unlike some, Donna isn't making a mint out of her brief encounter with infamy. In fact, she's been living with a

Opposite: *Donald Trump, said to have lost $25 million due to his love affair with 'Georgia peach' Marla Maples.*

Left: *Ivana Trump, who took her tycoon husband to the cleaners over his highly publicised affair with Marla.*

Below: *Openly unfaithful... Trump squired mistress Marla Maples to many showbusiness events during their dalliance.*

ceremony with Hart in which they 'brushed the front and back of our bodies with eagle feathers...it was sensual'.

Incredibly, once his reputation as a womanizer started to haunt his presidential campaign, Hart took the extraordinary step of daring the media to follow him in a bid to clear his name and show he was a hard-working politician.

'It was sensual,' confirmed the Comanche lady of a ceremony at which she and Senator Hart brushed each other's bodies with eagle's feathers

---

One newspaper, the *Miami Herald*, took him up on the offer, and their story about his weekend tryst with Rice rocked America. It became apparent that Hart and the leggy blonde had been 'friends' for four months, and had even been on an overnight sailing trip to the Caribbean aboard the aptly named *Monkey Business*.

Despite Hart's repeated denials of any impropriety, including the public show of support from his loyal wife, he saw his popularity go into a tailspin.

family in the Washington area and helps with the chores for pocket money.

Hart has largely retired to private life since his tryst with Rice. But the bubbly blonde wasn't the first woman the one-time senator knew intimately. Indeed, he admitted he had cheated on his wife, Lee, during two separations in 1979 and 1981.

The first liaison was with Diana Phillips, described as a professional hostess. The other was with Lynn Carter, prominent in Iowa politics. But during his presidential campaign one magazine also linked him to a 'radiant divorcee', whom he described as his 'spiritual adviser'.

Marilyn Youngbird, an American Indian, said she took part in a Comanche

Above: *Donna Rice hit the headlines and ruined Democratic presidential candidate Gary Hart's political career.*

Right: *Senator Gary Hart and his wife campaigning for the Democratic nomination. His smile turned to a scowl when he read of his affair with Donna Rice.*

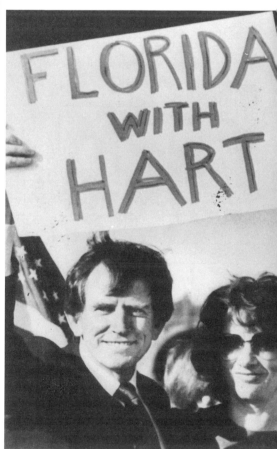

STARS OF SCREEN AND BEDROOM

Jan Parsons will never be a household name like Rice, but her sizzling one-night stand with actor Rob Lowe during the Democratic Convention in Atlanta in 1989 has been captured for ever on videotape.

Jan, who was just sweet sixteen when she, Lowe and another girlfriend engaged in a steamy *menage à trois*, dropped from sight soon after the scandal erupted. Lowe was later 'punished' for his misdeed with twenty hours of community service.

Jan used to work at the Super Hair Three-13 beauty salon, but her current whereabouts remain a mystery. She was a regular on the Atlanta nightclub scene when she met Lowe at the Club Rio, and was reportedly part of a group which engaged in kinky sex and devil worship.

In fact, in divorce proceedings between her parents, her mother, Lena Ann Wilson, claimed that Jan's father 'engaged in strange rituals in a hidden space in the closet'.

Although Lowe has made a couple of films since the scandal unfolded, his career has stalled.

Lowe's problems weren't the first time a Hollywood hero had fallen victim to a *femme fatale*. In fact Hollywood's greatest rogue, the dashing star Errol Flynn, saw his career sink to the bottom. Two sordid rape cases helped to shatter his screen persona and pushed him into a world of drugs and alcohol.

'I was attacked as a sex criminal,' he said after his 1943 trial for statutory rape. 'I knew I could never escape this brand, that I would always be associated in the public mind with an internationally followed rape case.'

He was right - even though he won the case, the Australian-born hell-raiser went into a decline. He was thirty-three when seventeen-year-old Betty Hansen and sixteen-year-old Peggy La Rue Satterlee cried rape to the Hollywood police.

Flynn's 'sexcapades' began early, and he was just seventeen when he left school - in a hurry. 'I was caught with the daughter of a laundress,' he recalled in his best-selling book, *My Wicked, Wicked Ways*.

When he was 'discovered' and brought to Hollywood, he was like the kid in the proverbial candy store, and fast became a

Top: *Movie actress Julia Roberts ditched her husband-to-be Kiefer Sutherland after his publicized party romps with a nightclub dancer.*

Above: *Kiefer Sutherland won and then lost the love of* **Pretty Woman** *star Julia Roberts because of his hell-raising.*

sought-after stud with his rugged good looks and colonial charm. He called himself 'a walking phallic symbol'.

'He was changing women as fast as his valet could change the sheets,' said Nora Eddington, the actor's second wife.

Seeing his accuser's hairy legs Errol Flynn knew that, drunk or sober, he could never have contemplated sex with her

---

He raged his way through Tinsel Town - fights, booze and women, always women. Even his yacht was named *Cirrhosis-by-the-Sea*, and his mansion on Mulholland Drive came complete with an orgy room and two-way mirrored ceiling. Flynn would later write that, as soon as he saw his accuser's hairy legs, 'I knew I was innocent. Drunk, sober, drugged, partly insane, these were not the legs Flynn would have next to his.' He died in 1959 at the age of forty-nine - his great energy and lust for life had been burned out.

And just recently, Hollywood actor Kiefer Sutherland saw his hopes of marrying *Pretty Woman* Julia Roberts go up in smoke, partly because of his relationship with a nightclub dancer called Amanda Rice.

Sutherland and Roberts were all set to be married in the splashiest wedding Tinsel Town had seen in years. The expected cost was put at $1 million.

According to his nightclub dancer friend, Kiefer Sutherland likened Julia Roberts to a corpse in bed

---

But just three days before the wedding Julia got cold feet because of her fears of failing at marriage, like her parents, and Sutherland's continued trysts with other women, particular Rice.

Amanda, a stripper, even blabbed to the media that Sutherland had told her that 'making love to Julia was like having sex with a corpse'.

HEAVYWEIGHT HUMILIATION

Mike Tyson was equally damaged by his brief, stormy marriage to Robin Givens (although she, too, suffered at the hands of the ex-champ). She publicly humiliated him by calling him a total basket case on national television and describing life with him as 'pure hell'. It's a reputation confirmed during Tyson's trial for the rape of an eighteen-year-old beauty queen in 1992, and Robin, who's still busy with her acting career, hasn't changed her opinion since the 1989 divorce.

'Mike should be required to wear a sign that says, "Caution: Mike Tyson is hazardous to women," ' she said. 'He's a demon underneath. He's got a terrible temper. I was terrified of him.' And, she claims, he put her mother, Ruth Roper, into hospital. 'He literally broke her heart,' she said.

Still, there are many who believe Givens contrived to marry the former

Opposite: Robin Givens humiliated husband Mike Tyson by calling him a 'basket case' on American television.

Below: Mike Tyson surrenders to the authorities after being indicted on rape charges in Indianapolis in 1991. In February 1992 he was found guilty of raping a 'Miss Black America' beauty contestant.

champ for his wealth, and was banking on divorcing him from the beginning. Her apparent rush to establish residence in California - which has strict communal property laws - did nothing to dispel these notions.

THE 'QUEEN OF MEAN'

Hotel magnate Harry Helmsley has had his reputation dragged through the mud by his own wife. While Leona Helmsley may not fit the physical mould of the average bimbo - she's not exactly young or beautiful - she has cost her husband untold damage because of her greed.

The 'Queen of Mean' made Harry a laughing stock. She unwittingly depicted him as a befuddled, senile fool who could

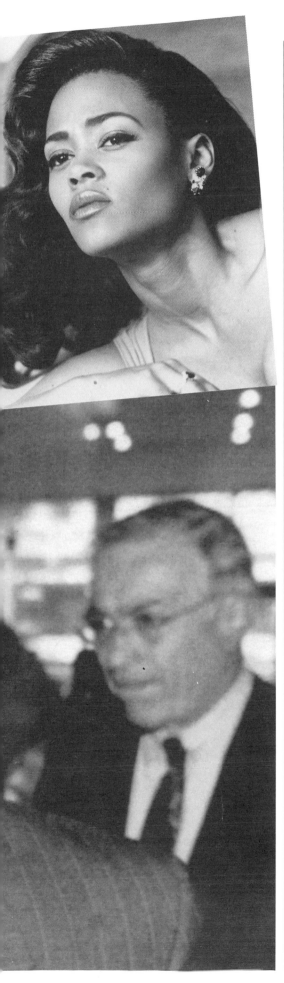

no longer run his empire.

Some long-time associates of seventy-nine-year-old Helmsley say the tycoon was a decent chap before his marriage to Leona in 1972. But afterwards Harry, a reclusive type, underwent a dramatic change, hitting the party circuit.

Actor Cliff Robertson remembers one of the parties that Leona threw. 'Leona ...showed us her pool, had photographers there as soon as you walked in,' he recalled. 'I just thought it was a rather ostentatious display of new wealth. I thought it was, in a way, rather sad. I felt sorry for Harry. He seemed very nice. I couldn't wait to get home, frankly.'

Leona, who was sentenced on multiple tax charges in 1990, moved a step closer to a four-year jail sentence in July 1991 when an appeals court rejected her plea to overturn the conviction.

Leona Helmsley's court battles have cost her husband Harry an estimated $20 million

---

However, the federal court left one small glimmer of hope for the seventy-one-year-old tyrant, by finding technical flaws in four of the thirty-three counts on which she was convicted. Still, federal prosecutors feel the ruling may only reduce her total fines and have no effect at all on her sentence.

So far, Leona's court battles have cost her and Harry an estimated $20 million.

But that's nothing compared to what Jessica Hahn cost Jim Bakker, the diminutive former television preacher.

HELLFIRE AND DAMNATION

Bakker was brought down by the former church secretary, whom he allegedly drugged and had sex with in a Florida hotel room a short prayer or two before he returned to the pulpit to admonish his flock for not following God's ways. The ensuing scandal eventually triggered a government probe into the good minister's fund-raising gimmicks, and resulted in a hefty prison term.

Hahn, meanwhile, has got on with her life. Following a few nip-and-tuck operations paid for by Hugh Hefner, she

Murphree, now thirty, a prostitute with a record in two states, was the woman whom Swaggart regularly paid to perform sex acts while he watched in a seedy New Orleans hotel - and she kindly re-created the poses for *Penthouse*. She even went on a national media tour to promote her story of their sexual liaison.

Murphree said the evangelist, who scoffed at Bakker's problems until he, too, was caught, patronized her for more than a year. She went along with his requests while he paid the going rate, but became enraged when he suggested that her nine-year-old daughter watch them.

Swaggart eventually went on national television and tearfully confessed he had committed an unspecified 'moral sin' and stepped down from the pulpit.

A few months later the Assemblies of God defrocked Swaggart for rejecting a Church order to suspend his preaching for a year, which he said would destroy his $140 million a year worldwide ministries. When he returned to the pulpit, Swaggart told his congregation that the Lord had forgiven him for his sins and 'what's past is past'.

DOWN ON THE STUD FARM

Even the famed House of Gucci has not been spared. Fashion mogul Paolo Gucci and his opera-loving wife split up in 1991 amid charges of illicit barn-yard sex and big-bucks spending sprees.

The very visible split erupted when Jenny Gucci claimed that the fifty-nine-year-old Paolo had moved a stable girl less than half his age into the fourteenth-century English country house they had shared since their marriage fourteen years earlier. And she has vowed to make him pay for his dalliance.

Jilted Jenny says the other woman is pretty twenty-one-year-old Penny Armstrong, who works for Gucci on his stud farm. 'I mean, what do they talk about - heavy metal rock groups? A thirty-eight-year age difference is pretty enormous.'

The fashion king calls the allegations preposterous. 'Jenny has become a shrewd, materialistic wife. Any feelings I had for her are gone now...'

Ironically, the Manhattan judge presiding over the battle is the same one

Top and above: *Roxanne Pulitzer and her husband Peter faced each other across a Florida courtroom while scandalous allegations were made of their millionaire lifestyle.*

posed nude in *Playboy* magazine, obtained work as a morning dee-jay in Phoenix, Arizona and has now launched her own telephone talk line. For the price of $2 anyone can call and get a recording of Jessica's hints for a better life.

'I wanted to be a saint and ended up a centrefold,' says the former church secretary who destroyed TV evangelist Jim Bakker

---

But the phone line also allows people to get to know the real Jessica. 'I want people to know that I'm not selfish. That I want to be useful,' she explained. 'I want to be used by God. I wanted to be a saint and ended up being a centrefold.'

Debra Murphree, the prostitute in the sex scandal that disgraced TV evangelist Jimmy Swaggart, never wanted to be a saint, but she too ended up a centrefold - in the rival *Penthouse* magazine.

who handled the drawn-out Trump split, which ended in Donald forking out almost $25 million.

At stake in the Gucci affair is Paolo's $50 million fortune. And both he and Jenny have vowed to fight to the finish.

'My wife has made a big mistake,' Gucci said. 'She is acting like Saddam Hussein. If she hadn't started a war, she would have got what she wanted. I have never denied her anything. But this is the way she paid me back - and now she is in danger of losing everything.'

Jenny, a tall English-born blonde who met the designer while studying opera in Italy, isn't deterred. 'I'm not acting like Hussein, he is. I'm Norman Schwarzkopf - and we all know who won.'

THE LOVE MATCH

In an unusual twist to the old story, tennis queen Martina Navratilova has also seen her name dragged through the mud by her lover, Texas socialite Judy Nelson.

Nelson has slapped a $10 million lawsuit on Martina and, in an historic move, filed a five-minute video recording along with the lawsuit.

Nelson, who gave up her husband to become Navratilova's lover in the 1980s,

Below: *Tennis ace Martina Navratilova and long-term lover Judy Nelson suffered emotional traumas as their affair ended in courtroom battles over money.*

says she and Martina were more than just bed partners. Her lawyer, Jerry Loftin, said: 'Judy is very saddened by the situation but there is no hope of a reconciliation. The contract was drawn up and filmed, and provides for an equal share of assets.'

Nelson is convinced she will win because she has film of herself and Navratilova signing their business contract

---

Nelson, who was dumped by Martina in 1991 for a younger woman, Cindy Nelson (no relation), also claims to have a tape of an interview in which Martina said that Judy was her partner 'in everything'.

Although Judy and Martina claim they were not 'married' at the time the contract was signed, some tennis insiders have confided that the couple did go through their own marriage ceremony, and actually exchanged rings.

Martina says Nelson's bitter lawsuit has put a shadow over what was supposed to be a satisfying conclusion to her magical career, which includes nine Wimbledon titles.

THE KENNEDYS
America's First Family

America's pride or America's shame? The Kennedy dynasty, the golden 'First Family', was involved with bootlegging, sexual debauchery, drugs and the Mafia - a web of vice and scandal that ultimately destroyed them as a political force

The Kennedy clan have been described as America's 'royal family'. For a country that has never enjoyed (or suffered from) a monarchy, the USA seems to have a strange yearning for the institution.

But if it is an oddity that such adulation exists at all, it is an even more imponderable enigma that, of all the candidates for such honours, it should be the Kennedys who emerged as the leading society lights. Because the family's background hardly lent itself to the elite role it came to follow...

The multi-million-dollar Kennedy dynasty was built on crime. Joseph Kennedy Sr, the colourful founder of the clan, was widely believed to have been a Prohibition-beating bootlegger in the twenties. Joe's grandfather made whiskey barrels and his father was a saloon keeper, so entering the drink trade himself was a natural step.

Nothing illegal was ever admitted or proved. How the Kennedys made their early fortune has always been kept a closely guarded secret. But claims of misdeeds in the Roaring Twenties have never been denied.

Whatever the source of his wealth, Joe was determined to be a winner and his activities amassed a fortune. Even now the family is still raking it in from a lucrative distribution deal struck fifty years ago which gave Joe the exclusive right to import spirits to the States. The deal still stands.

At the age of twenty-one, Joe borrowed money from friends to buy and

Above: *The Kennedy brothers: (from left) Robert, Edward and John. Robert and John would both be assassinated. Edward would have his presidential ambitions thwarted by the scandal of Chappaquiddick.*

Opposite: *Campaigning for election to the American Presidency, John F. Kennedy received rousing adulation wherever he went as he preached his new vision of politics.*

Left: *The Kennedy Clan of the 1930s....Joseph Kennedy with his wife and eight of their nine children.*

sell property and companies. He made killing after killing on the Stock Exchange. By twenty-five he was a bank president and by thirty-five he was a multi-millionaire.

Wealth also brought power, and he was appointed US ambassador to Britain. But the family's strong Irish roots and staunch Catholicism were pointers to a simmering dislike of the British. He opposed US entry into World War II and in 1940 told a reporter: 'Democracy is finished in Britain. The country will go socialist. If the US gets into the war with England, we'll be left holding the bag.' The remark forced him to resign his prestigious title of 'Ambassador to the Court of St James' and he was recalled to Washington with his tail between his legs.

Joe Kennedy swore he would be a millionaire by thirty-five, but by that age he had done so many times over

---

In his quest for power Joe had married Rose Fitzgerald, the daughter of Boston's first Irish mayor. Born into a rich socialite family in 1890, Rose was, in her own way, just as remarkable as Joe.

She married in 1914 and had nine children. She offered her children financial inducements not to smoke or drink until they were twenty-one - a prophetic action in view of their later history of boozing and philandering. She was once quoted as saying: 'I told the boys to study hard, and maybe they'll be President one day.'

Her Irish sympathies were also well known. When she and Joe were invited to spend a weekend as guests of the British royal family at Windsor Castle, she regarded it as a supreme irony, declaring: 'Living well is the best revenge.'

But as well as sharing Joe's political leanings, she also had to share him with other women. During their fifty-five-year marriage he had numerous affairs.

The most famous of his liaisons was with Hollywood star Gloria Swanson. The twenty-nine-year-old actress made all the running in what was to become a two-year affair in the late twenties. Joe handled her business affairs and successfully redirected her career.

Top: *Joseph Kennedy and sons John (left) and Joseph Junior arrive in London for a visit in 1937.*

Above: *Rose Kennedy, surviving matriarch of the Clan and mother of the assassinated John and Robert.*

It was the Catholic Church which ended the affair. In 1929 Gloria was picked up by a Kennedy aide and taken to a hotel room where she was introduced to Cardinal O'Connell, the archbishop of Boston and a friend of the Kennedys.

Extraordinarily, the archbishop told her that Joe had sought his permission either to divorce his wife or to set up a second household with Gloria - recognized and sanctioned by the Church.

O'Connell had declined and now told Gloria: 'I am here to ask you to stop seeing Joseph Kennedy. Each time you see him you become an occasion of sin for him.'

At an extraordinary meeting in a hotel room a Roman Catholic cardinal tried to break up the affair between Joe Kennedy and Gloria Swanson

---

Despite this weird attempt at ending their love affair, the transcontinental trysts continued until 1930 when two events occurred. One was that Gloria Swanson's hard-done-by husband warned he was suing for divorce. The other was that, at a dinner party, Gloria questioned one of Kennedy's business deals involving her career.

Joe exploded in rage, stormed out and flew to Boston, liquidating all his holdings in her movies.

THE CURSE OF THE KENNEDYS

Joseph Kennedy's sons inherited his sexual appetite. They also inherited his Irish republican sympathies. John once declared that his best overseas visit as President had been to Ireland. During his trip he was given a joke 'O'Kennedy' coat of arms. He had it made into a ring seal - but the only time he ever used it was on a letter to the Queen.

The Kennedy fortune is now reckoned to be approaching $1000 million, most of it tied up in trust funds, stocks and shares. But wealth has not saved them from the terrible curse that has dogged the dynasty. The family history is littered with scandal and tragedy.

Joe and Rose's third child, Rosemary, was born mentally retarded and spent most of her life in a home.

In 1944 came the greatest tragedy the family had yet known. Rose and Joe's eldest son, Joe Jr, died at the age of twenty-nine when his bomber blew up over the English Channel. Of all the tragedies that the old man witnessed in his life, the loss of Joe Jr hurt him the most.

Joe had been groomed for greatness by his ambitious father and would probably have been the President that brother John was later to become.

Disaster followed disaster. Four years after Joe Jr's death, Kathleen Kennedy was also killed in a plane crash.

Joe's dream of power was finally fulfilled in 1960 when John F. Kennedy became US President. At least the old man, who died in 1969 at the age of eighty-one, lived to see that proud moment. But tragedy struck again with the assassination of first the President and then brother Robert, the US Attorney-General.

It was only after their deaths that books were written posing questions about Robert's fidelity - and producing solid evidence about the philandering of JFK.

A PRESIDENT ON THE MAKE

In *The Crisis Years* by historian Michael Beschloss, JFK is depicted as a sex-crazy head of state who pursued his romantic pleasures regardless of national security. When he was a twenty-four-year-old naval intelligence officer during World War II, Jack Kennedy supposedly fell madly in love with Danish spy Inga Arvad Fejos, who was at that time working for the Nazis.

The tall, blonde ex-Miss Denmark was under FBI surveillance during their affair, and it almost cost Kennedy his position in the US Navy. It was only the intervention of his father that saved him.

A second shady affair occurred in 1963 when he started seeing Ellen Fimmel Rometsch, a twenty-seven-year-old West German who had been involved with two Communist groups. But when his brother Robert, then Attorney-General, heard of the affair he ordered the poor girl to be expelled from the USA.

Further astonishing evidence of the President's sexual adventures was related in a string of books which revealed his obsessions with film stars Marilyn

Below: *John Kennedy and Jacqueline Bouvier in the society wedding of 1953 at fashionable Newport, Rhode Island.*

Above: *Frank Sinatra, Robert Kennedy and brother-in-law Peter Lawford on their way to a fund-raising dinner in 1961.*

Monroe, Angie Dickinson and Jayne Mansfield. But lesser mortals were also the subjects of JFK's desires.

In the book *A Question of Character: A Life of John F. Kennedy*, Thomas C. Reeves provided evidence of a sex session with a new flame on the President's inauguration night and the hiring of a call girl immediately before Kennedy's famous television face-to-face confrontation with Richard Nixon.

Reeves alleged that CIA informants had told him of proof that JFK liked to get rip-roaring drunk while in the White House - as well as using 'marijuana, cocaine, hashish and acid'.

According to the CIA the President was no stranger to marijuana, cocaine, hashish and acid

---

Two things facilitated the President's astonishing philandering. One was the loyalty of the entire White House staff, including both his and Jackie's secret service guards who would alert him about his wife's movements and give due warning when he needed to break up a sex session.

The other was his friendship with Peter Lawford. Actor Lawford was JFK's

brother-in-law (he had married Jack's sister Pat) and lived in Santa Monica, California, where his beachfront home was headquarters for both Jack and brother Bobby's West Coast expeditions.

MARILYN: USED, ABUSED AND...MURDERED?

It was here that the two were introduced to the movie star Marilyn Monroe. It is generally believed that both brothers had affairs with Marilyn, and that they treated her cynically and dropped her harshly.

Lawford arranged many meetings between JFK and Monroe. When Kennedy won the Democratic presidential nomination he made an acceptance speech at the Los Angeles Coliseum, with Marilyn cheering him on. She then joined the young Kennedy for a skinny-dipping party at Lawford's beach house. Kennedy suddenly decided to stay on in California one extra day.

In May 1962 Jack Kennedy held his forty-fifth birthday party in Madison Square Garden. Marilyn was there at his side. She waddled on to the stage in a skin-tight dress and managed to blurt out a few lines of 'Happy Birthday'. She was scared and drunk. The crowd did not notice, but JFK did. Marilyn Monroe could become an embarrassment. She would have to go.

Soon afterwards poor Marilyn did indeed become an embarrassment. At thirty-six, she was turning more and more to drugs.

The Kennedys realized that, with her diaries and her knowledge of their Californian secret partying, the world's most popular blonde might be believed if she decided to break the presidential code of silence. Word was got to Marilyn that she must not attempt to contact either Bobby or Jack ever again.

It was enough to send the unstable movie star over the edge.

On the morning of 5 August, 1962, Marilyn was found dead at her home in Brentwood, Los Angeles. Did she, as the inquest found, die by her own hand? Was it accident or suicide - or murder?

Rumours of her affairs with Jack and Bobby Kennedy soon swept the world. According to one of her closest friends,

Robert Slatzer, Marilyn had two important meetings planned for the day following her death. One was with her lawyer; the other was a press conference.

At this conference, said Slatzer, Marilyn was going to reveal the truth about her love sessions with the President, or with the Attorney-General, or both. She felt that the brothers had used her, then abandoned her. The only thing that would have stopped her

revelations would have been a phone call or a visit from Robert Kennedy on the night of 4 August - her last day on earth.

That night a dinner party had been planned at the home of Peter Lawford. It was rumoured that Robert Kennedy was due to turn up. He never did. Nor did Marilyn. According to Lawford at the inquest, Marilyn told him on the phone she felt too tired.

At a press conference the day after her death Marilyn planned to tell all about her relationship with the Kennedy brothers

---

The theories that Marilyn Monroe had been silenced grew stronger. It was said that her house had been bugged by Robert Kennedy and by the FBI.

Monroe was believed to have had an abortion about this time, and the baby could have been Bobby Kennedy's. Marilyn had tried to contact him at the Justice Department in Washington on numerous occasions in the weeks before her death. The horrifying theory that secret agents killed Marilyn to protect the Kennedy brothers from disgrace was advanced by several authors.

Weird theories indeed. And not far removed from another well-recorded and fully admitted scandal, involving the President and a Mafia gangster's moll...

SHARING A MISTRESS WITH THE MAFIA

After JFK's death word leaked out of affairs that the President had conducted with secretaries, prostitutes, socialites, starlets, movie actresses, journalists and family friends. But no revelation caused more shock than the news in 1975 that Jack Kennedy had kept secret a two-year romance with a dark-haired, blue-eyed beauty called Judith Campbell Exner.

The affair was revealed when a Senate committee began investigating links between the CIA and the attempted overthrow of Cuban leader Fidel Castro. Those links led to Chicago Mafia boss Sam 'Momo' Giancana and his mobster friend Johnny Roselli...and still further down the chain of intrigue to Giancana's girlfriend Judith Campbell Exner. In secret

*Left: **Marilyn Monroe was the sex symbol of her age - and the plaything of the Kennedys.***

*Below: **The bed on which a legend died. Marilyn Monroe's body was found sprawled across it. Was it accident, suicide or murder?***

testimony she revealed not only her affair with Giancana but, unexpectedly, another at the same time with Jack Kennedy.

Judith claimed that she was Kennedy's link with the Mafia for most of 1960 and 1961, regularly carrying sealed packages between the President and her two Mafia bosses, Giancana and Roselli.

Exner said she was introduced to Jack Kennedy by Frank Sinatra

---

In her autobiography, *My Story*, Exner said she was introduced to Jack Kennedy in 1960 by singer Frank Sinatra at a Las Vegas party. Kennedy, who was then a Massachusetts senator, said their affair began almost immediately and continued across America, including Chicago, Los Angeles, Palm Beach and Washington.

Below: *Presidents past and present...John Kennedy with Dwight Eisenhower at the White House in 1962.*

One version of how the affair ended appeared in later reports from FBI sources. Exner, it seemed, had revealed that there had been many telephone calls between the President and FBI director J. Edgar Hoover.

What she may not have known was that some of them were warnings from Hoover to Kennedy that his continued liaison with Exner could destroy him.

A WRONG TURNING AT CHAPPAQUIDDICK

Youngest brother Senator Edward 'Teddy' Kennedy lost his chance of making the presidency when he took a wrong turn on Chappaquiddick Island, off the Cape Cod coast, on Friday night, 18 July 1969.

The thirty-seven-year-old Kennedy had looked as if he would put the family back on the political map as he gained in prestige as Democratic senator for Massachusetts. But the wrong turning he took proved also to be the turning point of his career.

Teddy Kennedy had spent the day sailing with friends before dropping in for a beer at a hotel in Edgartown Harbour. There he was joined by a party of friends, including his cousin Joe Gargan and lawyer Paul Markham.

As evening fell the three men took the short ferry ride across to the island of Chappaquiddick where a party was planned at a secluded, rented cottage. By 8.30 that night they had joined up with three other men and six young women.

Among the guests was Mary Jo Kopechne, at twenty-nine one of the 'boiler room girls' who had worked for Teddy's brother Bobby before his assassination the previous year. What happened as the night wore on may never be fully known...for the senator's recollection of events proved later to be strangely hazy.

Teddy Kennedy said he left the party shortly before midnight to return to Edgartown. He took with him Mary Jo, who had been staying at Edgartown's Dunes Hotel.

The route back to the ferry would have taken Kennedy down Main Street. He knew the road well. Yet Kennedy did not drive down Main Street. Instead of turning left at the crossroads just half a mile from the cottage, he turned sharp right - into Dyke Road and towards the beach.

His black 1967 Oldsmobile car began to cross the 85ft wooden, hump-backed Dyke Bridge, but midway the vehicle plunged off the side into the strong currents of Poucha Pond. A few seconds later, Kennedy emerged gasping for air. He crawled to the safety of the shore.

Later he was to recall that he dived repeatedly in an effort to reach Mary Jo, who was trapped inside the car.

Finally, exhausted and in a state of shock, he rested for fifteen minutes on the beach. Then he started running back towards the cottage where the barbecue was still in progress. He was never able to explain why he did not stop to raise the alarm at a house only two hundred yards away from Dyke bridge.

Instead the senator staggered back to the cottage and, dripping wet in the darkness, called Gargan and Markham outside to talk to him. Softly he told his two friends what had occurred.

Again, there was no attempt to reach a telephone - there being none at the cottage - to call the police and the fire service. The three men chose instead to drive back to the bridge and dive once more to the sunken car in an attempt to recover Mary Jo's body. In despair at having failed to reach her, the three men drove off, leaving behind Mary Jo almost certainly dead - but just possibly trapped in an air pocket and still struggling for life.

Edward Kennedy left the scene of the accident without raising the alarm at a nearby house

---

Further clues to the character of the man who might have been President then emerged. He told Gargan and Markham that he did not want the others to know of Mary Jo's death.

At Teddy's request, his two friends then drove him back through the crossroads, this time taking the correct turning to the ferry landing where again he shunned the use of a telephone. Instead he dived into the water and swam across the channel to the Edgartown side.

Above: *The moment that changed history as John Kennedy is assassinated on 22 November 1963. Jackie Kennedy leans over her dead husband.*

Right: *How America learned the worst. But soon the rumours began about conspiracies and cover-ups over the death of the President.*

Gargan and Markham said they assumed he had gone to raise the alarm and they drove back to the party.

On the Martha's Vineyard side of the channel, Kennedy was acting out another strange drama. He slipped silently out of the water and crept to his previously booked hotel room at the Shire Inn, in Edgartown, where he changed into fresh, dry clothes. He then wandered outside until he was noticed by the hotel's owner, who was working late.

Kennedy told him: 'I have been asleep. Something woke me up.' Then: 'I seem to have misplaced my watch. Can you tell me what time it is?' It was 2.25am. Kennedy thanked the hotel boss, bade him goodnight and went back into his room. The following morning Kennedy turned up in the hotel's small restaurant for breakfast at 7.30am, apparently none the worse for his ordeal. An hour after that, Gargan and Markham arrived.

According to testimony later, it was at this time that the group belatedly tried to ring a lawyer to report the accident. But Kennedy's Oldsmobile had already been discovered. Edgartown police chief Dominick Arena and his men had taken the ferry to Chappaquiddick.

His two men friends drove him to the ferry landing, where he slipped into the water and swam across to his hotel

---

At the bridge, Arena noted the skid marks and the Oldsmobile appearing above the ebbing tide. The tenant of the nearby house told him she had heard a car drive past around midnight.

Arena borrowed swimming trunks and a face mask and dived down to the car to see if there was a body inside but the 6ft 4in cop found that the strong current made the task too dangerous. He called up divers and radioed his headquarters with the number of the car, L78 207. The reply came back soon afterwards: 'It is registered to Senator Edward Kennedy.'

When diver John Farrar arrived from Edgartown, he examined the car. The driver's window was rolled completely down, the passenger's was fully closed, and the rear window was shattered. In the rear seat he found a girl's body.

In her handbag were keys to an Edgartown motel room, some cosmetics, dollars and a US Senate pass in the name of Rosemary Keogh - a friend. The police concluded that it was Rosemary and not Mary Jo whose body lay in the car.

Meanwhile, Arena received another radio message. Teddy Kennedy was sitting in Edgartown police station waiting to see him. Back in town Arena questioned Kennedy, but his replies were brief and elusive. He sat down and made a written statement.

He claimed that he had been unfamiliar with the route he had taken the night before and described how the car 'went off the side of the bridge'. He went on:

Below: Senator Edward Kennedy's career almost ended in the murky waters of Chappaquiddick Island when Mary Jo Kopechne died in his car in 1969.

Bottom: The turbulent marriage of Edward and Joan Kennedy meant strained moments in public for the feuding celebrity couple.

I attempted to open the door and window of the car but have no recollection of how I got out of the car. I came to the surface and then repeatedly dove down to the car in an attempt to see if the passenger was still in the car. I was unsuccessful in the attempt. I was exhausted and in a state of shock. I recall walking back to where my friends were eating. There was a car in front of the cottage and I climbed into the back seat. I then asked for someone to bring me back to Edgartown. I remember walking around for a period of time and then going back to my hotel room. When I fully realized what had happened this morning I immediately contacted the police.

Kennedy's curious police statement left so many questions unanswered that he was immediately assumed to be hiding his guilt

---

The statement left so many questions unanswered that a presumption of guilt was natural.

Meanwhile, the Kennedy machine swept into action to tidy up the rotten affair. Mary Jo's body was flown to

Pennsylvania in a plane chartered by the senator. He himself hid away at his nearby home at Hyannis Port.

Four days after Mary Jo's death, Kennedy flew to Pennsylvania to attend her funeral at St Vincent's Roman Catholic church. He was accompanied by his pregnant wife Joan and by his brother Bobby's widow Ethel. Kennedy surprised mourners by appearing at the funeral in a neck brace - worn, he said, because of injuries suffered in the accident.

Three days later he returned to Martha's Vineyard to plead guilty to the minor charge of leaving the scene of an accident. He was given a suspended two-month jail sentence and banned from driving for a year.

Kennedy's guilty plea saved him the embarrassment of giving evidence at the hearing. But it failed to silence press disquiet about what was seen as a cover-up. Kennedy was impelled to go on nationwide television and make a long, yet still evasive statement about the Chappaquiddick tragedy.

Kennedy's rambling apologia on TV made Life magazine accuse him of hustling heart-strings and trading on Kennedy credibility

---

He tried to 'explain' his strange actions after his car crashed into the water:

All kinds of scrambled thoughts ...went through my mind during this period. They were reflected in the various, inexplicable, inconsistent and inconclusive things I said and did, including such questions as whether the girl might still be alive somewhere out of that immediate area, whether some awful curse did actually hang over all the Kennedys... I was overcome, I'm frank to say, by a jumble of emotions - grief, fear, doubt, exhaustion, panic, confusion and shock.

And so on, ending with an equally rambling plea to be allowed to remain senator for Massachusetts.

He remained a senator, but his hopes of ultimate power died with Mary Jo Kopechne. Over the years Kennedy languished in a political pool flanked by bouts of boozing and womanizing.

His marriage to wife Joan ended in divorce in 1983. And tales of the senator canoodling with various young ladies in different parts of the globe became stock in trade for the popular tabloids.

CONTINUING THE FAMILY LEGEND

While Teddy hit the high spots, other Kennedy clan scandals continued. In 1983, Robert Kennedy Jr was arrested for possessing heroin. Shortly afterwards, brother David, twenty-eight, died of a drugs overdose in a seedy Florida motel room after a week of heavy partying. Cousin Teddy Jr fought cancer and had a leg amputated, only to be arrested a few years later for possessing drugs.

And in 1991 Edward Kennedy's nephew, William Kennedy Smith, was arrested over allegations that he had raped a woman at the Kennedy family mansion in Palm Beach.

After this latest shock a US poll revealed that the Kennedy name had by then become associated more with scandal and debauchery than with charitable or political achievements. But given patriarch Joseph Sr's beginnings in the bootlegging twenties, it is perhaps only reasonable to ask: had the Kennedy clan's reputation done any more than come full circle?

Below: *William Kennedy Smith listens in court to evidence about his alleged sex attack on a girl he invited back to the family's Palm Beach home.*

ELVIS – THE KING
The Death of a Legend

To millions of fans Elvis Presley was – and still is – the King. He was also an obese, violent drug addict with bizarre sexual tastes. What made him what he was?

His adoring fans see him as the all American boy, devoted son, model army recruit, generous friend and gifted entertainer. Others knew Elvis Aron Presley as an obese, violent monster, obsessed with death and kinky sex, a drug addict who popped pills by the bucketful to hide from the real world.

But all agree that he was the King.

He had it all. Fans, fame, fortune and an unmatchable talent. But he died aged only forty-two, grossly overweight, with an amazing total of thirteen drugs in his bloodstream. He took pills to go to sleep. He took pills to get up. He took pills to go to the lavatory and he took pills to stop him from going to the lavatory.

And he was in the bathroom when he

fell on to the thickly carpeted floor after a massive heart attack. Despite bodyguards, a live-in fiancee and a thousand so-called friends he lay there alone and cold for three hours before he was discovered. The King was dead. But who was the King?

At the autopsy a total of thirteen drugs were found in his bloodstream

---

In the last years of his life Elvis had become a bloated parody of the handsome, clean-living, pelvis-swinging star who had earned a billion dollars and was the idol of the world.

As his ex-wife Priscilla said, 'He became crazed with inactivity and boredom.' Night had become day for Elvis: he slept through the daylight hours and stayed up all night.

Above: *Elvis, Priscilla and their baby daughter, Lisa Marie - born on the 2 February 1968.*

Opposite: *Bloated and dependent on drugs to get him on stage, Elvis Presley ended his singing career as a sad shambling figure.*

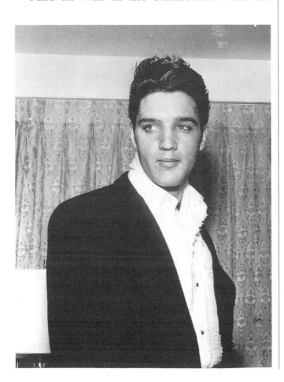

Left: *Fresh-faced and youthful, Elvis at the start of his career and on the trail to international superstardom in the Fifties.*

His sex-life became perverted. He was a voyeur, installing two-way mirrors in rooms through which he could secretly watch his friends engage in sexual acts with girls. He used video equipment to tape his own sex movies, some of lesbian activities.

But it was his drug addiction that killed him. Whenever he arrived in a new town he would send out his aides to find doctors to prescribe the huge daily doses of pills that he needed. Stepbrother David Stanley remembers what happened when the aides failed in Las Vegas:

He jumped on a table, pulled out his gun and said, 'I'll buy a goddam drug store if I want to. I'm going to get what I want. You people had better realize that either you're with me or you're against.

His concerts had become farces. Under the influence of drugs he forgot the words of numbers he had sung for years. He would ramble on incoherently to the audience. Hundreds walked out of a Las Vegas concert because he spent half-an-hour giving a karate demonstration.

It had been a sad decline for the ex-truck driver who, slim and sexy, had led a revolution in music twenty years earlier.

ADORED AND SPOILT

He was born on 8 January 1935 in East Tupelo, Mississippi, the only child of Gladys and Vernon Presley. Gladys, a sewing machine operator, knew she had been carrying twins but her doctor did not believe her. So when Elvis was delivered the doctor turned away and began cleaning up. Gladys was still in pain - a labour pain. A few minutes later Elvis's twin brother, Jesse Aron, was born dead.

His over-protective mother insisted on accompanying Elvis to and from school almost up to the day he left

---

Elvis always shared a close relationship with his mother. Gladys was over-protective of the spoilt young boy, taking him everywhere she went. He slept in her bed during his early years.

When Elvis started school, Gladys always insisted on walking him there and bringing him home in the afternoon. This daily ritual lasted almost to the end of

Above: *Elvis at 27 fishing in the Pacific waters of Hawaii during a break in the making of his film* **Girls, Girls, Girls.**

Below: *Presley's smouldering looks and singing talents at the height of his stardom in 1962.*

Elvis's schooldays and caused him a great deal of embarrassment. Finally, he insisted she should walk behind him and on the other side of the road, hidden by the bushes if possible.

MUSICAL BEGINNINGS

Vernon Presley, who did any jobs that came up, regularly attended the Assembly of God church with his wife. It was there that Elvis heard music - and sang - for the first time.

He won his first award for singing at a county fair. The young boy was placed second and won $5.

Given the choice, Elvis would have preferred the rifle - but since Gladys was paying it had to be the guitar

---

It was Gladys who went with Elvis to buy his first real guitar. It replaced the home-made model made from a lard can that Elvis had acquired in a swap with another youngster. When Elvis and his mother arrived at the hardware store, though, the birthday boy had his heart set on a rifle. Mother did not approve - and in the end prevailed.

When he was twelve, he was given encouragement by his teacher, Mrs Camp. She asked her class to take part in a talent show. Elvis, a new boy, shyly put up his hand and said he could sing a little and play the guitar. Next day he turned up with his guitar and sang his favourite song, 'Old Shep'. From then on he took his guitar to school every day.

The family moved to Memphis but life was always a struggle. In high school he learned to love football - and blues and country music. He began to wear his hair long and grew his famous side-burns for the first time. And he began to perform publicly for the first time. He would play at school and at the local boys' clubs.

Already there was no shortage of girls attracted to the shy, heavy-lidded, handsome young man. He fell in love for the first time - with a pretty fifteen-year-old called Dixie Locke. His parents even thought marriage was a possibility.

Once his schooldays were behind him - he was an average pupil - he got a job truck-driving for $41 a week. His route often took him past the Memphis Recording Studio, where you could make your own record for $4.

One Saturday in July 1953 Elvis took time off and turned up at the studio to cut two songs as a present for his mother. 'Who do you sound like?' asked the assistant Marion Keisker. 'I don't sound like nobody,' he replied. How right he was.

He recorded the two Ink Spots numbers 'My Happiness' and 'That's When Your Heartaches Begin' and made a big impression on Marion. She remembered him and constantly badgered her boss, Sam Phillips, about the teenager.

But it was a year before Phillips fixed up a recording session for Elvis. On 5 July 1954 he made the single 'That's All Right, Mama'. Two days later, a local radio disc jockey played the record fourteen times in a row.

'I don't sound like nobody,' said the young Elvis when he arrived at the recording studio - and indeed he was right

---

It was another case of a woman being a big influence in Elvis's life. He said later: 'If it wasn't for Marion I would never have got a start. That woman, she was the one who had faith, she was the one who pushed me. Sure, Sam had the studio - but it was Marion who did it for me.'

The first record order was for five thousand discs, and it climbed to number three in the Memphis country and western charts. Elvis and his group the Starlight Wranglers - later renamed the Blue Moon Boys - were in demand. Their second record didn't sell so well, but then along came Colonel Tom Parker.

ENTER COLONEL PARKER

He told the naïve youngster: 'You stay talented and sexy and I'll make amazing deals that'll make us both as rich as rajahs. Parker was a wheeler-dealer in the carnival/show-business world and he was telling the truth. The Colonel owned Elvis till the singer died: and he took 50 per cent of every dollar that Elvis earned.

It was Colonel Tom who insisted that Elvis developed his hip-wiggling style. And in Jacksonville, Florida he realized that he'd hit gold. It was there that

Below: *Elvis Presley and Frank Sinatra on the set of the 1965 movie* **Frankie and Johnny.**

Above: *Elvis married only once - to Priscilla. The couple later divorced but she kept his name.*

teenagers for the first time tried to rip off Elvis's clothes. He had become a sex star.

But one girl who was not impressed was girlfriend Dixie. When Elvis's career began to take off and he was spending weeks on the road, she found she wanted more than just loving phone calls. It broke his heart when she left him after eighteen months and married someone else.

Colonel Parker promised to make them both as rich as rajahs - no idle boast since he took a cool 50 per cent

---

Elvis's first appearance on network television in 1956 changed him into a national sensation. The older generation were repelled by Presley's mean, sexy image. He was attacked from pulpits and in editorial columns, and banned from radio programmes.

The teenagers, on the other hand, loved it all - particularly because their parents hated everything he stood for. Reluctantly show business had to accept him. After all, he was the country's No.1 recording star after 'Heartbreak Hotel' had sold a million.

He was already the King, Elvis the Pelvis or the Guitar-Playing Brando. There were Presley jeans, charm bracelets, guitars, T-shirts, bobbysocks, bermuda shorts. Presley was only twenty-one and already a millionaire.

GOODBYE TO GLADYS

In 1956, as well as 'Heartbreak Hotel', he released 'Hound Dog', 'Don't Be Cruel', 'Blue Suede Shoes' and 'Love Me Tender'. *Love me Tender* was the title of the first film he made with 20th-Century Fox. The record sold over 2 million copies.

In 1957 Elvis purchased Graceland, his home for the last twenty years of his life. He paid $100,000 for the building which had been previously used as a church. The two-storey mansion contained twenty-three rooms. He painted it blue and gold so that it glowed in the dark. And Mom and Dad moved in.

The fans may have wanted Elvis - but so did the US Army. In December 1957 he was drafted for two years. Elvis said he was quite prepared to 'do his share' and 'to protect his country'.

While doing his military service in Texas his beloved mother became ill. She returned to Memphis and was admitted to hospital where she was diagnosed as having 'acute severe hepatitis'. As days passed she sank lower while Elvis fought with the Army for a leave pass. At last they gave it, and he fought his way through the crowds to her bedside.

She died a few days later at the age of forty-six. Elvis was distraught. Vernon was there at her death and rang Elvis at Graceland. At the graveside Elvis collapsed several times. He leaned on the casket, weeping, and said, 'Oh God, everything I have is gone. Goodbye darling, goodbye, goodbye.'

Elvis never got over his mother's death, and his obsession with her prevented him from ever achieving emotional maturity

---

He was never to recover from the trauma. Author Albert Goldman described his relationship with his mother in these words:

Elvis's obsession with his mother lasted throughout his life, even though she died several years before he did. It was an unnatural obsession that ...certainly accounts for many of Elvis's later sexual problems.

It was a suffocating relationship that never really gave Elvis the chance to grow up a man.

THE SLIDE INTO SEX AND DRUGS

He left for Germany with the Army a few weeks later. It was while serving in Europe that stories of his sexual excesses began to emerge. His wild lifestyle began, says Goldman, in Paris in 1959 when he discovered the Lido nightclub and the Bluebell Girls' chorus line.

For two weeks Presley ate dinner at the club and then took the entire chorus line back to his hotel. 'He toyed with them till dawn,' he reports. And it was while he

Above: Elvis was once a truck driver on $41 a week. His route took him past the Memphis record studios where he found fame.

Below: Surprisingly Elvis Presley did not make London's Madame Tussauds waxworks exhibition until 1978. He stood in the Hall of Heroes.

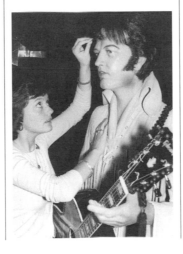

was serving in Germany that Elvis started popping pills for the first time.

He came back from two years' service having found a bride, Priscilla (although they didn't marry for another seven years), to find that the world still clamoured for him. Parker had done a good job while Elvis had been serving his country.

From the spring of 1961 to the summer of 1968 Elvis made twenty-one films and about $5 million. He worked and played hard. And he turned to pills for support.

Colonel Parker was nothing if not efficient. After two years as a GI Elvis went on to make twenty-one films and $5 million

---

In Hollywood, Colonel Parker set up Elvis and his bodyguards - dubbed the Memphis Mafia - in a Bel Air mansion which had belonged to Aly Khan and Rita Hayworth. 'It became the headquarters for the most intently partying group of bachelors in the history of Hollywood,' wrote Goldman.

The parties...would commence every night at about ten. The basic idea was to fill the house with attractive young women who had been specially selected to conform to Elvis's exacting criteria.

Elvis liked small, kittenish girls who were built to his ideal proportions. They were to be no higher than 5 ft 2 in and weigh no more than 110 lbs. What was critical was that the girls be as young as possible, certainly no older than eighteen, and that they be not too far removed from the condition of virginity. Elvis liked to see a pretty girl dressed all in white. White panties were Elvis's erotic fetish.

Elvis the nice guy was forgotten. He was turning into an arrogant, bad-tempered bore who insisted on respect and blind obedience. Elvis's trigger-sharp temper exploded into violence more than once against a girl who dared to answer back. He threw things at them like a hysterical woman - once a water melon; another time, more dangerously, a knife.

Once Elvis had made his way into the master bedroom with the pick of the litter, the Mafia were free to enjoy the remainder. While they did what comes naturally, Elvis was mostly content to watch his group of girls strip down to their panties and wrestle.

For fun Elvis had a 40 lb, 4 ft tall alcoholic chimp called Scatter who joined in the wrestling and was great for practical jokes. He once climbed up the drainpipe to the second-floor office of Sam Goldwyn. As he came swinging through the window, Goldwyn's secretary ran screaming in horror from the room. Scatter then enraged the legendary producer by leaping on to his desk.

Elvis bought one of the first home video cameras, and with co-operative young women made his own endless series of bedroom follies.

Elvis's alcoholic pet chimpanzee once shinned up a drainpipe and broke into Sam Goldwyn's office

---

But at the same time as these tacky bedroom antics, he was wooing the co-stars of his movies: Tuesday Weld, Ursula Andress, Yvonne Craig and Ann-Margret. He also dated Natalie Wood.

Elvis liked film work, but got more and more depressed as the films he made got cheaper and cheaper.

And so he turned to pills more and more. He ran a football club called Elvis Presley Enterprises. Everyone in the team would take two uppers. They then played four or five games straight off, said ex-bodyguard Red West. After the uppers came painkillers for the injuries. Inexorably the King was becoming a walking chemist's shop.

Musically, the mid-1960s was a period of decline for Elvis. His singles did not reach number one. There was more competition, especially from Britain and the Beatles.

MARRIAGE - AND DIVORCE

On 1 May 1967 the singer at last married Priscilla Ann Beaulieu, whom he always called Cilla. They had met when she was fourteen. Priscilla's stepfather was a captain in the US Air Force stationed with his family in Germany at the same time that Elvis was in the Army.

Priscilla was invited to Graceland for Christmas 1960 and then returned to

*Above: **Hundreds of statuettes of the King were turned out every month by the Zsolnay porcelain works in Hungary.***

*Below: **A bronze statue of Elvis got a public airing in London in 1981. It was valued at £25,000.***

Germany. Missing her, Elvis called her stepfather, and asked if she could finish her schooling in Memphis under his watchful eye. A year later he agreed, and she moved into Graceland in October 1962.

Elvis had proposed to Priscilla when she turned twenty-one on the insistence of Colonel Tom Parker. They married in Las Vegas and honeymooned in Palm Springs, California. They then moved into the West Coast Graceland in Beverly Hills. Nine months later their only child, Lisa Marie, was born.

Professionally, marriage gave Elvis new impetus. But in his private life he continued womanizing as before

---

Elvis slimmed down his staff, but that was the only change that the newly-wed star made to his personal life. His pill-popping continued at a destructive rate - as did his womanizing.

And author Albert Goldman says it was not long after the birth of Lisa Marie that Priscilla, fed up with Elvis's behaviour, got involved with another man: Elvis's friend and karate coach handsome Mike Stone.

But professionally, marriage seemed to give Elvis new impetus. He moved out of films and started recording and giving live shows again. On 31 July 1969 he started a sensational one-month engagement at the International Hotel in Las Vegas. He broke all attendance records: 161,500 people saw his show.

Touring again, he needed the amphetamines more than ever to call on his reserves of energy. As he put on weight, he took uppers to kill his appetite. Former body-guard Rick Stanley said: 'There were no half-measures. In 1972-73 he started getting into needles. That's when I really started to worry when he became a needle head. His body began to look like a pin cushion.'

Elvis was a stranger to moderation - once he started to inject his drugs his body quickly resembled a pincushion

---

Everything seemed to be booming for Elvis in the early 1970s. But the long tours of one-night stands brought him no great sense of fulfilment, although they did bring lots of cash. In 1974 he earned

Below: *Elvis in the film* **Change of Habit,** *in which he played a doctor who falls in love with a nurse.*

himself over $7 million gross. Of course he had to pay Colonel Tom his regular 50 per cent, but Elvis had a bizarre and extravagant life-style.

He bought fourteen Cadillacs in one night in Memphis and gave them away to friends, and then invited in an old Negro woman who happened to be passing to pick any car she fancied.

Said his old friend Jerry Shering: 'He still was not content. He loved performing live before a public, he liked being Elvis Presley and the adulation...'

In 1972 Priscilla could not take any more. Her affair with Mike Stone came out in the open. Elvis's drug-addled mind turned to murder. Says Goldman: 'When Priscilla finally asked for a divorce, Elvis was shattered. It wasn't so much the divorce itself, more devastation to his pride, the fact that the world could see that he was being rejected.'

Elvis sued for divorce and it was granted on 18 August 1973. When she told him that she was leaving, Priscilla explained to him: 'It's not that you've lost me for another man. You've lost me to a life of my own.' She was to go on to find stardom in the TV soap *Dallas*.

THE DRUGS TAKE OVER

As Elvis passed forty in January 1975 he literally ballooned. Living on a diet of junk food he lost control of his weight. He'd lost control of his drug-taking a long time before. He called it medication.

Nine days after his divorce came through he was admitted to the Baptist Memorial Hospital, officially for hypertension and headaches but in fact to be dried out.

At one time, Elvis was buying $4,000 worth of pills at a time. But his adoring public had no clue of his addiction until Elvis's father sacked bodyguards Sonny West, his cousin Red West and David Hebler. They co-authored a book called: *Elvis, What Happened?*

Published in 1977 just two weeks before his death, it revealed the full, shocking truth that had been hidden from the public for years. Said Hebler: 'No one forced the pills down Elvis's throat. It was the other way round...He was far from an unwilling victim. He demanded

drugs and he used pressure to get them.'

He was now sinking into a life of total debauchery. He ate only hamburgers, he was grotesquely heavy, and his last concerts were farcical. But the fans still loved him. Robert Hilburn of the *Los Angeles Times* wrote:

Blinded by love, cheered - instead of hooted - he strutted across the stage night after night in Las Vegas and in countless other cities in a glittery cape, 50 lb overweight and barely able to focus on the business at hand.

Elvis's bodily functions were so impaired by excessive drug-taking that his aides had to put nappies on him

---

Towards the end of 1976, Elvis had a new steady girlfriend - Ginger Alden, a runner-up in the Miss Tennessee beauty pageant. She was nineteen years younger than Elvis, and on 26 January 1977 she alleges they got engaged. Elvis proposed in the bathroom next to their bedroom, and gave her an 11½ carat diamond ring worth $60,000. They were due to be married, she said, on Christmas Day 1977. Elvis was never to make the date.

He was degenerating fast. His hair was dyed, and his mind and body were so mutilated by drugs that he had lost all control of his bodily functions and had to

be wrapped in nappies by his aides. He was regularly taken to hospital, needing treatment for an enlarged colon and a liver infection.

On 15 August 1977 Elvis played in the afternoon with daughter Lisa Marie who was staying for a fortnight's holiday. In the early evening he made an appointment with his dentist for himself and his girlfriend Ginger Alden. At 10.30 pm they arrived at his surgery. Ginger had X-rays, while Elvis had two fillings.

At 2.30 in the morning, after returning to Graceland, he stripped down to play two hours of energetic racquet-ball. At about 6.30am Elvis and Ginger retired to bed. At 9am she awoke briefly to find him still awake. Elvis told her that he was going into the bathroom to read.

Ginger said: 'Don't fall asleep.'

Elvis replied: 'OK, I won't.'

At about 2.20 in the afternoon she awoke and found that he had not returned. Calling 'Elvis' and getting no reply, she pushed open the bathroom door and found him on the carpeted floor, as if he had fallen from the black leather lavatory seat on which he had been reading.

His face was a grotesque purple mask. She told a reporter: 'I opened one of his eyes and it was just blood red.'

She called for Joe Esposito, Elvis's tour manager who tried to revive him. In the seven-minute ride to Baptist Memorial Hospital Elvis's personal doctor, Dr Nichopolous, kept on repeating: 'Breathe, Elvis. Come on, breathe. Please.' But it was no good. At 3.30pm Elvis was pronounced dead.

'Basically,' said the coroner, 'it was a natural death.' The illusion had to be preserved

---

Of the total of thirteen drugs found in his bloodstream one was merely an anti-histamine for nasal congestion and three - including morphine - had been created by the reactions of the ten that he had taken.

But within hours of his death the big cover-up started. Elvis's family, his sycophantic cronies, his doctors and Memphis itself were desperate to hide the truth about his last drug-filled hours.

Below: *Stepmother Dee Presley shocked the world with her book* **Elvis We Love You Tender** *in 1980.*

Despite the torrent of drugs in his bloodstream the verdict was Natural Death. Dr Jerry Francisco, the Memphis State Medical Examiner, said that death had been caused by an erratic heartbeat - 'cardiac arrythmia'.

It was two years later before the full extent of the cover-up was revealed when Dr 'Nick', who had so desperately tried to bring Elvis back to life, was charged with malpractice.

Tennessee public health inspector Steve Belsky said: 'Elvis Presley, from my experience, was issued more scheduled uppers, downers and amphetamines than any other individual that I have ever seen.'

Throughout the world Elvis's fans went into mourning after his death. Colonel Tom Parker immediately rang the grief-stricken Vernon Presley and made sure that he could continue acting for Elvis's estate. He went on to make Elvis richer in death than in life.

Close friends were allowed to see the bloated figure of Elvis 'lying in state' and hundreds of thousands attended the private funeral service conducted at Graceland. The confusion was so great that two mourners were run over by a car and killed.

The King was finally laid to rest beside the adored mother who was responsible for so much

---

Elvis's body was buried in Forest Hill cemetery, but after a body-snatching attempt and because of the large numbers of fans who came to visit his grave he was brought back to Graceland and laid to rest in the Meditation Gardens beside his beloved mother. On her gravestone Elvis had written: 'She was the sunshine of our home.'

Sex pervert? Drug addict? Narcissistic comic-book macho-man smothered by mother-love? Whatever the shocking truth and hidden secrets of Elvis Aron Presley, no one can ever deny him his title: the King.

Below: *Millions of fans pay homage to Elvis at his grave and the graves of his parents.*

JOYCE McKINNEY
A Story of Obsession

In 1977 the story of Joyce McKinney was Britain's No.1 headline-hitting scandal. Obsessed by a clean-living young Mormon missionary, she chased him across the Atlantic, kidnapped him and bound him in chains while she indulged her erotic passions

An alien visiting Britain in 1977 might have been forgiven for thinking that Joyce McKinney was the most important person on the planet. It was a rare day indeed during the final months of that year when you could buy a newspaper, turn on a radio or TV or walk into a pub and not read, hear, see or talk about the blonde with the infectious smile who had captivated the land.

Above: *Kirk Anderson, the object of Joyce McKinney's bizarre desires carries his Bible out of court in Epsom, Surrey in 1977.*

Opposite: *Joyce McKinney is driven away from court in tears and behind bars, suddenly the most written-about woman of the year.*

Left: *Hippie girl Joyce, the flower-power child, reveals the sensuous side of her character.*

On one day the *Daily Mail*, perhaps sensing that its own readership was suffering from McKinney overkill, ran a headline claiming it was 'the only paper WITHOUT Joyce McKinney'! But it was a short-lived break from the American woman whose lust for a young Mormon missionary called Kirk Anderson held gossip-hungry Britain spellbound.

STRICT UPBRINGING

Joyce McKinney was born in Minneapolis, North Carolina, in August 1950. Her father, Davies, was principal of an elementary school and her mother, Maxine, a former teacher of English there. Little Joyce's life was orderly and strict. She began the day with prayers and ended it the same way, and by the time she was four she could recite huge tracts of the Bible by heart. She attended Christian Bible Camp every summer.

By the time she was four the young Joyce could recite huge tracts of the Bible by heart

Her mother remembers her: 'Joyce had high morals. As she grew older she never smoked, drank or used any kind of drug. And if any boy tried to kiss her she would tell him off in no uncertain way. Never did I think she would blossom from tomboy into beauty queen.'

But blossom she did, and the Joyce McKinney who sang lustily in choir soon found her lust directed towards men. She won a beauty contest and her 38-24-36 figure was soon provoking admiring glances from many red-blooded men.

THE START OF AN OBSESSION

After graduating from the University of North Carolina, with a degree in science she moved to Brigham Young University in Utah, the heartland of the Mormon Church. Having met a Mormon family, Joyce thought she would find her own spiritual fulfilment at the stronghold town of the faith. 'What I found, though, was that I was having to fight guys off all the time to keep my virginity,' she said.

In July 1975 she met the man who was

Above: *Joyce at a London party with wild man of rock Keith Moon, drummer with The Who.*

spot. I turned to my girlfriend there and then and said: 'Hey, get out - I'm in love!'...He kissed me and it was bombs, firecrackers, the Fourth of July.

The man was Kirk Anderson, and within two years he would be kidnapped, sexually assaulted by her and forced to testify at one of the strangest criminal proceedings Britain has ever witnessed.

After that first meeting it seems that Joyce became obsessed beyond reason with the young Mormon. They made love and enjoyed dating each other, but there was pressure from the Church that made Anderson end the relationship.

His calling within the Church called for chastity, and he saw his bishop to confess his dilemma. He was advised to break off the affair.

'He kissed me, and it was bombs, firecrackers and the Fourth of July'

He saw Joyce for one last tearful time, and then flew to Britain in 1976 to embark on his work of spreading the word of his Church. Joyce meanwhile flew to Hollywood in a fruitless attempt at breaking into showbusiness.

In Tinsel Town she soon tasted the bitter fruits of frustration and rejection. She moved into an apartment with Steve Moskowitz in October 1976 after meeting him at a Hollywood party. He recalled: 'She looked beautiful and I wondered why she had no man with her. But when we began talking she told me about this guy Kirk Anderson, and I soon realized from the way she was going on about him that there was no other person for her...although I desired her like mad there was nothing sexual between us because of her love for Kirk.'

Moskowitz was perhaps the first person to realize the massive obsession growing inside her for Anderson. He went on:

Her whole life centred around meeting him again and getting him away from the grip of the Mormons. In February 1977 she got 15,000 dollars in compensation for some slight injuries she received in a car crash. She realized that at last she had the money to carry out her plan - to go to England and be with him.

to become her obsession - an obsession that would lead to her amazing collision with the full majesty of British law.

She had bought herself a new Stingray Corvette car and was trying it out around town with her girlfriend. She said:

We had pulled up outside of an ice cream parlour...when a white Corvette with a sandy-haired boy at the wheel pulled in beside us. He got out, came over to my car, and asked to drive. He leaned through the window, and I found myself gazing into the deepest pair of baby-blue eyes. He put Paul Newman to shame. My heart did flip-flops on the

...She told me her first aim in England was to give Kirk 'a sexual experience that he would never forget'. She started building up a collection of porno books and I had to take her to porno movies because she wanted to examine sex techniques.

'I had to take her to porno movies,' said Moskowitz, 'because she wanted to examine sex techniques'

After placing a bizarre ad. in a newspaper asking for a 'muscleman, a pilot and a preacher' to help her in a 'romantic adventure', Joyce teamed up with an impressionable, quiet-spoken trainee architect called Keith May.

May, who was twenty-two when he entered into this extraordinary plot with the twenty-seven-year-old Joyce, later admitted he was besotted with her. He said: 'I was floored by her looks and admit I would have done anything for her. I know she only wanted this Anderson guy, but I secretly hoped she would eventually fall in love with me.'

Joyce told May that Anderson secretly loved her but was unable to break free of the influence of the Mormon church. So she could - with the aid of her newly recruited sidekick - do nothing except break those bonds of the Church herself.

THE CRAZY PLOT UNFOLDS

The couple flew to England where they rented a room at a house in Hendon, North London - the base for her 'mission' for Kirk. On 14 September 1977 the whole twisted plot was set in motion.

The twenty-one-year-old missionary was based at the Church of the Latter Day Saints at Ewell in Surrey. Emerging from the church that evening, he was confronted by Joyce and May - May was brandishing a fake revolver. Later, at a pre-trial hearing McKinney was charged with kidnapping, entering Britain on a false passport and possession of fake firearms. Anderson testified that he was bundled off before awakening the following day in a strange bedroom.

He told Epsom magistrates' court in October of that year:

I felt May, who was using the name Bob Bosler, push something into my ribs and he grabbed my shoulder. I was startled and as I looked down I saw it was a gun. I was quite scared. He told me to come with him. I did not know then that the gun was an imitation.

He took me to a car parked about fifty yards away. I got into the rear seat. Joyce was in the front seat wearing a dark wig and she had another gun. I thought that was real too. She said something like how did I think eight thousand miles of ocean was going to keep us apart, or something to that effect. She got into the back seat with me and told me to put my head down. He told her to put a blanket over my head so I could not see where I was going.

Was Kirk Anderson a willing sex slave, or a rape victim in fur-lined manacles?

When I was allowed to remove the blanket I saw I was inside a garage and I was taken to a house adjoining it. I had no idea where I was. I was taken to the bedroom and allowed to sit while Joyce cooked some dinner...She told me she still loved me and wanted to marry me. She said I could be there for two or three months and she said she intended that we could just be together from that time onward. I spent that night with Joyce in the same room although nothing of a physical nature took place...The next day Bob Bosler - Keith May - placed a leather strap attached to a chain on my leg and he attached the chain to the bed. It was about ten foot long so I could in fact move off the bed but not very far. He said he had to chain me for her

Top: *The bed where Joyce's alleged sexual assault on the manacled missionary took place.*

Above: *The holiday cottage of Lower Holstock Farm, Devon where bespectacled Mormon Kirk Anderson was held.*

protection...Joyce told me if there was to be a ransom the ransom would be that I gave her a baby.

For the next ninety-six hours Kirk Anderson was either a willing sex slave to Joyce McKinney - or the prisoner of an obsessed woman who bound him in fur-lined manacles before ripping off his 'chastity vest' to force herself upon him.

The case ended up before Epsom magistrates' court because Anderson eventually escaped.

REVELATIONS IN COURT

The normally staid court was used to hearing speeding offences and burglaries - not the excitable outpourings of a woman who, as she told them, 'would have skied down Everest, backwards, with a carnation up my nose for him.'

During the committal proceedings journalists filled notebook after notebook with the lurid allegations. Anderson told how she manacled him and performed oral sex on him, how she begged him to marry her and how she dressed up in kinky clothes. She said she did it all for him.

When McKinney took the stand there were even more shocks in store. She said she had been made pregnant by the young missionary the first time they had met, but that she had miscarried.

In court McKinney described the kidnapping of Anderson as 'three days of fun, food and sex'

Describing the cottage affair as nothing more than 'three days of fun, food and sex', she went on:

My standards were quite high...I don't smoke, drink or use drugs. I wanted

someone who could read the Bible with me and have a family with me. I prayed for a very special boy to come into my life - and that is where Kirk comes in.

He was afraid of excommunication from the Church and that is why all these lies are coming in...

How could an eight-stone girl rape an eighteen-stone six-foot-two-inch man? His legs are as big round as my waist. Kirk wanted a holiday from his mission, with sex and food, but he had to go back and face his Church president. Kirk says I tempted him. He told Epsom police I was wearing a skin-tight leopard-skin jump-suit. I had black jeans with a scruffy-sleeved top - which has about as much sex appeal as a potato sack.

Referring to the bonds which secured him to the bed, McKinney said matter-of-factly that he had a hang-up about sex, and could not be satisfied until he was chained up.

THE LADY VANISHES

After two weeks it was decided that there was enough evidence to press for a full criminal trial for McKinney and May. But by granting them bail the magistrates ensured that they would never be seen in Britain again.

The trial was set at the Old Bailey for 2 May, but in April - posing as nuns - McKinney and May fled to Eire and from there to Toronto and New York. They kept up their disguises until she was back

in North Carolina. A storm of protest followed their vanishing act in England. There was bitter criticism of the bail system which allowed them to go free, and of inadequate immigration checks.

But since they had been dressed as nuns - and convincing nuns at that - there seemed little point in initiating a witch-hunt among the authorities.

A year later, in July 1979, she and May were tracked down to a caravan park in North Carolina by an FBI special agent, and they were charged with making false passport applications. But there was no attempt to bring them back to England.

Joyce received a £700 fine for her false passport application, and resurfaced in the news five years later when she was arrested outside the Salt Lake City, Utah, workplace of her unrequited love Anderson. She was ordered to undergo psychiatric tests but said: 'I love him...I will always love him.'

The world of scandal awaits to see what her next move will be.

Left: *Joyce celebrates her freedom with her parents. She slipped out of England dressed as a nun.*

Below: *Joyce McKinney's creed was: 'I believe you should give a man what he wants. What Kirk wanted I was willing to do.'*

ROCK HUDSON
A Secret Life

The hunky heart-throb screen star was gay, but kept his double life secret from his fans for decades. When Rock Hudson got AIDS, however, the truth could be concealed no longer

Right: *Rock Hudson with actor and singer Burl Ives.*

Right: *Rock Hudson with actor and singer Burl Ives.*

Just a few months after he had been forced to admit his innermost secret to a stunned world, Rock Hudson, the most dashing silver screen hero of his time, succumbed to AIDS at his stately Beverly Hills home. It was 2 October 1985 - and the day he died.

For almost forty years his fans had revered him as an indestructible, manly love god coveted by women and envied by men the world over.

The truth, however, was a far cry from his screen image. He was a homosexual, whose craving for taboo sex shattered forever his carefully crafted public persona and eventually cost him his life.

It was a secret that Rock had hoped to take to the grave with him. If it had not been for the effects of the disease, his wish might have been fulfilled.

Had it not been for the ravages of AIDS, Rock might have taken the secret of his homosexuality to the grave with him

---

But in the final weeks, not even he could hide the truth from outsiders any longer. His face was gaunt and ravaged. And his once strapping physique had been stripped to the bone.

But Rock did manage to hide the truth from most of the world - including his lover Marc Christian - for a full year.

It had begun as an irritation on his neck that refused to go away. But within a year, after going to a doctor in June

Opposite: *Rock Hudson shares a publicity cuddle with fellow film star Doris Day in 1960. He was one of the world's most popular actors.*

Below: *The tragic truth about Hudson's sexual preferences was a far cry from his screen image.*

1984, Rock was stunned by the truth. It was the first sign of Kaposi's sarcoma, a cancer that afflicts AIDS patients.

Yet the star refused to reveal his affliction to anyone but his most trusted confidants, including his long-time secretary Mark Miller.

Two months after the diagnosis, the dying star travelled to France for the Deauville Film Festival and a retrospective of his life in films. On the advice of his Hollywood doctor, Rock stopped first in Paris to begin an experimental treatment course with the drug HPA-23.

But his desperate bid for a cure failed, and by November his appearance had altered dramatically. At his fifty-ninth birthday party, which Christian hosted at their Hollywood love nest, guests couldn't help but notice the dramatic change in Rock's appearance.

He was drawn and weary. 'I've been on a diet,' he explained.

THE GAY YOUNG STAR

Of course, the world would soon know that his excuse was a lie. But then lying came easy to Rock, even when he was known as Roy Fitzgerald, one-time truck driver, vacuum cleaner salesman and Navy veteran, who had left his home town of Winnetka, Illinois for a crack at the bright lights of Hollywood.

Rock had been an only child growing

up in the Depression, the son of a car mechanic who left his young family when Rock was a small child. Young Roy grew up with a mother he adored and a stepfather he did not.

Although a popular lad, he maintained few ties to the town after he departed for the Navy and, later, Hollywood. That was in 1946, and the lonely, would-be actor would stand outside the gates of the movie studios hoping to be discovered.

Eventually, of course, he was discovered - but not outside a film lot. The following year, the twenty-two-year-old hopeful had gravitated to the gay community of nearby Long Beach. It was through this close-knit homosexual circle that he met Henry Willson, the legendary talent scout for the David O. Selznick Studio.

According to Hollywood lore Willson, who was also a homosexual, renamed his latest discovery for the Rock of Gibraltar and the Hudson River.

After Hudson shot to stardom, he could not even be seen dining out with his gay partner for fear of scandal

---

From the very beginning of his career, Hudson projected one image in front of the camera and another away from it, and went to extreme lengths to cover up his homosexuality in public. He and his two best friends at the time, George Nader - another struggling actor - and Mark Miller even developed code words so they could talk freely in public.

The charade fooled the public, but those working with Rock knew his secret.

'We all knew Rock was gay, but it never made any difference to us,' recalled Mamie Van Doren, a sexy starlet who was one of many young actresses to go on arranged dates with Hudson.

By 1953, when Rock had already appeared in several films but had not yet climbed the rung to stardom, he met and fell madly in love with Jack Navaar. Even though the two soon moved in together, Hudson could never show any public affection for Navaar.

The ruse would take its toll on the affair, especially in 1954 when Rock starred in *Magnificent Obsession*, the film which made him a headline star.

Above: *Hudson with Sophia Loren and Ruth Leunerik at a German film awards ceremony in 1962.*

Right: *Sexy Italian star Gina Lollobrigida regularly starred opposite Rock Hudson. They are seen here throwing grapes during a Hollywood party.*

Now firmly in the public eye, the actor could no longer even go out to dinner with Navaar. Inevitably, the romance ended within twelve months.

To safeguard his reputation as an all-American film hunk, Rock did not live with another man for ten years.

Despite carefully crafted smoke screens, however, in 1955 the scandal sheet *Confidential* was rumoured to be preparing an expose on the star's taboo lifestyle. Instead, Universal made a deal with the magazine: it traded information on Hudson for dirt on a lesser-known actor - his friend George Nader.

A MARRIAGE OF CONVENIENCE

The brush with scandal, however, had been too close for the studio executives. In a bid to silence any further whispers about Rock's sexual orientation, they hastily arranged a wedding between him and his agent's secretary, Phyllis Gates.

The ceremony took place on 9 November and went ahead even though neither Rock nor the studio bothered to tell Gates that he was gay.

It wasn't until the very end of their marriage, which lasted almost three years, that she even discovered Rock was a homosexual. Years later, after the star's death, she would also recall that he sometimes beat her - probably out of his inner rage at the studio-organized scam.

For much of the 1960s he continued his lusty adventures unabated, taking numerous lovers. Thanks to loyal friends, there wasn't even a hint of scandal...until the early 1970s when a callous jokester almost damaged his career and reputation beyond repair.

Rock sometimes beat Phyllis, probably because he was furious that the studio had forced him into marriage

---

The malicious prankster had sent out wedding invitations, inviting several noted show business columnists to attend the 'marriage' of Rock and his good friend singer/actor Jim Nabors.

It was an unfounded hoax, and even though Hudson's career was not damaged Nabors wasn't so lucky. Soon afterwards his top-rating television variety series was cancelled.

Rock's superstar status, the fact that he did not flaunt his homosexual lifestyle in public and his reputation for being 'a good soldier' for the studio saved him when other gay actors floundered.

But the Nabors tragedy did take its toll psychologically, and Rock became even more paranoid about his gay lifestyle. He came to shun nights out on the town, preferring to entertain at his Beverly Hills estate, nicknamed 'The Castle'.

By the mid-1970s Rock was limiting most of his acting to the stage, until he was offered the lead role as Police Commissioner McMillan in *McMillan and Wife*. It was filmed in San Francisco, the so-called 'Gay Capital of America'.

Here, at last, Rock found a sanctuary. With his closest friends he frequented gay discos and bars, and revelled in the more liberal climate. He became more confident in his homosexuality, so much

so that some confidants urged him to tell the world he was gay.

But Hudson refused, for business as well as personal reasons. He believed that movie-goers weren't ready to imagine that their leading man often rode off into the sunset with another man.

Hudson felt movie-goers weren't ready to be told that their favourite leading man had his own favourite leading man

---

By this time Rock was living again with a lover - publicist Tom Clark. Clark was a far cry from the pretty-faced men he usually courted. But he enjoyed the same hobbies of football, cooking and travelling as Rock did, and became the great love of the star's life. For the first time ever, Hudson could now actually take a man with him anywhere he wished - Tom had become the actor's manager.

'I can even introduce him to Princess Margaret,' Rock once boasted to friends.

Below: *Rock Hudson and Claudia Cardinale starred in the 1965 movie* **Blindfold.** *She was one of a string of pretty actresses he made movie love to.*

Although Rock was deeply in love with Clark, that didn't stop him from having what he called 'beauties' parties'. A dozen or so of the couple's closest friends would be invited, as well as up to fifty stunning young men for orgies.

After over-indulgence with sex and alcohol, Hudson suddenly had to reassess his life when he needed heart by-pass surgery

---

By 1977, however, Rock began his four-year slide into near-oblivion. Worried about his age and faltering career, he took to the bottle. But in 1981 his wild lifestyle came to a sobering end. He had to have heart by-pass surgery.

The operation had another effect, recalled old friend George Nader: 'He woke up from the drunkenness of the 1970s. The meanness and sniping fell

Below: Live on stage... Hudson and Juliet Prowse in I Do! I Do! a musical at London's Phoenix Theatre in 1975.

Below right: Rock and Juliet at the first night party of I Do! I Do!

away, and he was returning to the Rock we had known in 1952 - a warm human being who laughed and played games.'

ENTER MARC CHRISTIAN

But the actor had grown tired of Tom Clark, and the year after his operation began his last serious affair. The object of his affection was a younger, more virile man, Marc Christian.

Rock had met the twenty-nine-year-old Marc in October 1982 at a charity do in Los Angeles. 'I gave him my phone number, but he didn't call for three weeks,' Christian recalled years later. 'Finally he asked me out on a date. That date led to another. He was a true gentleman - it took quite a few dates before he even tried to kiss me.'

But early in the spring of 1985, Christian's good life came to an end. Hudson began to see less of him, as constant battles with flu and fatigue kept the actor frequently bedridden.

He had been diagnosed as having AIDS a year earlier, but Marc was left in the dark. 'That's when Rock began to lead a true double life,' said Christian.

Although Hudson's appearance began to change - he became dramatically thin - his appeal as a leading man did not. *Dynasty* creator Esther Shapiro successfully approached him to join the cast of the soap opera as a love interest for Linda Evans' character, Krystle.

But even when he did that now-famous scene in which he kissed Evans, Hudson refused to tell her he had AIDS.

In July 1985 Rock flew to Paris for more treatments, but he passed out in his

about Rock's disease until 'I heard it on the 6 o'clock news', was not allowed in to see him because Mark Miller had compiled a visitors' roster without his name on it.

But a few days later Marc confronted Miller in person and was finally given permission to see his ailing lover.

His lover Marc Christian was not allowed to see Rock in hospital

---

Marc recalled:

I asked him, 'Why didn't you tell me you had AIDS?' He avoided giving me a direct answer. There is no answer to that question. He said, 'When you have this disease, you're all alone.' I told him, 'You're wrong. You know that if you'd told me you had AIDS, I'd have helped you to get treatment...' He just looked at the wall and didn't say anything.

Eventually Rock went home...there was nothing doctors could do for him. When he could, he would take short walks beside his pool.

Although he had been raised a Catholic, Rock had let his religious beliefs slip. But on 25 September, a priest visited him at the estate.

The star made his confession and received Communion. Then he was administered the last rites. His once-strapping frame was deathly thin and covered with lesions and bed sores.

The day before he died, Elizabeth Taylor paid a visit, but Rock, who was being fed from an intravenous drip, was slipping into a coma.

The following morning, Rock awoke early and was dressed by a nurse. But Clark, who had returned to the estate to watch over his dying friend, didn't think Rock was well enough to get up. So he undressed him and put him back in bed.

Some thirty minutes later, Rock Hudson was dead.

WHAT PRICE LOYALTY?

But his greatest dread, that his fans would desert him once they knew the shocking truth, never did come to pass. Instead, they responded to his plight with sympathy, and a curiosity about this still-

suite at the Ritz Hotel. Finally, it was decided that Rock was too weak even to undergo another AIDS treatment, so the actor decided to return to Los Angeles. But before he did, it was at last announced to the world, on 25 July, that the ageing heart-throb had AIDS. The decision finally to tell the truth, confidants recalled, was Hudson's alone.

'The hardest thing I ever had to do in my life was to walk into his room and read him the press release,' said one of them. 'I'll never forget the look on his face...In his eyes was the realization that he was destroying his own image.'

When Hudson returned to Los Angeles, he came in the middle of the night aboard a chartered 747 jet from which he was removed on a stretcher. He was transferred by helicopter to hospital, where a procession of close friends, including Elizabeth Taylor, Carol Burnett and Tony Perkins later came to visit him.

Yet Christian, who had not known

Above: A moustached Hudson takes a break during the filming in Italy of **Il Vespaio - The Wasps Nest.**

Above: *Period piece... Elizabeth Taylor and Kim Novak were Hudson's co-stars in* **The Mirror Crack'd** *made in 1981.*

mysterious disease. On the day he died, the US House of Representatives passed a bill allocating almost $200 million for AIDS research in the following year. And Elizabeth Taylor galvanized Hollywood and the world into action with her plea: 'Please God, he did not die in vain.'

Rock's death at last made AIDS a front-page issue around the world

---

Of course, he did not. The revelation of his illness did much to spur on the fight against AIDS, as the disease finally moved to the front pages of newspapers around the globe.

That all meant little to Christian, however, who received nothing in the actor's will. Reportedly, Rock left the bulk of his estimated $27 million estate to Miller and George Nader.

But later that year Marc filed a claim against Rock's estate, saying he 'would not have risked death by continuing to engage in sexual relations with Hudson' had he known about the disease.

His attorney, famed divorce lawyer Marvin Mitchelson, categorized it as 'the most unpleasant lawsuit I've ever been involved with.'

In February 1989 a jury ruled that Rock was in fact guilty of 'outrageous conduct' for concealing his AIDS diagnosis from Christian, although he did not contract AIDS. Hudson's estate appealed, but in June 1991, an appeals court upheld his $5 million award.

Despite the rancour surrounding his final days, Rock Hudson is still considered one of Hollywood's brightest lights. His public, the fans he thought he could not trust with his deepest secret, remain as loyal to his memory as they were before. Rock had underestimated them - but they forgave him for that, too.

BIZARRE
AND
ECCENTRIC

PALACE INTRUDER
A Royal Audience

Despite security precautions at Buckingham Palace, the Queen of England was disturbed by an intruder as she lay in bed. How did a painter and decorator called Michael Fagan come to be chatting to his monarch as she desperately tried to summon assistance?

Buckingham Palace stands as more than a royal home in London - it is the essence of the monarchy, a symbol that draws hundreds of thousands of visitors a year.

Its imposing gates, and the high wrought-iron railings and barbed wire running along the perimeter walls of the garden are the visible guardians. Unseen are pressure pads, infra-red beams, attack dogs and police and military guards.

Yet every line of defence failed when an unhinged decorator called Michael Fagan decided he would visit his Queen in her bedroom. His break-in ranks as one of the most astonishing stories in the history of the British monarchy.

THE WRONG SIDE OF THE TRACKS

Michael Fagan was born at Paddington General Hospital on 8 August 1950 and was named after his building contractor father. His mother, Ivy, looked after their home on a run-down housing estate built after the war.

At first he seemed a bright boy, but that early promise waned at the tough Sir Philip Magnus secondary school near King's Cross, where he played truant and left at fifteen with no qualifications. Fagan drifted into a succession of handyman and decorating jobs.

In 1972 he married a Welsh girl called Christine, who already had two children by different fathers.

Over the next few years Fagan fathered four more children. Social workers' reports hinted at drug use by Fagan. But while his somewhat quirky lifestyle aroused their concern over his children's safety, there was never any evidence that he was abusive towards them.

Fagan and his bride existed on unemployment and supplementary benefits and child allowances. They moved twelve times in ten years.

The marriage began breaking up about two years before his palace 'visit'. There were angry scenes between him and Christine, which sometimes ended with her leaving the flat with the children. Ivy would console Michael and clean up the flat, which degenerated into squalor whenever he was left to his own devices.

In 1980 the Fagans' marriage started breaking up and Christine walked out on several occasions

---

On 26 June 1982, thirteen days before he broke into the Palace, he traced his wife to a sordid squat in Islington, North London. After angry scenes he was charged with assaulting his stepson.

But while he languished on remand in Brixton Prison he was visited by Christine and they made up.

Opposite: Michael Fagan, a no-hoper in trouble with the law, made his way one morning to the bed chamber of Her Majesty Queen Elizabeth II. He turned the knob and stepped inside...

Drop in opposite: Michael Fagan on his way to court.

Below: The grounds of Buckingham Palace are ringed by high walls and railings, trigger alarms, infra-red beams, attack dogs, police and military guards. Michael Fagan evaded them all.

But nobody knew that three weeks before the Islington showdown Fagan had been on a secret mission - an undiscovered break-in at Buckingham Palace! On 7 June security in London was allegedly tighter than a thumbscrew for a visit by President Reagan, yet he had scaled the fence undetected.

THE UNINVITED GUEST

Michael Fagan's second, more famous climb occurred in the early hours of Friday 9 July. As he hauled himself over the iron railings, he was seen by an off-duty policeman. The officer alerted his superiors, who immediately instigated a search - but without success.

Fagan first gained entry to the Palace itself through an open window on the ground floor, but the inner doors of the room he entered were locked so he climbed out again. Little did he know that the room housed the Royal Stamp Collection worth £14 million!

After shinning up a drainpipe and walking along a narrow ledge, he peeled back some wire netting to squeeze through a window into the office of the Master of the Household. The window had been opened only minutes earlier by a housemaid. Through this stroke of luck he had penetrated the heart of the Palace.

In his climb Fagan had triggered one of the infra-red alarms, but a policeman in the Palace switched it off, thinking it was a malfunction.

For the next fifteen minutes Fagan wandered unchallenged through the corridors and rooms of Buckingham Palace. He was seen by a maid who didn't think his behaviour was suspicious, so she did not report him.

Later he told police that he found his way to the private apartments by 'following the pictures' by Rembrandt, Turner and others which cover the Palace walls. Before he entered the Queen's bedroom he went into an ante-room and smashed a glass ashtray, cutting his hand.

At 7.15am, clutching a jagged piece of glass from the broken ashtray, he gingerly turned the knob on the Queen's door and let himself in.

The Queen was awoken as Fagan stepped across the floor to the heavy curtains and thrust them aside, letting the sun flood into the room.

What thoughts raced through Her Majesty's mind as she saw the sock-clad prowler, glass in his bloodied hand, can only be guessed at. She has never spoken publicly about the incident.

But it is a measure of her character that she remained level-headed and calm when many people would have screamed. The one thing she could not afford to do with the staring-eyed stranger was to lose her head or antagonize him.

What thoughts raced through Her Majesty's mind as she looked up from her bed and saw the prowler?

The Queen, well rehearsed in emergency procedures by the Royal Protection Squad officers who guard her, pressed the night bell connected to the police sentry on duty in the corridor outside. But at 6am the police sergeant - in accordance with Scotland Yard instructions - had left for the night.

The footman who would normally have been outside was away exercising the Queen's corgis, while a maid was vacuuming in another room.

Fagan sat at the edge of her bed in filthy jeans and a tattered T-shirt. What the Queen didn't know then was the plan that had gelled in Fagan's disturbed mind

Below: *Police guarding the Queen were slammed for their mistakes. Security at the Palace has since been improved.*

after he had smashed the ashtray. 'He intended to commit suicide on the Queen's bed,' said the police report.

The Queen pretended she wanted a cigarette - a habit she abhorred - and asked Fagan if he would like one. He replied that he would, and she then rang through to the Palace switchboard operator with a request that a policeman should bring her some.

Fagan later told his lawyer, Maurice Nadeem: 'We talked about our children. She told me she has a son called Charles who had a baby with Princess Diana. She said I must be very proud of my four children, that it would not be right for me to kill myself and leave them without a father. She was so kind to think of me in a situation like that.'

The first call went unanswered for six minutes. Her Majesty was furious. Everyone in the Palace knew that she did not smoke - so why on earth should she be ordering cigarettes from the privacy of her bedroom? She apologised to Fagan and phoned again, asking why her previous call had been ignored.

Chambermaid Elizabeth Andrews then entered the Queen's bedroom after cleaning in the other room, and is said to have greeted the Queen with the immortal words: 'Bloody 'ell ma'am! What's he doing in here?'

The Queen politely told her maid that Mr Fagan wanted a cigarette, and together they led him into a pantry where a footman came and chatted to him.

'Bloody 'ell, ma'am!' cried the chambermaid. 'What's he doing here?'

Within another two minutes first one, then another, police officer arrived and Fagan was led away. The nightmare had lasted less than a quarter of an hour.

AFTER THE EVENT

That there had been an appalling series of blunders was plain for all to see. A harshly worded internal Scotland Yard report laid the blame squarely at the door of the police.

Home Secretary William Whitelaw concurred, adding: 'It was an appalling

Top: *The Queen demonstrated her usual composure when the intruder walked across her bedroom to the curtains*

Above: *Fagan, who arrived wild-eyed at the Queen's bedside...clutching a jagged piece of glass from a broken ashtray.*

lapse of security. The Queen handled the intrusion with great composure.'

Assistant Police Commissioner John Dellow said: 'The cause of the breakdown of security was a failure by police to respond efficiently. If police officers had been alert Fagan would have been apprehended well before he got close to the private apartments.'

The unbalanced Fagan understandably was not prosecuted for the intrusion into the Queen's inner sanctum, and he was acquitted of stealing wine during the first trespass. However he still faced prior charges of assault and theft of a car, for which he served time in a mental institution until 1983.

His only public comment on his 'royal audience' was through a statement, read out by his lawyer, in which he dismissed speculation that the monarch's life was threatened. He never took up Fleet Street newspapers' offers to pay him thousands of pounds to hear his tale of a morning with the Queen.

JUNGLE SOLDIERS
The War that Went On

World War II ended in 1945, a fact that some Japanese soldiers never discovered. Fanatically loyal to their Emperor, they hid in the jungle for decades rather than risk the disgrace of capture

They were the descendants of the Knights of Bushido - Samurai warriors who excelled in war and knew no other life. Their creed was one of total obedience to their Emperor, their earthly mission none other than duty and death. Capture to them was the ultimate disgrace before Emperor and God, the humiliation that would brand them forever in the eyes of those whom they held in esteem - friends, family, officers, priests.

Such was the mentality of the average Japanese soldier in World War II - soldiers who fought to the death in their hundreds of thousands, or fell upon their own swords, rather than fly the white flag of surrender to the Allied forces.

For the Americans in particular, whose Marine Corps, Navy and Air Force crews

Above: US soldiers wade ashore from a landing craft onto a Japanese-held Pacific island.

Opposite: On 9 August, 1945 the United States dropped the world's second-only atomic device on the Japanese city of Nagasaki.

Below: The Japanese city of Osaka was devastated by American air raids as World War II drew to a close.

performed stupendous feats clearing the Pacific islands of the invaders, the names of places like Iwo Jima, Tarawa and Guadalcanal are written in blood on their memories. The Japanese turned these placid atolls into impregnable redoubts where every inch of sand was contested.

Thank God, said those who had lived through it, that it was all over in August 1945 when the Japanese Emperor Hirohito told his people to 'endure the unendurable' and lay down their arms in surrender.

But there were many soldiers who did not hear - and therefore could not heed - the call to surrender. For years afterwards they lived in the jungles and bush of the South Pacific and Indonesia, their Imperial Army uniforms reduced to rags on their backs, existing only to carry on the struggle against the Allies.

These men knew nothing of atom bombs which blasted apart their cities, nor the fire raids on Tokyo which levelled the metropolis. In their tropical lairs they did not know of a signed surrender on the USS *Missouri* in Tokyo Bay, nor of the occupation of their homeland. They slept at dusk and rose every day at dawn in the belief that the war was still going on.

Rumours of this lost legion of soldiers echoed down the years. Trappers in remote Philippine villages heard the tales of the 'devil men' living like jungle beasts in dens. In Indonesia they talked

大阪

*Above: **General Yoshira Umeza** signs the surrender documents on behalf of the Japanese Imperial Headquarters on the **USS Missouri** in Tokyo Bay on 1 September 1945.*

*Right: **The Allied Supremo General Douglas MacArthur** towers beside Japan's **Emperor Hirohito**. MacArthur remained effective ruler of Japan until 1950.*

A WORLD OF CONCEALMENT

It was on 14 October, 1944 that time froze for Masashi, Private 1st Class in the Army of His Imperial Highness the Emperor of Japan. He bent down to tie his bootlaces on a military road on the island as his comrades marched ahead...straight into an ambush sprung by Australian troops. As the sound of gunfire crackled through the undergrowth Masashi made a dive for the foliage with his comrade, Corporal Iroki Minakawa.

Over and over they rolled as the gunfire and sound of grenades echoed through the undergrowth. It was the start of their incredible sixteen-year game of hide-and-seek with the outside world.

For the first two months the private and the corporal existed on emergency rations and grubs that they scavenged from the forest floor. They drank rainwater collected in banana leaves, chewed the roots of edible plants for fibre, and occasionally dined on snakes caught in traps which they fashioned with wire from their backpacks and twigs.

During this early stage in their jungle exile they were hunted by Allied soldiers and later by native Chamorra aborigines with their wild dogs. At night they fashioned primitive hides and developed a new language - tongue clicks and hand signs which they considered the only safe form of communication.

They established a series of animal-like hides dug into the forest floor and covered with foliage. They lined the floor with dried grass and planted sharpened stakes in pits nearby to trap food.

To avoid being overheard by Allied troops they developed a language of tongue clicks and silent gestures

---

For an astonishing eight years they lived a nomadic existence.

Masashi later said: *During this harsh period we would often stumble across many other groups of Japanese soldiers who, like ourselves, had never given up the struggle. We felt sure that our generals had only made a tactical withdrawal and would one day come back with reinforcements.*

of the 'yellow ones' still roaming the dense undergrowth. The West, with its own problems of reconstruction, ignored these reports and they had adopted the aura of folk legends.

In 1961, however, sixteen years after the fall of Japan, a soldier named Ito Masashi emerged from the tropical jungles of Guam to surrender. Like a man emerging from some cocooned sleep, Masashi could not believe that the world he believed in so forcefully in 1945 no longer existed.

He had spent his years in hiding sure in the knowledge that his Emperor still needed him and that it was only a matter of time before his comrades came back for him.

We sometimes made fires but there was always the danger of the natives spotting them. The Japanese soldiers either died of starvation or disease, or were attacked and killed by the natives. I knew I had to stay alive because it was my duty to do so. It was only thanks to the good fortune of finding an American airbase's rubbish dump that we survived. The rubbish dump became a life-giving source for the fugitive soldiers. The extravagant GIs threw away an endless variety of food. They also found tin cans which they made into eating and cooking pans. Sewing needles were made from bedsprings, while primitive sheets were cobbled together from tents.

Every year the rainy season was their worst enemy, when for two months they would sit sullenly in their hides as the rains pelted down and they existed on berries and frogs which they drowned in pails of water. The tension between the two of them was almost unbearable during these times, said Masashi.

One day during the monsoon there was a terrible row between the men, forcing Minakawa to leave. Masashi recalled: *After he had gone I had an urge to scream at the top of my voice. I knew I could not survive without human company. For days I crawled through the dense jungle clicking my tongue until I heard his clicking signal. We embraced and vowed never to part again.*

The soldiers lacked salt in their diet so at night they sneaked down to the coast to boil sea water and eat the salt crystals.

MISTRUST AND DISBELIEF

After ten years they found leaflets on the island. They contained a message from a Japanese general whom neither of them had ever heard of, urging them to surrender. Masashi said: 'I knew that it was a ploy put out by the Americans to trap us. I said to Minakawa: "What kind of fools do they take us for?" '

The men's incredible devotion to a code of duty alien to many Westerners is illustrated by another incident Masashi recalls: *Once Minakawa and I thought about escaping by sea. We walked miles along the coastline looking for a boat in vain. What we did find was one of the*

two American barracks ablaze with lights. We crept near enough to see men and women dancing together and to hear the sound of a jazz tune. That was the first time that we had set our eyes on women in years and I was filled with despair at what I had been missing! Back in my shelter I began to carve the figure of a nude woman from a piece of old tree trunk. We could easily have walked over to the American camp and surrendered - I did not think then that they would harm us - but it was not in my spirit. I was bound to the Emperor and he would have been disappointed in us.

I still did not think the war was over but that the Emperor had merely pulled the troops out to fight elsewhere.

Masashi was shown a picture of his memorial in Japan, which stated that he had been killed in action

---

One morning, after sixteen years in hiding, Masashi's comrade put on his home-made wooden sandals and went off to steal a chicken. But twenty-four hours later he had not returned. Masashi was gripped by panic. 'I knew I could not survive without him,' he said. *I blundered through the jungle to search for him. I reached a military road, where I found Minakawa's rucksack and his sandals. I felt certain then that he had been captured by the Americans.*

Above: *Islanders on Guam captured soldiers Masashi and Minakawa. Both thought the war was still on 16 years after it had ended!*

Below: *Straggler Hiroo Onoda held out for 29 years in the jungle of Lubang island in the Philippines.*

Suddenly a helicopter swooped overhead and I scuttled back into the jungle, resolving to die fighting them. I climbed up a mountain and there were four Americans waiting for me. One of the 'Americans' was Minakawa with a freshly shaved face! He told me that natives had caught him stealing and had turned him over to the Americans. He said the war was over but it took me months in captivity before I would believe it. I was shown a picture of my memorial in Japan, saying I had been killed in action.

Reality was hard to take. All my youth wasted on a lost venture. I had so much living to catch up on. The first night I had a warm bath and a sleep between clean sheets . It was indescribably good.

FURTHER SURVIVORS FROM THE FORESTS

The emergence of Masashi was topped twelve years later, in 1972, by that of Shoichi Yokoi, a sergeant in the Imperial Army. He too had been on Guam.

When the Americans stormed the island he fled from his 77th Marine and Infantry Regiment and found a cave in the foothills of the mountains. He too found the leaflets littering the jungle floor urging Japanese soldiers to surrender in accordance with their

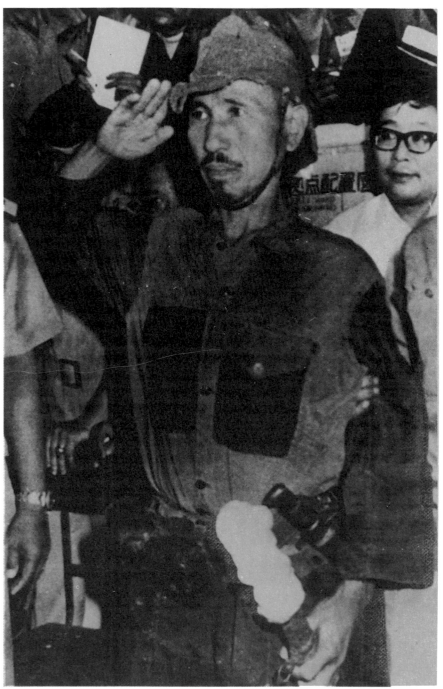

Above: *A gaunt-looking Lieutenant Onoda finally acknowledges that the war is over. He only surrendered when his former superior officer ordered him to do so.*

Left: *Onoda photographed when he was 23. He survived in the jungle by raiding villages for food and provisions - to the great terror of the villagers.*

Emperor's decree; and he, too, refused to believe them.

A hermit without the company of a fellow soldier, he hunted frogs and rats to survive. He wove clothes from tree-bark when his uniform rotted off his back, and shaved by scraping his face with sharpened flints.

He said: *It was so lonely for so many nights. I went to shout once at a snake that had crawled into the entrance of the cave and just a squeak came out. My vocal cords were so unused to being used that they had ceased to function. Every day after that I sang a little song or said a little prayer to keep them functioning.*

He was eventually caught by hunters in January 1972 when, aged fifty-eight, he was told that his exile had been futile. He broke down and wept. He knew nothing of atomic bombs, the surrender or the devastation of his homeland. When he was taken to hospital for a check-up - where he was pronounced A-1 fit - he was told he would fly back to Japan aboard a jet which would take three hours. 'What's a jet?' he asked.

When told he would be returned to Japan in a jet, Yokoi asked: 'What's a jet?'

The government in Tokyo was forced by public opinion to launch a drive to bring old soldiers out of their jungle lairs. So they embarked on Operation Cherry Blossom, dropping tons of leaflets on the Philippine islands and other remote atolls that had once been occupied by the Japanese Army. But it failed to flush out a single soldier – they still regarded the leaflets as propaganda by the troops.

THE REMNANTS OF THE IMPERIAL ARMY

Then in 1974 Lieutenant Hiroo Onoda, aged fifty-two, walked out of a Philippine jungle on remote Lubang island and into the arms of the local authorities.

It took his former commanding officer to come and finally talk him into believing the war was over. He asked to be allowed to retain his sacred ceremonial samurai sword, which he had buried on the island in 1945.

Six months before his capture Onoda and a comrade called Kinshicki Kozuka, had ambushed a Philippine Army patrol, mistaking them for Americans. His friend died in the ambush, and efforts to track down Onoda intensified.

Onoda was so bewildered by returning to the twentieth century that he spent four months undergoing intensive psychological counselling. He told doctors: 'I know that there are many of my comrades still out there, I know where they hide and I know their calling signs. But they will never come out for me because they will think that I have

gone soft and have surrendered. They will unfortunately die in those hills.'

Onoda said the only bright spot for him was an abundance of back pay and accumulated pension rights, which he pledged to spend on saki and sushi. There was an emotional meeting between him and his elderly parents back in Japan at which his father said: 'I am so proud of you. You did the right thing because your heart said to do it.'

A year later Lee Kuang-Huei, a native of Taiwan who had signed up for military service with Japan during World War II, was found in a home made hut, on an Indonesian island, sharpening the bamboo spears he used for fishing at night. He flung himself at the feet of the native intruders, who were accompanied by a local police official, and asked to be executed as he had now offended the Emperor by being captured.

If there are any soldiers left now they will be old men, weakening under the strain of such a harsh existence. But deprived of fatty foods, junk food, alcohol and additives, most of the survivors were amazingly fit when their war finally ended.

Nevertheless, at Japanese Shinto and Buddhist shrines around the country, it is a tradition to burn incense and light candles in remembrance of the 'lost ones', the boys who never came back and who never stopped fighting.

Below: *Fourteen years after the war a group of Japanese scoured the Philippine islands of Rabual and Lubang in the search for the two soldiers still hiding in the jungles.*

OCEAN DEATH TRAP
The Bermuda Triangle

Over a hundred aircraft and ships, their crew and passengers, have vanished for no reason in an area off the Florida coast - the infamous Bermuda Triangle. What strange and sinister force is at work here?

On the afternoon of 5 December 1945, the fourteen crewmen of Flight 19 climbed aboard their five US Navy Avenger bombers. It was 2pm and sunny when the aircraft's single engines roared into life and, in perfect flying weather, the planes soared skywards from their base at Fort Lauderdale, Florida, to begin a routine training mission over the Atlantic.

The only thing out of the ordinary was that one of the crew, for no apparent reason, asked and was permitted to be taken off the mission.

The squadron, led by Lieutenant Charles Taylor, thought little of the matter, made simple adjustments for a light north-east wind, then pointed their snub-nosed planes east towards the Bahamas.

The planes, each with enough fuel to cover 1000 miles (a healthy margin for any error), were to fly 160 miles due east, turn to the north for 40 miles, then head south-west back to their base. During their journey they were to make practice bombing runs at target wrecks on a bank called Chicken Shoals.

The five planes and their fourteen crew were never seen again.

Not, that is, until 16 May, 1991, when American treasure hunters seeking a Spanish galleon made an astonishing find. The explorers, diving from the San Francisco research vessel the *Deep See*

Opposite: *The fuselage of an Avenger aircraft resting on the sea bed. The plane is probably one of five that disappeared mysteriously off the Florida coast in December 1945.*

Below: *This Avenger torpedo bomber, photographed in June 1945, was the lead plane in the so-called Lost Squadron. These crewmen were the lucky ones, however - their places had been taken by others when the planes vanished.*

reported that they had located what may well have been the lost squadron which had disappeared forty-five years earlier. The sophisticated craft found the five planes in 750ft of water within two miles of one another, only ten miles off the Florida coast.

The discovery seemed to have put paid to one of the most enduring of the globe's mysteries - that of the notorious Bermuda Triangle. But had it?

EERIE LIGHTS AND STRANGE MALFUNCTIONS

More than a thousand other airmen, sailors and passengers have disappeared over the years, in more than a hundred lost aircraft and ships. Among seamen, the Bermuda Triangle is also known as the Triangle of Death, the Hoodoo Sea and the Graveyard of the Atlantic.

For centuries voyagers have been baffled by its mysterious calms and sudden storms, even from the time that Christopher Columbus entered this stretch of ocean and noted in his log that the crew had sighted peculiar glowing streaks of 'white water'. These eerie patches of lights and foam are still regularly sighted today.

Sometimes they are so bright that they have been detected from outer space. The Apollo 12 astronauts reported that this luminosity was the last light visible to them as they left the Earth.

Mysterious calms, waterspouts and unheralded storms have been chronicled by those bold enough to traverse the danger zone. Apparent instrument malfunction, spinning compass needles and inexplicable, localized deterioration of flying weather bedevil aviators. Often the only warning of these strange environmental changes is a weird yellow haze blanketing the horizon.

Even the fish get confused by the quirky magnetics of the region, and have been observed swimming upside down

---

The US Navy, which lost their five planes in 1945, still does not recognize the Bermuda Triangle as a danger zone, and the US Coast Guard insist that most of the tragedies and disappearances can be explained by the region's unique environmental features.

These include the swiftly flowing Gulf Stream current, the uncharted underwater canyons of that part of the Atlantic, and the terrifyingly violent storms that erupt there without warning.

The Bermuda Triangle is also known to pose a very real, physical threat to the unwary navigator on the sea or in the air. For it is one of the only two places on Earth where the compass needle points to the true, not the magnetic, north.

A navigator can be heading in the wrong direction while being absolutely certain that he is on the correct route. Perhaps this is why even the fish in the area can become confused; divers have reported erratic activity, with fish sometimes swimming upside down.

NO REASONABLE EXPLANATION

These are the logical explanations for the absolutely inexplicable. As officials of the US National Oceanic and Atmospheric Administration state in a report: 'Despite efforts by the US Air Force, Navy and Coast Guard no reasonable explanation to date has been found for the vanishments.'

And Richard Winer, who wrote *The Devil's Triangle*, a book that has sold 2 million copies, says: 'There are mysterious and strange things that are going on out there. I believe that not all the answers lie in human error, mechanical malfunctions, freak weather and magnetic anomalies.'

From the measured arguments of author Winer to those of John Wallace Spencer, an expert on UFOs, who wrote *Limbo of the Lost*, a book that has also sold 2 million copies. His explanations tend to be more fanciful.

Spencer argues that beings from outer space have established a colony under the sea. There, he claims, the missing ships, planes and their crews are kept for scientific research by these aliens of vastly higher intelligence. He says: 'Sure it sounds weird but it's the only explanation that covers all the facts.' Theories involving aliens from outer

space crop up time and time again in the sagas woven around the losses attributed to the Bermuda Triangle. Many claim that flying saucers spirited the ships and aircraft away, rather than sank them.

Such stories may be traced back to a naval board of inquiry called in to examine the mystery of the 1945 Lost Patrol. During the hearing one of the board reflected, 'They vanished as completely as if they had flown to Mars.'

Is this enigmatic stretch of ocean the site of the lost continent of Atlantis?

Another report given in evidence at the time was by a radio ham who claimed he had picked up the frightened voice of a pilot saying: 'Don't come after me - they look like they are from outer space.'

This intrigued Charles Berlitz, grandson of the founder of the Berlitz language schools, and a Yale graduate with a fascination for the legendary lost 'continent' of Atlantis.

Berlitz's theory was that the city that formed the core of Atlantis was powered by a giant solar crystal which now lies beneath the ocean floor. This crystal, said Berlitz, now sends false messages to the instruments of craft above - and sometimes sucks them to the depths.

Berlitz wrote the bestselling sixties book *The Bermuda Triangle*, itemizing over 140 known disappearances.

THE DOOMED SHIPS

But the actual label 'Bermuda Triangle' was first coined by Vincent Gaddis, the American author of a book on sea mysteries. He wrote: 'Draw a line from Florida to Bermuda, another from Bermuda to Puerto Rico, and a third line back to Florida through the Bahamas. Within this roughly triangular area most of the vanishments have occurred'.

Since his statement, reporters have 'stretched' the Bermuda Triangle into many contorted shapes to help explain - or dramatize - other historical disappearances. But this does not detract from the very many genuine mysteries that have sprung up within that precise, enigmatic and very dangerous 'Triangle'.

Take, for instance, the case of the British frigate *Atlanta,* which in January 1880 set sail from Bermuda for England with a crew of 290, most of them young training cadets. The ship vanished without trace, despite one of the most thorough searches of all time.

Six vessels of the Channel Fleet patrolled in line abreast, each only a mile apart, over the area where the *Atlanta* had disappeared. The search went on for four months, but not a single item of wreckage was found.

A year later came the first of at least a dozen instances of 'ghost' ships found floating crewless within the Bermuda Triangle. In 1881 the cargo ship *Ellen Austin* came upon a schooner with its sails billowing in the wind. Aboard was a full cargo of mahogany - but no sign of human life.

The captain of the *Ellen Austin* could not believe his luck. He decided the derelict ship would be his prize and put men on board her.

Suddenly a fierce squall caused the two ships to lose sight of one another. It was two days before the *Ellen Austin* saw its captured ship again - strangely, drifting once more. The crew who had been ordered aboard it were gone.

But the story does not end there. The greedy captain was determined to secure the schooner at all costs. After using all his powers of persuasion to get yet another crew on board, a further storm arose...and the mysterious ship plus her new crew was never seen again.

The first mystery that the twentieth century threw up was the disappearance of the supply ship USS *Cyclops* in 1918. On 4 March this state-of-the-art piece of engineering, all 500 ft and 19,500 tons of her, set sail from Barbados for Norfolk, Virginia with a valuable cargo of manganese ore and a crew of 309.

Because World War I was still in progress when the *Cyclops* vanished, it was first thought that the vessel had been the victim of a German mine or submarine. But this theory was later dismissed when access was made available to German war records. Careful study revealed that no mines had been laid nor any submarine positioned in

Above: *The US Navy supply ship* **Cyclops** *vanished in March 1918, during the last months of World War I. At first, it was assumed that a U-boat or mine had sunk it, but research in German records after the war showed that no U-boats or mines were anywhere in the vicinity.*

those waters at that time.

At the time of her disappearance the weather had been fair, the seas moderate and winds light, ruling out the obvious explanations of storm damage or shifting cargo.

The Royal Navy reported: 'The disappearance of the ship has been one of the most baffling mysteries in the annals of the Navy.'

As the century grew older, more examples were recorded of the jinx afflicting the area yet to be labelled the Bermuda Triangle.

In 1925 the American freighter *Cotopaxi*, bound for Havana from Charleston, simply disappeared. The following year the cargo tramp *Suduffco* never completed its journey from Newark, New Jersey to Puerto Rico.

The Norwegian freighter *Stavanger* vanished off the face of the earth with its

in cargo, size and age. But they had two things in common - none of them gave out any distress calls at all, despite all having radios on board. And there were no severe weather or storm conditions when they disappeared.

What we do know is that extensive searches throughout the waters of the Triangle have never produced any evidence of a cause for these vessels or their crews going missing.

The pattern, however, was broken in the case of the Japanese freighter *Raifuku Maru*. During the winter of 1924 she gave out a chilling message from somewhere between the Bahamas and Cuba.

The last words heard from her were: 'Danger like a dagger now...Come quickly...We cannot escape...' No one has ever discovered what that danger was. Even more mysterious was that a ship steaming towards the *Raifuku Maru* after hearing the distress call found nothing: no wreckage, no bodies. The Triangle had claimed another victim.

FLIGHT TO OBLIVION

Because of heightened military security during World War II less public awareness was created about the so-called Hoodoo Sea. Until 5 December 1945, when the five US Navy Avenger bombers set off on their ill-fated flight.

An hour after take-off, with their mock bombing runs completed, the Fort Lauderdale control tower received an urgent radio message from Lieutenant Charles Taylor. 'Calling tower,' he radioed. 'This is an emergency. We seem to be off course. We cannot see land. Repeat, we cannot see land.'

Tower: 'What is your position?'

Taylor: 'We are not sure of our position. We cannot be sure just where we are. We seem to be lost.'

Tower: 'Assume bearing due west.'

As long as the aircraft were off the Florida coast, this would inevitably have brought the planes back to landfall.

Taylor: 'We don't know which way is west. Everything is wrong...Strange... We cannot be sure of any direction. Even the ocean doesn't look the way it should.'

Although most of his colleagues were

crew of forty-three in 1931. Its last recorded sighting was somewhere south of Cat Island in the Bahamas.

In 1932 the schooner *John and Mary* was found bobbing quietly in calm seas fifty miles south of Bermuda, its sails neatly furled but with not a soul aboard. Another schooner, the *Gloria Colite* from the West Indian island of St Vincent, was found abandoned in 1940.

No distress signals were picked up from any of the vessels, despite having radios on board

---

And in 1944 the Cuban freighter *Rubicon* was similarly found drifting off the Florida coast - its only occupant a dog.

Every one of the vessels mentioned so far was completely different. Each varied still under instruction, Lieutenant Taylor was a highly experienced pilot. It was an unbelievable admission that he did not know his own position and his direction of flight.

About fifteen minutes later, at 3.30pm, a flight instructor at the airbase listened in to the radio and heard, over the static, a conversation between one of the lost pilots and a colleague. The first pilot was asking for compass readings and the second pilot responded with: 'I don't know where we are. We must have got lost after that last turn.'

Increasingly concerned for his seemingly bewildered airmen, the flight instructor desperately attempted to get a message to Lieutenant Taylor. Eventually he succeeded.

Taylor told him: 'I'm sure I'm in the Keys but I don't know how far down.'

We cannot be sure of any direction. Even the ocean doesn't look the way it should

---

By now those commanding the Fort Lauderdale naval station were incredulous. The Florida Keys begin more than a hundred miles to the south - so far off the planes' route as to be unthinkable. If they were heading westwards for 'home' they would find themselves hopelessly lost in the Gulf of Mexico.

The Fort Lauderdale instructor reached Taylor once more and told him to turn to the north.

'We have just passed over a small island,' Taylor reported shortly afterwards. 'No other land in sight.' From that moment onwards, the base was unable to speak to the pilots.

But through the static they were able to pick up snatches of conversation between the airmen. It appeared from the tangle of voices that Taylor had handed over command of the squadron to another senior pilot, Captain Stiver.

At one stage the new leader said: 'We are not sure where we are. We think we must be 225 miles south-east of base. We must have passed over Florida and be in the Gulf of Mexico.'

Later Stiver was heard to say that he

was turning 180 degrees in the hope of heading north to hit the Florida coast. No one at base could understand why, in fine weather, the pilots were not using the sun to navigate themselves out of trouble.

The last faint words from the lost squadron were: 'Entering white water. We are completely lost...'

As far as Fort Lauderdale could calculate, the squadron had turned west and begun a flight to oblivion - straight out across the endless wastes of the Atlantic Ocean - while the last of their fuel burned away.

A Martin Mariner flying boat with a crew of thirteen was sent up to hunt for the planes. It radioed back that it had encountered strong winds at 6000ft. Then there was silence.

Coast Guard cutters, destroyers, submarines and Royal Air Force planes, plus a host of private craft, all joined the search. But neither the squadron nor the flying boat was ever seen again...

Until 1991, when the underwater explorers of the research vessel the *Deep See* reported: 'We think we've found the lost squadron.' First underwater cameras and then robots were sent down and confirmed the Fort Lauderdale numbering on the planes. A figure 28 was clearly seen on video. It was Lieutenant Taylor's aircraft.

The fate of Flight 19 was suddenly back in the hands of the living. And some of the mystery that had hung like an enigmatic haze over the Bermuda Triangle had suddenly evaporated.

At least, that is what the experts were saying. Just as they were saying it in 1955 when twelve of them - all Japanese scientists with the most advanced equipment that money could buy - launched an expedition into the Triangle to debunk, once and for all, the legendary curse. They were never heard from again.

Since the disappearance of the ill-fated Flight 19 on 5 December 1945, an astonishing catalogue of mysteries has emanated from the Bermuda Triangle. Here are some of those lost in the graveyard of the Atlantic...

1947: A US Army C54 Superfort disappeared a hundred miles off Bermuda without broadcasting a word to indicate it was in any difficulty.

1948: A British airliner, the *Star Tiger*, a four-engined Tudor-Four, radioed four hundred miles north-east of Bermuda: 'Expect to arrive on schedule.' The thirty-one passengers and crew were never found.

1949: The *Star Ariel*, sister plane of the *Star Tiger*, was flying from London to Santiago in Chile via Bermuda and Jamaica. Radio contact was lost 380 miles south-west of Bermuda. Its last words were: 'All's well.'

1950: The SS *Sandra*, a 350ft freighter, sailed from Savannah, Georgia for Puerto Caballo, Venezuela with 300 tons of insecticide. She passed St Augustine, Florida and then disappeared without trace.

1954: A US Navy Lockheed Super Constellation vanished while flying from Maryland to the Azores.

1955: The yacht *Connemara IV* was found mysteriously abandoned four hundred miles west of Bermuda.

1956: US Navy patrol of Martin seaplanes P5M disappeared with a crew of ten near Bermuda.

1962: US Air Force tanker KB150, flying from Langley Field, Virginia to the Azores, never arrived.

1963: The *Sno-Boy*, a 63ft fishing boat with forty aboard, sailed from Kingston, Jamaica for North-East Cay eighty miles south, but vanished with all hands.

1963: Two new US Air Force KC135 four-engined Stratotankers from Homestead Air Force Base, Florida, heading for a classified refuelling range in the Atlantic, were lost three hundred miles south-west of Bermuda.

1963: AC132 Cargomaster vanished *en route* to the Azores.

1965: AC199 Flying Boxcar with ten aboard vanished in the south-east Bahamas.

1967: The *Revonoc*, an all-weather 46ft racing yacht, disappeared within sight of land.

1967: The owner and passenger of the cabin cruiser *Witchcraft*, disappeared while the vessel was at a harbour buoy just one mile from Miami.

1970: The *Milton Latrides*, a freighter *en route* from New Orleans to Cape Town, vanished.

1973: The *Anita*, a 20,000 ton freighter with a crew of thirty-two, sailing from Newport News to Hamburg, disappeared.

1984: The brig *Marques*, 88ft, foundered during the world-famous Tall Ships Race and was lost with eighteen crew on the northern borders of the Bermuda Triangle.

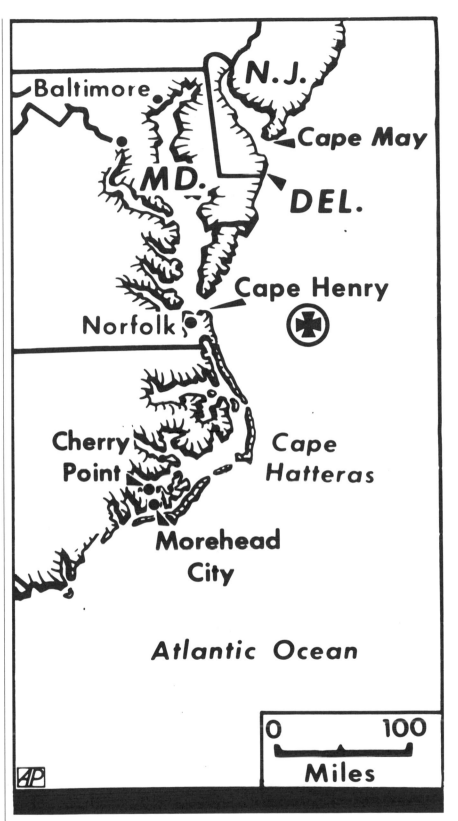

Above: *A map shows the spot where the USS* Cyclops *disappeared during World War I. The ship had been sailing between Barbados in the West Indies and Norfolk, Virginia.*

CASPAR HAUSER
Mystery Child

The enigma of Caspar Hauser was a topic of animated discussion throughout the drawing rooms and taverns of nineteenth-century Europe. Was he of royal blood, as some believed, or a child of the devil?

By the early nineteenth century, the Southern German city of Nuremberg was a bustling provincial centre. Its wide cobbled streets were lined with elegant houses, its fine squares graced with ornate churches and fountains. Into this 'Treasure House of Germany' came a shabbily dressed waif, a pauper who may have been a prince...

THE ENIGMA ARRIVES IN NUREMBERG

On a bright May morning in 1812 a cobbler called Georg Weichmann squinted across the square outside his home at the shambling figure which emerged from an alleyway. It was a boy of about sixteen, dressed in a torn topcoat and tattered knee-breeches. He hobbled unsteadily in a pair of ill-fitting boots.

The kindly cobbler instantly took pity on the lad and walked over to where he stood, staring wildly about him as though in a panic. 'Are you lost? Where are your parents?' asked Weichmann.

All the cobbler's questions produced merely strange, unintelligible whispers until, suddenly, the child thrust an envelope into his hand. The address read: 'The Captain of the 4th Squadron, 6th Cavalry Regiment.'

Puzzled, the cobbler led him to the Captain's house nearby. The Captain was not at home, and while they waited his servant offered them food.

Weichmann was amazed when the waif, thin as he was, refused to touch a plate of meat and sausage in front of him, but instead grabbed a dry bread roll and ate it ravenously.

Eventually the Captain arrived and tore open the envelope to find two letters.

The first was dated a few days before. It read: 'I send you a boy who is anxious to serve his country in the Army. He was left on my doorstep as a baby. I have ten children of my own to bring up and can care for him no longer.' The note ended callously: 'If you do not want to keep him, kill him or hang him up a chimney.'

The second letter was dated 1812 and purported to be from the child's natural mother. It said simply: 'Take care of my child. His father was in the 6th Cavalry.'

'If you do not want to keep him,' ran the letter, 'kill him or hang him up a chimney'.

The Captain took one disdainful look at the child and decided to wash his hands of the whole strange affair. Despite the protestations of the kindly cobbler, the boy was promptly marched off to the nearest police station and thrown into a cell. For several days, while his fate was being decided, a jailer watched the child and was struck by what he saw.

'He can sit for hours without moving a limb,' he observed later. 'He sits rigidly without growing at all uncomfortable. Also he prefers darkness to light and can move about in it like a cat.' The jailer gave the child a scrap of paper on which he scratched the words 'Reiter' - the German for cavalryman - and 'Caspar Hauser'. This, police assumed, was the boy's name.

In many of his actions he would appear babylike, often tottering on his feet and falling like a toddler who was only just learning to walk. Yet Caspar seemed to have a bright, alert mind. The patient jailer spent hours every day teaching him to speak and write.

A STRANGE TALE

Within six weeks Caspar could at last relate the story of the first sixteen years of his wretched life, and the jailer summoned the city Burgomaster to hear his sad tale.

Above: *Caspar Hauser arrived with a note in his hand at the city of Nuremberg one morning in May 1812...an enigma was born.*

Opposite: *The young Caspar remembered being kept in a tiny darkened room, slumbering on rags laid across a straw bed. He was fed on bread and water and was possibly drugged.*

Above: *Hauser admires a wooden horse watched over by Professor Daumer in this early print. Under caring tuition, this backward boy became a youthful academic.*

One day some boots and an envelope were thrust into his hand and soon he found himself hobbling painfully through the centre of Nuremberg.

WILD RUMOURS

Caspar's story swept the taverns like wildfire. Suddenly he found himself the star of Nuremberg. The city council published a much-embellished account of Caspar's strange upbringing. It broadcast an appeal throughout the land for clues to his true identity. But many gossip-mongers and tittle-tattlers had already made up their minds who Caspar was. Some puritans said he was a child of the devil; mystics asserted that he had been sent from an alien planet; others were convinced Caspar was of royal birth.

There was certainly some circumstantial evidence for this last theory. In 1812, around the time that baby Caspar was dumped on the labourer's doorstep, the ruler of the province, Grand Duke Karl and the Grand Duchess Stephanie, had a baby son. But he died of meningitis - at least according to the doctors.

Had the true heir to the Grand Duke been spirited away at birth by rival claimants?

The couple had no more children, and when the Grand Duke died in 1829 the succession passed to the male line of the Countess of Hochberg. Only weeks after the Grand Duke's death, a year since Caspar's arrival in Nuremberg, an incident occured which seemed to support the theory.

AN ASSASSIN'S VICTIM

Casper arrived in Nuremberg, was now living at the home of Professor George Daumer, a respected philosopher and educationalist. In a short time the professor had transformed Caspar from a backward child into a bright, articulate young man, a prized guest in Nuremburg's drawing rooms.

One night the professor returned home to find Caspar lying in a pool of blood on

Caspar could remember being kept locked up all day and all night in a small darkened room about six feet by four. He slept in rags on a straw bed, and neither saw nor heard anyone come or go.

Whenever he awoke there would be a plate of bread and a jug of water by his bedside. Sometimes the water would taste brackish and it would send him into a deep sleep. When he woke up, he would discover his hair had been cut and his nails trimmed.

Only once did he ever come into contact with another human being. A hand came around the door of his cell with a pen and a piece of paper. It guided him to write the three words which he had first shown the jailer: 'Reiter' and 'Caspar Hauser'.

the basement floor. He had been stabbed several times in the face and neck and was lucky to escape with his life. Caspar told the professor that a masked man had broken into the house and attacked him.

The gossips had a field day. This surely was the work of a would-be assassin hired by the Countess of Hochberg to do away with the rightful heir to the late Grand Duke's title.

Some people resented the acclaim being heaped upon Caspar. A waif with a mysterious upbringing was one thing, an interesting diversion at high society parties. A young man with pretensions to royalty was quite another. Some even whispered that he had faked the attack in the basement to surround himself with an even greater aura of mystery.

This band of cynics grew when, after the assault, the frightened Caspar was given a police guard at a secret address. The city was beginning to tire of the boy.

NEW 'PROTECTORS'

Then the eccentric English earl, Lord Stanhope arrived. He was fascinated by the remarkable story of the Child of Nuremberg, and managed to persuade the city council to allow him to become Caspar's legal guardian. In 1831, with Caspar in tow, he set off on a tour of the minor courts of Europe, parading the boy to the delight of dukes and princes.

But after two years on the road, the noble lord tired of his charge. Not for the first time in his wretched life Caspar was unceremoniously dumped. Lord Stanhope decided to lodge him with a mean-spirited puritan pastor named Meyer in the town of Ansbach, fifteen miles from Nuremberg. Caspar, now twenty-one, was put to work as an apprentice bookbinder, which he is said to have enjoyed.

THE MYSTERY REMAINS

One evening in December 1833, as he walked home from work through a park, Caspar was approached by a stranger who plunged a knife repeatedly into his ribs and ran off.

Mortally wounded, Caspar staggered to his lodgings where, incredibly, the pastor refused to believe his story. He accused Caspar of trying to gain attention by inflicting the wounds himself. Caspar was put to bed and the police were never called. Three days later, Caspar Hauser died in agony.

The pastor insisted that Caspar's terrible stab wounds were self-inflicted and did not call the police

---

The police found a black wallet near the scene of the crime. Inside was a note, in mirror writing: 'Hauser will be able to tell you who I am. To spare him the task I will tell you myself. I am from ... on the Bavarian border ... My name is MLO.' The assassin was never found.

Hearing of Caspar's death, the Grand Duchess Stephanie is reported to have broken down and wept, sobbing that she believed he was indeed her long-lost son.

Caspar was buried in the tiny country churchyard at Ansbach. His grave is still there to this day. The simple epitaph on his tombstone reads: 'Here lies Caspar Hauser, Enigma. His birth was unknown, his death mysterious.'

Below: *The cradle that would have been Caspar's if the boy had been of royal birth. Was the child from nowhere really heir to the title of Grand Duke.*

T.E. LAWRENCE
Arabian Sands

White-robed Lawrence of Arabia was one of the great heroes of World War I. What made this enigmatic man enlist in the ranks afterwards? And was his death in a motorcycle crash really an accident, or was he 'eliminated'?

Right: *Lawrence of Arabia poses for the camera in Arab headgear and flowing robes. This was the image he wished to present to the world.*

Opposite: *An avid British public devoured every scrap of information about Lawrence. This photograph, which was captioned 'The Kingmaker', fed their adulation.*

Below: *Colonel Lawrence stands with other military dignitaries behind the Emir Feisal. Such local leaders used Lawrence's martial expertise to maintain power.*

The powerful Brough motorcycle accelerated through the winding lanes of the Dorset countryside. The rider enjoyed the sensation of speed, the almost sensual thrill of dicing with injury or death. In under a minute the machine

Above: Simple Bedouin Sheiks rallied to his call. Here Lawrence confers with a group of them as they outline their strategy in the sand.

had roared the mile or so from his cottage to Bovington Army Camp.

The soldiers on the gate knew him well by sight. He greeted them, dismounted and walked to the camp post office to send a telegram inviting a friend from London to visit him the following day. He returned to his machine and headed back towards his cottage.

Just 400 yards from home the rider swerved to avoid two boy cyclists, hit the verge and somersaulted over the

Right: Encamped in the desert with tents and camels...Lawrence's exploits became the stuff of legend. At the time he gloried in it.

handlebars of his motorbike. Without a crash helmet he hit the road, fracturing his skull.

Six days later he died in the local hospital without fully regaining consciousness.

Thus ended the life of RAF Aircraftman Shaw, T. E., serial number 7875698. The hundreds of people who packed the tiny local church at Moreton for his funeral a week later, including generals, famous literary figures and even Winston Churchill, knew Shaw better as Colonel T.E. Lawrence - Lawrence of Arabia.

It was only the funeral of a low-ranking airman, but the church was packed with major public figures

---

The enigma of Thomas Edward Lawrence - to some a *Boys' Own* hero, leader of an Arab army and literary genius; to others a charlatan and a masochist - still divides historians today. Either way the legend survives.

His life inspired David Lean's epic film, *Lawrence of Arabia*. His death provoked a welter of theories, including murder and suicide.

OUT OF WEDLOCK

Lawrence was born in Tremadoc, Wales, in August 1888. His father, Thomas Chapman, an Irish landowner, had run off with the family nanny, Sarah Lawrence, taking her surname and leaving behind a wife, four daughters and most of his wealth. When T. E. was born to Sarah the family had to live on the comparatively modest income of £300 a year from Thomas's former estate.

The young Lawrence won a scholarship to Oxford University where he read history at Jesus College. One of Lawrence's tutors, Ernest Barker, got an insight into his student's character. He concluded that Lawrence's studies were merely 'a hurdle to be jumped on the road to action'.

On a research trip to France, he claimed, his sketches and maps got him mistakenly arrested as a spy. In his next year at Oxford he enrolled in the university shooting club and the Officer Cadet Training Corps. Lawrence's future was being shaped.

FAME AND ITS PRICE

By the outbreak of World War I, Lawrence was an expert on the Middle East. He had spent five years working on archaeological

Left: *Lawrence (left) in full desert robes, with colleague Lowell Thomas.*

Below: *One of Lawrence's own photographs of troops advancing in the desert with him. The original is in the Imperial War Museum, London.*

sites in Syria, the Lebanon and Palestine. He had also, it has recently been revealed, been part of a spying network on the progress of the Berlin to Baghdad railway being built by the Germans.

Excavating an archaeological site gave Lawrence a cover for spying on the German-built railway in Mesopotamia

---

Lawrence was in a group ostensibly funded by the British Museum to carry out a dig at Carchemish in Mesopotamia, now Iraq. He was armed with a camera

Below: A smiling T.E. Lawrence, 'soldier and administrator', at British Headquarters in Cairo.

Below right: A rare unposed photograph in which he has not dressed for his role as an Arab military leader.

and telephoto lens, while 'excavating' conveniently close to the railway line.

His almost unrivalled knowledge of the Arab world and its leaders meant that by 1916 Lawrence was appointed a special adviser to Sherif Feisal, who later became King of Iraq. Together they stirred up a rebellion against the Turks, allies of the Germans, in Arabia.

Lawrence's exploits are now the stuff of legend. Gradually discarding his British Army uniform for Arab garments, his armoured cars for camels, Lawrence led his 'Arab Army' against formidable Turkish opposition - and won.

He captured the key port of Aqaba on the Red Sea coast and cut a swathe through Turkish lines up to Damascus in Syria.

The personal cost to Lawrence was something which would affect the rest of his life. On a spying mission in the town

*Above: **Lawrence of Arabia's English retreat: Clouds Hill, Dorset, as seen from the Rhododendron Wood above the isolated cottage.***

of Deraa, a key rail junction between Amman and Damascus, Lawrence was captured, whipped and apparently homosexually raped by the town's Turkish military governor, Hajim Bey, and his henchmen.

Captured by the Turks, Lawrence was first beaten and then homosexually raped by a group of soldiers

---

He wrote in his famous book *Seven Pillars of Wisdom*, that he was first whipped: 'The men took me up very deliberately, giving me "so many", and [would] then... ease themselves and play unspeakably with me.' He added: 'At last when I was completely broken they seemed satisfied.' With the ordeal over the corporal then kicked him. 'I remember smiling idly up at him, for a delicious warmth, probably sexual, was swelling through me,' he wrote.

Lawrence escaped from the evil Turks' clutches. But never from the torment, of both the pain and the pleasure which he had experienced.

After the war, and with Lawrence hailed as a hero - the gruesome details of his capture had by this stage not been made public - he became a special adviser on Arab affairs to Winston Churchill, who was chairman of a British Government Committee on the Middle East. With Churchill he attended the 1921 Cairo Conference, which established the new post–war order in the region.

DISAPPEARING INTO THE RANKS

The following year he wrote to his friend, the poet Robert Graves, that he wanted to become 'ordinary', to escape from his own fame and responsibilities. He then wrote to Air Marshall Sir Hugh Trenchard, Chief of the Air Staff, asking if he could enlist as an ordinary airman in the newly formed RAF. Trenchard was surprised, to say the least. But Lawrence's determination was so great that Trenchard eventually gave in and sent the following memo to his chief of RAF personnel:

'It is hereby approved that Colonel T. E. Lawrence be permitted to join the Royal Air Force as an Aircraft Hand under the alias of John Hume Ross. On receipt of any communication from him asking for his release, orders are to be issued for his discharge forthwith.' At least, if he didn't like it, Lawrence had a return ticket.

To his amazement, the legendary leader of the revolt in the desert was declared medically unfit for the RAF

When Lawrence arrived at the RAF recruiting office in London's Covent Garden two weeks later he was amazed when a medical officer decided he was unfit to serve. He had indeed spent the previous months sweating over his book, which had taken its toll, but Lawrence of Arabia unfit to be an ordinary airman? Finally, an officer who had been told of Lawrence's true identity took the medical officer to one side...and Colonel Lawrence became Air Hand Ross. He was posted to the air photography school at Farnborough in Kent.

But someone blew the whistle on

Above: *One of the two bicycles that Lawrence swerved to avoid before his fatal motorcycle accident.*

Right: *Albert Hargreaves who was riding one of the bicycles escaped the accident unscathed.*

Opposite: *Idolized even beyond death...an effigy of Aircraftman Thomas Edward Shaw in his better-known role of Lawrence of Arabia.*

Airman Ross. the *Daily Express* broke the story on 27 December 1922: 'LAWRENCE OF ARABIA - FAMOUS WAR HERO BECOMES A PRIVATE' Three weeks later Lawrence discharged himself from the RAF.

Lawrence went back to his writing, but there was something about the discipline of the life of a 'squaddie' that he still yearned for. In March the following year, Lawrence changed his name to T. E. Shaw and joined the Tank Corps.

Lawrence realized that at the age of thirty-three and with an upper-class accent he would not survive five minutes in a barrack room. So he took along with him an eighteen-year-old Scot called John Bruce as a 'minder'. Bruce later admitted that part of his job was to administer the birch to his master.

Lawrence took a young 'minder' into the Army with him - his duties included birching his employer

---

By early 1925 Lawrence had suffered enough at the hands of his Tank Corps brothers-in-arms and appealed to his well-placed friends at the Air Ministry to get him back into the Air Force. By this time, however, there was a Labour government, which regarded Lawrence as something of a snob and an imperialist. His request was refused.

HOUNDED BY THE PRESS

But in June that year an American magazine came out with a story headlined: 'LAWRENCE OF ARABIA - NEW DISGUISE' and revealed that he was now a private in the Tank Corps. The magazine also revealed details of his flogging in Deraa, without going into the more unsavoury parts of the incident. Lawrence was scared, and his old friend Sir Hugh Trenchard was moved enough to get him a job back in the RAF. Trooper Shaw of the Tank Corps now became Aircraftman Shaw of the RAF.

In his new disguise Lawrence was posted to India, probably to get him out of the way. He served first in Karachi and was then moved to defend an airstrip at Miranshah on the North West Frontier.

But again news leaked out. Amazing rumours reached governments all over the world that the famous Colonel Lawrence had been sent to India on a series of secret missions. He was stirring up an Afghan rebellion. He was spying on the Russians. He was, in fact, a war waiting to happen. Questions were asked in the House of Commons, and Lawrence's activities were front page news every other day.

In fact, Aircraftman Shaw was happily engaged in obeying his NCOs, guarding his airstrip on the North West Frontier and trying to write a book. But the scandal was too much for the British government. Lawrence was ordered home on the next boat out of Bombay.

There is no doubt that the incident made him many enemies both at home and abroad. The Russians, who had been trying to gain a foothold in northern India, were convinced that Lawrence was behind an Afghan uprising against Bolshevik influence in their country. At home many senior officials, both in the military and in the government, regarded the erstwhile hero as an embarrassment.

Lawrence remained in the ranks of the RAF until February 1935, tinkering with engines at a seaplane squadron on the south coast. The publication of *Seven Pillars of Wisdom* had brought him great literary acclaim. He left the RAF and took Cloud's Hill Cottage, set on a hill above Bovington Camp.

UNANSWERED RIDDLES

Many unanswered riddles surround his death. How could Lawrence, an experienced motorcyclist, crash while swerving to avoid two cyclists travelling in single file on the other side of the road? Who was driving a mystery black car which he is said to have swerved to avoid seconds before the crash?

The question of the car, spotted by a soldier from Bovington who was just yards from the accident, was discounted at the inquest, which was held with unprecedented haste on the morning of Lawrence's funeral. It is also fairly certain that Lawrence's vast experience and intellect were being used to help formulate a new policy to gear up the RAF to a war footing following German rearmament. Did the Germans know this and decide that Lawrence was too dangerous to live? Alternatively, had the Bolsheviks finally got their revenge for his alleged involvement in Afghanistan?

Indeed, had the British government itself decided that Lawrence now knew too much and could not be trusted?

Or had he finally succumbed to the pressure of his fame and the torment of his fascination with the whip? Did Lawrence of Arabia take his own life?

NOBLE ODDITIES
Foibles of the Rich

The British aristocracy has bred countless oddities from harmless eccentrics to dangerous lunatics. One Duke lived in underground tunnels like a mole.
A famous society hostess believed she was Queen of the Jews. There was an Earl who dined in splendour, his dogs seated at table with him...

Money may not make you mad - but it has certainly had a stunning effect on the upper classes. Britain's eccentric aristocrats have had the millions to indulge their every bizarre whim - and the arrogance to ignore the stunned reactions of their fellow countrymen.

LORD ROKEBY.

Above: Lord Rokeby, whose holiday to a spa led him to become an 'amphibian'.

Opposite: Wanting to wed the Messiah, Lady Hester Stanhope shunned London society.

Left: The family of prime minister Lord North produced more than one eccentric.

SENDING IT UP IN SMOKE

Sometimes their inheritance has literally gone up in smoke. Take the amazing case of the rebellious young grandson of Lord North, the eighteenth-century Prime Minister.

Resenting his family's background, he ran away from their country seat - Rougham Hall in Norfolk - and joined the navy. When his father died he returned home to claim his inheritance.

But the young Lord North packed the cellars of the Hall with the gunpowder, lit the fuse and destroyed the house.

THE UNDERGROUND ARISTOCRAT

But in one celebrated case the family fortunes went underground. William John Cavendish Bentinck Scott, the fifth Duke of Portland, was obsessively shy. He loathed meeting people, and visitors were barred from his home, Welbeck Abbey in Nottinghamshire.

The Duke decided there was only one thing to do: burrow. He built a series of subterranean rooms, including the largest ballroom in the country, a huge library and a billiard room that could house a dozen billiard tables. And like a human mole he linked his underground kingdom with fifteen miles of tunnels. One tunnel, a mile and a quarter long, connected his coachhouse with Worksop railway station.

In a black carriage with drawn blinds he would travel through the tunnel from Welbeck to the station. Still seated in the carriage he would be loaded into a railway truck. At his London home in Cavendish Square the servants would be sent out of sight as he climbed from the carriage and rushed into the privacy of his study.

Born in 1800, he spent his early years as a normal young man and he became an MP. But slowly his shyness took control of his mind. When the Duke moved into Welbeck he cleared the vast halls of their treasures and portraits and dumped them in a huge pile. He lived alone in five bare rooms in the west wing.

But if the Duke lived for most of his eighty years in the utmost privacy, in death he became a very public person in a bizarre court case. He had been buried simply and quietly in Kensal Green cemetery in North London. And soon, because of his mysterious lifestyle, the rumours of a double life began sweeping the capital.

Then up stepped a widow, Anna Maria Druce, who claimed that the dead Duke was really her late husband, Thomas, a shopkeeper. She swore that Thomas's funeral at Highgate cemetery had been a trick so that her husband, who had become disenchanted with his shopkeeper role, could return to his

Below: The poet Lord Byron was, of course, a genius as well as an eccentric. After years of wild living in England, he fled to the Continent where he carried on a series of steamy love affairs. He died nobly, however...in Greece, where he had gone to aid the cause of independence. He was just thirty-nine.

reclusive role at Welbeck Abbey. The coffin, she said, had been empty - except for a hundredweight of lead. And she claimed the Portland title and all its lands. The case lasted for years but was dismissed when Thomas Druce's grave was ordered to be opened up, and there he lay.

THE WATER-LOVER

If the Duke of Portland would have preferred to be a mole, Lord Rokeby would have liked to be a toad. He believed that he should spend as much of his life as possible under water.

It was a holiday in the spa town of Aix-La-Chapelle that changed him from mammal to amphibian.

For years he had led the good life as one of the landed gentry of Kent. He came into the Rokeby title after the death

given a half-crown to reward them for their excellent taste.

The water-loving aristocrat attempted to keep his strange obsession a secret. And in the end he built a vast swimming pool in his garden - covered by glass - where he would spend his day.

Lord Rokeby was a terrible embarrassment to his family, who feared him appearing in public displaying his strange habit of eating a leg of roast veal while immersed in the water.

His sister, Mrs Elizabeth Montagu dreaded that he might 'exhibit his amphibious and carnivorous habits at Bath'. She could not stand the thought of a 'gentleman's bathing with a loin of veal floating at his elbows'.

His strange habit of eating a leg of roast veal while swimming gave rise to rumours of cannibalism

---

Many thought he was a cannibal because of the meat that he ate while bobbing around in the water. His love of water obviously did the trick. He died at the grand old age of eighty-eight.

QUEEN OF THE JEWS

But there were aristocratic women who were eccentrics too. Lady Hester Stanhope, niece of Prime Minister William Pitt the Younger, was an extraordinary example.

An extremely attractive hostess in London society, she had one belief - that she was to be Queen of the Jews.

It was in 1810, when she was thirty-three that she left England to go and fulfil her destiny. Astrologers and fortune-tellers in London had assured her of her fate.

She set out on her voyage with a group of friends including a young man, Michael Bruce, who was to become her lover. Rumour has it that, when they reached Athens, Lord Byron dived off the rocks to greet her.

But soon after setting sail from Constantinople for Cairo they were shipwrecked close to the island of Rhodes. All their clothes were lost and Lady Hester opted to wear Turkish male

of an uncle who had been Bishop of Armagh and Primate of Ireland. The new Lord Rokeby was a picture of responsibility. But then came his foreign holiday to 'take the waters'.

Every day afterwards he would spend hours in the sea off the beaches of Kent. His servants had difficulty dragging him out on to dry land.

His favourite bathing place was on the sands of Hythe, three miles from his home at Mount Morris. His builders constructed a beach hut there for him. And he started to swim so much that he often fainted and had to be rescued.

He started to grow the most enormous beard. It hung down to his waist and was so thick and wide that it could be seen from behind.

He insisted on walking to the beach wearing peasant clothing. But behind him would come his carriage with a servant kitted out in the most splendid finery. If it rained the servant would ride in the carriage - but Lord Rokeby enjoyed getting soaking wet.

He had drinking fountains installed on the pathway so he could always have his beloved water at hand. And if he came across anyone drinking at them they were

Above: ***When Lady Hester Stanhope tired of travel, she settled in a disused monastery near Sidon in Lebanon to await the new Messiah to claim her as his bride.***

Above: *The eighth Earl of Bridgewater believed that nothing was too good for his pets, which were waited on by teams of servants.*

clothing for the rest of her life.

They were rescued by a Royal Navy frigate and taken to Cairo, and so started an extraordinary series of adventures in the Middle East. Money was no object. Lady Hester played the part of an enormously wealthy haughty princess. The saddle of her horse was covered in crimson velvet inlaid with gold.

When all her clothing was lost in a shipwreck Lady Hester decided to wear Turkish male garb for the rest of her life

---

Some thought she was a boy because they could not understand how a woman could break all the rules of the Middle East. But she didn't care about rules, and broke them with such style that she was

treated with great respect. Fascinated crowds poured coffee in front of her horse as she rode by, side-saddle, and in Jerusalem the doors of the Church of the Holy Sepulchre were thrown open to her.

She became more royal than royalty and began to think of herself as Queen Hester. After an historic voyage across the Arabian desert she was welcomed as queen of the desert and crowned.

But in 1914 she grew tired of her meanderings, settled down in a disused monastery near Sidon in Lebanon and waited for the new Messiah to come to claim her as his bride. She died penniless at the age of sixty-three, her pathetic dream as Queen of the Jews unfulfilled.

THE LORD WHO STAYED IN BED

The rich eccentric aristocrat can do anything he wants. Or nothing at all, as the new wife of Lord North discovered.

Their September wedding at Westminster was followed by a very successful Caribbean honeymoon. Returning to Burgholt House in October Lord North announced to his American bride that he was going to bed. 'That suits me just fine,' she said.

She was somewhat surprised the next day to find that she was up before he was. But dutifully she prepared his breakfast and took it up to him where he was not asleep but just lying there.

'You needn't have disturbed yourself,' said the butler. 'Breakfast in bed is already prepared for his Lordship. You see, October the ninth is the day on which he starts his hibernation.'

Shocked, she asked how long the hibernation lasted. 'Until March the twenty-second unless spring is very pleasant,' he replied. And he confirmed that Lord North spent all that time in bed. 'He just doesn't like the winter,' he added.

He ended: 'If you will forgive me, I must put the dining table in place.' When the amazed Lady North got upstairs she found their bedroom occupied a 25 ft Hepplewhite dinner table with a strangely cut hole towards one end. 'Sixteen to dinner tonight,' said the horizontal Lord North, 'and that's where I'll be sitting.' And he went on to explain.

'You see, my dear, no North has got out of bed from October to March since my ancestor lost the American colonies. Perhaps if he had hibernated as well, we might have been able to go on ordering you Yankees about instead of having to marry you.'

FOUR-LEGGED DINNER GUESTS

Francis Henry Egerton, the 8th Earl of Bridgwater, had no time for women. Or for his fellow men for that matter. He much preferred the company of his dogs. Nothing was too good for them. He even bought them the finest soft leather boots to protect their paws.

For if the Earl's first obsession was his dogs, his love of boots and shoes ran a very close second. He wore a new pair every day of the year. And when he kicked them off at night he ranged them around the walls and used them as a calendar.

His dogs were his only friends and every day he took half a dozen of them for rides in his carriage. Then at night he would dine with them in the great hall.

The huge table would be laid for twelve and his dogs would be led in - with crisp white napkins around their necks. Servants stood behind their chairs to dish out their food on to the family silver. The Earl would engage them in conversation as if they were friends and relatives.To cynics who commented on his madness the Earl would reply that his dogs were better behaved than any gentleman.

The Earl lived for many years in Paris, where he upset his neighbours by his shooting habits.

As his eyesight grew worse he would clip the wings of pigeons and use them for easy target practice.

Baron De Rothschild's superb chateau in Buckinghamshire was home to many creatures great and small. In the 1860s guests could expect to be driven up the long drive in a carriage drawn by four zebras.

Inside snakes writhed around the bannisters, and a supposedly tame bear had a habit of slapping women guests on the bottom. But the most amazing incident in the Baron's animal kingdom happened in the 1890s at an important political dinner for Lord Salisbury.

A tame bear had the habit of slapping female guests on the behind

Seated around the the long table each of the twelve guests noticed that there was an empty chair beside them. Obviously their dinner neighbours were

Below: *Sir Lionel Walter, the second Baron Rothschild, would transport guests in a carriage drawn by four zebras*

late in arriving. Suddenly the great doors at the end of the dining room opened, and in walked twelve immaculately dressed monkeys to take up the spare seats.

THE MANIAC BUILDER

Mega-rich William Beckford had a very different type of obsession - his foible was building tall spires that promptly crashed to the ground. And he had no shortage of cash to satisfy his ambitions.

At the age of ten when his father died in 1770, he inherited £1 million in cash and property in England. Not to mention large sugar plantations in Jamaica. His investment income was £100,000 a year - an absolute fortune in those days.

Beckford did everything in a hurry. Highly intelligent he wrote books in a couple of days. As he said after finishing one novel in French: 'I never took off my clothes for three days and nights. This severe application made me very ill.'

He travelled widely and was particularly impressed by the giant spires he saw on religious buildings in Spain and Portugal. And when after a disastrous marriage he settled at his family estate in 1795, they became the examples that he intended to emulate. At Fonthill he planned an enormous Gothic abbey, a private folly with a vast tower as its centrepiece. Beckford boasted that he was going to have the highest private home in Britain. But first he built a wall

Top left: William Beckford inherited a fortune and spent it in a hurry building edifices that did not even survive him.

Above: Author William Beckford maintains a moonlit vigil over the madcap building work at Fonthill. But his vast Gothic abbey turned a costly folly.

seven miles long and 12 ft high around the estate to keep out inquisitive eyes. Then he started in earnest - and in a rush. He couldn't wait for proper foundations to be dug. He decided, against his builder's advice, that the foundations that had been dug for a smaller house would be satisfactory. He used cement and wood instead of stone and brick because they were quicker to work with.

Five hundred labourers were employed, with one shift working by torchlight through the night. He even poached 450 building workers away from work on St George's Chapel at Windsor when he estimated that things were going too slowly. But he gave them too much beer as a bribe to work faster, and most of the time they worked on the great tower blinded by ale.

He demanded the use of every cart and

wagon in the area - much to the frustration of local farmers. After six years the great building was complete. The magnificent spire soared to 300 ft above the beautiful abbey.

But then the first gale blew. The spire literally snapped in two and hurtled to the ground. Coolly, millionaire Beckford announced that he was sorry he hadn't seen it crashing down - and gave orders for a new tower to be started immediately.

Seven years later the new tower was finished. But this time he had used stone to give it strength. Inside the dazzlingly decorated abbey he lived a bizarre life alone with one servant - a Spanish dwarf. But every day his dining table was set for twelve. And the cooks would be ordered to prepare food for twelve.

On his first Christmas in the newly built abbey he said he would only eat Christmas dinner if it was cooked in new kitchens. His builders told him it was not possible to finish them in time. But that wasn't any answer for the eccentric aristocrat.

On Christmas Day the fires were lit in the ovens. The mortar was hardly dry, the bricks had not settled and the timbers were not securely fixed. Dinner was in due course served. But as the small army of servants cleared the plates a crash reverberated around the abbey. The new kitchens had collapsed.

In 1822, after a slump in sugar prices, Beckford was forced to sell his dream folly to an ammunition dealer, John Farquhar, for £330,000. But the new owner did not get a good deal. Within months of his arrival the giant spire came crashing down again.

Beckford moved to Bath, but was disappointed to find that his new home was missing one essential - a tower. He promptly built one, but made sure that it was a mere 130 ft high. The great folly builder died in 1844 aged eighty-four. And for once his tower outlived him. It is still there today.

THE DRESSED UP LORD

Lord Cornbury, the 3rd Earl of Clarendon, was Queen Anne's cousin. And she gave him the plum job of representing her as Governor of New York and Jersey in America.

But he took it all a little too seriously. As he told friends: 'In this place I represent a woman, and in all respects I ought to represent her faithfully.' This was his excuse for turning up at the opening of the New York Assembly in 1702 in a blue silk gown and satin shoes, and carrying a fan.

He loved to show off on the streets wearing a hooped skirt, but his long-suffering wife did not have such a happy time. All his money went on his clothes, and he gave her none for hers. She was forced to resort to stealing.

He was ordered to return to England in 1708 to pay his debts but stayed a favourite of Queen Anne.

And he didn't change his habits upon his return, he was spotted in Worcestershire 'in a gown, stays, tucker, long ruffles and cap'.

Below: *When the Earl of Clarendon, Viscount Cornbury was sent by his cousin Queen Anne to represent her as Governor of New York, he arrived in America dressed as a woman.*

CHILD PRODIGIES
Infants Who Amaze

What creates a Mozart, composing music when most children cannot write their own names? How can an illiterate peasant child perform complicated mental arithmetic at speed? For centuries child prodigies have fascinated scientists and public alike

C hild prodigies have been astounding society for centuries with their amazing, almost magical abilities to understand things beyond the comprehension of even the most intelligent professors, maestros and theorists. These young wonders, who are literally one in a million, can solve the most complex mathematical problems, compose intricate symphonies, quote extensive passages of literature - and all before they reach their teens.

Zerah Colburn, for instance, took just four seconds to calculate how many seconds there were in eleven years.

Above: *Possibly the greatest composer who ever lived Wolfgang Amadeus Mozart playing the piano accompanied on the violin by his father.*

Opposite: *George Bidder was known in his youth as 'a calculating boy'. He grew up to become a renowned civil engineer.*

Left: *The English Methodist divine and hymn writer Charles Wesley. He was a musical prodigy who played harpsichord at the age of three.*

Wolfgang Amadeus Mozart could play the violin and piano brilliantly at the age of three. Arthur Greenwood knew the alphabet when he was just twelve months.

But these unique gifts do not come without their costs. Many prodigies had their brief day of fame, only to disappear from view, and never to fulfil their early expectations. Others died young. In many cases, the infant wonders were literally worked to death by over eager parents who hoped to cash in on their stunning talents, never allowing their offspring the time to explore the simple pleasures of youth.

Child genius is far more common in boys than in girls, probably because infantile gland disorders - thought to be responsible for creating the amazing talents - are mainly found in males. Medical authorities believe prodigies produce an exceptional level of hormones in certain glands, including the pituitary and adrenal. These child wonders, then, peak at an early age because their nervous systems reach their pinnacle long before the rest of their bodies develop.

Although some prodigies have graced the world of literature and fine art, they are extremely rare, experts say, and usually burn out quickly. Englishwoman Daisy Ashford was one. When she wrote *The Young Visiters* (sic) at the age of nine it was hailed as a masterpiece. She never came close to matching its brilliance.

Rather, young geniuses seem to excel in the fields of maths and music - because neither of those disciplines requires experience of life.

MUSICAL GENIUSES

Though a vast majority of child wonders fade into oblivion after a brief blaze of glory, musical child prodigies, many descended from eminent musical families, fare better because their works often live on.

The greatest of these was Mozart, arguably the finest composer who ever lived. Receiving practically his entire education from his father Leopold, himself a fine musician, the young Wolfgang was just three years old when he first became an attraction in Salzburg. By the time he was four, he could remember every note in every solo of the concertos he heard and liked.

His reputation as a musical genius soon brought him to the attention of the Austrian Emperor, and by the time he was six he, his father and sister Maria Anna, herself an accomplished pianist at the age of eight, embarked on a lengthy tour of Europe, playing for the crowned heads and aristocracy of several countries. Everywhere they went, Wolfgang caused a sensation with his exquisite touch - whether it was on the piano, violin or organ.

Despite the boy's amazing gifts, however, Wolfgang's father could not secure him an appointment equal to his status and talent. So, at the age of twenty-five, Mozart decided to try for himself.

Above: *Polish pianist and composer Frederick Chopin first performed for an audience at the age of only eight.*

Below: *Dr Richard Strauss, his wife and grandson. Strauss composed music from the age of six right up until his death.*

He left Salzburg for Vienna, where the following year he married a singer named Constanze Weber.

The marriage took its toll on Mozart's finances, which were meagre, but even when he was in the grip of poverty he continued to compose some of the most beautiful music the world has ever heard. In fact he left more than six hundred works. Within a few hours of his death, at the age of thirty-five in 1791, he was still working on his unfinished Requiem.

He was once asked to explain by a friend how he composed his sonatas and symphonies. Mozart replied, much to his friend's surprise, that he had no idea.

'When I am in particularly good condition, perhaps riding in a carriage, or in a walk after a good meal, and in a sleepless night, then the thoughts come to me in a rush and best of all,' he said.

'Whence or how - that I do not know and cannot learn: those which please me, I retain in my head and hum them perhaps to myself - at least, so others have told me. Then it goes on and I keep on expanding it and making it more distinct and the thing, however long it be, becomes almost finished in my head.'

Charles Wesley, nephew of the founder of Methodism, was another musical prodigy. Like Mozart, he showed an uncanny talent at the tender age of three

by playing for his startled father a tune on the harpsichord.

His genius quickly developed to the extent that, whenever he heard a tune or melody on the street, he would race home and play it - even though he never

studied music. When he was just four his father introduced him to the leading musicians of his day in eighteenth century London, and two years later he was being tutored by a master in Bristol.

Young Charles became so adept at playing the works of Handel and Scarlatti that at the age of twelve he was regarded as the most accomplished interpreter of their works in the world. He went on to enrich the musical world with many hymn tunes of his own.

When asked by a friend to explain how he composed music, Mozart replied that he had no idea

---

There were, of course, many other precocious musical prodigies. Chopin made his public debut when he was eight. Weber was appointed conductor of the Opera at Breslau when he was seventeen. Richard Strauss was composing music from the age of six and continued until his death. Haydn too composed from the age of six. Sir Yehudi Menuhin was playing the violin with ease by the time he was three and at thirty-two was

Above: *Franz Josef Haydn composed from the age of six. Here his nautical experience inspires his great works:* The Four Seasons *and* The Creation.

Left: *British conductor Sir Ronald Landon, born in 1873, could play the piano before he could even talk.*

considered a virtuoso. And Sir Landon Ronald could play the piano before he could even talk.

Not all great young talents are remembered by history, however. One of the most remarkable reports of a musical prodigy appeared in the *Encyclopedia of Psychic Science*. It told of Blind Tom, a five-year-old black child, the son of slaves, dazzling pre-Civil War America by playing two tunes on the piano at the same time - one with each hand - while he sang a third!

YOUNG MATHEMATICIANS

Still, providence was on the whole far kinder to musical prodigies than to those who excelled in mathematics. Most of the latter faded into obscurity once their moment of glory passed.

Ampère, the great French physicist and mathematician whose name is now used to measure electric current, is a notable exception - for many reasons.

Not only did he achieve lasting fame and recognition, but he also showed amazing talents in more than one discipline. A voracious reader, he raced through every book his father could get him, but loved nothing better than devouring a twenty-one-volume encyclopedia - most of which he could recite verbatim many years later.

In 1786, when he was just eleven, he was already studying advanced mathematics. Within seven years he had mastered the intricate complexities of Lagrange's landmark publication, *Mechanique Analytique*.

During the remainder of his life - he died in 1836 - Ampère revolutionized mathematics, discovered the fundamental laws of electrodynamics and wrote important papers on chemistry, poetry and psychology.

Carl Friedrich Gauss, born in 1777 to a poor German family, is also remembered. At the age of twenty-four he published his *Disquisitiones Arithmetica*, which is considered a milestone in numerical theory.

Regarded as the premier mathematician of the nineteenth century, Gauss showed his promise amazingly early when, at the age of two, he mentally corrected his father's mistakes when working out the

Above: *Andrè Marie Ampère, the French physicist and mathematician whose name is now used as a measure of electric current. He could recite an encyclopedia verbatim.*

wages of some workmen. The boy became a local celebrity in his home town of Braunschweig and, thanks to some kindly noblemen, was given the chance to attend school, mastering the classical languages by the time he was eleven.

But maths was his real forte. Once a new mathematics teacher told him not to bother coming to lessons, because he couldn't teach him anything he didn't already know. By the time he was fourteen, he had been called to the court of the Grand Duke of Brunswick, where he entertained the aristocracy with his amazing memory and astonishing speed at solving difficult calculations.

But even Ampère and Gauss were no match for some of the most amazing mathematical prodigies, even if the latter

Zerah Colburn,
Aged 8 years,
Remarkable for solving Arithmetical questions.
Copied by permission from the original.
Pub. April 7 1813, by R. S. Kirby, 11, London House Yard, S.t Paul's

following problems, which he solved in mere seconds, and always in his head - and remember, he could not perform even the most simple multiplication on paper.

Given that the distance between Boston and Concord is 65 miles, how many paces must it take, assuming each step is three feet? The answer, 114,400, was given in ten seconds.

What number multiplied by itself will produce 998,001? In less than four seconds he answered: 999.

While able to solve intricate mathematical problems at lightning speed in his head, he could not do the simplest sum on paper

---

Colburn's fame soon spread to Europe, and in 1812 his father took him to England, where the greatest mathematicians of the day quizzed him. The young prodigy answered every question correctly, and so quickly that the man appointed to take down the results had to ask him to slow down.

For instance, when asked the square root of 106,929 he answered '327' immediately - before the poor note-taker could even record the original figure! They tried another. What is the cube root of 268,336,125? Without a second's thought, he replied '645'.

In another incredible feat, he proved that the number 4,294,967,297 was not a prime number - one that could only be divided by 1 and itself - even though it had long been asserted that it was. In his head, he worked out that the number was equal to 641 x 6,700,417.

Give the square of 999,999? Answer: 999,998,000,001. In five seconds, he worked out the cube root of 413,993,348,677 (7453).

The questions kept coming. How many times would a coach wheel, 12 feet in circumference, turn around in 256 miles. And how many minutes are there in 48 years? He answered both in less than four seconds. To the amazement of everyone present, with the second of these two answers he gave the number of seconds as well!

Inexplicably, within two years of his dramatic performance before the great

never fully bloomed into greatness. Zerah Colburn, for example, lost his powers of calculation when he was just ten, but his wondrous feats still amaze. Born in Vermont in 1804, Colburn had no mathematical education, and yet by the time he was six was giving public demonstrations of his skills. Consider the

Above: *Zerah Colburn at the age of eight was asked 'How many minutes are there in 48 years?' He answered correctly in four seconds.*

minds of Europe he lost his amazing powers entirely. As a young man he tried his hand at acting, but failed, so in 1821 he returned to America where he was ordained a deacon in the Methodist Church. For the next fourteen years he served as an itinerant preacher until appointed as a language professor to a small seminary college. He died at the age of thirty-five.

The young prodigy answered the questions so quickly that the note-taker had to ask him to slow down

---

One of the greatest English child prodigies was George Bidder, who was born in Moretonhampstead, Devon in 1805. Billed as the 'Calculating Boy', Bidder showed extraordinary abilities at the age of four, even though he could not even count to ten until he was six! Nor could he read figures, and his command of language was so poor that he did not even know there was such a word as 'multiply'.

But he so dazzled everyone who met him that his father took him on a tour of England, and soon everyone was clamouring to see the 'Calculating Boy' who answered every poser with consummate ease:

What is the compound interest on £4444 for 4444 days at 4 1/2 per cent per annum? In two minutes, he gave the answer: £2434, 16 shillings and 5 1/4 pence.

How long does it take to fill a cistern with a volume of one cubic mile at the rate of 120 gallons per minute? Again in two minutes came the reply: 14,300 years, 285 days, 12 hours and 46 minutes. Bidder even took leap years into account!

If a clock pendulum vibrates the distance of 9 3/4 inches in a second, how many inches will it vibrate in 7 years, 14 days, 2 hours, 1 minute and 56 seconds, if each year is precisely 365 days, 5 hours, 48 minutes and 55 seconds? In less than a minute, Bidder replied 2,165,625,744 3/4 in.

If a flea jumps 2 ft 3 in in every leap, how many hops would it take to go around the world, whose circumference is 25,020 miles? And how long would it take, given that it hops once every second without a break. In seconds, the answers came: 58,713,600 leaps, and 1 year, 314 days, 13 hours and 20 minutes.

Bidder, who eventually spent some time in school and was then privately tutored, rose to great heights, becoming one of England's greatest engineers. He was largely responsible for founding the London telegraph system, constructed the Victoria Docks, and became the President of the Institution of Civil Engineers.

His amazing powers actually increased with time, and in problems where some special properties played a role he was equalled only by Ampère.

Two days before his death, in 1878, a friend posed the following problem. Given that the speed of light is 190,000 miles a second, and the wavelength of the red rays is 36,918 to the inch, how many of its waves must strike the eye in one second? As his friend pulled out a pencil

Below: Philosopher John Stuart Mill in a photograph taken in 1860.

to calculate the answer, Bidder reportedly replied: 'You need not work it out. The number of vibrations will be 444,433,651,200,000.'

Unusually for a former child genius, George Bidder retained his amazing abilities until he died in his seventies

---

Unfortunately, history has not always recorded the exploits of prodigies so well as those listed above. Nevertheless, enough remains of their legendary abilities for even twentieth-century men and women to admire their genius.

Miguel Mantilla, a Mexican-born infant, was just two years old when he could answer questions like: 'In what years did, or will, 4 February be a Friday?' He could rattle off the answers in less than ten seconds.

George Watson, a native of Buxted in Sussex, was born in 1785. He was considered almost an idiot in everything except calculation and memory. Although he could neither read nor write, he performed in his head the most difficult mathematical problems and could answer correctly, without hesitation, any questions concerning what day of the week it was for any date in history. If the date happened to be during his lifetime, he could also say where he was and what the weather had been. He could also describe and count every church and public house in every village, town and city throughout the neighbouring counties.

Some prodigies have exhibited all-round amazing skills. Christian Heinecken, who was known as the 'Infant of Lubeck', startled everyone in Germany when, a few hours after his birth in 1721, he began talking. Before he was a year old, it is reported that he could remember all the major events in the first five books of the Old Testament. And by his second birthday he could name all the historical happenings in the Bible, as well as knowing Latin, French and geography.

John Stuart Mill, the nineteenth century philosopher and economist, could read Greek at the age of three. By the time he was ten was completely at ease with the complex works of Plato and Demosthenes.

Thomas Macaulay was one of England's all-round geniuses. At seven he had already written a universal history, at eight composed a thesis on how to convert the natives in Malabar to Christianity, and at fourteen he could recite all of Milton's 'Paradise Lost'.

Blaise Pascal, the French philosopher and mathematician, was likewise an all-round wonder child. Before he was twelve, he was writing theses on acoustics, and he invented the first calculating machine at nineteen. By the time of his thirtieth birthday, just nine years before his death in 1662, he had written several books on religion.

Today eleven-year-old Ganesh Sittampalam, who lives in Surbiton, Surrey, could well lay claim to being the world's smartest child. He's already the youngest university student on the planet, and is currently speeding through his course even though he only attends lectures once a week. At his present pace, he should have his Bachelor of Science degree by the time he's thirteen.

Above: *Blaise Pascal was a seventeenth-century French mathematician and religious philosopher.*

STAR FOLLIES
'Showbiz' Shockers

Voracious sexual appetites, dangerous practical jokes, black magic rituals and a terrible fear of growing up - hallmarks of some of the freaky superstars of twentieth-century showbusiness

With more money than sense, the glitzy stars of showbiz and pop enjoy themselves with a vengeance. Cash is the last thing on their minds when they set out to indulge their eccentricities. Bizarre, freaky, wild, sexy or just plain daft, the household names of screen and record often outperform their screen characters in their own lives.

KEITH MOON

The drummer with the Who rock group was a lunatic on stage - and off it. On stage he regularly wrecked his drum kit. Off stage he thought nothing of

Opposite: *Greta Garbo was the ultimate sex symbol...mysterious, unattainable, who always wanted to 'be alone'.*

Below left: *Rolling Stone Mick Jagger has a pretty good line in eccentricity himself - but he also once suffered at the hands of Keith Moon. Moon interrupted his honeymoon night with Bianca.*

Below: *The Who's drummer Keith Moon started his day with two bottles of champagne before tackling a couple of bottles of brandy.*

wrecking his car by driving it into a swimming pool.

Whenever he stayed in hotels he went on orgies of destruction. He dropped firecrackers down the loo, blowing holes in the floor. He chopped furniture into firewood and threw TVs out of the window. He earned a fortune - but spent it before he could count it.

The clown's antics in hotels cost him £200,000! He explained his bizarre behaviour simply: 'The momentum is still there when I come off stage. I'm like an express train or an ocean liner. It takes me two or three miles to stop.'

Moon was like a child who could permanently misbehave and knew he would never be punished. His cash would always protect him. When asked what he feared most, he replied: 'Having to grow up.'

Born in August 1947, the son of a London motor mechanic, he moved from job to job until he joined The Who in the 1960s. He got an audition with the group

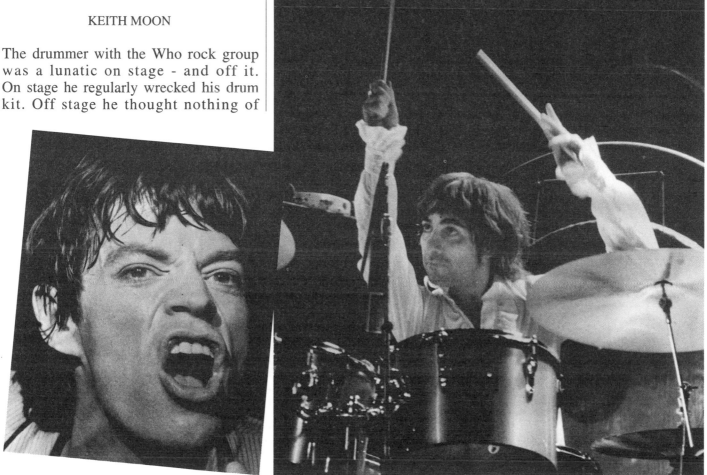

Above: *Keith Moon in action with his co-stars in The Who. He was found dead by his Swedish girlfriend in his London flat in 1978 at the age of 32.*

simply by saying that he was a better drummer than the one they had. Lead singer Roger Daltrey remembered that Moon turned up with orange hair and wearing an orange suit. They called him the Gingerbread Man.

He ended the audition by smashing up his drum kit. It was to become his trademark at concerts worldwide. Moon became known as the wild man of pop.

He started the day with a Bucks Fizz - champagne and orange juice - out of a mug, lying back in a black velvet, monogrammed dressing-gown. It was just a warm-up for his daily intake of two bottles of champagne and a couple of bottles of brandy. And then the fun started. Moon didn't care who were the victims of his pranks. Mick Jagger exploded with rage after Moon ruined a honeymoon night after the Stone's wedding to Bianca. The couple were asleep in their eleventh floor hotel room in Hollywood when they heard movement on their balcony. Mick took a gun from under his pillow and aimed it at the curtains.

Suddenly they were swept aside and

there was Moon. 'Good evening,' he said. The madcap pop star had climbed from balcony to balcony, hundreds of feet up, to offer his wedding congratulations.

When Moon blew up his drum kit on stage with gunpowder, Bette Davis fainted in the wings

---

His antics were often explosive. On American TV Moon decided that The Who's performance would end with a bang. He arranged for a special effects man to blow up his drum kit with gunpowder. Unfortunately Moon kept on plying him with drink. And with every drink more and more gunpowder was poured into the explosive device.

The result was dramatic. Moon was thrown backwards through the scenery. Lead guitarist Pete Townsend stood petrified, his hair ablaze. And when Moon lurched forward out of the scenery to take his bow he was covered in blood, with pieces of drum kit embedded in his arms. Screen star Bette Davis, who had been watching from the wings, promptly fainted with shock.

Dressing up was another of his favourite pranks. The police were not amused when they got involved in one of his stunts. A Rolls-Royce had drawn up in London's Oxford Street. Two huge but smart, obvious villains jumped out and leaped on an innocent-looking, middle-aged clergyman.

They gave him a kicking and beating worthy of the East End.The crowds on the pavements did nothing while the vicar was dragged screaming and kicking into the back of the Rolls. He was heard to yell: 'Have you no respect for the cloth?'

Two youths eventually gave chase and, seeing the vicar pinned in the back, called the police. When stopped at a roadblock, out stepped the vicar, unharmed. It was Keith Moon.

'I love to make people laugh,' he said. The police didn't.

In the mid-seventies after years of living in an alcoholic haze, Moon tried to cut back on drink with the help of fellow drummer Ringo Starr. But he still managed to get himself kicked off a British Airways jet after trying to break into the pilot's cabin demanding to play his drumsticks on the control panel.

One night in 1978 he went to a party and announced his engagement to blonde Swedish model Annette Walter-Lax. Next morning he was found dead of natural causes. He'd always said that he was going to die young. He was thirty-one.

ERROL FLYNN

A generation earlier, film star Errol Flynn was the swashbuckling hell-raiser who set new standards in showbiz for eccentricity - and scandalous behaviour. He designed himself a house of pleasure in the Hollywood Hills - a fortress for erotic amusements. The kinky Flynn even installed two-way mirrors in the ceilings of the bedroom so that he and his friends could observe his guests making love.

Flynn said of the visitors to Mulholland House: 'Strange people wended their way up the hill. Among them pimps, sports, bums, down-at-the-heel actors, queers, athletes, sightseers, process-servers, phonies, salesmen, everything in the world.' And of course, pretty girls.

In the later 1930s Flynn had taken over the role of handsome film hero John Barrymore. Said producer Jack Warner: 'He had mediocre talent, but to the Walter Mittys of the world he was all the heroes in one magnificent sexy animal package... actor or no actor, he showered an audience with sparks when he laughed, when he fought or when he loved.'

Flynn may have made the perfect screen Robin Hood. In real life he was a drunk with brittle bones and permanent piles. But he had an image to keep up as a rake. And he set about living up to it with spirit - mainly Scotch whisky. But his disgraceful philandering was to catch up with him in 1943. He was charged with rape after complaints from two Hollywood groupies, Betty Hansen and Peggy Satterlee.

Below: *Errol Flynn was a disgraceful philanderer. But his amorous activities rebounded in 1943 when he was charged with rape.*

Betty alleged that Flynn had raped her at a sex-and-swim party, while Peggy said that they had made love on the *Sirocco* in front of every porthole. Betty told how Flynn had undressed to have sex with her - but had kept his socks on. This caused some amusement amongst film-goers of the day. Flynn's last film had been *They Died with Their Boots On*. After the reputations of the two 'victims' had been destroyed by Flynn's lawyer, the jury had no difficulty acquitting him.

From the early 1950s it was downhill all the way. Drink and drugs pushed Flynn towards an early death.

JIMMY PAGE

While Errol Flynn built his house of pleasure Led Zeppelin guitarist Jimmy Page bought his dream home, which more accurately should be described as

Below: *How Aleister Crowley saw himself. This self-portrait of the man who called himself 'The Beast'.*

the House of a Thousand Nightmares: It had previously been owned by the character known as the Wickedest Man in the World.

Boleskine House, overlooking Loch Ness in Scotland, had been owned by Aleister Crowley, the English public schoolboy who became the King of Satanism. He was known as the Great Beast, 666, or the English Beelzebub.

Page, an authority on Satanism, was so obsessed that he bought Crowley's former temple, a brooding, sinister place haunted by the ghost of a man beheaded there. But the evil vibrations of the house and Page's dabbling with black magic had a deadly effect. It was as though Led Zeppelin had angered the devil, and it was cursed.

Heavy rock band Led Zeppelin were formed in 1968 after Jimmy Page's group the Yardbirds collapsed. Within a couple of years they had taken America and Europe by storm. In the seventies they were outselling the Rolling Stones albums by three to one. And indulging in the sex and drugs which went with success in the rock 'n' roll world.

Sex and drugs were also the keys to the working of Aleister Crowley's evil mind. Through them he sought a higher plateau of gratification.

But heroin and booze were taking their toll. Bonham was so chronic an alcoholic that a doctor had to travel with him. And then the run of bad luck started.

In August 1975 the car carrying Plant, his wife Maureen, their children and Jimmy Page's daughter crashed into a tree on the Greek island of Rhodes. Maureen fractured her skull, her husband broke an ankle and elbow, and the children fractured various limbs. Plant could not walk for six months.

Had Page's dabblings in black magic caused an awful curse to be laid on him and the members of Led Zeppelin?

The rumours began about Satan's curse on Led Zeppelin. At Boleskine House a caretaker had killed himself. And the man who replaced him went mad. In July 1977 a freak respiratory complaint killed Plant's five-year-old son Karac. Had

Jimmy Page upset his evil masters, and were they hitting back?

The final blow came in September 1980 when John Bonham was rehearsing at Page's other home at Windsor. On his way he dropped into a pub for lunch. With his sandwiches he drank sixteen vodkas. At the rehearsal, which turned into a party, he drank vodka after vodka until he collapsed in a coma. He never woke up. He was thirty-one.

The original Led Zeppelin would never play again. Had the Wickedest Man in the World returned for his final evil revenge?

GRETA GARBO

Movie star Greta Garbo was the ultimate recluse, mysterious, unattainable, a superstar who valued her privacy more than all the money in the world. She announced, 'I want to be alone,' and for the last forty years of her life she did not make a film.

Instead she became a legend, an enigma living a lonely life in Manhattan on the riches she had earned during her twenty-year Hollywood career.

She had an ex-directory phone number and even those who had it were always answered with 'Miss Garbo isn't in' by the ex-actress. She rarely went out. When she did, she flitted around the streets like a beautiful ghost. Her eyes were always shielded by dark glasses, and a slouching coolie-style straw hat covered most of her pale face.

Even in her death she insisted on being mysterious. Officials at New York Hospital, where she had been on a kidney dialysis machine, said it had been her wish that no details should be given.

She was very rich but very mean. When she went out to buy clothes it was at a sale, and she even sold back to the newsagent magazines she had bought and which she found on inspection to be without interest. In her last interview she said: 'I don't want any kind of attention from anybody, except that I know that someone likes me. Otherwise it's sickening.'

She was born Greta Lovisa Gustafsson in Stockholm, Sweden on 18 September, 1905, daughter of an uneducated labourer who was often ill or unemployed. She

left school at fourteen to help pay for his medical treatment, and vowed then to build her life so that she would never be financially dependent on anyone.

She began making her living in a barber shop, lathering men's faces. Her big break came at seventeen in the hat section of the department store where she then worked, when she was chosen to appear in a filmed hat advertisement. The stage-struck youngster enrolled at Stockholm's Royal Dramatic Theatre and haunted film studios seeking work.

Her career took off when Maurice Stiller, then Sweden's leading director, became besotted by the tall, angular beauty. He made her his protegee, changed her name to Garbo and starred her in his 1924 silent movie *The Atonement of Gosta Berling*.

She had light brown hair and greyish green eyes, and always kept her Swedish accent - which meant she could never pronounce her Ws. Said Hollywood director George Cukor: 'She could let an audience know she was thinking things

Top: *Greta Lovisa Gustafsson was the daughter of an uneducated and often unemployed Swedish labourer. Later she was to haunt film studios seeking work.*

Above: *The haunting beauty of Garbo...'She could let an audience know she was thinking things and thinking them uncensored'.*

Above: Michael Jackson was a superstar before he even reached his teens. He has since been making up for his lost childhood.

getting into his stride when the Swedish actress suddenly pushed him away and leaped out of bed. She then proceeded to perform energetic aerobic exercises while singing an obscure Scandinavian peasant song.

When her bewildered lover asked her what she was doing, Garbo explained that it was her mother's tried and tested method of avoiding getting pregnant. It obviously worked for Garbo.

Garbo stopped making films in 1941 at the grand age of thirty-five. In her films she had always played ladies of mystery. Now she started playing the part in real life. The eccentric enigma spurned her adoring public totally and locked herself away in an apartment on East 52nd Street, New York. It was furnished in bare Swedish functional style with a few valuable paintings, Renoirs and Modiglianis. A cleaning lady came twice a week; otherwise she had her wish: she was alone until her death in 1990.

MICHAEL JACKSON

Megastar singer Michael Jackson did not have a childhood. He was a star by the age of ten. But he's been making up for it ever since.

As a child he was so busy singing that he never visited a zoo. So now he's bought himself one. Chimpanzee Bubbles is his favourite animal - Michael treats him like the child he so badly wants. The private zoo also boasts a giraffe called Mahali, snakes, llamas and peacocks.

He wanted a fire engine. So Wacko Jacko spent $150,000 on one for his ranch in the Santa Ynez valley, California. He wanted a train set. So he paid $7 million for a home which has its own railway track running up to the front door from the tennis courts.

In the past fifteen years he has undergone over a dozen operations and paid plastic surgeons more than $250,000 to transform his image. He has spent $90,000 on a pressurized oxygen chamber so that he can breathe pure air at his home. He takes regular naps in it, so that he can live to be 150.

For exercise he dances for hours, copying the movements of his animals for new dance steps. Said Jerome

and thinking them uncensored.'

Garbo stepped on to US soil in 1925 and had American audiences drooling from her first appearance in the silent movie *The Torrent*. She was a superstar within two years. But the coming of sound movies was a worrying time for Garbo. Would US audiences accept her foreign accent?

She made her first 'talkie' in 1930. Garbo's first lines in *Anna Christie* were: 'Gimme a vwisky vwith chincher ale on the side; and don't be stinchy, beby.' She became nicknamed the Swedish Sphinx, surrounding herself with mystery. She also earned a fortune.

Garbo never married, but had numerous love affairs. One of her lovers, Polish poet Antoni Gronowicz, told of her strange bedroom antics. He was just

The first hit record, 'I Want You Back', came in 1970. Two years later he went solo - and those golden eggs kept on coming. His *Thriller* album published in 1982 sold 37 million copies. When its sales had reached 25 million it was estimated to have earned him $50 million. On a worldwide tour in 1988 he was earning £200 - a second!

No wonder he can afford to indulge himself with a weird lifestyle. Chimpanzee Bubbles has been trained to smile, roller-skate and ride a horse.

Jackson may be freaky himself - but he has an interest in other freaks too! While in London he showed a morbid fascination for the Victorian sideshow freak known as the Elephant Man. He visited the London Hospital in Whitechapel and stared for half an hour at the tragic remains of John Merrick, whose story was told in the film starring John Hurt.

When he returned to the US he ordered his staff to buy the preserved remains - whatever the cost. The London Hospital politely declined to sell. So Jackson bought two ancient Egyptian mummies instead.

Jackson has created a fantasy world with pet animals as a shield against his greedy human entourage

---

Howard, former president of the Jackson companies, 'Watch him next time you see him dance - you'll see the movements of Michael's menagerie right there on stage.' Added Jerome, 'Jackson lives in his own little world with his animals. He confides in them, not people. He's created a fantasy world to protect himself from the money-hungry, cut-throat humans around him who do anything they want to keep their goose laying those golden eggs.'

Michael Joe Jackson was born on 29 August, 1958 in Gary, Indiana. And he's been laying those golden eggs from the very beginning. His domineering dad, Joe, decided that his family were going to be stars, and everything was sacrificed to his dream.

His first career break came when he won a talent contest at high school. Michael's recording debut came singing with his brothers as the Jackson Five on a record called 'I'm a Big Boy Now' in 1968.

It is hardly surprising that many friends say that the key to understanding the eccentric superstar is in his troubled relationship with his father. But the singer was to get his revenge years later when he sacked his father as his manager.

Above: A young Liz Taylor pictured by renowned photographer Baron in 1954.

He has spent his life looking for love. Michael is devoted to singer Diana Ross, who is credited with discovering the Jackson clan. Liz Taylor was next on his list. He turned one room at his mansion into a shrine to her, covering the wall with her photographs and installing a giant video screen to play her movies twenty-four hours a day. In 1987 he stunned her by proposing marriage. Liz rejected him.

Soon after this, he made enquiries about adopting four children. But it came to nothing. Then he instructed lawyers to find a surrogate mother to have his child - without sex. According to his aides, the mother would have to be one in a million - black, spiritually and physically beautiful, and with a high IQ.

Perhaps only when his child is born will Michael Jackson find true happiness and give up the bizarre childlike existence in which he so shyly hides.

ECCENTRIC FLAIR
Cranks and Crackpots

Paranoid about germs, Howard Hughes lived in a hermetically sealed environment - yet managed to run a business empire. Frank Buckland fed his pet monkeys beer in the week and port on Sundays. Cranky these two may have been, but they were not unique...

Left: *Howard Hughes and his TWA boss Joseph Bartles set off on a record-breaking Los Angeles to New York flight. Naturally the plane was filled with starlets.*

Opposite: *Film magnate, aircraft manufacturer and aviator Howard Hughes as he liked to be photographed - in the days when he allowed himself to be photographed at all.*

Below: *Starlets like the young Ginger Rogers were escorted by Howard Hughes who, with oil riches, took Hollywood by storm.*

Eccentrics have brightened every age. And now that conformity is the order of the day, with faceless bureaucrats watching and commanding our every move, they bring fresh air to our regimented lives.

HOWARD HUGHES

The twentieth-century crank Howard Hughes was one of the greatest mysteries of the modern world. He was so obsessed by germs that he cut himself off from the outside world for twenty years.

A billionaire, he lived in luxury hotels where he would always book the whole penthouse floor. He was surrounded by guards who were never allowed to see him. TV cameras monitored every possible entrance.

And inside he sealed himself off in his own prison with the most extraordinary thoroughness. All furniture was removed except for his bed and a chair. The windows were covered, so no light entered his room, and then the windows were taped to keep out germs. He had no books or photographs: just a film projector and a vast box of tissues to dust down surfaces constantly. And yet he ran a worldwide business empire with a rod of iron.

Hughes was born rich in Houston,

Above: *Visitors to the home of naturalist Frank Buckland would find alligator, mice, squirrel and ostrich on the menu.*

Texas. When his father died he left the young man an oil-drilling tool company. And twenty-one-year-old Hughes took off for Hollywood to invest in the new boom industry of movie-making.

He was an instant success, producing *Scarface*, with George Raft, and *Hell's Angels*, the first film to star Jean Harlow. She became one of his many Hollywood lovers. Hughes was charming, witty, irresistible and seriously rich. He bought apartments for his lovers as easily as some men would buy them dinners.

It was good news for a starlet to be seen with him, and he was spotted out with young hopefuls like Ava Gardner, Ginger Rogers, Mitzi Gaynor and Elizabeth Taylor.

But if he treated Hollywood and showbiz as his hobby, big business was his life. A keen pilot, he owned two aircraft companies: Trans World Airlines and Hughes Aircraft. He also saw himself as an engineer.

He designed a monster plane called Hercules to move troops in World War II. It was an eight-engined flying boat which could carry seven hundred soldiers and weighed 200 tons. But it was just too heavy. Hughes himself was its pilot for the one mile it ever flew.

But he was already showing signs of eccentric behaviour. A police officer in Louisiana refused to believe that the scruffy tramp in front of his desk was Howard Hughes. The man was unshaven, wearing a crumpled, filthy suit, and on his feet were a scruffy pair of gym shoes.

The Louisiana police couldn't believe that the scruffy tramp in front of them was the famous billionaire businessman

---

Hughes had been taken to his police station as a vagrant. He'd crashed his private plane and, despite having $1200 in his pocket, had no identification. The police officer refused to release him until he was identified by a friend.

After his second marriage ended with a $1 million pay-off Hughes became more and more reclusive. He hired a loyal group of bodyguards who were all Mormons. They became known as the Mormon Mafia as they protected him at his bungalow in the desert near Las Vegas. Visitors were rare. But for those he dealt with, it was highly unusual. One big airline boss was driven miles into the searing heat of the desert, the car windows firmly closed. Even the air vents were sealed by paper handkerchiefs - so that their conversations could not be overheard!

For the last twenty years of his life he wandered from one luxury hotel to another with his Mormon Mafia always in attendance. To move him they often used private ambulances, with Hughes strapped to a stretcher as he left or entered his new 'home'.

His eating habits were getting stranger. Hughes was reducing himself to a skeleton. He would have an obsession about chicken soup, for instance, and that was all he would eat for weeks. Then he would go on an ice cream diet.

He only had his hair and fingernails cut twice in ten years - his nails grew to a horrendous four inches long, and his greasy hair and beard hung down his chest in a vile dirty black mass. Yet he insisted that the hairdresser clean up like a surgeon before approaching him.

He died, aged sixty-eight, on the plane which was taking him back to his birthplace in Houston, Texas. It was the one secret that he couldn't keep from the world.

FRANK BUCKLAND

Howard Hughes may have had bizarre eating habits but they were nothing compared to those of nineteenth-century naturalist Frank Buckland. He would eat anything at all - from elephant trunk to roast giraffe.

Strange eating habits ran in the family. His father, Dr William Buckland, was said to have eaten a chunk of Louis XIV's embalmed heart! Buckland senior, a clergyman and Dean of Westminster, thought the worst thing he'd ever tasted was mole - it ran a close second to stewed bluebottles.

Animals were always part of his life. He was born in 1826 and lived in a large house on the quadrangle of Christ Church, Oxford, where his father was then canon. It was full of live - and many dead - animals. Snakes and frogs were kept in glass cases in the dining room where the most extraordinary meals were served up. Alligator, mice on toast and roast ostrich were often on the menu.

Though fond of mice in batter, he could not abide fried earwigs

---

At the age of four Frank was given a small natural history cabinet which he used to store his dissections and stuffed animals. Later, while at public school, at Winchester College, he would be so hungry that he would often eat squirrel pie or mice in batter.

He kept live animals too. In his room he had a buzzard, an owl, a raccoon, jackdaws and a magpie. While he was at Oxford his pockets were stuffed with slow worms living in moss. They had a disconcerting habit of poking their heads out when he was talking.

Below: Watching, not eating... Buckland examines caged monkeys at his home. He introduced new breeds of animal to Britain; some wandered free, others he cooked.

Left: *Shropshire squire John Mytton went out hunting stark naked - even in winter - and drank up to eight bottles of port or brandy a day.*

Below: *Sir Francis Galton's* **Art of Travel** *was full of helpful hints. If you want to light your pipe while travelling in a high wind, just get your horse to lie down and use the creature as a windshield.*

FRANCIS GALTON

Cranky scientist Francis Galton worked so hard that he was worried he would suffer from 'strained brain'. So he invented a strange hat ventilated with holes so that the cool air could circulate around his head as he studied. It had little retractable shutters which were opened by a valve, operated by a small bulb in the end of a rubber tube which hung down from the top of his head.

It seemed to work for the eccentric scientist. He was an expert in medicine, mathematics and metereology, to name just a few of his interests. He wrote prolifically, and received many academic honours as well as a knighthood.

Buckland became a popular surgeon at St George's Hospital, London but began to spend more and more time as a naturalist, writing and lecturing on animals. He became a founder member of the Society for the Acclimatization of Animals in the United Kingdom.

At home the living room was like a private zoo. The eccentric naturalist kept monkeys by the fire and allowed them to roam free, causing immense damage. He gave them beer every night and they had a glass of port on Sundays. Pet rats romped on his desk and a mongoose ran wild round the house.

Amidst this chaos he would work on his learned treatises, puffing away at a huge cigar and wearing a bowler hat - but with bare feet. He hated shoes and boots.

London Zoo gave him plenty of samples for his cranky menus. He insisted that a dead prize panther was dug up so that he could try panther steaks. And he was delighted when the giraffe house burnt down, because then he could try roast giraffe.

In the 1860s an interest in fish took over his life. Buckland hatched thirty thousand salmon in his kitchen and became the Inspector of HM Salmon Fisheries on the personal recommendation of Queen Victoria. He travelled around Britain by train, but he always had the carriage to himself because he smelt so appallingly of fish.

FRANCIS GALTON

But the dotty scientist will always be remembered for one serious discovery. He was the man who realized that every human being has a different set of fingerprints, a revelation that was to change the face of police detective work. His system of classifying them is still used today.

One of his most successful works was a book called *The Art of Travel*. Published in the 1840s, it suggested a cure for feeling under the weather while travelling in foreign countries: drop a little gunpowder into a glass of warm soapy water, and drink. It will tickle the throat, he said, but clear the system.

He had many such helpful suggestions. How do you keep your clothes dry in a downpour? Take them off and sit on them. Blisters on the feet? Make a lather of soap bubbles in your socks and break a raw egg into each boot.

How do you light your pipe in a heavy wind? Get your horse to lie down and use it as a windshield. To cure wasp stings: take the gunge from your pipe and smear it on the skin.

Galton was born in 1822 into a rich scientifically minded family. After Cambridge University he travelled in Syria, Egypt and the Sudan. He acted the typical Englishman abroad, while at the same time taking his scientific research seriously.

There were no carpets, curtains or wallpaper in Galton's home because he regarded them as purposeless dust-traps

---

He wanted to know why the Hottentot women had such large bottoms. Seeing a suitable example bathing one day he set to work to do some serious research. At a distance he measured her rear with his sextant and then using trigonometry and logarithms, calculated her shape in comparison with the standard English woman. It made a very solemn paper for the Royal Geographical Society.

At his London home in South Kensington, he insisted that everything should have a practical purpose. He refused to have carpets, curtains and wallpaper - because they collected dust and had no purpose. He had no comfortable chairs, just wooden benches.

Diners at his Rutland Gate home were also unwitting victims of his experiments. He had a theory that if people were attracted to each other they would lean towards each other like metal to a magnet. If they weren't attracted they would sit bolt upright. He installed pressure pads on the sides of his dining room chairs, and after his guests had left took readings to judge if they had got on.

JOHN MYTTON

Shropshire squire, John Mytton drank up to eight bottles of port or brandy every day. He used to say that it kept him warm while he was out hunting stark naked ... whatever the weather.

Mytton was born in 1796, and when his father died he was left the family seat, Halston Hall, near Shrewsbury, £60,000 in cash and an income of about £10,000 a year. It was a fortune in those days, but he got through the lot in fifteen years.

He dropped bundles of notes around his estate. He gave money to his servants without asking them to account for it. After winning thousands of pounds at Doncaster races he lost it all when it blew away as he tried to count it.

Squire Mytton rode a light carriage around as if he was a Roman charioteer. He purposely drove into a rabbit hole to see if it would turn over. It did.

To the local people he was a hero, to the county set he was an idiot. But he didn't care what they thought. He would shock his friends by arriving at posh dinner parties in full hunting gear and riding a brown bear. On one occasion he was spurring on his steed so hard that the bear turned round and bit him.

But in 1830 Mytton ran out of money. Sodden with drink, with the creditors closing in on him, he escaped to France. There he had one last escapade that is remembered. Getting hiccups one night, he recalled that a sudden shock would cure them. So he set fire to his nightshirt. The hiccups vanished instantly but he was badly burned. .

After returning to England he was sent to a debtors' prison. He died in 1838, aged only thirty-eight.

TWINS
Double Identity

Twins - identical, non-identical and Siamese - must be the ultimate examples of shared lives. Telepathic communication, fear of the outside world, and sinister control of each other often figure in their strange existences

The number of twins born every year is growing - and no one knows why! A study in Britain revealed that 7452 pairs arrived in 1990. That works out at about one set in every ninety pregnancies. Now doctors are trying to discover exactly what is causing the upsurge in these bumper bundles.

Twins are created by the fertilization of two separate eggs by two separate sperm, and develop in two separate placentas. They may be no more alike than any other brothers and sisters.

Such twins may run in families, usually on the mother's side. More fascinating are identical twins, caused when a single egg, fertilized by a single sperm, divides into two. The babies share the same placenta and are always the same sex. The chances of having twins increases over the age of thirty-five. And the likelihood of twins increases with the more babies a mother has.

That is the medical explanation and definition of twins. But to mothers throughout history - and nowdays to an increasing number of them - having two-in-one-go means double trouble and amazing stories that are worth a second look.

Opposite: *Identical twins are caused when a single egg fertilized by a single sperm divides into two.*

Below: *Greta and Freda Chaplin eat, work and sleep in unison. If separated they cry. By their teens they had synchronized every single movement.*

BRITAIN'S ODDEST COUPLE?

Perhaps the most famous twins of the 1990s are Greta and Freda Chaplin. They speak and eat in unison, do literally everything together and cry if they are separated for even a moment.

When they dress they face each other as if looking in a mirror. If Freda wears a bracelet on her left wrist, then Greta will wear one on her right. If one breaks a shoelace, the other immediately pulls the lace from her opposite shoe. They buy the same-size shoes, even though Greta's feet are larger than her twin sister's. If Freda grazes her right arm and needs a plaster, Greta will put one on the same spot on her left arm.

Every movement, down to fastening the last button, is carried out in absolute unison. When they sweep the floor they both hold the vacuum cleaner. When they make tea they both carry the pot to the table. If they are given clothes that are slightly different they alter them to make them match.

For instance, if one twin is given black gloves and the other green gloves, they will

Right: *Film-maker Emeric Pressburger wanted identical twin girls for his movie* **Twice Upon a Time.** *These two were at the audition.*

Below: *A children's party was one of the test scenes for* **Twice Upon a Time.** *Here some 200 twins watch a conjuring show to make them less self-conscious.*

swap one. They even exchange the buttons on their coats so that they appear identical.

When they eat they insist on having exactly the same-size portions on their plate. If they're having fish and chips they will both pick up a chip at exactly the same time.

When they walk, their footsteps are in precise rhythm. They brush their teeth at exactly the same time and pace. Their hair is pinned up in exactly the same way and their clothes are identical down to stockings, handkerchiefs and underwear.

A social worker once gave the twins two different-coloured bars of soap, and they burst into tears. Both bars had to be

cut in half and divided between them before they would use it.

And the twins get through a lot of soap. One of their obsessive rituals is bathing. They like to spend up to two hours a day washing each other, and get through fourteen bars of soap a week.

If one woman falls ill, so does the other.

The Chaplins are obsessive about their bathing ritual and get through fourteen bars of soap a week

---

The Chaplins say they can remember nothing about their schooldays - they went to their local Derwent Junior School and Birnholme Secondary School in York - or indeed their growing years. But it is believed that the sisters, who were forty-eight when their lifestyles were first fully studied in 1991, developed their strange obsessions because of the strictness of their mother.

From the time they were babies their mother treated them as one and encouraged their total dependence on each other, virtually to the exclusion of the rest of the world. The toys they played with as little girls were identical - right down to their twin dolls. Ask the women what advice their mother gave them, and they reply in unison: 'She told us to always stick to each other and never to go with men.'

The sisters were even told that if they went to the shops they had to buy two of everything. If only one purchase was available, they had to go without.

If one sister wanted to read and the other didn't, neither was allowed to read. Even their individual names were dropped and both were simply called 'Twin'. They were discouraged from finding outside friends.

It was hardly surprising then that by the time the girls were fifteen their every movement was totally synchronized. And although their bizarre pattern of behaviour was caused by their obsessive mother Elsie, it had now become too much for her to cope with.

After much deliberation, she and her retired bus driver husband Jack decided that the girls should be put into care. The Chaplin girls were then to spend more

than a decade cooped up in various hostels - a strange existence for a strange couple.

Sadly though, right up until their parents died in 1989, the twins would make the journey every week to their old home on the Tang Estate in York. After getting off the bus, they would walk to the semi-detached house and simply stand and look. They had long given up ringing the doorbell. It was never answered.

They could see their mother in the house fully aware her estranged daughters were outside but refusing to accept their presence. She acted as if she couldn't see them.

But still the sisters visited. They just looked, sometimes standing motionless for hours before finally both turning away at the same moment and going home.

At fifteen the twins were rejected by the mother who had brought them up in such a bizarre fashion, and were put into care

---

The Chaplin twins now live quietly in London and do not like attention or being surrounded by people, despite the fact that their very lifestyle and appearance draw attention to them. Shopping is an ordeal, as they feel that everyone is staring at them. Sometimes they will go out of their front door and head straight back inside again because they both instinctively feel that something is not right. They do not need to speak a word.

Above: *Allie and Marnie Anderson were the twin teen daughters of a London film producer. Many such twins find life unsettling.*

Above: *Being a mother of identical twin babies can be doubly joyful - or just double trouble.*

Together, they say: 'We don't like being stared at. Sometimes we shout: "Go away! What are you looking at?"'

They have had other obsessions, too. They hit the headlines when they latched on to a next-door neighbour, Kevin Iveson. They followed the unfortunate man everywhere, pestered him at his working men's club and even threw themselves in front of his van.

Despite doing all he could to deal patiently with the odd couple who followed him everywhere, sixty-six-year-old war hero Mr Iveson finally snapped. After all, he had put up with their continual presence for a staggering fifteen years.

During that time the women had trapped his hand in a door and written him a series of poison pen letters. On one occasion when they hurled abuse at him, Mr Iveson turned on his tape recorder. He reckoned no one could possibly believe what he had to endure. That recording was used in evidence when the twins

were taken to court in November 1980.

But despite the foolproof evidence, the twins repeatedly denied the allegations, stunning the court with their constant interruptions (in unison of course) of: 'He is a liar. We have never been near him.'

A consultant psychiatrist said there was no medical explanation or solution to their problem. The Chaplin women were convicted of causing a breach of the peace. They were released from prison early when they promised to stop pestering Mr Iveson. They were also terrified that being in prison would one day mean separation.

Despite Kevin Iveson's tapes of the abuse the two women had hurled at him, in court they denied all knowledge of him

---

Their unique case created much publicity and the twins withdrew even more into their singular, secret world. They couldn't understand why people were taking an interest in them and it scared them. They ignored the strangers who wrote to them. All except for one man who was to provide the women with a more normal lifestyle and help to bring them back into the real world.

They had no reason to trust retired engineer Jack Davenport, but something inside them told them they should. And Jack felt genuinely sorry for the women.

He offered them accommodation in his London house. 'I felt I could help them,' he said. 'They seemed starved of kindness, affection and understanding. I was ready to offer all those things.'

Greta and Freda arrived for what was initially to be a trial visit. But Jack proved to be their saviour and the three became good friends. For the first time in their lives the women learned how to open tins of food, how to cook properly and how to look after themselves. Jack became their protector and father figure.

And he gave them the confidence eventually to move out to a place of their own, although they still visit him daily.

The women still cannot be separated. If that happens, even for a moment, they become hysterical and run around in circles. They don't like crowds, and are still unable to contend with abuse and stares.

An even greater criminal dilemma was the case of baby-faced identical twins Craig and Timmy Good. They were just fifteen years of age when their father William and grandmother Cleo were shot dead in their trailer home on Saluda Island, South Carolina. Hauled before a court accused of the murders, the twins blamed each other for pulling the trigger of the .22 rifle.

The boys had been double trouble ever since their birth in 1973. They seemed to have a psychic knowledge of whatever the other was thinking or doing. At school they would swap classrooms to confuse their teachers.

By the time they were nine they were already selling drugs for their father, William. On the few occasions when they managed to attend school they were often suspended for smoking marijuana, fighting, drunkenness or setting off the fire alarms.

William Good, long separated from his wife Robbie, bought the boys rifles for Christmas just before he was killed. William and his sixty-year-old mother Cleo were murdered on 20 February 1989. Her rings were wrenched from her fingers and her chequebook and pick-up truck stolen. Police believed a psychotic killer was on the loose and began a search for what they assumed would be the butchered bodies of the twins. In fact they found them stoned on drugs, living in the laundry room of an apartment block. A social worker said he believed the boys had killed their father and grandmother 'so they could party with their drug-smoking, school-cutting, beer-drinking friends'.

Police assumed a psychotic killer was responsible for the murders and expected to find the twins dead too

---

The twins were tried as adults. Timmy testified that his brother fired the fatal shot. Craig, however, refused to take the stand but in a statement said he saw his father and grandmother 'fall' - though he did not see Timmy pull the trigger.

Below: *Identical twins can share a form of telepathic communication. Even when they are far apart they often seem to be aware of the other's feelings.*

The prosecutor, district attorney Don Myers, told the jury that it did not matter which twin actually pulled the trigger - both were equally guilty. He said: 'It was sickening to have to sit and listen to these twins talk casually about the murders as if they were nothing. They have no remorse. They think it's a big joke and their only regret is getting caught.'

The jury took four hours to decide whether or not only one twin had undertaken the killings while the other took no part. In the end they agreed with district attorney Myers and found them both guilty of murder. They were each sentenced to life imprisonment for the killings, and sixty-five years each for armed robbery and stealing an automobile.

When Eric Bocock and Tommy Marriott met for the first time in thirty-eight years, they looked at each other in amazement. Separated at birth, the identical twins greeted one another wearing the same hairstyle, the same neatly trimmed beard and gold-rimmed glasses.

Both were dressed in velvet jackets, white shirts, grey trousers and black shoes. Both were 5ft 6in tall and both weighed exactly 12st 6lb.

It was even more bizarre for them to discover that they had both been chargehands at engineering works for twenty-one years. Both had their hair cut by their wives, both had an allergy to house dust and both liked horse racing.

Their astonishing meeting was recorded for television in 1983 when a TV company helped Eric trace his long-lost brother. Professor Thomas Bouchard of the University of Minnesota, where doctors were carrying out a study of identical twins, said it was the most striking case of 'twinned lives' he had ever witnessed.

FOR EVER JOINED

But the most fascinating twins of all are those known as 'Siamese' - or in scientific jargon, pygopagous. Britain's first and most celebrated Siamese twins (although at that time they were not known as such) were 'Ye Maydes of Biddenden' in Kent.

Born around 1100, they were joined together at both the hips and the shoulders. The girls, Eliza and Mary Chulkhurst, lived for thirty-four years and expired within six hours of each other - the longest-surviving twin supposedly declaring: 'As we came together we shall also go together.'

To this day they are remembered by locals in the village, who bake Biddenden Maid cakes every Easter Monday.

The Biddenden Maids never married or even fell in love, as far as legend has it. But Siamese twins can and do form romantic attachments - sometimes causing trouble in double doses, sometimes not.

Rosa and Josefa Blazek were born in 1880 in Czechoslovakia. They were joined together at the pelvis, having two lungs and two hearts but only one stomach.

In 1907 the twins met a German officer. Rosa married him and had a baby boy, Franz, who was seven years of age when his father died in World War I. The sisters went on to earn a fortune by touring with circuses and peep shows throughout Europe and North America. They had very different personalities, but never allowed them to interfere with their calm and trusting relationship. For instance, Josefa drank only beer while her sister could take only wine; this caused considerable upsets in their single stomach but not once in their friendship!

When one twin got jaundice, their shared stomach enabled the other to eat for two

---

In 1922 Josefa contracted jaundice while appearing in Chicago. Rosa ate for two in order to keep up her sister's strength but she refused to allow surgeons to separate them to save her life. She said: 'If Josefa dies, I want to die too.' She did...only fifteen minutes after her twin.

The most famous twins of all time were Chang and Eng, the Siamese twins born to Chinese parents on 11 May 1811, in the province of Mekong, Siam. Joined firmly at the chest by a six-inch-long band of flesh, the children were

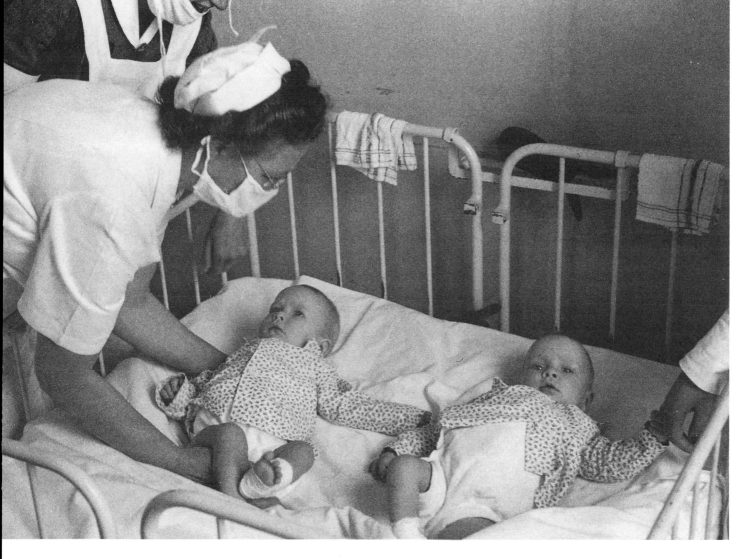

sentenced to die by the King of Siam who believed them to be an omen of ill fortune for his country.

Instead, a Scottish merchant named Robert Hunter took them to America where they grew up to become two utterly different personalities.

Chang was an extrovert with an early thirst for life and a later thirst for bourbon whiskey. Eng, on the other hand, was a feeble child who had a struggle to survive and who later abhorred his brother's wild ways. He was, as one might expect, strictly teetotal. Chang once faced a prison sentence for a drunken assault but was let off because the judge thought it unfair on Eng.

The twins became a sideshow attraction, touring the world. In France they caused a furore because it was believed their appearance could cause deformation of unborn children. In England, which they visited in 1829, they were feted by the nobility and gawped at by the common crowds. Eventually, tiring of their lives on the road, they settled down as farmers in North Carolina,

assuming the surname Bunker.

At the age of 44 they married two expatriate English sisters, Sarah Ann, aged twenty-six, and Adelaide Yates, twenty-eight. They all shared a very large bed and the sisters gave birth to no fewer than twenty-one children, all of them perfectly healthy. To show that there was no impropriety in the relationship with their wives, they purchased two houses - one for Sarah Ann and one for Adelaide - and they stayed with the sisters on alternate weeks.

A newspaper report of the time states: 'A most pathetic characteristic of these illustrious brothers was the affection and forbearance they showed for each other until shortly before their death.

'They bore each other's trials and petty maladies with the greatest sympathy, and in this manner rendered their lives far more agreeable than a casual observer would suppose possible.'

Their death, when it came on 17 January 1874, was peaceful. It is believed that they both died of old age at exactly the same moment.

Above: *Three-week-old Siamese twins Folkje and Tjitske de Vries start life apart in hospital in Holland after they were separated to begin a normal life in 1954.*

SALVADOR DALI
Surrealist Prankster

The most outrageous showman of the twentieth-century art world, Salvador Dali turned his whole life into an expression of Surrealism - presenting the grotesquely improbable as a normal everyday event.

Salvador Dali, the great Surrealist painter, was as eccentric and splashy as his fantastic and memorable dreamscapes. In fact, when he died in January 1989 at the ripe old age of eighty-four, he left behind a legacy of bizarre behaviour to match his enigmatic works - a fitting epitaph for one of the leading artistic showmen of this century.

Unlike many of his peers, the Spanish-born genius was a perennial attention-seeker, and was often pilloried as a madman who was far more interested in cold hard cash than in art. The 'Divine Dali', as he liked to call himself, was an unforgettable character with his long, slicked-down hair and waxed moustache, and a true international oddball, flitting between New York, Paris and a castle in Spain, sporting an ermine cape and a silver-handled cane.

'Every morning upon awakening, I experience a supreme pleasure: that of being Salvador Dali'

But in a career that spanned almost six decades he produced approximately two thousand serious artistic works, wrote and illustrated books, poems and essays, did stage designs for plays and ballets, produced commercial advertisements, wrote an autobiography and designed

Opposite: *Renegade surrealist artist Salvador Dali relaxes characteristically in a six-legged chair at his home near Cadaques on the Spanish Coast.*

Below left: *Dali with his Russian-born wife and constant source of inspiration, Gala Dimitrovna Diaharoff.*

Below: *He used skulls, bones and entrails in his paintings. Here he wears one of his props while clowning at his Mediterranean beach home.*

everything from jewellery and furniture to glass and china.

THE ECCENTRIC EGOTIST

Beyond his undeniable talent, Dali was wonderfully, almost uniquely, weird and egotistical, repeatedly claiming he was the greatest artist of modern times. 'Every morning upon awakening, I experience a supreme pleasure: that of being Salvador Dali, and I ask myself, wonder-struck, what prodigious thing will he do today,' he once said.

On his first visit to America in the early 1930s - with money borrowed from his colleague Pablo Picasso - Dali unveiled for reporters who met him at the ship a nude painting of his companion, Gala Dimitrovna Diaharoff, with lamb chops on her shoulder. Asked about the chops, he replied: 'Very simple. I love [her] and I love lamb chops. Here they are together. Perfect harmony.'

Just days later, while giving a lecture in New York, he appeared in a deep-sea diving suit and helmet. 'The better', he explained with grave seriousness, 'to descend into the depths of the subconscious.' Unfortunately, he almost suffocated because he'd forgotten to bring along an air pump.

In 1974 Dali, who seemed willing to do just about anything if the price was

Above: *His paradise villa at Port Lligat where he 'descended into the depths of subconsciousness'.*

Below: *He called himself the Divine Dali. His detractors called him a cash-orientated showman. His admirers saw him as a genius. The world found him unforgettable.*

right, signed on with a US advertising agency for a television commercial in which he painted a leotard-clad model to illustrate how Alka-Seltzer works.

Later, after leaving New York for France, he was seen carrying a 5 ft tall, purple Bugs Bunny doll that had been given to him as a farewell present. 'This is the most ugly and frightening animal in the world,' he said. 'I will paint it with mayonnaise and make it an object of art.'

When a reporter once visited him at his home on Spain's Costa Brava, the artist waved him into the garden and suggested: 'Let's climb that tree where we can be comfortable.' Two armchairs were hanging in the branches!

Although he was married to Gala until her death in 1982, he had no children, and he had always maintained he didn't want it any other way. 'Great geniuses always produce mediocre children, and I do not want to go through that experience,' he said. 'I am only interested in inheriting myself.'

He would say anything to shock and outrage. He once exulted: 'Sometimes I spit on the portrait of my mother from sheer pleasure.'

Dali's eccentricity was a by-product of his refusal to take art as seriously as his fellow artists did. When other Surrealists

announced they were Communists, Dali come out as a fervent Spanish royalist. When other artists said the only real path to artistic prominence was through poverty and bohemian simplicity, he could not resist telling everyone he met that he was in it for the money and the luxuries it could bring. And when modern artists said that the truth could be arrived at through avant-garde experimentation, Dali announced that he was actually an old-fashioned painter.

Through it all, Dali insisted he was about the only sane person in the world, as he revealed in his 1976 autobiography, *The Unspeakable Confessions of Salvador Dali*: 'The clown is not I, but rather our monstrously cynical and so naively unconscious society that plays at the game of being serious, the better to hide its own madness. For I - I can never repeat it enough - am not mad.'

Dali's greatness as an artist probably reached its zenith between the mid-1920s and the early 1940s, when the Surrealist period was similarly at its peak. Many of his paintings of that era were famous for their strange placement of unrelated objects in an environment where they did not belong, such as *The Persistence of Memory* of 1931 - which many critics still regard as one of the finest examples of Surrealism – in which he draped limp watches over various objects, including a branch of a dead tree. Dali, who loved to babble, said the watches were 'nothing else than the tender, extravagant, solitary, paranoiac-critical Camembert of time and space'.

THE PRECIOUS GENIUS

Salvador Felipe Jacinto Dali was born into a middle-class family in the town of Figueras in Upper Catalonia, Spain, on 11 May 1904, two years after the death of a brother who was also named Salvador. But in his crazy way, Dali would even argue that fact. Instead, he often said that he was born two months earlier because, he was quite certain, he began to think while still a seven-month-old foetus. 'It was warm, it was soft, it was silent,' he claimed. 'It was paradise.'

From a very early age, he wished to be an artist, and by the time he was ten he

had already completed two flamboyant oil paintings, *Helen of Troy* and *Joseph Greeting His Brethren*. But he was also a rather weird youngster, and loved the attention he got from stunts like flinging himself down a long flight of stairs at school. And his favourite place at home was a big tub in the laundry room, where he would sit for hours, thinking and painting. He also liked to wear his hair long under a large black hat, and would later describe himself as the world's first hippie.

When he turned seventeen, his father sent him to the San Fernando Academy of Fine Arts in Madrid, where he not only won several prizes but also managed to get himself suspended for twelve months for allegedly inciting other students to riot over the appointment of a professor who he thought was unworthy. He returned a year later, only to be kicked out for good in 1926 for what the academy said was his support for revolutionary causes.

Although his early years were influenced by a variety of styles, in 1928, on a visit to Paris, he was introduced to

Top: *Dali claimed that he began to think while still a foetus. What he was thinking in later life was to most people much more of a mystery.*

Above: *His long, waxed moustache was the trademark of a man who courted publicity - which helped his improbable works sell for millions.*

Surrealism by his fellow Spanish artist Joan Miro. Founded in 1924 by the French poet Andre Breton, the Surrealist movement advocated the 'systematic exploration of the subconscious imagination' and Dali soon became one of the leaders of the movement.

SEXUAL IMAGERY

In 1929 he painted *The Great Masturbator*, one of his more significant paintings of the period. It depicts a large, wax-like head with pink cheeks and closed eyes with very long eyelashes. A huge nose leans on the ground, and instead of a mouth there is a rotting grasshopper

Below: *Publicity seeker Dali poses with a local fisherman's son and starfish on the rocks near his home. The bay was given to the artist by Spanish dictator General Franco.*

crawling with ants. For much of the 1930s, sexual and scatological images were a common theme in his work, and he had a bizarre fondness for including in them grasshoppers, telephones, ants, keys, melting torsos, crutches, bread and hair. Dali called his technique the 'handmade photography of concrete irrationality' and it was based, he said, on 'the associations and interpretations of delirious phenomena'. Not surprisingly, even he said he didn't understand all his images!

During the 1930s his fellow Surrealists grew worried about Dali's preoccupation with Hitler's genitals

Although his work was well received by critics who praised the deep vistas of his paintings, critical success did not bring instant profit. Instead, Dali plied the streets of Paris vainly trying to find buyers for his bizarre inventions - devices like women's shoes with high steel springs, fingernail-shaped looking glasses, and even a plaster head of a roaring lion with a fried egg in its mouth.

His eccentricity, however, led to a falling out with his fellow Surrealists, who expelled him from the movement in 1934, claiming he had developed an unhealthy interest in money and was guilty of 'vulgarisation and academicism'.

DECLINE AND DISARRAY

Over the remaining decades of his life, he spent more and more time on a variety of business and commercial affairs. For several years he did one large painting a year - usually for a huge fee - and became involved in everything from selling lithographs to designing shirts and bathing suits to making airline commercials. 'Dali sleeps best after receiving a tremendous quantity of cheques,' he used to say. He must have slept like a baby because he lent his name to perfumes, body-freezing schemes, brandy bottles and furniture and fabrics. His commercials led most critics to agree that the last two decades or so of his working life were remarkable more for their plain silliness than for any real artistic accomplishment.

In later life his lust for money became an obsession and he lent his name to everything from perfumes to body-freezing schemes

One of the sillier schemes was his painting in 1973 of the wall panels for a fleet of Iberia passenger planes. In the years just prior to his death Dali suffered from a variety of health problems, including Parkinson's disease, deep depression and malnutrition. After the death of Gala, he spent most of the time at his twelfth-century castle at Pubol, north of Barcelona, but in August 1984 a short circuit in a device he used to summon his nurses set fire to his bedclothes. Badly burned and too weak to stay at the castle any longer, he was moved to a wing of the Dali Museum in Figueras, where he had been born, by his assistants. Tragically, for the next five years he lingered largely in a horrid limbo, confined to a wheelchair and fed through a tube. The hands that had painted some of the most important art of the twentieth century shook uncontrollably.

His professional life was similarly in complete disarray. Secretaries and agents milked him for all he was worth, selling copyright and reproduction rights to his works all over the world - with much of the profit going into their own pockets.

Left: *The artist slumbers. He once said, 'Dali sleeps best after receiving tremendous quantities of cheques.' He did.*

Below: *Dali and his wife Gala. After her death he spent most of his time at his 12th century castle north of Barcelona. His final years were spent in pitiful decline.*

Dali's unfortunate habit of signing blank sheets of paper led to a flourishing trade in fakes

Fake Dali lithographs were everywhere - a process encouraged by the artist's disheartening habit in the 1970s of regularly signing blank pieces of paper. Dali could and did sign more than 1800 an hour, according to one associate.

Not surprisingly, the art world was scandalized by forgeries of his works, and Dali himself was said to have signed thousands of blank sheets of paper for easy conversion into bogus Dali 'originals'. By some estimates, the forgeries of his work ran into hundreds of millions of dollars.

Still, Dali himself was not perturbed by the furore. 'No one would worry if I were a mediocre painter,' he sniffed. 'All the great painters have been falsified.' Indeed, he remained overwhelmingly popular with art lovers, and in 1979 and 1980 a major retrospective drew more than a million visitors in Paris and 250,000 in London.

And for all his failings, Dali remains, even in death, an unforgettable character, who made eccentricity an art form. As the critic Winthrop Sargeant once remarked: 'There is nothing abnormal about Dali. He is simply antinormal!'

RASPUTIN
Peasant Turned Seer

Before the 1917 Revolution St Petersburg society was scandalized by a newcomer in its midst. How did a filthy, semi-literate peasant from Siberia, member of a sex-obsessed 'holy cult', exert a hypnotic influence over the ruling family of Imperial Russia?

Right: *Asked by Princess Murat for the secret of his powers, he wrote: 'It is love, my little dove.'*

Opposite: *An honoured equal...Rasputin the 'mad monk' seated with Captain Von Lohman of a crack cavalry regiment and Prince Pontiatine, chamberlain of the royal palaces.*

Below: *Dressed as a monk, Grigori Rasputin held an eerie power over weak-willed Tsar Nicholas II.*

Rarely has an individual wielded as much power as the 'mad monk', Grigori Rasputin, over a monarch and supreme ruler. The weak minded Nicholas II, Tsar of all the Russias, saw his wife, the Tsarina Alexandra, fall under his spell and witnessed his own influence wane as the demonic-eyed holy man exerted more and more sway over the court. In death, as in life, Rasputin defied belief. It took poison, gunshots, a beating with chains and finally drowning to polish him off.

THE SIBERIAN PEASANT BOY

Rasputin was born in the farthest of Imperial Russia's outposts: Siberia. He was christened in the Russian Orthodox Church as Grigori Novykh, only later answering to the name of 'Rasputin' which, translated, means 'debauched one', a tag he wore with evil delight.

The name 'Rasputin' means 'the debauched one', and he delighted in it

Siberia then, as now, was the home of exiles and banished enemies of the state. Life was brutal and harsh among the villages dotting the endless plains: particularly harsh in the village of Pokrovskoye, where Rasputin's parents tilled miserable plots of thin soil and raised a few chickens. In 1872 Anna, a Mongol girl from Tobolsk, gave birth to her third child, Grigori.

The boy was destined for a life of hard work, rustic living and probably an early death. But two things marked him out: his intense, burning eyes and an incredible, seemingly insatiable, lust for the opposite sex.

He lost his virginity to a Russian general's wife, Danilova Kubasova, who, with the aid of six handmaidens, seduced him in her bedchamber in their stately home near his village.

After that his sexual exploits among the local populace were legendary. He frequently promenaded with prostitutes in his native village, and earned the scorn of all when he was caught frolicking in a pond with three girls: even though then, at the age of twenty, he had already married a local girl, Praskovia Feodorovna.

Below: *Two things marked Rasputin out, right from the start - extraordinarily piercing eyes, and an unshakable lust for women.*

Rasputin claimed that his religious transformation took place while bathing naked in a pond with some village girls

---

It was during his cold-water dip with the village maidens, Rasputin would later claim, that a religious transformation overcame him. This sudden enlightenment caused him to uproot and take to the primitive roads and farm tracks of Russia, leaving behind his three children, to preach the heretical and somewhat confused gospel of the strange religious sect of a group known as the Khlisti. Rasputin entered a Khlisti monastery at Verkhoture where his debauchery was honed.

Bizarre sexual customs, multi-partner relationships and orgies were all part of their gospel: they believed that in order to be redeemed, man must first sin. It was a perfect cult for the over-sexed Rasputin.

Thus converted, Rasputin began the wanderings that would eventually lead to the court of the Tsar. Russia was then a primitive, pre-industrial land, and news of Rasputin's deeds was spread largely by word of mouth. He took on the eminence of a holy man, becoming imbued with undeserved mysticism as he doled out snake-oil cures to the peasantry and preached the gospel of indulgence.

He began preaching about 'redemption

through sexual release' and told the poor people whom he encountered that it was their duty before God to surrender to him their wives, daughters and any other female relations.

ARRIVING IN ST PETERSBURG

Soon he landed up in St Petersburg, the glorious Western-style capital of Imperial Russia. For Rasputin, St Petersburg was the natural place to be. He set himself up in an apartment on a fashionable street and invited ladies - his reputation by then, 1903, was considerable - to dine at his table before inviting them to what he dubbed his 'holy of holies', the bedchamber!

Upper class women discovered a new and thrilling sensation in making love with this filthy, drunken 'holy man'

Typically, day after day Rasputin could be found in his house, surrounded by beautiful young women: he called them his 'disciples'. More often than not he sat with one on his lap, lecturing about the 'mysterious resurrection' that awaited all his conquests.

To understand his entry into the very highest circles of Russian political and social life it is necessary to understand the mind of the monarch himself. Tsar Nicholas was a charming, autocratic, sensitive but weak leader, out of step with the great social and political changes sweeping the world. He had been brought up to revere the divine right of kings, to believe that he was God's missionary on earth to look after the great mass of peoples that made up Holy Russia. He was sadly deluded.

His rule started in 1894 with a pronouncement that he would reign as his forebears had: as a total autocrat. He paid no heed to the growing dissatisfaction within his country, the great revolutionary movement that was growing daily, even though his secret police force, the Okhrana, warned him of the danger of Marxism and Leninism.

Two years after Rasputin's arrival in St Petersburg, revolution occurred in Russia. Workers, hungry for bread, marched peacefully on the grand Winter

Palace. Dozens were cut down by gunfire outside the gates by loyal Cossacks and police; the snow turned red with their blood as they tried to present to their ruler a petition demanding change.

Unmoved by the dead the Tsar said afterwards: 'Under no circumstances will I ever agree to a representative form of government, for I consider it harmful to the trust of God.'

Tsar Nicholas believed he had been invested with a divine right to rule his people, and rejected all other forms of government

---

Tsar Nicholas was striving to preserve an old order that guaranteed poverty and misery for the masses and splendour and indulgence for the aristocracy. It was the latter which attracted Rasputin, who had garnered a reputation for himself as a holy man with healing powers.

Tales were told of biblical-style 'laying on of hands' performed by Rasputin in the villages and towns he passed through. Whether or not he actually had any attributes other than an over-sized sexual appetite is not known. But at the time he seemed a blessing to the Tsarina Alexandra as she worried for the health of the young Tsarevitch, the Crown Prince Alexis: for the boy was a haemophiliac.

Above: *The mad monk surrounded by his fawning court followers. The faithful were granted a 'laying on of hands' by the mystical Rasputin.*

Below: *A drawing of Rasputin by the Princess Lucien Murat. The monk preached a philosophy of self-indulgent sex worship.*

Alexandra was strong-willed and the true power behind the Romanov throne. Summoned by the Tsarina to test his powers of healing, in 1908 Rasputin made his first visit to the Winter Palace to see the ailing Tsarevitch.

When Rasputin first appeared at the Winter Palace it was during one of the boy's bleeding fits. He paid no heed to protocol in his visit and arrived unkempt from a bedroom session with the wife of a general. By some means, probably crude hypnotism, those who witnessed him calm the young lad testified that he did indeed possess strange and mystical powers. The boy's internal agony ceased, and the bleeding stopped.

The mad monk arrived at the Winter Palace dirty and dishevelled, straight from the bed of a general's wife

---

For the Tsarina his arrival and miracle working were a blessing she would never forget. From that day forward the fortunes of Holy Russia, the Romanov dynasty and the unholy fakir were inextricably bound together.

Conservative ministers and nobles, outraged by his behaviour with some of the highest women in the land, pleaded with the Tsar to banish him: but at first to no avail. Finally, he was forced to see reason when his chief minister Stolypin sent him a dossier of Rasputin's sexual misdeeds. This time the Tsar had no choice but to exile Rasputin.

But his departure in 1911 signalled a turn for the worse in the health of young Alexander. Within six months the Tsarina had gained his release from internal exile and he was once again admitted to the grand salons of the Winter Palace. He reached the pinnacle of his power four years later as Russia was bleeding itself to death on the battlefield against the Tsar's cousin Kaiser Wilhelm. The situation was so dire that the Tsar left St Petersburg for the front to assume command. Alexandra was left behind to assume supreme power. But although she was the acting head of state, it was Rasputin who became the real ruler of Russia. His influence ranged from the appointment of Church officials to the selection of cabinet ministers.

THE MADMAN WHO WOULD NOT DIE

His conduct outraged the nobles, who saw him as an affront to civilized behaviour: but they were powerless while he held the Tsarina in his sway. In 1916 Prince Feliks Yusupov, husband of the Tsar's niece, formed a conspiracy to end the mad monk's life.

Together with Vladimir Mitrofanovich Puriskevich and Grand Duke Dimitry Pavlovich, the Tsar's cousin, Yusupov decided to invite Rasputin to his home for supper: a final poisoned repast that would snuff the life from him. Rasputin accepted readily.

In the basement of the Moika Palace, at midnight on 29 December, Rasputin tucked heartily into food sprinkled with cyanide. While 'Yankee Doodle Dandee' played on a phonograph in the room above, Rasputin asked for more. Then he began to look drunk, his eyes swimming, and he asked the prince to sing for him!

Yusupov ran to his friends in the room above to tell them Rasputin had not died, and went back with a loaded revolver. The prince then fired two shots into him and he went down. 'But he was not dead,' said Yusupov. 'He was gasping and roaring like a wounded animal and grabbed me by the throat.'

Above: *Ragged-bearded Rasputin was found guilty of a catalogue of sexual indiscretions with the wives of noblemen. He was banished to the hinterland in 1911.*

He staggered through the doorway into the freezing courtyard where the victim showed remarkable stamina by surviving four more bullets. He was still alive when the prince and other conspirators finally silenced him by beating him with chains. He was then weighted down and dragged to the Neva River.

With his death the conspirators hoped that the Tsar would disentangle the political and social mess created by his wife under Rasputin. It had gone too deep into Russian society; within months the entire Romanov dynasty was dead.

History's epitaph for Rasputin was best summed up by the moderate revolutionary Alexander Kerensky, who said: 'If there had been no Rasputin, there would have been no Lenin.'

MYSTERIES

TUTANKHAMUN
Curse of the Boy King

Those who 'defile' the tomb of the Egyptian boy king Tutankhamun have suffered misfortune, disease and sudden death. Are they the victims of a three thousand-year-old curse?

Above: *Howard Carter stands above the excavations at the tomb of Tutankhamun in 1923.*

Right: *Archaeologists discuss their findings during the excavations.*

Opposite: *Howard Carter kneels before the wonder of Tutankhamun's yellow quartzite sarcophagus.*

Below: *Howard Carter leaves the White House after a meeting with President Calvin Coolidge in 1929.*

With trepidation among the watching throng, the tomb of the Egyptian pharaoh Tutankhamun was reopened in the summer of 1991 after being closed for nine months because of a growth of fungus within the ancient vault. As research work was resumed on the tomb at Luxor in southern Egypt, the world wondered whether the amazing seventy-year sequence of bad luck, sickness and death attributed to the legendary curse of the pharaoh would strike yet again.

DREADFUL WARNINGS

The so-called Curse of Tutankhamun first fascinated the public in the early twenties as plans were laid to reopen the tomb for the first time in three thousand years.

The amateur archaeologist, fifty-seven-year-old Lord Carnarvon, was well aware of the curse as he prepared to excavate the fabled, treasure-laden tomb. While still in Britain before the start of his exploration, the fanatical Egyptologist had consulted the celebrated mystic of his day, Count Hamon, who delivered to him this message: 'Lord Carnarvon not to enter tomb. Disobey at his peril. If ignored will suffer sickness. Will not recover. Death will claim him in Egypt.'

Carnarvon, however, was intent on continuing the biggest and costliest expedition of his lifetime. His team had worked on the project for years, ever since being granted a concession to excavate the most heavily dug site in the whole of Egypt - the Valley of the Kings.

The Earl and his American partner Howard Carter started digging in earnest only in 1917. But during five disappointing seasons they discovered only some alabaster jars inscribed with the names of Rameses II and Meremptah.

The partners debated whether to attempt a sixth season's dig...and decided to give the project one last try.

THE TOMB OF THE BOY KING

The one area on the site where Carnarvon and Carter had not attempted a dig was so churned up by past excavations that no one had thought it worthwhile to investigate further. The partners ordered the removal of some disused huts.

Carnarvon had returned to England when the first hut was demolished - to reveal beneath it a step cut into the rock. Carnarvon was telephoned, and the excited peer persuaded Carter to reseal the site while he made the three-week journey back to Egypt.

The two explorers now embarked on the most nerve-racking week of their lives. By now it was clear that the greatest archaeological discovery of the century was within their grasp...the revelation of the tomb of an obscure, adolescent pharaoh, untouched from the day when his frail body had been sealed up by the slaves of ancient Egypt.

The awe and superstition surrounding the find caused its own problems. As they neared their golden goal, the Westerners had difficulty keeping their team together as waves of fear swept through the native diggers.

The sense of dread was heightened when an inscription above the entrance to the tomb was translated. It read ominously: 'Death will come to those who disturb the sleep of the pharaohs.'

The breakthrough came on 17 February 1923, when the archaeologists entered the funerary chamber of the boy king. Carter exclaimed: 'Things, wonderful things!' as he gazed in awe at the sumptuous treasures.

*Below: **The boy king's tomb with the hills of the Valley of the Kings in the background.***

*Bottom: **A later photograph of the excavation and the Valley of the Kings. The tent is the 'police headquarters'.***

'Things, wonderful things!' exclaimed Carter as he gazed in awe at the rich treasure around him

---

In an antechamber were golden boxes and caskets, golden chairs, a golden throne, golden couches, statues, animal heads, alabaster vases and a golden snake. A further chamber was opened and, when a torch was shone through, the archaeologists reported what appeared to be a wall of gold.

Three doors led from this shrine. Two were bolted and sealed, and these the explorers left for the moment. Instead they unblocked a small passageway which opened up another chamber of treasures, all in gold, depicting gods and goddesses and visions of the afterlife.

Still to be discovered was what lay

with the poison and fever from a mosquito bite.

As he passed away, the lights of the city mysteriously flashed on and off. And back home at his country house in England, a dog howled pitifully in the middle of the night. It awoke the entire household before, gasping for breath, the animal lay down and expired.

It was not until the winter of 1925 that Carter could resume his work, entering first one and then the second of the final sealed and bolted doors leading to the sarcophagus. What was revealed to Carter is described in his own words.

The ancient Egyptian builders had carefully numbered each of eighty component parts of the shrine

---

With intense excitement I drew back the bolts of the last and unsealed doors. They slowly swung open and there, filling the entire area within...stood an immense yellow quartzite sarcophagus. Specially striking were the outstretched hand and wing of the goddess sculptured on the lid as if to ward off an intruder.

The lid of the sarcophagus weighed more than half a ton, and there was a further delay as hoists were called in to raise it. The shrines had to be dismantled and removed, a task made easier by the fact that their eighty component parts had

behind one of the two remaining sealed doors - the solid gold coffin containing the mummified body of young King Tutankhamun. That revelation of ancient splendour beyond belief was yet to come.

THE CURSE STRIKES

Opening the tomb had uncovered ancient riches beyond belief. But it had also released a mysterious, dark force that had lain dormant for three thousand years.

Two months later Carnarvon was dead. He had taken to his bed at Cairo's Hotel Continental, complaining: 'I feel like hell.' His son cared for him in his last hours, the archaeologist's body racked

Above: *A local helper emerging from the tomb bearing the statuette believed to be of Tutankhamun's queen, a daughter of the earlier pharoah Akhenaton.*

Below: *Howard Carter, assisted by two local helpers, uses pillows to protect the gilded sidepieces of Tutankhamun's royal coach. A seated Lord Carnarvon looks on.*

all been carefully numbered by the original builders.

When the lifting gear took the strain and gently raised the lid of the coffin, all that could be seen was a bundle of rotting linen cloth. But beneath was a golden effigy of Tutankhamun on the lid of a coffin - the famous effigy glitteringly restored and photographed and now known around the world.

No wonder Howard Carter's descriptions of his discovery were so euphoric. But his words were soon overshadowed by the astonishing catalogue of tragedy that followed the disturbance of the pharaoh's remains.

For it was not only Lord Carnarvon who met his premature fate soon after entering the outer shrine of King Tutankhamun. Fellow archaeologist Arthur Mace, who had been there when the tomb was opened, died shortly afterwards. He too was taken ill at the Hotel Continental, complaining of extreme fatigue.

A close friend of Carnarvon's, George Gould, travelled to Egypt to pay his last respects. He collapsed with a fever just hours after taking a look at the tomb. Radiologist Archibald Reid, whose equipment was used to determine the age of the tomb, was sent back to England complaining of fatigue. He died soon after disembarking.

Six years after revealing Tutankhamun, twelve of those who had witnessed the opening of the tomb had died. And the curse continued to take its toll.

Above: *Tourists hunt for souvenirs in the Valley of the Kings.*

Below: *The closing of the tomb of King Tutankhamun following a dispute between Howard Carter and the Egyptian government.*

Within a decade only two of the original excavation team survived, and about twenty-five others connected with the expedition had died unexpectedly. For a while the curse seemed content with the victims it had claimed.

...AND STRIKES AGAIN

Then in 1966, on the eve of an international exhibition of the relics, Egypt's director of antiquities, Mohammed Ibrahim, begged that the treasures should be kept in the country. He had dreamed of death should they go on their planned trip to Paris. He was over-ruled. Leaving a final meeting in Cairo, Ibrahim was hit by a car and died instantly.

Only six years after the opening of Tutankhamun's tomb, twelve of those present had died

---

The fear was revived in 1972 when the golden death mask of King Tutankhamun was being sent to London for an exhibition. Dr Gamal Mehrez, successor to the dead Mohammed Ibrahim, was in charge of the despatch from Cairo.

Dr Mehrez had no fears of any curse, saying: 'I, more than anyone else in the world, have been involved in the tombs and mummies of the pharaohs. Yet I am still alive. I am the living proof that all the tragedies linked to the pharaohs were pure coincidence.'

Sure enough, the arrangements for the removal of King Tutankhamun's golden relics went ahead without problems. The collection was packed and loaded on to lorries to be taken to the airport.

That evening, Dr Mehrez, having overseen the end of the preparations, breathed a justified sigh of relief as he prepared to leave the Cairo museum. Moments later he slumped to the floor and died of 'circulatory collapse'.

Whoever scoffs at the curse seems to become its next victim

Strangely, of all those associated with the relics, the excavation co-leader, Howard Carter, defied the curse and died of natural causes in 1939.

There have been many theories about the Curse of King Tutankhamun. Some say poisonous substances were sealed in the tomb. An atomic scientist, Professor Louis Bulgarini, postulated that the ancient Egyptians may have used radioactive material to safeguard the sacred burial site.

He said: 'It is definitely possible that the Egyptians used atomic radiation to protect their holy places. The floors of the tombs could have been covered with uranium or the grave could have been finished with radioactive rock.'

But most chilling of all is the theory of author Phillip Vandenburg. In his book *The Curse of the Pharaohs* he says that the pyramids and tombs were the perfect breeding ground for bacteria which created a fatal virus. It is certainly a theory that those who had the task of reopening Tutankhamun's tomb in 1991 could not forget...For the reason it was shut down was the spread of a virulent fungus, caused by bacteria from the breath of millions of visitors.

Above: *The Egyptian cabinet and their followers gather for the official reopening of the tomb after Carter's return to London.*

Below: *Sixty cases of invaluable artifacts are removed from the tomb en route for the Cairo museum.*

CROWHURST
Ocean-going Fraud

Drummed out of the RAF and the Army, failed as a businessman, Donald Crowhurst thought he could redeem himself with a lone voyage round the world. When his venture seemed doomed to failure he perpetrated a colossal fraud that in the end even he could not handle.

In 1968, in the aftermath of Sir Francis Chichester's historic single-handed voyage around the globe, the conquest of the oceans caught the imagination of the world. Not since the days of Henry the Navigator or Columbus had people been so stirred by tales of tough men in ships battling against the lonely sea and the sky; not to explore new worlds, but rather to discover themselves.

As one lone sailor of the time, a romantic Frenchman, put it: 'When one has listened for months to the hum of the wind and the sea, to the language of the infinite - one is afraid of being brutally cast back into the company of people...'

Above: *Francis Chichester prepares to sail out of Sydney Harbour on board the famous* **Gypsy Moth IV** *on his voyage back to England in 1967.*

Opposite: *Inspired by Chichester, adventurer Donald Crowhurst decided to seek fame with a lone ocean voyage.*

Below: *Francis Chichester sails up the Thames, heading from Greenwich to the City of London on board* **Gypsy Moth IV.**

Some, with rather more faith than nautical wisdom, climbed into beer barrels or bathtubs and paddled forth to brave the elements - only to be turned back by the first loudhailer from an exasperated lifeboat skipper.

Others set sail in sleek, expensive craft, using the ultimate in twentieth-century marine technology, and were never seen again. Donald Crowhurst was one of these - but he was no maritime hero. His was one of the most bizarre voyages ever undertaken by a lone sailor.

THE MAN WITH A CHIP ON HIS SHOULDER

In May 1967 Crowhurst was not among the crowd who stood on Plymouth Hoe and cheered Francis Chichester's return to fame, fortune and a knighthood from his round-the-world voyage in *Gypsy Moth IV*. At the age of thirty-five, Crowhurst was himself a fairly accomplished sailor. He admired Chichester and had read all his books.

What Crowhurst resented was the money that Francis Chichester was making out of his epic voyage

But, instead of driving the short distance from his home in Bridgwater, Somerset, to see the triumphant arrival of his hero, Crowhurst spent the day in a perverse fit of jealousy sailing his own small yacht in the Bristol Channel.

He told friends that he could not understand what all the fuss was about.

not last long. After a night out on the town he borrowed a car to get back to his barracks and was stopped by police. He was asked to resign his commission.

After trying his hand at various jobs, Crowhurst joined an electronics firm in Bridgwater as chief design engineer, married Clare, a charming, intelligent Irish girl, and rapidly had four children.

Still the wild ex-serviceman could not settle down. A naturally gifted scientist, Crowhurst would spend hours tinkering in his shed with electronic equipment. On days off he would sail his twenty-foot sloop *Pot of Gold* off the Devon coast.

A pot of gold was precisely what Crowhurst hoped to make by realizing his dream of starting his own business. He had designed a pistol-shaped gadget called a Navicator, a radio direction-finding device for yachtsmen.

After he crashed his new Jaguar and suffered head injuries Crowhurst's personality changed for the worse

---

Crowhurst persuaded his widowed mother to sell her house and lend him money to launch his new firm, which he called Electron Utilization. At first business boomed. He employed up to six people and bought a new Jaguar car, but in true Crowhurst fashion he drove it too fast and had a nasty crash in which he sustained head injuries.

He recovered, but his wife Clare claimed that his personality changed after the accident. Crowhurst, normally a mild, affable man, would fly into fits of rage or simply stare moodily out of the window.

Certainly his business suffered, and by 1967 Crowhurst had to go cap in hand to a local businessman, Stanley Best, to borrow £1000 to keep it afloat.

This, then, was Donald Crowhurst on the day Francis Chichester sailed up Plymouth Sound. A failed airman, a failed Army officer, and shortly, it seemed, to become a failed businessman.

Donald Crowhurst read the plaudits for Chichester in the following day's newspapers and decided that here was a way of gaining publicity for himself and his ailing company and at last finding that elusive pot of gold.

What Crowhurst resented most was the money that Chichester was making out of his voyage. He was receiving sponsorship, royalties and advertising contracts from companies who wanted to attach his name to their products. Chichester was likely to become a very rich man. And Donald Crowhurst was broke.

Born in India in 1932, the son of an expatriate railway official, Crowhurst had been commissioned into the RAF as an electronics engineer. He was later asked to leave the service after several breaches of discipline.

The young Donald promptly joined the Army, was again commissioned and settled down to take a course in electronic weaponry. His new career did

Above: Gypsy Moth IV was opened to the public in a new dry dock alongside the famous clipper Cutty Sark at Greenwich in 1968. Crowhurst yearned to sail Chichester's yacht.

A WAY OUT OF THE MESS

Within months of Chichester's return, scores of yachtsmen began working out how they could go one better. The most obvious feat would be a *non-stop* round-the-world voyage. The most obvious...but also the most daunting.

Even if they succeeded, each of them knew they would not see another human being for up to ten months. They would have to sail their tiny craft single-handedly for thirty thousand miles across every ocean of the world.

They would face all these dangers alone - yet still there were men who were desperate to make the attempt. And Donald Crowhurst was one of them.

The only problem was, he didn't have a proper boat. Nor the means with which to buy one. Certainly his own little yacht, the *Pot of Gold*, would barely make it across the English Channel, let alone around the world. And his funds were, to put it mildly, extremely low - Stanley Best was beginning to rue the day he had

Above: *Old man of the sea Sir Francis Chichester stands on his head for cameramen to launch his keep-fit book in London in 1969.*

been talked into investing in Crowhurst's business, and was now asking for his money back.

Crowhurst, ever the optimist, decided he knew exactly where he could find the right boat - and it had only had one careful owner.

It had been decided that *Gypsy Moth IV* would be placed in dry dock at Greenwich as a permanent memorial to Sir Francis Chichester's epic voyage. Crowhurst wrote to the town clerk of Greenwich, asking if he could borrow the boat for a year. Chichester, however, made discreet enquiries about Crowhurst among the yachting fraternity. When he discovered that hardly anyone had ever heard of him, *Gypsy Moth* was duly launched into a sea of cement and Donald Crowhurst was left without a boat.

Desperate for a suitable boat, Crowhurst even tried to borrow Chichester's *Gypsy Moth IV*

In March 1968 the *Sunday Times* decided to hold a non-stop round-the-world race for the Golden Globe trophy. Because yachtsmen would be leaving at different times and from different ports there would be two prizes: one for the fastest voyage and another for the first yacht home.

To avoid any accidents with bathtub sailors a panel of judges was set up to vet entrants. A Mr Chay Blyth applied and they could hardly turn him down - he had, after all, rowed across the Atlantic. John Ridgway, a tough ex-SAS officer who had been Blyth's rowing companion, was also a safe bet. Robin Knox-Johnston, a twenty-eight-year-old Merchant Navy officer, was again a highly experienced sailor. And when the vetting panel received an entry form from Mr Donald Crowhurst, how could they turn him down? Had he not tried, sadly in vain, to put to sea in *Gypsy Moth IV*?

Crowhurst had indeed applied to join the race. The problem was he still did not have a boat, or the money to buy one.

He solved both problems in characteristic style by persuading his long-suffering backer, Stanley Best, to lend him another £6000. He convinced

Best that it would be the shrewdest financial move he had ever made.

In a letter, Crowhurst wrote:

On the basis of the declared entrants so far I could win both prizes. The really exciting prospect is the possibility of a trimaran... which has three hulls... being equipped with various safety mechanisms which I have designed...

Best agreed to lend Crowhurst the money. He said later: 'My wife tells me I must have been mad. But Donald was the most impressive and convincing of men.'

With cash in the bank Crowhurst quickly found two boatbuilding firms who between them could handle a rush job. It was already early May, and according to the race rules all entrants had to set sail by 31 October.

In his heart of hearts Crowhurst knew he had bitten off too much, but to call it a day was too much for his ego

---

During the frantic weeks that followed, Crowhurst became increasingly frustrated as he watched first Ridgway, then Blyth and Knox-Johnston set sail. Royal Navy Commander Nigel Tetley, with the only other trimaran in the race, soon followed.

Crowhurst spent the time attending classes in radio-telegraphy. He hired an ex-Fleet Street reporter called Rodney Hallworth, who ran a news agency in Teignmouth, Devon. Hallworth arranged for Crowhurst to be adopted by the town of Teignmouth. Crowhurst's boat would be called *Teignmouth Electron*.

As the weeks passed and the boat still remained unfinished, Crowhurst's behaviour became bizarre. He would shout and swear at friends, then go into maudlin fits of depression. It was as if he had suddenly realized what he had committed himself to. But it had all gone too far. He couldn't back out now.

First the boat smashed one of her hulls trying to avoid a ferry. Then various faults showed up in the *Teignmouth Electron*: bolts and screws would come loose at certain speeds.

Over the next few days Crowhurst became more and more distracted, and it was soon obvious to local seafarers that his voyage was doomed.

On 30 October, the night before Crowhurst was due to sail, right on the race deadline, he told his wife: 'I am not happy with the boat, she's not right. I am not prepared.' He then burst into tears.

She said later: 'I was such a fool.' She believes it was a cry for help, a last chance to abort the whole trip.

THE START OF THE ILL-FATED VOYAGE

The following day, with the whole town of Teignmouth lining the quayside, Donald Crowhurst set sail in his untried, untested trimaran - the 9ft by 8ft cabin still littered with unopened boxes of equipment and stores.

Surprisingly, considering the haste of his departure, Crowhurst made steady progress. Within two weeks he was off Portugal, but already the *Teignmouth Electron* was revealing her faults.

Water was leaking into one of the three hulls. Worse that than, loosened screws had made the self-steering gear virtually useless. Crowhurst pirated screws from other parts of the boat to fix it.

Then disaster struck a third time. His Onan generator, the only source of electric power on the boat, failed after being drenched in seawater. It meant no lights - and no radio communication.

No further from home than the coast of Portugal, Crowhurst was without some of his most essential equipment

---

On Friday, 13 November, while he was still off the coast of Portugal, Crowhurst put his thoughts in writing:

This may look like a load of excuses for stopping. That's not what I want to do. If I stop I'll disappoint a lot of people - Stanley Best most importantly...and then my family.

And then he decided:

I will continue south and try to get the generator working so that I can talk to Mr Best before I commit myself to any particular course or retiring from the race. If the whole thing goes quite sour: Electron Utilization bankrupt... ten years of work and worry down the drain, I would have Clare and the children still...

By this time, Crowhurst had covered

some 1300 miles but by such a tortuous route that he had only made about 800 miles of his intended course. He was hopelessly behind all the other race starters. And, with all his problems aboard the *Teignmouth Electron*, he still had 28,000 miles to go. He must have realized then that he could not possibly complete the race, let alone win. His only recourse was, in his words, to save face.

Several days later Crowhurst managed to get the generator working. He learned over the radio that Knox-Johnston was off New Zealand, and Tetley was rounding the Cape of Good Hope. Crowhurst, now off Madeira, was thousands of miles behind. He booked a call to Stanley Best.

According to his log he had planned to plead with Best that he could only retire from the race; that he would try again next year after proper preparations; that he must have one more chance. In fact he said none of these things. Everything was going well, apart from one or two technical problems, and he warned that there might be a period of radio silence because of generator trouble.

It was the first clear hint that Donald Crowhurst had planned a new route for his round-the-world trip.

THE FACE-SAVING CON TRICK

On 10 December Crowhurst sent a telegram to Rodney Hallworth, his press agent, claiming the new speed record for a single day's sailing of 243 miles. The story appeared in all the national papers the following day. There was, of course, no way of checking it.

No one could possibly know that back on the *Teignmouth Electron* Crowhurst was now filling in two logbooks. One showed his real course and position, which every seaman must do to help with navigation. The other consisted of the route he would show the race judges when he returned in triumph.

While the rest of the world believed that *Teignmouth Electron* was churning through the white horses of the Roaring Forties, Crowhurst was drifting aimlessly in the South Atlantic, making sure that he kept well away from passing ships.

He was killing time, waiting for the moment - months hence - when he could announce to the world that he had sailed the globe, rounded the Horn and was on his way home.

After cabling about generator trouble he started to fill in two logbooks, one genuine, the other fake

---

By the end of January, when he was officially reckoned to be somewhere in the Indian Ocean, Crowhurst realized he would have to repair his damaged third hull, otherwise he would sink. He did not have the proper equipment to do it on board, and he began to sail slowly towards the coast of Argentina.

He figured that if he landed at some remote spot on the South American coast it was unlikely that anyone would recognize him or remember who he was.

Below: *Donald Crowhurst poses with his wife Clare and their children Rachel, 6, Simon, 9, Roger, 8, and James, 11, before his ill-fated voyage.*

Above: *Royal Navy Commander Nigel Tetley with his wife Eve. Tetley set sail on the epic voyage shortly before an impatient Donald Crowhurst.*

For several days Crowhurst meandered around the Argentine coast, just out of sight of shore, and pored over a book called *The South American Pilot* which listed all the possible landing places.

After much indecision he picked his spot - Rio Salado, which according to his book consisted merely of a group of sheds and buildings. He landed his battered craft there on 6 March.

He was in luck. The tiny fishing village was a hundred miles from nowhere and had no telephone. The easy-going coastguard, while mentioning the visit of an eccentric English sailor in his log, did not think the incident worth reporting. Crowhurst spent several days stocking up with supplies and repairing his boat, then set sail again.

Maintaining strict radio silence - under the guise of his broken generator - Crowhurst spent the next month sailing aimlessly around the Falkland Islands. He had worked out that the earliest

possible date he could reveal his position would be 15 April.

What of the other race yachtsmen? On 6 April, Robin Knox-Johnston was spotted by a passing tanker in the South Atlantic on his way home. He was now favourite to win the Golden Globe. The only other yachtsman left in the race, Commander Tetley, was reported homeward-bound 150 miles from the Falklands...where Donald Crowhurst was lurking in *Teignmouth Electron*.

Back home, Crowhurst's press agent Hallworth was having a worrying time. He had not heard from his protege for nearly three months. There had been no sightings. And he could only assume that Crowhurst was somewhere near Australia or at the bottom of the Pacific.

Then, on 9 April, Crowhurst decided to test the water. He was still not sure if his stopover in Rio Salado had been reported. He sent a cable, via Buenos Aires, which said simply: DEVON-NEWS EXETER HEADING DIGGER RAMREZ LOG KAPUT 17697 WHATS NEW OCEANBASHINGWISE.

It was a masterpiece of non-information. But Hallworth pounced upon the message. Digger Ramrez he took to mean the tiny island of Diego Ramırez, south-west of Cape Horn.

No one could raise Crowhurst to confirm his position, but these sparse details were enough for Hallworth. He filed a story to all the national papers that his boy was rounding the Horn and was on target for the fastest time. Donald Crowhurst was back in the race.

On 30 April he reached the spot he had planned and broke his radio silence with a cable congratulating Knox-Johnston on being the first man home. Now he was racing Nigel Tetley for the prize for the fastest time. But Crowhurst, alone in his cabin, had worked it all out. He did not want to win.

THE FINAL DECEPTION

By now he had realized that his fake log - with details of non-existent storms in the Indian Ocean and phoney squalls in the Pacific - would not stand up to the judges' scrutiny. If, however, he came in a close second to Tetley he would be hailed as a hero anyway. And, more importantly, he would not have to present his log to the race organizers.

Crowhurst deliberately dawdled as he headed home up the Atlantic. But Tetley had been told that *Teignmouth Electron* was hard on his heels, and pushed his already-battered boat to the limit. Off the Azores he hit a storm and sank.

It was the final dilemma. He couldn't lose - he was already two months ahead of Knox-Johnston's time. He couldn't win. The judges would spot his fraud.

He sent a telegram commiserating with Tetley, who had been rescued in his rubber dinghy. Then Donald Crowhurst, failed serviceman, failed businessman and now a failed round-the-world yachtsman, simply stopped sailing.

Ironically his radio really did break

Below: *Renowned yachtsman Robin Knox-Johnston fights the wind and waves with his yacht* Suhaili *towards the end of the race.*

down, and he wrote in his log that he was desperate to talk to his wife Clare. He could still receive messages, however, and it must have added to his sense of impending doom when he was cabled by Hallworth that Teignmouth was putting out the flags for his homecoming.

As one by one his rivals dropped out Crowhurst was faced with a terrible dilemma - if he won, his fraud would be exposed

---

By 22 June Crowhurst had drifted into the eerie stillness of the plankton-green Sargasso Sea. He had managed to get his radio working and sent off routine messages to Hallworth, his wife and the BBC. Then, within twenty-four hours, Crowhurst went mad.

Over the next few days he wrote twelve thousand words of gibberish about the cosmos, the mind and mathematics.

The log entry finished at 11.20am on 1 July. No one will ever know exactly what happened then, but it is widely believed that Donald Crowhurst, insane with guilt, remorse and loneliness, climbed up on deck, walked to the rail and plunged into the calm Sargasso Sea.

Nine days later the *Teignmouth Electron* was spotted by a Royal Navy vessel, the *Picardy*. The trimaran was deserted, and in the cabin lay Crowhurst's damning logbooks.

When the news broke, the nation mourned the loss of one of its bravest sons of the sea. A fund was set up to help the Crowhurst family, and Knox-Johnston donated his £5000 Golden Globe prize. It was not until the logbooks were examined back in England that Crowhurst's amazing fraud was exposed.

To this day there are some who believe that Donald Crowhurst secretly made a raft from flotsam gathered from the Sargasso Sea and set sail for the nearest landfall, the Cape Verde Islands. For many years afterwards his wife did not believe her husband was dead.

Over the years there have been alleged sightings of him in the Azores and the Canary Islands. Certainly it would be ironic that Captain Conman Donald Crowhurst even cheated his own death.

ROBIN HOOD
Prince of Thieves?

The hero of the greenwood, who robbed the rich to pay the poor - or a murderous brigand idealized by later generations? What's the real truth about the romantic, swashbuckling figure known as Robin Hood?

Left: Life in the green wood - subsisting by illegal hunting of the king's deer.

Six hundred years after his death, a footnote in history was written about a small-time crook who roamed woodlands in central England.

This villain of the piece hardly warranted a mention in chronicles of the time; his exploits were less than dramatic in such a violent age. And his story would, understandably, have gone untold in a period when wars, plague and famine were not uncommon.

But for some unfathomable reason, the legend of this crook has been writ large in history. His name, all these centuries after his death, is better known today than it was when he was alive. The name ... Robin Hood.

DEBUNKING THE MYTH

In March 1988 the town council of Nottingham in the East Midlands issued a report on the most famous inhabitant of their city. Since over the years they had received thousands of requests for information about Robin and his Merry Men, the council decided to issue the definitive statement on the matter.

Extraordinarily for a place that owed its repute to the ages-old story, the councillors took it upon themselves to cast some doubt on the veracity of the legend of the elusive Master Hood.

According to Nottingham's assiduous researchers, the dashing hero who robbed the rich to help the poor never even met his paramour, Maid Marian. Friar Tuck, they said, was a myth. Little John was grumpy and short-tempered - nothing like the happy-go-lucky character of folklore. Their survey went on in this vein...

But when the town councillors debunked the legend that was one of their few claims to fame, they found that they were only the latest in a long line of cynics. For when examining the history of Robin Hood, it is almost impossible to separate fact from fiction. Many before them had researched this fascinating story - and still the ghost of Robin Hood has not been laid to rest.

So what is the myth and magic of the lad in Lincoln green whose daring exploits still thrill to this day, in books and films and on television? One can accept what serious researchers have unearthed - that Robin plundered from travellers riding the Great North Road near Barnsdale in South Yorkshire, and that he forayed with his outlaw band thirty miles away in Sherwood Forest. Or one can accept the romantic version that this handsome hero really did rob from the rich only to give to the poor.

THE HISTORICAL FACTS

Robin's minor rule of the English 'badlands' reputedly occurred around 1261. But the first mention of him did not come until a century later when he was briefly referred to by the Scottish

Opposite: The Robin Hood statue in the city of Nottingham.

Below: Design for a stage costume of Robin Hood from 1904.

historian Fordun, who died in 1386. Further written word of his exploits came in the sixteenth century.

According to the chronicler John Stow, he was an outlaw in the reign of Richard I. He supported a hundred men, all tall and good archers, with the spoils he took, yet he 'suffered no woman to be

oppressed or otherwise molested. Poor men's goods he spared, abundantlie relieving them with which by theft he got from abbeys and houses of rich earles.'

Let's start by taking the most charitable view of his history. The tale must begin with records which show that a Robin Hood did exist - in Wakefield, Yorkshire, in the thirteenth and fourteenth centuries.

This character is documented as being born in 1290 and christened Robert Hood. The family surname is spelt three ways in the old court records: Hod, Hode and Hood. But it is clearly stated that Robin's father was a retainer of Earl Warenne, lord of the manor of Wakefield.

So how did history's most famous petty thief launch himself on his rewarding road to robbery?

In 1322 Robin got a new landlord, Thomas, Earl of Lancaster. When the Earl led a revolt against the weak and ill-advised King Edward II, Robin, like his fellow tenants, had no choice but to obey his lord's call to arms. But the revolt was crushed, and Lancaster was captured and

Left: *Robin Hood and Little John illustrating the 'Roxburghe Ballads' of around 1600.*

Below: *Romanticized view of a rustic couple, possibly Robin Hood and Maid Marian.*

beheaded for treason. His estates were confiscated by the King and the Earl's rebellious servants were outlawed.

Robin found a haven in Barnsdale Forest, an ideal hiding place covering 30 square miles of Yorkshire. And here we have the beginnings of the famous Sherwood Forest link.

Robin became an outlaw after a failed uprising against the unpopular King by his lord, the Earl of Lancaster

---

Sherwood was a neighbouring Nottinghamshire area of around 25 square miles. The two forests were served by the Roman-built Great North Road, used frequently by travellers who were obvious targets for outlaw robbers. The legend of Robin Hood, dressed in Lincoln green for camouflage in the forest, was born.

THE LEGEND GROWS

Stories of Robin's death-defying, heroic antics became rife. There was the escapade involving the stuffy Bishop of Hereford, who was making his way to York when he came upon Robin and his men roasting venison poached from the King's hunting forests.

Thinking they were simple peasants the bishop ordered them to be seized immediately. The outlaws were unruffled, saying they were too busy to be arrested

and that food was uppermost in their minds. The bishop's aides then rounded them up, ignoring their pleas for mercy. But with one blast on Robin's horn the rest of the gang emerged from the forest, the bishop was taken prisoner and a ransom demanded.

Determined to get as much fun as possible from his hapless hostage, Robin made the bishop dance a jig around a large oak tree. To this very day, that spot is known as Bishop's Tree Root.

When the Bishop of Hereford tried to arrest Robin and his men they told him they were too busy eating stolen venison

---

We hear, too, of the day Robin, accompanied by his closest friend Little John, paid a visit to Whitby Abbey. The abbot asked them to display their much-heralded archery skills by shooting from the monastery roof. Robin and Little John were happy to oblige.

One of the best-loved stories about Robin, passed down from peasant to peasant, concerned his meeting with Edward II. Legend has it that the King, dismayed at his royal deer disappearing from under his eyes into the stomachs of the outlaws, made up his mind once and for all to clean up the forest.

He and his knights dressed up as monks and rode into Sherwood, knowing that Robin Hood and his band would be

Above left:King John in a legendary confrontation with the Abbott of Canterbury. Ever since Sir Walter Scott published **Ivanhoe** *in 1819, storytellers have thought of Robin Hood as contemporary with John and his elder brother Richard Coeur-de-Lion.*

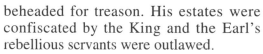

Above: *The men in Lincoln green take it easy with an armoured knight.*

Above: *Robin Hood depicted in combat with a foe. Their weapons are quarter staffs.*

Right: *Robin Hood and his band of outlaws face the wrath of King Richard in this undated version of the Sherwood myth.*

waiting for unfortunate travellers such as them. They were right. The outlaws intercepted them and demanded money.

The disguised king said that £40 was all he had (a small fortune in those days, anyway). Robin took £20 for his men and handed the rest back to the King.

Edward then produced a royal seal and told the outlaw leader that he was summoned to Nottingham to meet the King. Robin and his men dropped to their knees, swore love and allegiance to Edward and invited the 'monks' to dine with them - on the King's own venison!

Edward finally realized that Robin's unwittingly cheeky antics had thwarted him in his mission. He revealed his true identity and pardoned them, on condition that they all serve him at court if ever he called for them. This story sounds pure fantasy, dreamed up by admirers of Robin Hood over the centuries. But it may not be entire fiction, after all.

It is revealed in *A Lytell Geste of Robyn Hood*, published in 1459, and we know for a fact that the King was in Nottingham in 1332. We know too that the name Robin Hood appears in Edward's court accounts a few months later in 1324.

After that it seems he did one of his famous disappearing tricks, back into the forest and back once more into folklore.

The secret network of routes in the forest was marked by trees known only to Robin and his followers

---

And so the daring tales continue. There was Robin's visit to St Mary's church in Nottingham, where a monk recognized the outlaw and alerted the sheriff. Robin single-handedly slew twelve soldiers with his trusty sword before being captured. He must have known even then that his loyal followers would not abandon him. Before Robin could be brought to trial Little John led a fearless raid, repatriating Robin his leader to his outlaw 'family'. Just for good measure, they tracked down the monk who had 'grassed' on Robin - and murdered him.

THE COMPANIONS OF THE GREENWOOD

We cannot talk about Robin Hood without giving due credit to his Merry Men and to his legendary female companion Maid Marian. Robin's closest aide was Little John, supposedly not a merry man at all but a rather miserable, touchy fellow. It has always been believed that Little John was so called as a jest, and that he was in fact tall of stature. This was proved when his grave was opened at Hathersage, Derbyshire in 1784, and was found to contain the bones of an exceptionally tall man.

Friar Tuck is now believed to be a composite character of two fat friars, or perhaps even a single, jolly fellow who enjoyed morris dancing. He may even have been Robert Stafford, an early

fifteenth century Sussex chaplain who used the alias Friar Tuck to carry out his part-time business of outlaw.

As for Maid Marian, the latest research shows she was the product of a thirteenth-century French poem and, sadly, never kissed her sweetheart in the leafy glades of Sherwood Forest.

Her existence could also fit in with the theory that Robin was in fact 'born' out of a character depicted in May Day ceremonies. Maid Marian may simply have been Queen of the May.

WILL THE REAL ROBIN HOOD PLEASE STAND UP?

Robin Hood's legendary, leafy exploits in England's most famous forest continued until around 1346. He is reputed to have died, ill, at Kirklees Priory - his death hastened when the prioress, his cousin Elizabeth de Stainton, bled him until he

Above: *This engraving, entitled 'Courtesy of Little John', shows the outlaw apparently abasing himself before a knight - or possibly waylaying him in order to rob him.*

was too weak to recover from his crippling pains.

That's the romantic view of Robin Hood, valiant do-gooder. But there seems to be a strange Anglo-Saxon propensity to debunk their heroes, and Robin is one who has suffered more than most.

One expert, Graham Black, director of Nottingham's *The Tales Of Robin Hood* exhibition, said: 'We are now close to knowing Robin's true identity.'

According to Black, the real trail of Robin Hood starts in 1261 when William, son of Robert the Smith, was declared an outlaw in Berkshire. The court clerk who wrote the order gave him the nickname William Robehood or Robinhood.

Other court documents have been found which refer to people with the name Robinhood, and most of them were criminals. This suggests, say the scholars, that if the original Robin Hood existed he must have been active before that time.

The strongest candidate for this dubious honour, according to Graham Black, is Robert Hod, tenant of the Archbishopric of York, who fled from justice in 1225. He appears in records two years later as outlawed Hobbehod.

So where does the more romanticized version of the legend come from? Robin is generally thought of as being a contemporary of King Richard I, known as the Lionheart, who ruled from 1189 to 1199. But he was only placed there by Sir Walter Scott in his 1819 novel *Ivanhoe*.

In some versions of the tale Robin was a nobleman, the Earl of Huntingdon. But this again was an invention - of a playwright who in 1597 wanted to attract the nobility of the day to his theatre. Until that time Robin had been described as a yeoman, a retainer to a lord.

The elevation of Robin as the greatest archer in the land comes from wandering storytellers, who relayed to the simple people of rural England five ballads written between 1450 and 1500.

Maid Marian's virginal reputation was acquired only in the nineteenth century when the Victorians decided her act needed cleaning up

---

As for pure, chaste, virginal Maid Marian, she is supposedly the beautiful ward of evil Prince John, and first met Robin when she was ambushed by his Merry Men. But this theory is disregarded by academics, who say she first emerged in a thirteenth-century French poem as a shepherdess with her shepherd Robin.

It was not until two hundred years after the French poem was written that she was finally adapted to fit the Robin Hood legend. And Maid Marian's virginal reputation followed long after when the prudish Victorians cleaned up her act!

As for Friar Tuck, according to legend he was a jolly figure who ate huge meals, amused the outlaws with his jolly japes and fought doughtily with a staff. Indeed there was a real-life Friar Tuck. But he

Below: *This ancient drawing appears to show a soldier helping the collection of taxes from a penurious peasantry.*

was, in fact, a murderer and robber who was the chaplain of Lindfield parish in Sussex. He took the alias of Friar Tuck when a royal warrant demanded his arrest in 1417.

James Holt, professor of medieval history at Cambridge University and author of a book on Robin Hood, says: 'Records show that Friar Tuck organized a separate outlaw band 200 miles away from Sherwood Forest and hundreds of years after Robin Hood was active. And really, there was nothing jolly about Friar Tuck - he is believed to have burned and pillaged the homes of his enemies.'

Meanwhile Little John, generally regarded as a gentle giant who was Robin's right-hand man, was actually capable of brutal murder. John once slew a monk suspected of betraying Robin - then cut off the head of the monk's young servant so there would be no witness. He did perform one valiant act, however, when he rescued his master from the mightily fortified prison presided over by the notorious sheriff of Nottingham.

The jolly Friar Tuck was really a murderer and robber with a warrant out for his arrest

---

As for Robin, Professor Holt says: 'He was nothing like he is portrayed. He wore a hood, like a monk's cowl. There is absolutely no evidence that he robbed

from the rich to give to the poor. That was added to the legend two hundred years or more after his death. He was widely regarded as being a riotous marauder.'

Lovers of folklore much prefer Robin Hood's reputation to be that of fighting for the underdog, taking from those with money to give to those who had none, and all the while thumbing his nose at authority. Which is why it is nice to believe that, after a lifetime of daring deeds, whether for good or ill, our hero really did summon up enough strength as he lay dying to blow his horn and bring his faithful friend Little John to his side.

Above: *Robin Hood in the title page of an old volume. The Victorians maintained a highly romanticized version of the legend of the 'noble savage'.*

Left: *Could this be Robin and Maid Marian beneath a mighty forest oak? Only if tailors and hairdressers were in his merry band.*

DINGO BABY
Outback Injustice

'A dingo has got my baby!' cried distraught Australian mother Lindy Chamberlain. But her story was not believed. Were the family victims of prejudice and a cover-up by the authorities?

The news made just a few paragraphs in the world's press. And although it was a somewhat hollow victory, it was the closing chapter of a nightmare story for a young Australian mother.

Famous 'Dingo Baby Case' mum Lindy Chamberlain was awarded £210,000 damages for wrongful imprisonment. The compensation was reported in July 1991. It ended eleven years of fighting to see justice done.

But it was much less than Lindy felt she deserved. Three years of her life had been lost while she languished in jail for a crime she did not commit.

All the time, Lindy protested her innocence, telling anyone who would listen that it was a dingo, a wild dog, in the Australian desert that had taken and slaughtered her nine-week-old daughter. Followers of the case were shocked.

So too was Lindy. She couldn't understand how fellow human beings who had read her story and sat in judgement of her in court had decided she had committed such a wicked deed.

No one had believed that her screams were those of a mother at seeing her new baby dragged off by a wild animal. Yet the words Lindy Chamberlain cried that moment were to go down in history: 'A dingo has got my baby...!'

'DINGOES ARE WILD'

It was a scorching hot evening on 17 August 1980 when what had begun as a happy family camping holiday turned into tragedy. Lindy, her Seventh Day Adventist preacher husband Michael, and their three children Aidan, Reagan and baby Azaria were on a picnic near the mysterious Ayers Rock.

The Chamberlains had only casually glanced at a sign saying 'Dingoes are wild' and warning visitors not to encourage them by putting down food. Michael Chamberlain remained around the barbecue area when Lindy decided to return to the family tent to check on baby Azaria. The child had been left contentedly in her cot.

When Lindy entered the tent the scene before her eyes was too horrific to take in at first. She saw a dingo shaking her child violently in its clenched, bloody teeth. Then it ran off dragging the baby with it.

Fellow campers, visitors and other volunteers - three hundred in all - took part in a desperate search of the area. But no evidence of the poor child could be found on or around Ayers Rock, the sinister monolith sacred to the Aborigines.

Although there was no body, Alice Springs coroner Des Sturgess found at the inquest that 'in the time they went to the campsite and the time Mr Chamberlain was at the barbecue area, the death was caused'. Lindy could not be comforted. Her newborn baby had gone, dragged to a wild creature's lair somewhere and eaten.

When Lindy entered the tent she saw a dingo dangling her new baby Azaria from its bloodstained muzzle

That first inquest was gruelling enough for the Chamberlains, but the support of friends from Michael's Church and their families was a great help. What was to follow, however, was not only to invade their private grief but to lay it bare before an accusing world.

A year later they had to relive their baby's disappearance all over again. For some reason, Australia's Northern Territory police had not been satisfied with the inquest verdict. They worked towards disproving it and had, over the months, been gathering new evidence against Lindy Chamberlain. That

Opposite: Lindy Chamberlain arrives at court in Darwin, Australia, for the inquiry into the death of her baby daughter Azaria - the so-called Dingo Baby.

evidence was considered important enough to be presented before a second inquest in 1981.

The Chamberlains found themselves at the coroner's court again. This time a plastic bag lay on the table. It contained little Azaria's playsuit which had been found in shreds and blood-drenched outside a dingo's lair close to the campsite several days after the baby disappeared. What hadn't been found was the white matinee jacket Lindy said her child had been wearing.

The police forensic department had discovered a handprint the size of a woman's on the tiny garment. The team had come to the conclusion that the child's clothes had been touched with hands wet with blood. This could easily have been explained by the fact that Lindy, hysterical at what had happened, had clutched the baby's suit after accidentally smearing her hand in the blood that spattered the tent.

But more evidence was being compiled against her. They said they found blood on the door handle of the Chamberlains' car, on the carpet, under hinges and under the dashboard. Some traces were fetal blood, they said - the blood of a newborn baby.

ACCUSED OF MURDER

The authorities now felt they had enough proof that a murder had taken place. They alleged that thirty-three-year-old Lindy Chamberlain had invented the dingo snatch story in a bid to get away with cold-bloodedly killing her baby.

Without body or motive, and with only circumstantial evidence, the police decided Lindy had killed her own baby

---

The investigations crossed the world. British forensic expert Professor James Cameron, of the London Hospital medical school, was called in to give a second opinion. It was claimed that Lindy had slashed her baby's throat with a pair of scissors as she sat in the family car. The bloodied child had then been held by human hands.

It is rare that a murder charge can be brought without a body being found. In this case there was no body, no motive and no weapon. But on 2 February 1982 the Alice Springs coroner, this time Gerry Galvin, made an announcement that stunned the Chamberlains. He ordered that Lindy should stand trial for murder. Michael was indicted as an accessory.

Even before that hearing, public feeling towards Lindy changed. She was no longer a mother who had lost her child in tragic, freak circumstances and therefore deserving of support and sympathy. She was now the cold and calculated killer of her very own baby.

By the time Lindy and her husband went to court on 19 April 1982 her cause had fiercely divided the nation. The case was discussed everywhere. Newspapers reported that Ayers Rock, sacred site for the Aborigines, was used for initiation and childbirth rites.

And it was revealed that the Chamberlains had visited other Aboriginal sites in the same area. Newspapers couldn't believe their luck when they heard that one of these sites was called Cut Throat Cave and that Azaria was the Aboriginal word for 'sacrifice in the wilderness'.

The name Azaria, according to the journalists, meant 'sacrifice in the wilderness'

It was obvious that Lindy and Michael Chamberlain, granted bail of £13,000 each, had the odds stacked against them for a fair hearing in Alice Springs. The authorities decided they should go to court in Darwin in a bid to get them impartial justice.

Their trial lasted seven weeks. The jury consisted of nine men and three women. They listened as the Chamberlains were first damned with the forensic evidence and then exonerated as loving parents, the victims of a tragic circumstance.

Prosecutor Ian Marker said Lindy killed her baby, buried her in the desert and then, with the help of her husband, dug the body up to tear off the clothing. They then placed the suit near a dingo's lair. He called Lindy's dingo claims a 'fanciful lie'.

Professor James Cameron did not waver from his conclusions. He stood by his original statement that, judging by Azaria's babysuit, death had been caused by an incised wound to her neck. In other words, by a cut throat.

Below: *Lindy and Michael Chamberlain's devout Seventh Day Adventist faith helped them through the nightmare ordeal that shattered their lives.*

Prosecuting evidence came from campsite witnesses, forensic scientists, police and lawyers. The defence called twenty-eight people to the stand. Among these were ten who said that Lindy was very loving towards Azaria.

Another two witnesses gave evidence that, the day before the baby went missing, two children at the campsite were confronted by a dingo that, obviously used to humans that put out food for it, showed no fear. It grabbed the trousers of one of the children.

The case seemed to be going well for the Chamberlains when a young man called Kyth Lenehan took the oath and told in a matter-of-fact way how he had been in an accident in June 1979, and that the caring Chamberlains had taken him to hospital in their car. He had bled quite heavily from a head injury. That would explain traces of blood found in their car.

Much later, forensic scientists were to be greatly embarrassed when the 'fetal blood' found under the car's dashboard turned out to be a bitumen substance used to dampen engine noise. And the holes in the baby's clothing were consistent with marks made by dingo teeth.

Mr Justice James Muirhead's summing up took a staggering six hours. Then the jury was out for several hours more.

Lindy and Michael showed no emotion when they were both found guilty.

In prison Lindy gave birth to another daughter - taken from her only forty-five minutes later

---

Michael was found guilty of being an accessory and given an eighteenth-month suspended sentence. He was also bound over in the sum of £300 to be of good behaviour for three years.

The harsh sentence on Lindy shocked even those who had already believed her guilty - not just because she was still a young woman and the mother of two small children, but because when sentence was passed, on 29 October 1982, Lindy was just a month away from having another baby.

She gave birth to daughter Kahlia in prison. Forty-five minutes afterwards, her baby was taken away from her. Two days

later, Lindy was freed on bail pending an appeal. Lindy's appeal was rejected on 30 April 1983.

She was taken back to Berrinah jail in Darwin to 'resume her sentence as soon as possible'.

NEW EVIDENCE OVERTURNS THE VERDICT

Then came a dramatic twist. In February 1986, climbers searching for the body of British tourist David Brett, who had fallen to his death on Ayers Rock, found a tiny bloodstained matinee jacket. It was the jacket of Azaria Chamberlain.

The police forensic scientists who had tried so hard to convict Lindy were now called in to examine what was delicately referred to as 'organic material' found near the jacket. It was human remains.

Lindy was let out of jail. One of her first actions was to instruct legal advisers to institute yet another inquiry.

The Royal Commission Inquiry began in May 1986 and lasted nearly a year. Heading it was Mr Justice Morling, who found many faults with the case presented by the prosecution. The Chamberlains were granted a pardon.

After all she had endured, this was not enough for Lindy. She said: 'There is no satisfaction in getting a pardon for something you didn't do... I want the conviction quashed and the authorities to admit I was wrongly accused.'

'There is no satisfaction getting a pardon for something you didn't do in the first place,' declared Lindy

---

Lindy and Michael were reunited while the legal system geared itself up for yet another hearing. Lindy talked of her time in jail. She said: 'I used to think I'd be out in a few days - that it was all a big mistake. The major thing that has got me through is my faith in God.'

On 15 September 1988, it took just ten minutes before three judges declared Lindy and Michael completely innocent of all charges.

As the verdict was announced, Lindy stared intently ahead. But as the court rose she almost fell back in her seat.

Then she and Michael met the cheering crowd outside the Darwin court before going into hiding to pray.

The couple's lawyer announced he would institute proceedings to win compensation for all the time they had lived under sentence of killing their own baby. And he pointed out the true meaning of the baby's name, Azaria, which he said was 'Blessed of God'.

Lindy and her husband had fought for and won justice. But they were not yet able to retreat into a quiet life, biding their time until financial compensation was awarded.

TELLING THE STORY

Thousands of miles away in London, film producer Verity Lambert had followed the Chamberlain story closely. She had read *Evil Angels* by Melbourne lawyer John Bryson, one of the nine books to be written about the infamous Dingo Baby Case. 'I felt very strongly there had been a miscarriage of justice and wanted to put the record straight,' she said.

Having set her heart on the story, Verity went to Australia to meet the Chamberlains. The film she eventually made was a £10 million production called *Cry in the Dark*.

Ignorant prejudice against Seventh Day Adventists had cooked up tales of ritual human sacrifice

---

The film won honours for its star, Meryl Streep, who was given the best actress award at the 1989 Cannes Film Festival. To prepare for the role, Meryl arranged a meeting with Lindy Chamberlain and said afterwards: 'The moment I read the story I knew I wanted to do the film. There was no question in my mind when I met her that she was innocent and I was very moved.'

Lindy also wrote her own version of events, in a 768-page book called *Through My Eyes*.

In 1991 the first reports of Lindy and Michael's cash settlements started to come through. In June that year the Northern Territory government agreed they could have £195,000. The couple

had asked for £690,000. The government had originally refused to pay anything, saying the Chamberlains had failed to declare all their assets accumulated from the sale of their story.

Lindy accused the authorities of deliberately delaying payments. She said: 'They know they have done me a wrong and have wronged the rest of my family, and that I'm innocent.'

Before the compensation award Michael Chamberlain had to cut firewood for a living and the children had no shoes

---

The Chamberlains desperately denied reports that they had made fortunes out of their story. Said Lindy: 'People laugh at you and some say "We know you've got money" but we just don't have any.'

The couple were heavily in debt to the Seventh Day Adventist Church. Michael was cutting up firewood for £15 a bundle, a job he was doing right up until the compensation award.

They did have a car, however - the 1970s vehicle in which Lindy was accused of murdering her baby. It was returned by the police authorities - minus its gearbox and engine.

Today the family still live in their bungalow in Cooranbong. Lindy maintains that her story of what really happened that night in 1980 was discredited by the authorities to protect its fledgling tourist industry and plans to develop facilities at Ayers Rock.

Lindy just wants an end to it all, but she says: 'You know, it never really did come out in evidence about a number of attacks on children before Azaria's death. The site where we camped is now part of an Aboriginal reserve. But I am told dingoes still come into tents...'

Above: *Even after Lindy Chamberlain was cleared of the murder of her baby, she had to convince a still - suspicious public that she had not made a fortune from her tragedy.*

NESSIE
Myth or Monster?

For many centuries Scottish folklore has told of a monster living in the murky depths of Loch Ness. Even modern hi-tech investigations have failed to prove whether Nessie and similar creatures from North America are fact or fiction

The existence of Nessie, the friendly monster of Loch Ness, was officially announced in 1933. But for countless generations dating back to the Dark Ages folklore had recounted the legend of the loch.

Deep, dark and forbidding, Loch Ness is a giant tear in the earth's surface cutting across the centre of Scotland. It is in an area as impenetrable and hostile as is possible in this modern age.

The Loch, 300 metres deep, 24 miles long, with water as black as pitch, was gouged out ten thousand years ago by the last of the Ice Age glaciers. And since man learned to pass on stories it has been home for mysterious monsters.

THE LEGENDS BEGIN

The first written record of a water monster in the loch came as long ago as AD 565. In his biography of St Columba the then Abbot of Iona described how the saint triumphed over a 'water beast' in the River Ness. St Columba had been working to convert the heathen Picts and Scots from his new monastery on Iona, off the west coast of Scotland.

On his travels he came to Loch Ness and found local people burying a neighbour who had been badly mauled by Niseag - to give the monster her Gaelic name - while out swimming.

The corpse had been brought to the shore by villagers armed with grappling hooks to ward off the monster. But one of the saint's followers was foolhardy enough to swim across the narrows at the head of the Loch to get a small boat. As he swam out, 'a strange beast rose from the water something like a frog, only it was not a frog'.

St Columba is said to have ordered the great beast to turn back - and succeeded

---

St Columba, wrote the Abbot, faced the monster and ordered him: 'Go no further, nor touch that man.' Meekly, the monster turned on his tail and fled.

It was the beginning of the legend of the Loch Ness monster.

For centuries Scottish folklore has recounted tales of kelpies, malignant

Above: *Was this the Loch Ness monster - four dark humps in the water - photographed in 1952?*

Opposite: *In 1934, London gynaecologist Robert Wilson took four photographs of a strange creature rising from the depths of Loch Ness.*

water sprites, which lurked by the waterside disguised as horses, waiting for human victims.

Local people living near Loch Ness even now can remember being told as children not to swim in Loch Ness because of the kelpie.

DETAILED SIGHTING

But it was in the spring of 1933 that Nessie was 'born' with the first famous detailed sighting, by Mr and Mrs John MacKay, which was reported in the *Inverness Courier*. In the same year a road had been blasted along the north shore and trees and undergrowth cut down to give a better view of the massive expanse of water, the largest freshwater lake in Britain.

In an interview in the *Daily Mail* fifty years later Mrs MacKay relived that dramatic day. She said:

I was the only one who saw it. It was March 1933 and we were hurrying back from a house sale in Inverness. Suddenly at the seven-mile stone... you couldn't believe what we were seeing, never having seen such an enormous thing.

It was just an enormous black body, going up and down. You could not put a name to it. It could have been an

Top: *Headquarters of the Loch Ness monster investigation team set up in 1968. Later expeditions were to use ever more sophisticated equipment.*

Above: *Members of the team of monster hunters watch the loch's surface, eager for any sign of the creature's existence.*

elephant or a whale. I was yelling to John to stop, stop - whatever words came into my head - but he only thought that a bee was bothering me on my wind-screen, you had to remember it was the old road, very narrow and by the time he stopped...

'Just ripples...' said her husband. He swore her to secrecy, explaining: 'If that got round they'd all be saying we've been imbibing. Put more water in it, they'd say.'

But Mrs MacKay did tell her story. She said 'I told someone in the strictest confidence, who then told someone else and the water bailiff Alex Campbell got to hear of it. He was local correspondent for the *Courier*.'

If they told their amazing story, Mr MacKay thought, people would shake their heads in disbelief and say the couple had been drinking

---

The editor printed the story under the headline 'Strange Spectacle of Loch Ness', and for the first time described it as a monster. It caused a sensation - and an explosion of sightings.

THE SIGHTINGS MUSHROOM

In the next fifty years there were over three thousand serious claims that Nessie was alive and well. Could they all be mistaken?

Just two months after the MacKay sighting a gang of workmen engaged on blasting operations were startled to see Nessie going up the centre of the lake in the wake of a passing drifter. They said that it had an 'enormous head' and a large, heavy body.

And in August of the same year three witnesses noticed a disturbance on the surface of a very calm Loch Ness. There were several humps in line, rising and falling with a slightly undulating motion suggesting a caterpillar.

Sightings came thick and fast. In 1938 a steam tug captain and his mate were astonished to notice a huge, black 'animal' shaped rather like a hump-backed whale emerge on the surface and keep up with their vessel.

The creature had two distinct humps, but after a brief disappearance it resurfaced with seven humps or coils and sped past the tug 'at terrific speed' leaving large waves.

On 13 August 1960, the Rev W.L. Dobb had just finished a picnic lunch with his family beside the lake when they all saw large waves moving along the water. A few seconds later they all saw a large black hump. It quickly disappeared - to be replaced by two humps.

It is as though Nessie is playing a tantalizing game of hide-and-seek with sightseers and scientists.

PHOTOGRAPHIC EVIDENCE

But beside eye-witness reports there is photographic evidence to support the existence of the mysterious monster.

Photographers began arriving to picture Nessie within months of the MacKay spotting. In November 1933 the Rev N. Dundas, who saw Nessie with his wife, tried to photograph the beast - but when the photo was developed the monster was missing.

The first photograph alleging to show Nessie was taken by Hugh Gray, also in 1933. Gray took five pictures - but four were blank. When his photograph was published in various newspapers Kodak staff signed a statement that the negative had not been tampered with.

In 1934 came the famous 'Surgeon's Photograph'. Robert Wilson was a London gynaecologist on holiday with a friend. They were driving to Inverness and had stopped on the road by the Loch.

Suddenly he noticed a commotion in the water 'between 150 and 200 yards from the shore where the head of some strange animal rose up out of the water'. He managed to take four photographs before the object sank from view.

Below: *Even submarines have been used in the hunt for Nessie. Some detected strange, moving objects in the loch's depths.*

Above: *Fiction not fact...
A film-maker touches up the
paintwork of a plastic
Nessie on the lochside, for
the spoof movie,* **The Private
Life of Sherlock Holmes.**

The third important photograph
supporting the theory that Nessie does
exist was taken by Lachlan Stuart in July
1951. He was employed by the Forestry
Commission and lived close to the Loch
with his wife and children and a lodger,
Taylor Hay.

Given the huge quantity of detailed
evidence from eye-witnesses, can they
all have been mistaken?

But sceptics say that photographs of
Nessie are either faked or misinterpreted.
Logs in the water, the wake of passing
vessels or wind changes could cause
images similar to Nessie, they argue. But
the sheer volume and intensity of eye-
witness evidence from Loch Ness cannot
be ignored. Is it possible that they are all
liars or just plain mistaken?

Some eye-witnesses believe that
Nessie can live on land as well as water.
As a child during World War I Margaret
Cameron heard 'crackling' in the trees
and saw a creature slither down into the
water. She said, 'It had a huge body and
its movement was like a caterpillar.'

It had a shiny skin, the colour of an
elephant, and two short round feet at the
front. After lurching to one side it put
one foot after the other into the water.

Mr and Mrs George Spicer from
London described it in 1933 as a
'loathsome sight'. It looked like a huge
snail with a long neck, he said. And it
was carrying what looked like a dead
lamb in its mouth.

Sceptics say the 'Monster' is merely an
otter, and that the peculiar light on the
Loch plays tricks with people's eyes

Some experts have used these land-
based sightings to argue that Nessie was
nothing but an otter and witnesses were
confused by tricks of the light.

The Loch itself does present problems
because of its situation. It can play tricks
on the eyes. It is a large mass of water,
sometimes completely calm in a way that
the sea rarely is, and its high shoreline
casts deep shadows and reflections.

HI-TECH COMES TO LOCH NESS

The locals in the area - ever ready to coin
a shilling as only a Scotsman can - have
been only too willing to boost their
tourist industry with less than scientific
evidence of the monster's existence.

Modern technology, however, has
made the hunt for the truth about Nessie
more scientific and reliable. Two cine
films of the Loch, which are far more
difficult to fake than still photographs,
were submitted to the Joint Air
Reconnaissance Intelligence Centre by
David James of the Loch Ness
Investigation Bureau.

The first was shot by Tim Dinsdale and
shows a hump moving slowly away from
him and then fast across his field of
vision while submerging. The analysts
concluded that the object was 'probably
animate'. They said that the object was
nearly 5 ft 6 in wide and moved at about
10 miles per hour.

In 1970 underwater photography was
used as an investigative aid for the first
time. But the murkiness of the peaty
water and the limitations of equipment
make it difficult.

This photographic expedition was led
by Dr Robert Rines, president of the
Academy of Applied Science in Belmont,

Massachusetts. Rines stayed two weeks, and two years later produced photos showing a fin or flipper.

His second visit, in 1975, resulted in a picture which could be interpreted as the upper torso, neck and head of a living creature. But other investigations into the circumstances of how the photograph was taken have tended to denigrate the veracity of the picture.

Is Nessie a plesiosaur, a relic from before the last Ice Age 70 million years ago?

However it was enough for naturalist Sir Peter Scott, who had helped launch the Loch Ness Phenomena Investigation Bureau in 1962. He announced: 'There are probably between twenty and fifty of them down there. I believe they are related to the plesiosaurs.'

The plesiosaur has not been seen on earth for 70 million years. Monster hunters concluded that Nessie and her ancestors were cut off from the sea when the Loch was formed at the end of the last Ice Age. But other experts argued that the plesiosaur could never have survived in the conditions of Loch Ness, or would never have coped in its original form and would need to have mutated drastically to live.

NESSIE'S RELATIVES ABROAD

But while Nessie may be the most famous of her breed there are other water monsters haunting lakes and seas all over the world. She is not alone.

In Lake Okanagan in British Columbia, near the US-Canada border, reputedly lives a monster named the great Ogopogo. In fact verifiable sightings were being recorded a long time before Nessie's notoriety.

The first reports of the monster of the lake originated with the Indians in the seventeenth century. They described a large, dark-coloured creature with a long neck and a humped back.

The beast's name means 'remorseful one', for in Indian legend he was a murderer who had been changed into a water serpent in punishment.

Below: *The Japanese are obsessive Nessie hunters. Here she is represented, complete with spouting nostrils, in Dago Park, Fukuoka City, Kyushu.*

The modern spate of sightings started in the 1870s, when Susan Allison saw what she thought was a log suddenly swim up-lake against the wind. In July 1890 Captain Thomas Shorts was sailing the steamer *Jubilee* through the lake when he saw an animal off Squally Point, about 15 ft long, with a ram-like head and the sun shining through its fins.

Arthur Folden, a sawmill worker, was driving his wife home on a sunny day in August 1968 when they saw something large and animate moving through the calm water of the lake. Folden stopped the car and and took out his 8mm cine camera.

For a minute he filmed the object, which was swimming about 200 yards from the shore. Scared of the publicity, he waited a year before he was persuaded by relatives to show the film publicly.

In Indian legend the Ogopogo was a murderer who had been turned into a water monster to punish him

---

In 1976 there was more photographic evidence. Ed Fletcher was on the lake when an object cut across his bow. He recorded: 'If I hadn't shut the engine off I could have run him over or jumped on his back. The boat drifted to within 30 feet of him.'

Fletcher and his daughter, Diane, had time to return to shore to pick up a camera. When they returned, Ogopogo appeared from the depths again.

Fletcher, his daughter and another passenger whom they had picked up at the same time as the camera watched for an hour. 'He would submerge, swim at least two city blocks, then surface and all the while we chased him.'

He said that the serpent surfaced a dozen times. Fletcher took five photographs. He reported that it swam coiled up and then it stretched out.

His daughter described the skin as smooth and brownish like that of a whale, with small ridges on its back. As it swam it turned like a corkscrew. And the witnesses also talked of its head which, they said, had 'two things standing up from the head like the ears of a Dobermann pinscher'.

MORE WATER MONSTERS

A monster named Manipogo - presumably a relation of Ogie - is believed to inhabit the two lakes of Manitoba and Winnipegosis in Canada. Again, it was originally seen by Indians. Most descriptions give it a flat, snake-like head, dark skin and three humps. Some reports have even given it a mate and offspring.

Some reports say that the creature known as Manipogo has a mate and young

---

Lake Champlain, which straddles the Canadian-US border, is also famous for monster sightings. 'Champ' was first spotted by Samuel de Champlain, after whom the lake was named, in 1609. He thought it looked like a 20 ft snake with a horse's head.

An amazing picture allegedly of Lake Champlain's mystery creature was taken by Sandra Mansi in 1977. Some sceptics try to suggest that the head and neck are

really the fin of a small whale rolling on its side. Others contend there was a sand-bar just below the surface, implying that it was a hoax.

One set of experts said the photograph was genuine. Another said the creature was as real as the tooth fairy

---

The Optical Sciences Centre at the University of Arizona examined the print and said it was genuine. But Professor Paul Kurtz of the State University of New York said he thought that the monster was as real as the tooth fairy.

Ireland, too, has its lake monsters. Even three priests swore that they'd seen an unknown being in Lough Ree. On 18 May 1960 the three Fathers - Daniel Murray, Matthew Burke and Richard Quigly - were fishing off the Lough in the River Shannon.

Suddenly the peace was shattered by a large flat-headed creature approaching them. It was about 100 yards from where they sat. All three of the priests could see it quite clearly.

THE MYSTERY GOES ON

But as sightings continue all over the world, even the great advances of science do not seem to be getting us any nearer proving - or disproving - the existence of Nessic and her colleagues.

In 1933 E.G. Boulenger, Director of the Aquarium at London Zoo, said that reports of Nessie were 'a striking example of mass hallucination'. He pointed out that once Nessie was seen by a few people, she would be reported by many more. People see what they want to see, he argued. But can so many thousands be deceived worldwide?

Scientists have argued that there is no fish, reptile, mammal or amphibian known to them which matches the descriptions of the monsters of the lakes.

We know that the giant monsters who lived on land died out because they could not adapt. But we do not know what happened to the species who were at home in the water.

Perhaps down there lazing in the dark depths of Loch Ness and other lakes around the world lies the answer.

Above: *A sea 'monster' spotted off the coast of California. Sightings of Nessie-like creatures have been reported from all over the globe - and are increasing.*

GHOSTS
Terrors of the Night

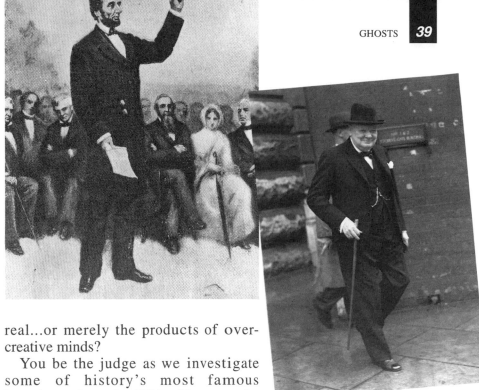

Why did an English schoolboy's furniture move spontaneously about his bedroom? What did a tough sailor see in an empty house that frightened him to death? Believe them or not, you have to agree that these stories of the supernatural are bizarre - and scary

Ghosts, haunted houses and castles, things that go bump in the night, poltergeists - they are the stuff of our worst nightmares. Eerie, pale reminders of our own mortality and the uncertainty which awaits us all. Are they real...or merely the products of over-creative minds?

You be the judge as we investigate some of history's most famous hauntings...from the White House to the Bank of England to the tiny town of Amityville, Long Island, to Hollywood.

THE WHITE HOUSE APPARITION

Winston Churchill has seen him, so has visiting Dutch Princess Juliana. And Maureen Reagan, the former President's first daughter, swears by him. Who is he?

*Above left: **The apparition of assassinated American President Abraham Lincoln has been seen regularly in the White House over the years.***

*Above: **Winston Churchill claimed to have seen the ghost of Abraham Lincoln.***

*Opposite: **The ghost of Dorothy Walpole is said to haunt Raynham Hall in Norfolk. This photograph showing what seems to be a ghostly presence coming down the stairs was taken in 1936.***

*Left: **Too much familiarity with the spiritual could be dangerous in 17th-century Salem, Massachusetts. This painting depicts the trial of George Jacobs, one of Salem's infamous witchcraft trials.***

Well, according to those who have caught a glimpse of the apparition, it's none other than Abraham Lincoln, America's greatest President.

'I'm not kidding,' says Maureen Reagan. 'We've really seen it.' She and her husband, Dennis Revell, often slept in Lincoln's Bedroom when they visited her parents in Washington, and claim to have seen the apparition, which is sometimes red, sometimes orange. Maureen and her husband claim it's Lincoln's ghost.

The Reagans' dog refused ever to set foot in the Lincoln Bedroom, where their daughter had seen an apparition

---

Neither President Reagan nor Nancy ever saw the apparition during their eight-year stay in the White House, and nor have President Bush or First Lady Barbara. Mrs Reagan scoffed at the notion that Lincoln's spirit still wandered the historic building, but she does recall that the family dog, Rex, often barked in the bedroom's direction - and refused ever to set foot in it.

THE GHOSTS OF FLIGHT 401

Ghosts, however, aren't restricted to houses or castles. One of the most famous of all spooky tales is that of the Ghosts of Flight 401. In December 1972, an Eastern Airlines TriStar crashed into a murky Florida swamp, killing 101 people

Above left: *James Brolin played the part of George Lutz in the film version of* **The Amityville Horror.**

Above: *Police guard the house at Amityville, Long Island, that became the focus of the horror story industry.*

Below: *Margot Kidder and James Brolin portrayed the couple who bought their dream home, only to have it turn into a nightmare.*

including the pilot and his flight engineer. But since the accident Captain Bob Loft and engineer Dan Repo have been spotted on at least twenty other Eastern TriStar jetliners by crew members.

Startled TriStar crew members have claimed sightings of the pilot and engineer of the ill-fated Flight 401

Most of the sightings - by highly trained aviators who are hardly prone to panic - have occurred on planes that were fitted with parts of Flight 401 that were salvaged. And many of those who swear they have seen the ghosts of Loft and Repo knew both men personally.

HOLLYWOOD'S BRUSH WITH THE SUPERNATURAL

More than 25 million Americans claim to have seen a ghost, so it comes as no surprise that many Hollywood stars have also had brushes with the supernatural. Actress Elke Sommer actually bought a haunted house in Beverly Hills - though she had no idea it was home to a ghost before she moved in.

But soon after she and Joe Hyams moved in, as they were lying in their bedroom, they began to hear weird noises coming from the dining room downstairs. Every night was the same, until a few weeks later when they were suddenly awakened by a loud knocking on their bedroom door. Hyams jumped out of bed, opened the door and saw nothing - nothing except a cloud of thick black smoke coming from downstairs.

Startled, he raced down the stairs, and found the dining room ablaze. No one knows what happened for certain, but several mediums told the couple that the ghost had probably started the fire as a prank, but then changed his mind and raced upstairs to warn them.

Did the ghost in Elke Sommer's Beverly Hills mansion start a fire as a prank, and then warn the inhabitants?

Oscar-winner Ellen Burstyn, who starred in *One Flew Over the Cuckoo's Nest*, has also had a run-in with a ghost - but not only was this ghost friendly, she knew him. She recalled that shortly after the death of Lee Strasberg, the famed acting tutor, in 1981 she was staying with his widow in the Strasbergs' apartment.

As she tried to fall asleep, his ghost appeared to her and spoke. 'I suddenly felt a pull on my shoulder, and Lee appeared,' she said. 'He said to me, "Be strong. Yes, grieve, but death is part of life, and not the end." '

Even more frightening, however, was the experience of James Brolin, star of *The Amityville Horror*, who claims the movie was surrounded by evil during its making. He recalled:

On the very first day of filming I stepped in the elevator in my apartment block and pressed the button for the lobby floor. Before we'd gone three floors it shuddered to a grinding, screeching halt, the lights flickered and I was plunged into frightening darkness. I screamed for help, but no one could hear me. It was an eerie, frightening experience. You imagine all sorts of hair-raising things in silent darkness. It seemed an eternity.

Thirty minutes later the elevator restarted, and a relieved Brolin went to the set of the film.

GHOSTLY HORRORS

The macabre story chronicled in Brolin's film was, of course, far scarier than anything that ever happened to the actor. The story of *The Amityville Horror* still ranks as one of the most terrifying ever.

The tale began one November night in 1974 when Ronald DeFeo, then twenty-three, gruesomely slaughtered his family of six in their six-bedroom house in suburban Long Island. Thirteen months later, land surveyor George Lutz and his

Below: *Ronald DeFeo is led from Suffolk county police headquarters accused of gruesomely slaughtering his family of six.*

Bottom: *Just as the owner George Lutz claimed to have done, actor Brolin takes on the characteristics of murderer DeFeo who previously lived in the Amityville house.*

family moved into that very same house - and within twenty-eight days, they would flee for their lives.

The story of 112 Ocean Avenue, which Jay Anson developed into a best-selling book, stunned America. The Lutzes' eerie account included green slime oozing from the walls, large numbers of flies, doors coming loose off their hinges, the sounds of a band playing in the living room and pigs snorting in the windows. Finally, after they and their young children could take no more of the horrifying haunting, they fled, leaving behind virtually everything.

'I switched on my lamp,' recalled Matthew Manning, 'and saw to my horror that the cupboard was inching out from the wall towards me'

Englishman Matthew Manning had a similarly terrifying experience with unseen forces in Cambridge, beginning in 1967. When he was just eleven, the house he shared with his parents was suddenly overtaken by strange events. His father, Derek, noticed that every time he reset a silver mug on a shelf it would fall to the floor. Over the next few weeks other objects were found in places they shouldn't have been, and gradually the off-putting disturbances became more than frightening. Heavy objects, like chairs and tables, began moving about

Left: *Ronald DeFeo leaves court, convicted of murder. Thirteen months later, surveyor George Lutz and his wife bought the death house.*

Below: *No. 112 Ocean Avenue, Amityville, drove the Lutz couple away within twenty-eight days of their purchasing the six-bedroom house.*

The next day, he and his parents awoke to find the house a shambles: furniture was strewn about, pictures had fallen from the walls, a table had been turned upside down and there were ornaments scattered about the floor.

Eventually, the sinister events became even more frightening. Water pools appeared on the floor and, most eerily, writing began appearing on the wall. One message warned: 'Matthew Beware'.

Incredibly, however, when Matthew left for boarding school the poltergeist went with him, doing the same bizarre things to the dormitory as it had done to his parents' house. It wasn't until 1971 that Matthew began to develop psychic skills of his own, and gradually the poltergeist activity ceased.

Not all poltergeist appearances are so terrifying, however. The story of Francis Martin and his family would seem to bear that out. In October 1963, Mr Martin noticed a damp area appearing on the wall of the living room in his home in Methuen, Massachusetts.

Suddenly there was a loud popping sound and a gush of water burst from the wall, lasting for some twenty seconds. After a few days of sudden water spurts, the anxious family moved into a relative's house nearby.

***

The Martin family moved to a relative's house to escape the strange happenings - but their poltergeist came with them

***

Whatever had caused their problem followed - and soon the second house was spurting water! A deputy fire inspector came around to investigate and checked the structure for leaky pipes, but found none. Not wanting to inundate the relative's house, the Martin family returned to their own home...but not before turning the water off at the main and draining the pipes.

It did no good, however, and the bizarre water flow from the walls continued unabated. The strange phenomenon occurred on and off over the next few weeks, but then stopped as suddenly as if someone - or something - had turned off a tap.

and tipping over. Matthew, who recounted some of the frightening moments in his book *The Link* recalled:

I had gone to bed...I suddenly heard a scraping noise coming from the direction of the cupboard, which continued for almost thirty seconds. Having listened to it for a moment, I switched on my lamp and saw to my horror that the cupboard was inching out from the wall towards me. When it halted, it had advanced about eighteen inches. I switched off the light and almost simultaneously my bed started to vibrate violently back and forth...[then] the vibrating ceased, and I felt the bottom end of my bed rising from the floor to what I estimated to be about one foot.

Above: *Popular conception of a ghostly apparition. In a survey, more than 25 million Americans claimed to have seen a ghost.*

HAUNTED LONDON

While America has its fair share of ghostly doings, London is probably home to more famous ghosts than any other city in the world. From out-of-the-way back streets to famed landmarks like the Tower, the Bank of England and Kensington Palace, the city is haunted with literally hundreds of spirits.

The Bank of England, for instance, has been haunted by the Black Nun, an apparition that wanders around the Bank garden. The ghost is said to be Sarah Whitehead, the sister of a former Bank employee, Philip Whitehead, who was arrested in 1811 for forging cheques. Whitehead was sentenced to death, and the tragedy so traumatized his sister that for the next twenty-five years she went daily to the Bank to look for him.

When she died, she was buried in an old church inside the Bank grounds, which later became the Bank gardens. In the 150 years or so since, she has been sighted on numerous occasions - still wandering in her eternal search for her long dead brother.

Probably the most famous and scariest of all the city's ghosts is the one which haunts a house in Berkeley Square - an apparition that reportedly scared at least three people to death. One of the stories surrounding the Berkeley Square ghost tells of a young child who was either tortured or frightened to death in the house's nursery. His ghost, still sobbing

Above left: Matthew Manning was haunted by poltergeist activity from the age of eleven.

Above: Matthew Manning's poltergeists only left him alone when he began to develop psychic powers of his own.

Below: One of Manning's more remarkable psychic gifts was 'automatic' drawing. This is a rhinoceros drawn by him in the style of the Renaissance artist Albrecht Dürer.

and wearing a kilt-like garment, is said to make periodic appearances.

Another story claims the ghost is actually that of a young woman, who shared the house with her lascivious uncle. In an attempt to free herself of his immoral advances, she threw herself from a window on the top floor. People claimed to have seen her ghost hanging on to the ledge and screaming.

Is the Bank of England's ghost the sister of an employee sentenced to death for forging cheques?

A third story recounts the bizarre tale of a white-faced man whose appearance was so ghastly, that a sailor was literally frightened to death by the apparition when he visited the house with a crew mate.

The building was vacant at the time, so the two seamen decided to sleep there - only to be awakened by the sound of footsteps coming up the stairs. Someone - or something - walked into their room, causing one of the poor chaps to panic so much that he fell from a window to his death. The second sailor, who survived the terrifying ordeal, was later found on the street, unconscious from fear.

The house was so famous in Victorian days that it actually became a tourist spot of sorts. One well-heeled citizen, Lord Lyttleton, actually spent a night inside the haunted room, armed with two rifles which he had loaded with buckshot and

silver sixpences, which he believed would guarantee him protection against whatever evil lurked inside. He survived the night, but later recounted firing at an apparition that leaped at him from the dark. He also claimed he tracked down a woman who had been driven insane after spending a night inside the house.

Armed with buckshot and silver bullets, Lord Lyttleton spent a night inside the notorious Berkeley Square house

---

Throughout the long and macabre history of the house, two other people are said to have died from fright. One, a housemaid, was found inside the haunted room, hysterically weeping on the floor. She was taken to St George's Hospital, where she died the very next day.

But before her death, doctors tried to ascertain what had scared her so much. She refused to discuss it, saying only it was 'just too horrible' to describe. Not long after, a volunteer agreed to spend a night in the room to learn what may have happened. He was found later that night - his eyes agape in horror, and dead.

Whatever evil lies in wait inside the house in Berkeley Square, it has reportedly been dormant for many years.

The Theatre Royal in Drury Lane is another of London's famous haunted landmarks - but the three centuries-old building may have more than just one

Top: One message that appeared mysteriously on Manning's bedroom wall warned: 'Matthew Beware'.

Above: 'Slavery', a monkey - another of Matthew Manning's automatic drawings.

unearthly visitor. The most famous, of course, is the Man in Grey, who has been spotted by dozens of startled actors and patrons in the past two hundred years.

He appears in knee breeches, frock coat and tricorn hat, and is most often seen walking along the gangway from one side of the theatre to the other - where he disappears through the wall. Occasionally the Man in Grey has been spotted in one of the seats. His ghostly appearance at the beginning of a show is said to forecast a successful run. Most of the cast of *The Dancing Years* claim they saw him when they gathered on stage for a photo shoot.

The appearance of the Man in Grey at the Theatre Royal, Drury Lane is supposed to ensure a successful run

---

According to theatre historians, about one hundred years ago, a small room was discovered inside the theatre, containing the skeleton of a man with a knife between his ribs. They believe he was the victim of a ruthless eighteenth-century manager of the theatre.

The theatre is also thought to be haunted by the ghost of Dan Leno, the comedian-dancer. In the dressing room he used during his tenure at the theatre - the number of which is kept a secret in case it upsets the current tenant - a face sometimes appears in the mirror. Those who have seen it swear it is Leno's.

There have been a number of peculiar happenings at the theatre which would tend to support those who claim to have seen at least one of the ghosts. Some actors swear they have been pushed or nudged by 'unseen hands' while on stage, and Michael Crawford said a hand assisted him during one difficult scene. Indeed, theatre archivist George Hoare has claimed the unseen hands tugged on his coat as he was leaving his office.

The Drury Lane Theatre may be the most famous of London's haunted theatres, but it's by no means the only one. In fact, five other theatres claim to have ghosts, including the spirit of John Buckstone, whose appearance is also said to guarantee a show's success.

Buckstone, who was actor-manager at

The ghost who haunts the Coliseum is said to be a young soldier of World War I, who appears to take his seat in the dress circle on the anniversary of his death. It's said he spent his last night in London at the theatre, watching the pretty ladies of the show. The next day, he left for the battlefield and was killed.

ROYAL APPARITIONS

From clowns to kings - London has them all. At Kensington Palace, numerous people over the years swear to have seen the face of King George II looking out of the window over the main entrance.

Nearing death, the King was said to stare longingly out of the window at the weathervane, in the hope that the winds would signal a good breeze for the ships bringing him despatches from his beloved Germany - despatches he dearly wanted to read before the end came. But on 25 October 1760 he died - with the winds still unfavourable to shipping.

His sad, ghostly face is said still to peer out occasionally at the vane, hoping for a change in the wind.

Above: *The Bank of England is said to be haunted by the ghost of 'the black nun'.*

Below: *The Tower of London housing the royal jewellery collection, scene of several hauntings.*

the Haymarket Theatre, was a favourite of Queen Victoria. His ghost, which is considered very friendly by those who have seen it, appears in one of the boxes, and his old dressing room door opens and closes by itself. The Haymarket is also haunted by the ghost of Henry Field, who was an actor-manager there during the eighteenth century.

Of course, no discussion of famous London hauntings would be complete without reference to the Tower - which has been home to numerous bizarre events over the centuries.

One of the eeriest reports of strange goings on comes from Edward Swifte, Keeper of the Crown Jewels for almost forty years until his retirement in 1852.

Swifte recalled that one night, in October 1817, he was dining with his family inside the sitting room of the Jewel House when they saw the most bizarre sight: 'A cylindrical figure, like a glass tube' hovering above their table for as long as two minutes. Suddenly, the 'tube' - which Swifte described as having been filled with a dense, blue-and-white liquid - began moving around the table. Mrs Swifte screamed: 'Oh, Christ! It has seized me!' At that, Swifte jumped to his feet and swung at the object with his chair. In the blink of an eye, the mysterious tube vanished.

Incredibly, neither Swifte's son nor sister-in-law had seen a thing!

Field Marshal Lord Grenfell saw the ghost of Anne Boleyn - and was court martialed for being drunk

One of the most astonishing apparitions inside the historic landmark is an actual execution. According to those who have witnessed the frightening spectacle, the execution is that of the Countess of Salisbury, who was beheaded by order of King Henry VIII.

The apparition appears only on the anniversary of her death, and eyewitnesses say she can be clearly seen and heard screaming in terror as she is chased by her ghostly executioner. The ghastly apparition ends with her decapitation.

Not surprisingly, the Bloody Tower is home to most of the Tower of London's ghostly sightings, including those surrounding the two little Princes, King Edward V and his younger brother, Richard, Duke of York. They were murdered on the orders of Richard, Duke of Gloucester, later King Richard III. Their tiny ghosts have been spotted many times, walking hand in hand, on their eternal quest for peace.

The headless body of Anne Boleyn, one of several executed wives of Henry VIII, has been seen in several places throughout the Tower of London.

Field Marshal Lord Grenfell, who was stationed at the Tower as a young lieutenant, swore that he saw Anne's ghost, outside the King's Houses, where she was kept on the evening before her execution. He said her headless body appeared in front of him, and then he fainted. His superiors didn't believe him, claiming he was drunk, but at the subsequent court martial, when other guards told similar tales, he was acquitted.

Below: *Churches too have their fair share of hauntings. This picture which seems to show the ghostly figure of a priest was taken at Eastry, Kent, in 1956.*

SPACE INVADERS
UFOs and Aliens

Is there intelligent life elsewhere in the universe? And if so, are UFOs - Unidentified Flying Objects - a sign of its existence? Sceptics may mock, but the weight of evidence is mounting and governments take the matter very seriously indeed

Left: *Former US President Jimmy Carter is a firm believer in UFOs - he claims to have seen one.*

Opposite: *Four supposed UFOs appear as glowing blobs above a car park and factory in 1950s America.*

Below: *This photograph, allegedly showing five UFOs flying in formation, appeared in a weekly Dublin newspaper for teenagers.*

The first encounters hardly compared with Steven Spielberg's vision. There was no meeting of minds, no mother ship; there were no bug-eyed humanoids - not even a lyrical conversation between computers.

Instead, the first telltale meeting, which came on 24 June 1947, was nothing but a fleeting glimpse on the horizon. Idaho businessman Kenneth Arnold, who was piloting his own small plane, was flying over Washington State when he saw nine 'saucer-like things' which were flying in formation, at speeds he would later estimate at some 1200 miles an hour.

His sensational report, which gave birth to the term 'flying saucer', began the twentieth-century fixation with Unidentified Flying Objects, which in less than fifty years has resulted in thousands of sightings.

Everyone, from policemen via pilots and astronomers to former President Jimmy Carter, claims to have seen the mysterious objects - while others swear they have actually made contact with the 'extraterrestrial' visitors. President Carter, who sighted a UFO on the night of 6 January 1969, while he was still Governor of Georgia, has said: 'I'm convinced that UFOs exist, because I have seen one.'

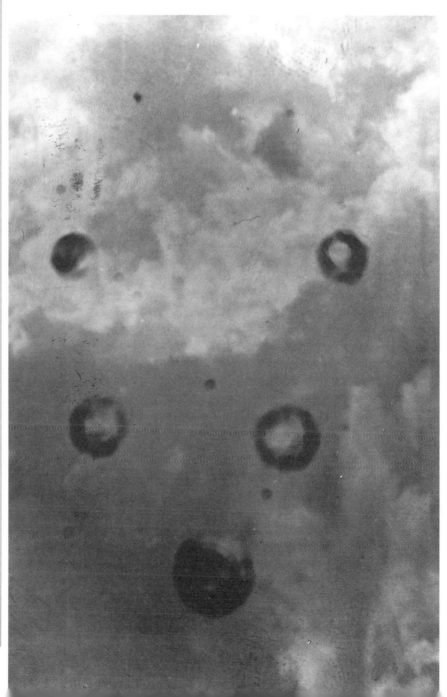

ARE WE ALONE?

But before any serious discussion on the existence or otherwise of UFOs can be undertaken, our first question must be: are we alone?

The answer, of course, has never been conclusively proven...and yet even the most learned of scientists calculate the odds heavily in favour of us not having the universe entirely to ourselves. Planet earth and our entire solar system are part of one average-size galaxy called the Milky Way, which contains 200 billion stars similar to our own sun. Since most of these stars are believed to have satellites or 'planets' of their own, even the most cautious scientist will admit that millions of planets in our galaxy may be capable of supporting some type of life form in some stage of evolution.

Above: *The charred remains of a supposed alien, found in Mexico by Charles Wilhelm and his wife Geri.*

Right: *UFO sightings have been reported throughout the world - and sometimes people have provided photographic 'evidence'. This picture was taken in Denmark.*

So given that intelligent life almost certainly exists elsewhere in the universe, the argument for the existence of UFOs becomes even more plausible.

But that is not to say all such sightings are real. In fact, even firm believers in UFOs admit that some 95 per cent of all 'sightings' are easily explainable in earthly terms - that is, they are the result of natural phenomena or natural objects misidentified. According to scientific studies, the most common sources of UFO misidentifications are meteors, stars and planets, airplanes, weather balloons, clouds, satellites and simple mirages.

The Milky Way, of which our solar system is merely a part, contains 200 billion stars similar to our sun

---

But what of the remaining 5 per cent - which even the most ardent debunker cannot fully explain away? Where do they come from? And why?

No one knows whence they come, but some UFO proponents believe they know why. According to their scenario, the most common theory is that these extraterrestrial beings have been monitoring earth at intervals for hundreds of years. Indeed, advocates note that in 1270 the citizens of Bristol recorded seeing a strange flying craft over the city - and that one of its occupants was 'burned and asphyxiated' by the earth's atmosphere when it got out of the craft!

In 1561 the citizens of Nuremberg in Germany claimed they had seen several circular objects which 'appeared to fall to

the ground as if all was on fire and everything consumed amid a great haze'.

One night in 1716 the astronomer Halley witnessed an object so bright that he was able to read by its light

---

In March 1716 the great English astronomer Edmund Halley recorded seeing an object so intensely bright that it lit up the night sky as if it was day. Halley even noted that the light was so bright he could read a book by its glow.

In the Persian Gulf, on 15 May 1879, sailors aboard the British warship *Vulture* saw two giant, glowing objects in the sky. They described them as wheel-shaped, and claimed they spun slowly until descending almost to sea level. The mysterious objects were clearly visible to all, and seen for more than thirty minutes.

On 17 November 1882, the Greenwich Observatory reported seeing a large green disc hovering in the sky. Astronomers throughout Europe also reported viewing the object.

THE TOP BRASS INVESTIGATE

The US government's involvement in the quest to authenticate or positively refute the existence of UFOs began in 1947, after the Arnold sighting. Senior military men first feared that the objects were secret Russian weapons. They threw a security cordon around their investigations, and passed off reported sightings as either simple misidentifications or the products of over-fertile imaginations.

But behind the closed doors of the Pentagon, the military brass was as baffled as anyone and set up a top-secret unit called Project Sign to look into the phenomena. Five years later, after a record number of sightings, the US Government set up Project Blue Book - another top-secret investigation.

According to the latest disclosures, it now seems apparent that it is still actively investigating mysterious, unexplained UFO encounters, despite years of official denials and ridicule of such sightings.

The government is secretly funding a massive investigation to determine if some UFO sightings are real, and decide once and for all if alien life is visiting the earth. Indeed, it has been reported that a top-secret panel, codenamed the UFO Working Group, is spending millions of dollars in the search, and has checked out dozens of spectacular sightings.

Cold War fears that the unexplained objects might be of Soviet military origin soon had to be laid aside

---

This Working Group is said to be an elite panel of military and civilian experts, which meets regularly in a

Below: *In the 1980s an English company had the idea of producing its own flying saucers which it hoped would eventually be able to carry cargo. This prototype was flown under radio control in a giant hangar in Bedfordshire.*

heavily guarded room deep inside the huge Pentagon complex. Their mission is simple: to determine if there is life out there in space.

One of the most fascinating, unsolved cases in the Group's files concerns a series of strange sightings - which had occurred many years earlier - over the small Wisconsin town of Elmwood.

Two undercover CIA operatives were sent in to test the validity of the sightings, and then threw a veil of secrecy over the probe as the government tried to contain it. 'One of the most impressive witnesses was policeman George Wheeler, a former World War combat flier,' said Howard Blum, a former correspondent for the *New York Times* and author of a book on the government's interest in UFOs. 'In April, 1975, Wheeler was patrolling the streets when he saw a huge ball of flame coming in the night sky. He raced after the object - and saw a craft, shaped like two cereal bowls together as big as a football field, hovering about 1500 feet above the ground. He reported that the strange craft took off at tremendous speed, performed amazing acrobatics and then disappeared in an instant.'

The US government takes the sightings so seriously that it has set up a top-secret working group to investigate them

---

A year later Officer Wheeler had a second encounter, this time observing a bright orange flame on the outskirts of the town. Thinking it was a fire in the distance, he radioed headquarters. Blum says when the officer got to the top of a small hill at the edge of town, he radioed: 'My God! It's one of those UFOs again. It's huge. As big as a two-storey house.'

The author said Wheeler described it as 'silver and 250 feet across, and a bright orange beam was coming from its domed roof'. Police chief Gene Helmer went to investigate the object, while his wife, Gail, manned the radio at headquarters.

'I'll never forget that night,' she said. 'George said he was looking at a UFO and it was obvious he was very excited.' As Wheeler described the craft to her it began to lift from the ground, then fired a

Above: *This apparent UFO, photographed over the mountains of the Polish-Czechoslovak border, has a simple explanation. It is, in fact, a cloud of a kind that does occasionally form over mountainous terrain.*

Right: *This UFO was said to have been photographed over the Clarence River in New Zealand.*

blue ray towards his squad car. 'He was knocked unconscious,' said Blum. 'And when he came to, he was in bad shape. He complained of severe pain in his arms and legs, and had severe headaches. He believed he was the victim of radiation poisoning from the ray. Before physicians could find a cause for his pain, he died suddenly.'

Although the US Government officially denies the existence of any top-secret UFO panel, it openly admits to an interest in searching for extraterrestrial life, which is no longer considered a scientific 'twilight zone'. In fact NASA has made the goal a priority.

As the police chief described the amazing sight over his radio, the craft fired a blue ray towards his squad car

---

The Space Agency's interest in the hunt for other intelligent life forms got a shot in the arm in 1988, when astronomers discovered that planetary systems were not confined to our own sun and nine orbiting planets, and that those distant relatives may also have given birth to life in some form. 'That is the circumstantial evidence that life

Above: *This photograph was taken by the manager of a photographic studio in Bulawayo, Zimbabwe.*

Below: *A somewhat hat-shaped UFO, photographed over a North American town.*

exists elsewhere,' said Michael Klein, a member of the NASA team.

For almost three decades, astronomers from Harvard and Ohio State University have been monitoring parts of the universe, hoping for that elusive radio signal. 'We've picked up quite a few strong signals, but they're never repeated,' said Skip Schwartz, a field station manager for the Harvard team. 'It's as frustrating as coming home to a ringing telephone. By the time you reach the receiver, the other party has hung up.'

EXPERT WITNESSES

Millions of people around the world - from England to Australia to the United States to Russia - firmly believe the 'aliens' are already making limited contact. And there are some disturbing incidences of UFO sightings which even the experts cannot disclaim.

One of the most graphic sightings came on 15 August 1950, in Great Falls, Montana, when a local baseball team manager, Nicholas Mariana, and his secretary saw two brilliantly glowing objects appear over the park in broad daylight. The strange craft moved in unison across the sky.

One up on previous UFO witnesses, Nicholas Mariana had a home movie camera with him and managed to film his encounter

---

However, unlike previous witnesses to such encounters, Mariana had proof - he filmed more than 15 seconds of the spectacular aerial display with a 16mm home movie camera. The film, which is considered by UFO investigators as one

Right: *Another UFO sighting that was captured on film - this picture was taken from a car.*

Below: *Mrs Irmgard Lincoln hit the headlines in 1976 with her claims that Martians were planning to pay the United States a visit. Here she holds up photographs as 'proof' during a news conference.*

of the most impressive pieces of evidence ever gathered, shows two metal-like objects dancing across the sky.

In 1957, on a USAF training flight over the border between Mississippi and Texas, the crew of an RD-47 jet flying at 30,000 feet reported a radar signal moving upwards on their screen. Both the captain and co-pilot then noticed a bright light heading towards them, and their sighting was confirmed by a radio report from the ground.

Twenty minutes later the pilot again saw the bright light, this time it was some 5000 feet below his plane - then, suddenly, the radar blip split in two. Seconds later, it was again one. The entire incident was later confirmed by a third installation, an air defence radar station in Duncanville, Texas.

There was no need for radar confirmation in an incident recorded over Boianai, in Papua New Guinea, in June 1959. Some thirty-eight people saw the two-day aerial display by several UFOs - and their inhabitants! - including an Anglican priest, William Gill, who had the good sense to make notes.

The first instance came on the night of 26 June, when Father Gill noticed a bright white light in the sky which appeared to be coming towards him. As it drew closer, he recalled it resembling a saucer-shaped disc, and being accompanied by several smaller objects. The 'mother-ship' was so bright that it lit up the night-time clouds.

The following night, a startled Gill and other witnesses were again privy to the encounter. 'We stood in the open to watch,' he wrote.

Although the sun had set, it was quite light for the following fifteen minutes. We watched figures appear on top - four of them - there was no doubt they were human. Two smaller UFOs were seen at the same time, stationary, one over the hills, west, and one overhead. Two of the figures seemed to be doing something in the centre of the disk - they were occasionally bending over and raising their arms as though adjusting or setting something. One figure seemed to be standing, looking down on us.

Could an Anglican priest have made up such a story? If so, why? And how could almost forty people witness the same strange incident?

And how could a highly trained Army helicopter pilot put his craft into a steep descent - only to find it climbing at more than 1000 feet a minute? That happened to Captain Larry Coyne on 18 October

1973, over Mansfield, Ohio, when he and three other crew members reported a near-collision with a UFO. It was shortly before 11pm when Coyne noticed a bright red light coming from the east, growing ever closer on what seemed to be a collision course.

When a highly trained Army helicopter crew reports being 'taken over' by a UFO, even the sceptics have to listen

The helicopter pilot estimated the UFO's speed at more than 600 knots and, with little time to spare, threw his craft into a steep dive to avoid a mid-air catastrophe. He looked up, and described the UFO as 'approximately 50 to 60 feet long, about as big as our aircraft. The leading edge of the craft was a bright red light. The trailing edge had a green light, and you could delineate where the light stopped and the gray metallic structure began. You could see because there were reflections of the red and green off the structure itself.'

Shortly afterwards, as the UFO broke off its 'surveillance' and disappeared into the night sky, Captain Coyne was startled to discover his helicopter was ascending, instead of descending. 'We were supposed to be going down,' he said. 'But we were going up!' Somehow, the alien craft had drawn the chopper upwards. Given the training and experience of the Army crew, the case caused a firestorm of controversy, but none of the four aviators ever changed their stories.

One of the most telling 'encounters' occurred in the early hours of 31 December 1978, over the South Island of New Zealand. An Australian television crew, retracing the flight path of several earlier planes whose crews had reported seeing strange, bright objects, actually filmed one of the mysterious lights.

The object, which also appeared on the plane's radar, was filmed on 16mm colour film, and could be clearly seen zipping through the night sky at speeds in excess of 3000 miles an hour.

The film caused a sensation, and was brought to the USA where scores of experts scrutinized it for signs of fakery or explainable phenomena. The team

Above: UFO researchers Michael Lickman and Bill Knell claimed that aliens landed in the Queen's district of New York City in 1989.

Below: Vasya Surin from Voronezh in the former Soviet Union claimed that he had seen a UFO hovering over his home town in October 1989.

unanimously agreed that it could not have been faked, or explained away in earthly terms.

EVEN CLOSER ENCOUNTERS

But visual sightings and radar confirmations of UFOs - no matter how incontrovertible - pale into insignificance when compared to stories of physical contact with extraterrestrials...stories often retold in stunning detail under hypnosis.

Certainly the most sensational account of such an encounter comes from a Brazilian farmer, Antonio Boas, who claims he might have fathered an extraterrestrial child. Boas, who was twenty-three at the time, told his incredible tale to Dr Olavo Fontes, who was treating him for what seemed to be radiation poisoning - a rare disorder for a farmer in the jungles of South America.

According to the deposition Dr Fontes recorded, the very close encounter occurred shortly after midnight on 15 October 1957. Boas was up late, ploughing a field on his tractor, when a

Above: *Frenchman Frank Fontaine went missing for several days in 1979. Later he claimed that he had been abducted by aliens in a UFO.*

'luminous, egg-shaped object' some twelve yards long and eight yards wide hovered over him briefly before landing in the paddock. The tractor engine and lights failed as the craft came to rest on three metal 'legs'. Suddenly four aliens, clad in helmets, descended from the object and dragged the stunned farmer up a ladder into the ship.

Brazilian farmer Antonio Boas claimed he was abducted by aliens and subsequently fathered an extraterrestrial child

---

Inside there were five aliens, whom Boas described as humanoid, and who spoke in 'a series of barks, slightly resembling the sounds made by a dog'. They were small, about five feet tall, and clad in 'very tight-fitting overalls'. He claims he was stripped naked, and blood

taken from his chin (Dr Fontes did indeed find two small scars on the farmer's chin during his examination).

Shortly afterwards, Boas recounted, a beautiful naked woman came into the room...and they made love. 'Shortly after we had separated,' he claimed, 'the door opened. One of the men appeared, and called the woman. Then she went out. But before going out she turned to me, pointed at her belly, and then pointed towards me and with a smile (or something like it), she finally pointed towards the sky.'

The best-known, and probably the most extensively documented, case of 'alien abduction' occurred thirty years ago, in Whitfield, New Hampshire. Barney and Betty Hill were on their way home to Portsmouth, New Hampshire, after a holiday in Canada. As they were driving south along US Route 3 late at night they saw a bright light moving erratically in the sky. Perplexed, they none the less drove on, although the light seemed to be following them. As they reached the White Mountains, the object, which had grown much larger, began to close in on them.

Barney stopped the car, and got out to observe the strange craft through a pair of binoculars. Incredibly, he saw up to eleven figures moving behind the rowed windows of the object. 'I don't believe it! I don't believe!' he repeated to his incredulous wife. He recalled the beings as humanoid, dressed in shiny black uniforms and visored caps.

By now, the UFO was less than twenty-five yards away, and Barney dashed back into the car, screaming: 'They are going to capture us!' He started the engine, and accelerated as fast as the vehicle would go...but suddenly the car began to shake, and the Hills lapsed into drowsiness. Two hours later, and some thirty-five miles away from where Barney had stopped the car, they regained total consciousness. They drove home, thoroughly bewildered by the experience and the 'missing' two hours.

For the next two years, they were plagued by nervous disorders and terrifyingly real dreams of being aboard an alien spaceship. Finally, unable to cope any longer with their anxiety, they visited Dr Benjamin Simon, a Boston psychiatrist who specialized in treating disorders through hypnotherapy.

For six months, beginning in January 1964, they were under the supervision of Dr Simon, and gradually their bizarre story came to light.

Both told identical tales of that night. Their car was stopped, and they were dragged out by a group of humanoids, less than five feet tall, with triangular heads and grey skin. Their eyes were large, slanted, and their mouths were nothing but tiny slits. Somehow, their language was translated into English in

Below: *The dramatic scenery of Hawaii forms a fitting setting for this alleged UFO sighting.*

the Hills' minds. They took their two 'guinea pigs' aboard the craft, where they were given a thorough physical examination, then released.

After sighting a UFO and its occupants they lost consciousness and woke up two hours later, thirty-five miles away

However, Betty recalled something else - something which continues to amaze and baffle UFO experts. When she asked the 'leader' of the aliens where they were from, he pointed to a 'star map', which she later redrew under hypnosis. It wasn't until several years later, based on new astronomical data that was not available in 1961, that it was learned Betty had drawn an amazingly close map of a newly-discovered cluster of stars called Zeta Reticuli.

SOVIET SIGHTINGS

While most of the more sensational accounts of UFO sightings and close encounters have been reported in the West, the advent of Glasnost in the former Soviet Union opened up a whole new world for UFO researchers.

Indeed, in 1989, the news agency, TASS reported that three aliens had visited a park in the city of Voronezh. Several residents told TASS that the visitors stood about 10 feet tall with 'very small heads'. A later report in the newspaper *Sovetskaya Kultura* added more details: One alien had 'three eyes, was clad in silvery overalls and boots the colour of bronze'. The creatures, TASS said, 'made a short promenade' around the park - accompanied by a small robot - before retreating to their spaceship.

These are a few among the growing numbers of people who claim to have seen UFOs or to have been abducted by their inhabitants. Does this mean that visitors from space are real? Or does it signal some form of mass hysteria? No one really knows. The answers may come in a generation, or tomorrow. Somewhere, up in that dark sky, there may be those who do know. But for now, mankind can only wait...and wonder.

CAMELOT
Arthur's Lost Court

The romantic tales of King Arthur and his Knights of the Round Table are familiar to most of us. Is it all the product of a storyteller's fertile imagination - or is there some truth behind the ancient legends?

...'Tirra lirra', by the river
Sang Sir Lancelot.
She left the web, she left the loom,
She made three paces thro' the room,
She saw the water-lily bloom,
She saw the helmet and the plume,
She looked down to Camelot.

The mystery and romance of Camelot, as captured in the epic poem by Alfred, Lord Tennyson, 'The Lady of Shalott', shows that in the nineteenth century, as in this one, the enduring mystery of King Arthur and his Knights of the Round Table had lost none of its

appeal. The legends of virtue, decency and manliness, are clung to by school-children and romantics, convinced that somewhere in the violent, disease-ridden and dangerous past that was pre-medieval England there existed a kingdom that flourished under the wise King and his righteous followers.

But is it all mere hocus-pocus, of the kind that might have been conjured up by the court wizard Merlin?

Was there an Excalibur, a Round Table, a Lady Guinevere and a Sir Lancelot? Or are these tales of fancy born in an age of despair to brighten up otherwise dismal lives?

THE LEGEND IN LITERATURE

King Arthur and his court are referred to by scholars as the Arthurian Legend, and the first reference to the King seems to be in the epic Welsh poem *Gododdin*, which appeared around AD 600. In the poem, some tales are told of a 'mighty warrior'. Other early works show this mighty warrior as a Celtish chieftain who fought bravely against Saxon invaders of Britain.

In 1135, in *Historia*, Geoffrey of Monmouth mentioned King Arthur as the conqueror of western Europe, and afterwards Wace wrote another historical work called the *Roman De Bru*, which

imbued Arthur with the aura of chivalry and romance that has surrounded him ever since.

Then, in the next century, the French poet Chrestien de Troyes wrote five romances dealing with the knights of Arthur's court. His *Perceval* contains the earliest literary version of the most famous Arthurian odyssey, the quest for the Holy Grail, the chalice from which Christ is supposed to have drunk at the Last Supper.

The story of Perceval is the quest for the Holy Grail - the chalice from which Christ is said to have drunk at the Last Supper

---

Two medieval German poets were subsequently important for perpetuating the Arthur legend - Wolfram von Eschenbach and Gottfried von Strassburg, the latter writing the story of Tristan and Isolde. Sir Tristram was an Arthurian knight sent to Ireland to bring back Isolde the Fair to Cornwall to be the bride of his uncle, King Mark. The Cornish element in the story is important in later beliefs that the seat of King Arthur - Camelot - was in fact in the West Country.

After 1225 the legend seemed to grow thin with the Europeans, but it continued to thrive in Britain. *Sir Gawain and the Green Knight*, which appeared around

Top: The Arthurian Legend was a favourite theme for Victorian artists - this painting depicts Sir Tristram being admitted into the fellowship of the Round Table.

Above: A 14th-century reconstruction of the Round Table from the Great Hall of Winchester Castle. It was painted for a visit by the Emperor Charles V in 1522.

1370, is one of the best of all Middle English romances and fully embodies the romantic ideal of chivalry and honour.

That was followed by the last really important medieval work on the subject, *Morte d'Arthur*, by Sir Thomas Malory, whose tales became the source of many of the later Arthur tales.

No important works were written after this for several centuries until Tennyson's *Idylls of the King*. Later again, the German composer Richard Wagner used the Arthurian legends as the inspiration for many of his great operas.

THE CELTIC MYTH

So, knowing that Arthur was written up as fable by a succession of writers, can there possibly be some foundation in fact? Most definitely yes, say those Arthurian Legend scholars who believe that only truth could have been the basis for such closely interwoven tales.

It is a truth founded not in English, but in Celtic, history. Research has shown that Arthurian legends were spread all over Europe by the twelfth century, broadcast by Breton minstrels from the north west French coast, whose dialect was - and is - remarkably similar to the now extinct Cornish language.

But before examining its roots, here is

what the Legend of King Arthur is all about. Arthur was the illegitimate son of Uther Pendragon, King of Britain, and his lover Igraine.

After Uther's death Arthur - who had been brought up in secrecy and was not known to his people - ascended the throne by declaring himself the rightful heir and withdrawing a mighty sword, Excalibur, from a block of stone. This was a feat that no pretender had been able to accomplish before him.

Merlin, the court wizard, then declared his parentage, bowed down before him and pronounced him King. Arthur reigned at Camelot and proved himself to be just, honest and decent, and evolved the egalitarian concept of a Round Table for his knights.

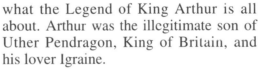

Arthur slew his arch-enemy Mordred, but, mortally wounded, was borne away to the magical Isle of Avalon

---

Arthur had several enemies including Morgan le Fay, his treacherous sister, and his nephew Mordred. Morgan was a sorceress and a schemer who plotted against Arthur for the throne. Mordred seized Arthur's throne while the King was away in battle.

In terrible combat King Arthur slew Mordred, but not before he was mortally

Left: *Sir Galahad, son of Sir Lancelot, and one of Arthur's most loyal followers.*

Above left: *Sir Gawain, Arthur's nephew, was the hero of one of the finest of medieval English romances -* **Sir Gawain and the Green Knight.**

Above: *The theme of chivalry has been a constant source of inspiration. This painting of a knight errant, by Sir John Gilbert, hangs in London's Guildhall.*

Above: *The magician Merlin with the wily temptress Vivien in a 19th-century engraving by the Frenchman Gustav Dorè.*

Above right: *Illicit lovers Sir Lancelot and the Lady Guinevere - a line engraving after a miniature in an 11th-century manuscript at the Bibliothèque Nationale in Paris.*

wounded himself. His body was borne away to the Isle of Avalon where it was said that his wounds would heal and from where his subjects believed he would have a second coming.

His two most devoted knights were Sir Tristram and Sir Lancelot of the Lake - who besmirched his chivalrous reputation by carrying on an affair with the Lady Guinevere, Queen of England and wife of Arthur.

Other knights included Sir Pelleas; Sir Gawain, Arthur's nephew; Sir Balin and Sir Balan; Sir Galahad, Lancelot's son; Sir Kay, Arthur's villainous foster-brother; Sir Percival, Sir Gareth, Sir Geraint and Sir Bedevere.

There are no historical records of such people, nor of a court of Camelot, nor of a king who ruled England with bene-volence and chivalry. But back in the mists of time, among the fierce tribes of Wales, it is believed that the legend was born out of reality.

THE HISTORICAL REALITY

Eminent Arthurian scholar Alfred Nutt, in *Studies on the Legend of the Holy Grail,* and Professor Sir John Rhys, in his *Studies in the Arthurian Legend,* theorize that the King was born in Celtic folklore based on tribal leaders. The earliest Celts, who arrived in Britain in about 500 BC, were called Goidels and came from Gaul. It is from these hardy, warlike people that the Arthurian Legend stems.

In AD 410 Rome gave notice that internal problems in Italy made it impossible for her troops to govern any longer and so, after 360 years of occupation, they were withdrawn. With the Romans gone the land became a battlefield, invaded by Saxon raiders, Jutes and Angles, while Picts and Scots teemed over the deserted Hadrian's Wall.

It was in this time of turmoil that, in 443, an appeal was made to Rome for assistance. It fell on deaf ears. The bold Scots and Picts forayed as far south as Kent where they drove the Kentish chief, a Celt called Vortigern, to desperation. Too tired for war, he fled westwards to Wales and built himself a citadel.

Determined to make it impregnable, Vortigern consulted his magicians and soothsayers. They advised him to sacrifice an orphan child and bury it in the foundations of his fortress. The boy he chose, Ambrosius, son of a Roman couple of consular rank, saved himself by displaying a gift for prophecy.

This is fact - but the legend goes on to say that the boy was Myrddin, Welsh for Merlin. Others believe that the citadel may have been the Camelot of legend.

Nennius, a ninth-century historian, wrote that a descendant of Vortigern fell at the Battle of Mount Badon fighting the Saxons. Historians have searched ever since for Mount Badon, and suggestions

*Below: **King Arthur bids farewell to his beloved Guinevere in a convent. She conducted an affair with Sir Lancelot behind Arthur's back.***

as to its whereabouts include Bath, Badbury near Swindon and Badbury Hill near Farringdon. Some theorize that this descendant may have been King Arthur.

In the twelfth century, as King Arthur fever gripped the imagination of a wretched peasantry, the remains of a Celtic man and a woman were found within the walls of Glastonbury Abbey. This, said the monks at the time, was the Avalon of legend, and they had found King Arthur and his wife Guinevere, who had been buried there at a later date.

There were many links between the Arthurian legends and the details of Celtic history

---

The Celtic connection has parallels with many of the details in the Arthur stories. The Round Table, for instance, was typical in Celtic communities where the tribal elders sat in a circle with the chieftain in his 'scat perilous' - he had to be challenged in combat for his seat to be taken by another. The Holy Grail may have been based upon the simple drinking vessels used by the Celts.

The battle at which Arthur died, called the Battle of Camlann, may have been fought near Cadbury in Somerset, and countless excavations and man hours have gone into examining the area - without much luck. Finally, the Celtic religion played an important part in Celtic life, and certainly the Arthur of legend was a devoted Christian and 'defender of the faith'.

So fact or fiction, myth or memory? American Arthurian scholar James Dunsford suggests:

The King Arthur we know in Hollywood mythology and English folklore was very different from the real King Arthur, who represented strong ideals in a bad world. But I am convinced that there is indeed something in these stories and that Camelot did exist, as did the knights, or warriors who served him. But it was an age when nothing was recorded, nothing preserved. I venture that one day we may have more concrete evidence than this, but until then King Arthur will be more widely remembered as a story than as a reality.

CORN CIRCLES
Mysteries of the Fields

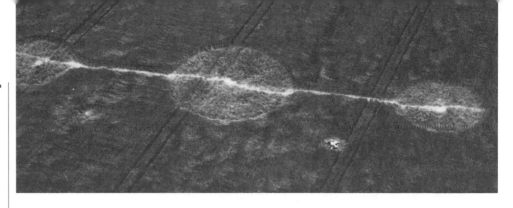

The great corn circle debate began centuries ago. Now it has gripped the imagination of the public and the press. Are these strange phenomena created by freak weather conditions, aliens from outer space - or hoaxers?

Practical jokers, whirlwinds, hedgehogs, mating foxes or Unidentified Flying Objects...everyone has a theory about the unexplained phenomenon of corn circles. It is a mystery that caused a stir throughout the eighties but which burst afresh into the public eye with a rash of sightings at the start of the nineties. The mainly elliptical circles varied from 10ft to 200ft and more in diameter. More than a thousand circles, some surrounded by up to four outer rings, were recorded in a handful of English counties between 1980 and 1990. Although flattened, the crop was not damaged and the curves had an unnerving neatness to them.

In the late seventeenth century fairies and the devil were still under serious consideration as causes

---

Scientists, meteorologists and farmers came up with an astonishing array of explanations for the seemingly instant appearances of these circles and other patterns in fields of crops. A £10,000 reward was even offered by a British national newspaper. But the mystery went unsolved.

While all this was going on, what no one seemed to appreciate was that the crop circle phenomenon was not entirely 'news'. In fact, the riddle taxed great minds three hundred years ago and more.

In 1686 Robert Plot, Professor of Chemistry at Oxford University, wrote a book called *The Natural History of Staffordshire*. In it he searched for some 'higher principle' to explain crop circles rather than the current theories such as rutting deer, urinating cattle and fairies.

Professor Plot did not entirely debunk such myths, saying that 'the Fairies so much tak't about' might indeed be to blame. He wrote: 'They may indeed

Above: *A couple caught 'making hay' in a corn circle. Not the answer to the mystery!*

Opposite: *Corn circles began to be reported in great numbers in 1980.*

Below: *Although flattened, crops are rarely damaged.*

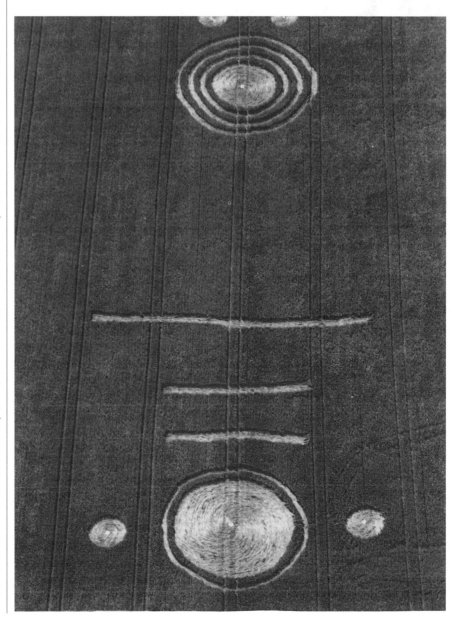

occasion such circles', but added that the repetitive plodding of animals was a far more believable cause.

However, after intense deliberation, Professor Plot concluded: 'They must needs be the effects of lightning, exploded from the clouds most times in a circular manner.'

The pent-up energy would be emitted from the cloud 'so as at due distance to become a circle and in that forme to strike the Earth'.

And what about the crop marks that were not circular? That was due to the fact that sometimes lightning got forced out of clouds in a rectangular shape!

Below: *A pamphlet published in 1678 blamed Satan for crop circles.*

Bottom: *In the 1980s, the theory that UFOs were behind crop circles was the most widely discussed.*

CONFLICTING MODERN THEORIES

Why then did the whole crop circle debate go dormant for almost three centuries afterwards? Fewer explanations are offered here than for the corn circles themselves. But it was certainly true that, until the eighties, the crop circle argument had been less than lively. Then, when more and more people began reporting sightings, a whole array of suggestions were put forward to capture the imagination of the public.

For three hundred years the debate lay dormant, ignored by scientists and public alike

---

In place of fairies and devils, UFOs became the most popular explanation. Mating animals was also a suggestion. So was the theory that hedgehogs had been driven to circular motion by dementia. Another theory voiced was that aliens had decided to communicate through the Sumerian sign language of tribesmen who lived around the borders of Iraq some five thousand years ago.

Perhaps not so strange was that the theories most favoured by scientists were those linked to weather conditions.

Consultant meteorologist Dr Terence Meaden, head of the Tornado and Storm

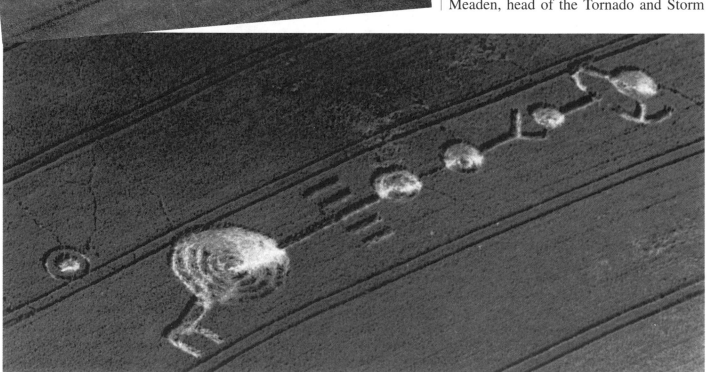

us even more than the others because the flattened crops grew back in a dartboard formation. There were seven concentric rings of crops, with a series of perfect spokes going out from the centre.'

After a later discovery of a vast formation of crop circles and other patterns, a worried Colin Andrews said that the molecular structure of some of the plants had been changed. He said: 'We have written to the Ministry of Agriculture asking them to take the affected crops out of circulation. It is possible that molecular contamination has taken place.'

On another major investigation, Mr Andrews and his partner Pat Delgado borrowed equipment from the Army to keep lengthy surveillance on fields likely to be affected. They reported that the circles were being caused by 'some form of higher intelligence'.

Some scientists believe the phenomenon may be caused by the recent hole in the earth's ozone layer

---

Andrews said: 'They are caused by some sort of high energy but we don't know what. The shapes are becoming more and more complex and I believe that what we are heading for is circles in the form of snowflakes or flowers. The shapes we have seen recently are just the start of what is to come.'

Research Organization believed that other weather conditions - and wind energy in particular - were a factor.

He announced to a conference at Oxford Polytechnic in 1988 that the mystery had been solved. He told his audience that the circles were formed by sudden whirlwinds. Most of the circles were formed near hillsides, the explanation being that wind gusts on only one side of a hill, creating vortexes of gyrating air which move suddenly downwards to create the circles.

*Above: **Meteorologist Dr Terence Meaden claimed in 1988 that whirlwinds caused such precise patterns as this.***

Have demented hedgehogs run in circles, or is something from 'out there' communicating in an archaic Middle Eastern sign language?

Another leading investigator, Colin Andrews, disagrees with the whirlwind theory. In 1983 he and his team of eleven scientific colleagues set out to research phenomena in central southern England.

Reporting their findings in 1989, he and his team ruled out hoaxers, aliens, helicopters and whirlwinds. They said they believed that unprecedented atmospheric conditions caused by the newly discovered hole in the earth's ozone layer were to blame for the farmland phenomena.

Andrews, an electrical expert with the local authority in the Test Valley in Hampshire, said: 'We now believe that the shifts in the earth's electromagnetic conditions caused by the ozone hole may be responsible. One of the circles that appeared recently in Hampshire amazed

*Below: **In 1989 a team of investigators cited atmospheric complications caused by the depleted ozone layer as the cause of crop circles.***

had found themselves with first-hand knowledge of how the circles are created.

Gary and Vivienne Tomlinson, of Guildford in Surrey, were strolling along a footpath at the edge of a Hampshire cornfield when the crop started moving...the couple were being caught in the eye of a brand-new corn circle.

Vivienne Tomlinson recalled:

There was a tremendous noise. We looked up to see if it was caused by a helicopter but there was nothing. We felt a strong wind pushing us from the side and above. It was forcing down on our heads - yet incredibly my husband's hair was standing on end. Then the whirling air seemed to branch into two and zig-zag off into the distance. We could still see it like a light mist or fog, shimmering as it moved. As it disappeared we were left standing in a corn circle with the corn flattened all around us. Everything became very still again and we were left with a tingly feeling.

Husband Gary added: 'We didn't speak for ages, and we told no one about the incident until three days later.'

It was three days before the Tomlinsons could bring themselves to tell anyone what had happened

---

When the Tomlinsons did eventually speak of their experience, Dr Terence Meaden immediately took them back to the site, near Hambledon. He reported: 'There is a perfectly logical explanation for this. It is that when a strong gust of wind blows over a hill, it rushes into the still air on the other side and causes a spiralling column.'

The crop circle debate has tended to centre on southern England. But similar markings have been reported from North America, Australia and Japan. Japanese scientists who visited Britain to investigate the phenomenon have taken the ozone layer theory seriously. But they have come up with other explanations.

Professor Yoshihiko Ohtsuki, from Tokyo's Waseda University, said in 1991: 'The circles are caused by an elastic plasma, which is a very strong form of ionized air. In an experiment...we created a plasma fireball which, if it touched a plate covered in aluminium powder, created beautiful circles and rings, just like the ones seen in fields.'

AN UNNERVING EXPERIENCE

On a sunny August day that same year a couple out for a walk found themselves in the middle of a crop circle in the making. It was the first time that anyone

Above: *Some people have put forward the theory that crop circles are signs left by aliens using an ancient Middle Eastern language.*

Below: *A crop circle in Wiltshire, one of the two English counties most affected by the phenomenon.*

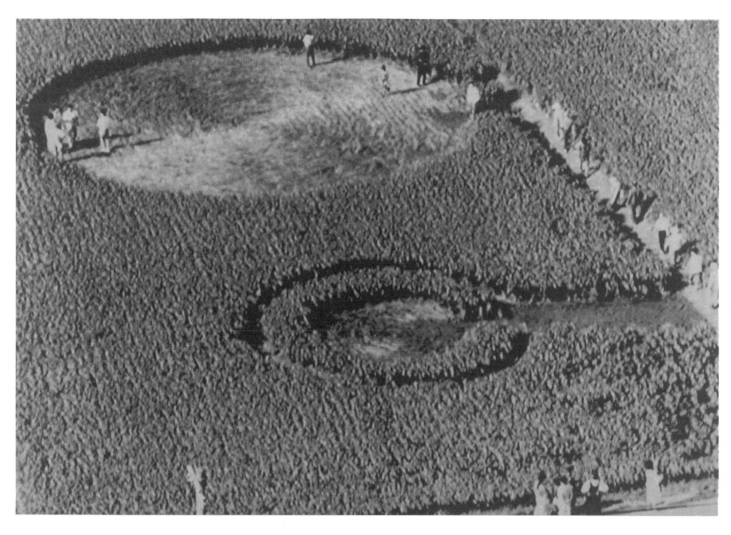

HOAX OR GENUINE?

The summer of 1991 was a vintage period for corn circles. Circles even appeared on farmland at the Prime Minister's country retreat, Chequers. The local who found them said: 'If they were made by humans it is extraordinary that the perpetrators were not caught by security men guarding the Prime Minister.'

If the circles at Chequers were made by humans, it seems odd that security guards noticed nothing

---

The most extraordinary sighting, however, was one reported by Eddie Wise, of Bristol, who spent four nights in a Wiltshire field trying to solve the mystery...and claims he saw an alien spacecraft land. He said: 'It was enormous. There were no lights but I could see what appeared to be windows. A long object was lowered from the base of the craft and when it touched down in the field everything became quite still.'

Some British farmers were upset by the rash of corn circles. Each one, on average, costs them £60 in damaged crops, they say. Others cashed in on the boom, however. Suddenly signs sprang up outside farm gates, offering parking facilities for passers-by who wished to visit sites.

Are the crop patterns created in recent years no more than elaborate middle-of-the-night hoaxes? It has always been obvious that many of them were hoaxes - the work of elaborate practical jokers.

Indeed in 1991, two British artists, Dave Chorley and Doug Bower, claimed to have created all the major corn circles found over the previous thirteen years. They claimed to have fooled Japanese scientists, farming organizations and government departments. Using poles, boards and ropes, they recreated a corn circle in a field in Kent. It fooled the experts...but failed to silence the debate.

Above: *Even ancient man was mystified by crop circles, believing they were a sign from the heavens. We are not much wiser today.*

YETIS
Tracks in the Snow

Hairy beasts, half-ape, half-man, have long been reported from Siberia, the Himalayas and western North America. What lies behind the legends of the Chinese Wildman, the Abominable Snowman and Bigfoot?

The International Society of Cryptozoology in Tucson, Arizona, has only about three hundred members - but is the subject of a great deal of cynical comment. The reason is the strange work of the organization.

'Cryptozoology researches sightings of strange creatures,' says the society's secretary, anthropologist Richard Greenwell. 'It also studies a culture's literature and folklore of reports of strange creatures that may not be known to scientists.'

In short, Mr Greenwell and his fellows believe in monsters. And to admit that Bigfoot or the Wildman of China actually exists is to leave oneself open for a bit of mickey-taking.

If the pygmy elephant is a recent zoological discovery, why shouldn't the Abominable Snowman turn out to be genuine too?

It is only when recently collated evidence is studied that many laymen too begin to believe in the unbelievable. A number of new species of beast have already been discovered, say the cryptozoologists. Among them are the pigmy elephant of central Africa, which is one third the size of a normal elephant, and the onza, a fierce variety of mountain lion which had been legendary for years among Mexican peasants.

The pigmy hippopotamus, the white rhinoceros, the giant panda and the komodo dragon are other examples of

Above: A recent reconstruction of the hairy creature of the Far East - variously called a Yeti, Wildman of China, Meti, Yeren and Abominable Snowman.

Opposite: The blurred outline of one of the Yeti's cousins, the Sasquatch or Bigfoot, running through the forests of Oregon, North America.

Left: The indefatigable traveller and explorer Sir Francis Galton, whose interests included the study of strange and unusual species.

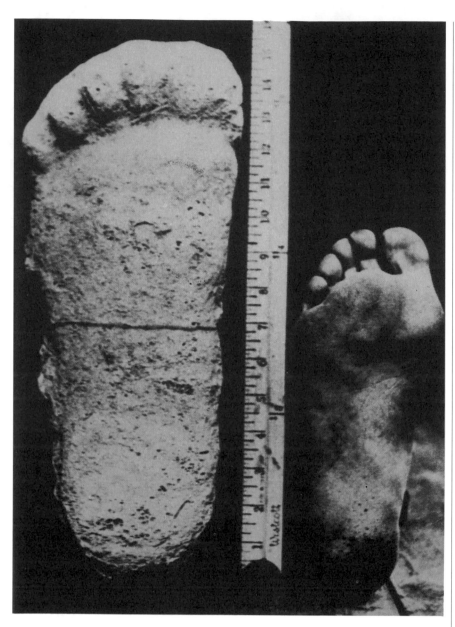

Above: *Plaster cast of a Bigfoot's tracks found in North America, compared with the size of a human foot.*

discoveries of hitherto unknown wildlife. 'These bizarre animals were proved not to be the stuff of imagination,' says Richard Greenwell. 'So why should there not be even more mysterious creatures out there?'

Among these, three wild creatures have gripped the imaginations of ordinary people more than any others. The reason could be that reports describe them as half-man, half-beast.

These creatures are known variously as Bigfoot, Sasquatch, Shookpa, Alma, Meti, Yeti, Abominable Snowman, Kang-mi, Migo, Yeren and the Wildman of China. Few scientists took reported sightings of these animals too seriously until recent evidence arose from an unexpected source...

THE WILDMAN OF CHINA

Sightings of a creature the Chinese call the Yeren have been made by peasants over the centuries. A man-like primate with human features, the Yeren (or Wildman of China) stands 6ft tall and may possess toolmaking and basket-weaving ability. Hundreds of sightings by farming folk in central China were largely ignored by scientists. But recent hair samples may prove that the creature really does exist.

Until the late eighties, Western scientists had not been allowed access to the desolate forest area where a wealth of evidence about the monster had been collected by Chinese researchers. Then six countries, including Britain and the United States, invested £250,000 to send a team to the region to look at the evidence and bring back hair samples for high-technology analysis.

Gene Poirier, professor of anthropology at Ohio State University, was one of those who, like Richard Greenwell, was persuaded to travel to central China to collect data on the existence of a forest version of the Himalayan Yeti. What they uncovered was the most exciting find of their lives.

Poirier himself was a reluctant hunter. As a renowned scientist, he had always dismissed reports of such a beast. But his teaming up with Englishman Greenwell led to a fascinating two-year quest. And an independent London television film-maker, Geraldine Easter, was there with her camera team to record the evidence.

Sophisticated analysis of a few hairs proved the existence of a hitherto unknown higher primate

---

Evidence of the creature's existence consisted mainly of hair samples collected by farmers who had seen the monster on their land. Shanghai's Fudan University first discovered that the samples were from neither a man nor an ape. Yet they were certainly animal hairs.

The hairs were then sent to Ohio State University and to England's Birmingham University, where work was carried out by the Department of Space Research and Physics under Dr Rangeet Sokhi. The results of the tests were announced in November 1990. The scientists' conclusion was dramatic. The samples were from a creature which was neither man nor ape...which proved that the Wildman of China actually existed.

As further tests began to analyse the structure of the hair's chromosomes, the basic structures of life, Professor Poirier said: 'We have established that the animal does not fall into any known category. This is the first evidence of the existence of a new higher primate.'

The latest breakthrough from central China suggests that a creature called Gigantopithecus, which existed half a million years ago - long before man - has managed to survive in extremely remote areas. Jawbones and more than a thousand teeth of this early 'ape man' have been found across China, and Vietnam and India.

Geraldine Easter says: 'The Chinese Wildman is either a beast we know nothing of or he is Gigantopithecus, which has somehow managed to beat extinction in these areas alone. He was a contemporary of the panda bear - and pandas have survived.'

EYE-WITNESS ACCOUNTS

In 1981 the China Wildman Investigation and Research Society was established in Hubei province. Among the eye-witness reports collected by the society are these:

On the morning of 19 June 1976 Gong Yulan, a woman farmer from Qunli village in Fangxian county's Qiaoshang township, went into the mountains with her four-year-old child to cut grass for her pigs. As she climbed a strip of land between the hills she suddenly noticed a reddish-brown creature was scratching its back against a tree only six or seven metres away. When the creature saw Gong Yulan and her child it rushed towards them. Gong fled down the mountain and later described the creature to the investigation group. She said it was taller than an adult human at 1.8 metres. The hair on its head was comparatively long and both its hands and feet were hairy. It walked erect like a human and it took long strides. It was a

male and its appearance terrified her. When she was shown a photograph of an erect orang-utan, Gong said: 'It looked just like this.' When she was shown photos of a bear, she shook her head.

A Chinese peasant woman, shown a photo of an orang-utan, said the creature that had scared her looked just like it

---

Zhu Guoqiang, a stockman from Huilong township in Fangxian county, gave this evidence:

On 16 June 1974 I was herding four oxen over a ridge at Longdonggou when I suddenly came face to face with a creature resembling a human but covered with brown hair. I aimed my gun at it but it grabbed the barrel. I pulled and pushed but I couldn't make it let go, so I fired anyway but missed. It opened its mouth wide, making a frightening face and showing its yellow teeth, which were similar to a human's but a bit wider. My legs turned to jelly. Three of the oxen had moved away but a large black bull, which had previously gored people, snorted and rushed at the creature as it stood still

Below: *Rant Mullens from Washington State with wooden replicas of a Wildman's feet. He had carved them from wood.*

clutching the end of my rifle. The beast dropped the gun and ran away.

In the Qinling Mountains in north-west China, in the early 1950s, Fan Jingquan was working as part of a geological prospecting team for the Ministry of Heavy Industry. During his two-year contract he met many locals who had seen Wildmen and who had even fed them. He persuaded one old man to take him to a chestnut grove where the creatures roamed. This is his story:

The young male Wildman showed no fear, and ran up to the old man to take the chestnuts he was carrying

---

As expected, a creature arrived. She was at least 1.6 metres tall and had a young one with her. Maybe because my clothes were different to the old man's she seemed particularly wary of me. But the young boy creature was fearless, running up to the old man for the chestnuts he was carrying. The mother called it back. The sound she made was neither like a horse nor a donkey.

Zhang Yujin, from Hongta township in Fangxian county, once helped kill a Wildman. He says:

I was eighteen years old and an orderly in the local Kuomintang army cadre. In the spring of 1943 I was with a hunting group of fifty or sixty soldiers when we came across a house in the hills. The owner told us that a creature had been crying on the slopes behind the house for half a day. The county magistrate, who was leading our hunt, ordered myself and another thirty soldiers to take three machine guns and surround the place. But when we arrived we saw not one but two creatures. One was sitting down with its head lowered and crying. The other was walking round the first and touching it every now and then. We watched for half an hour and then opened fire. The one that had been walking fled immediately and the other fell dead. When we examined it we found it was male, as tall as a human and its entire body was covered in dark red hair.

Many tales of the Chinese Wildmen speak of tears rolling down their cheeks

---

Tales of the crying Wildmen have a common theme. Liu Jikuan told investigators how she had seen a captured pair of creatures paraded in 1942.

I was thirteen that year and went to the centre of town to see the strange monsters which had been captured by the Kuomintang army and were tied up with a chain. They were a male and female. Their heads were bigger than a human's and their hair hung down to their shoulders. The female had big breasts and the male had tears rolling down its cheeks. We gave them an ear of corn and they ate it.

This sort of evidence is easy to question. The eye-witnesses tend to be peasants and the antiquity of their stories arouses suspicion of embellishment. But recent provincial expeditions in the Chinese hinterland have been carried out in a thoroughly scientific manner.

Recently the Department of Biology at Huadong University organized several expeditions which collected first-hand evidence of Wildman footprints, caves, hair and 'nests' - strangely woven wooden constructions, sometimes assembled dozens at a time, and assumed to be the homes of the Wildmen.

Below: *Supposed Yeti footprints. A belief in the Yeti is still fairly widespread among Tibetans.*

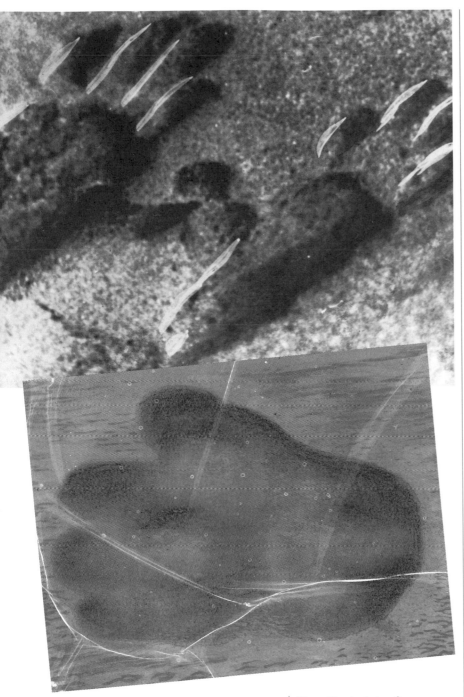

THE ABOMINABLE SNOWMAN

The Wildman of China came to Western attention only in recent years. But across the Himalayas lives a creature whose existence was first reported to the West way back in 1832.

An adventurous Briton, B.H. Hodgson, went to live with the Nepalese high in the mountains and wrote home about a tall, erect, ape-like creature covered in thick hair. In Britain, it was assumed that the imaginative adventurer was mistakenly referring to the Himalayan red bear or

Top: *Footprints of an Abominable Snowman which appeared in western Sikkim. Other marks on the photo were made by the party that discovered them.*

Above: *Simulation of a footprint found in the Himalayas by the explorer Eric Shipton in 1951.*

perhaps the large langur monkey. But in a scientific journal Hodgson described how some Nepalese porters had 'fled in terror' from an erect, tail-less creature with shaggy hair that ambled up to them.

They called it a *rakshas*, the Sanskrit word for 'demon'. They told him that references to Wildmen went back to the fourth century BC.

Half a century went by before another Briton, Major Lawrence Waddell of the Indian Army Medical Corps, reported seeing remarkable footprints which were 'said to be the trail of one of the hairy men who live in the eternal snows'. He discovered the tracks 17,000 ft up in north-east Sikkim.

Reports from remote regions are often dismissed as the exaggerations of superstitious peasants

---

In his book *Among the Himalayas* he wrote: 'The belief in these creatures is universal among Tibetans. None, however, of the Tibetans I have interrogated on the subject could ever give me an authentic case.'

In his conclusion, Waddell insisted that the hairy Wildmen were simply vicious, meat-eating, yellow snow bears that frequently preyed upon yaks.

The next recorded sighting of tracks by a European was in 1914 when J.R.P. Gent, a British forestry officer stationed in Sikkim, wrote of discovering footprints of what must have been a huge and amazing creature.

The sightings sparked worldwide curiosity, and mountaineers headed for the area in strength throughout the 1920s and 30s. They returned home with even more details of the astonishing Yeti. It was at this time that a newspaper reporter coined the phrase 'Abominable Snowman' to describe the beast.

Nepalese villagers, Tibetan lamas and the hardy sherpas had plenty of stories to tell. They told visitors that Yetis had always lived along the snow line that separates the wooded lower slopes from the desolate, icy wastes above.

Reports differed. Some said the animals were anything up to 12 ft high but extremely agile. Others described the

Above: *This 1955 picture shows a Nepalese official holding a large animal's scalp, kept at Thangboche monastery for about a century.*

One villager's report of the time said:

On catching sight of us, he stood up to his full height. He was very tall and lean, over six feet, and dressed in deerskin. He had a mop of unkempt hair and very long arms. His face was as big as a human's but his forehead was small and protruded over his eyes like the peak of a cap. His chin was large and broad, far bigger than a human's. Other than being a little taller, he was very much like a human. The next moment he ran away. He ran very fast, leaping high after every third step, and he was barefoot.

Siberian villagers went on a berry-picking expedition and discovered a strange hairy creature which had had the same idea

---

But how much of this was hearsay? It was very difficult to find hard proof for the existence of an Abominable Snowman. Tibetan lama monasteries were rumoured to have scalps, skins and even mummified bodies of the creatures, but no Westerners had been able to get their hands on any of these bizarre relics to bring them back home for analysis.

Then in 1921 Colonel C.K. Howard-Bury became the first European ever to see a real live Yeti...

The colonel was heading a British expedition attempting to climb the world's highest mountain in the first Everest Reconnaissance Expedition. He and his team were clambering over a ridge some 21,000 feet up when they spotted a strange group of creatures on the Lhapka-La Pass.

The sherpas immediately jumped to the conclusion that this must 'the wild man of the snows' When they reached the spot where the creatures had been, they discovered huge footprints in the snow, 'each of them about three times the size of a human print'.

On his return to Britain, Howard-Bury read up on the ways and customs of the Himalayan 'wild man'. He discovered that naughty Tibetan children were threatened into behaving themselves with warnings about the massive creature.

Said Howard-Bury: 'The children are told that to escape from the creature they

creature as walking with its head held high but with a lolloping gait, its long arms swinging by its sides.

Villagers said the creatures were shy and only approached areas of human habitation when hunger forced them to do so. Their diet was mainly rodents and lichen, and they disembowelled their prey before consuming it - a peculiarly human trait. Furthermore, said the villagers, a Yeti would make a distinctive yelping sound when scared.

This, then, was the Abominable Snowman as described by local inhabitants. But where was proof of his existence?

FROM HEARSAY TO PROOF

In the 1920s a Chuchunna (a name meaning 'outcast' given to the man-beast in the Yakutiya region of eastern Siberia) was seen by villagers. The creature was picking berries, and stuffing them into its mouth with both hands.

have to run very fast down the hill because then his long hair falls over his eyes and he can't see them.' He also learned that the females of the species were hampered by the size of their breasts. One sherpa reported: 'We followed the track of two female Yeti and their breasts were so large they had to throw them over their shoulders before they could bend down.'

Female Yetis, said the sherpas, had to throw their massive breasts over their shoulders before they could bend down

---

In the spring of 1925 a sighting was made by British photographer N.A. Tombazi. He observed one of the elusive creatures 50,000 feet up the Zemu Glacier and, since he was a Fellow of the Royal Geographical Society, his testimony was not be laughed at.

In his book *Bigfoot* - the name later associated with the ape-like creatures of North America - John Napier quotes Tombazi as follows:

Unquestionably the figure in outline was exactly like a human being...It showed up dark against the snow and, as far as I could make out, wore no clothes. Within the next minute or so it had moved into some thick scrub and was lost to view. Such a fleeting glimpse, unfortunately, did not allow me to set the telephoto camera, or even to fix the object carefully with my binoculars. But a couple of hours later, during the descent, I purposely made a detour so as to pass the place where the 'man' or 'beast' had been seen. I examined the footprints which were clearly visible on the surface of the snow.

In 1936 the expedition of Ronald Kaulback confirmed the widespread existence of mysterious footprints. A year later the first photograph allegedly showing a Yeti's footprint was taken by Frank Smythe.

During World War II, five Polish prisoners being held in a Siberian labour camp escaped from their Soviet captors and made an incredible march across Mongolia and Tibet to Bhutan where, in

Below: *Thangboche monastery at the foot of Mount Everest in the Himalayas has been the base for many mountaineering expeditions - and the source of many yeti reports.*

1942, they crossed the Himalayas to India. They recounted a strange episode which had occurred in the mountains.

They said they had looked down from a ledge and spotted two burly ape-men only a few feet below them. The creatures were aware that they were being observed but showed no emotion and, seemingly ignoring the strangers, continued to shuffle through the snow.

Prisoners escaping from a Siberian labour camp watched a pair of Yetis at close range for over two hours

---

This was just another story which intrigued Yeti followers throughout the world. But the only real evidence was still the 1937 photograph. No first-hand evidence about the Abominable Snowman had yet been obtained.

HARD EVIDENCE

On 8 November 1951, however, all that was to change. Mountaineer Eric Shipton was climbing with fellow Briton Michael Ward and Sherpa Sen Tensing in the Gauri Sankar range. They came across a trail of crystal-clear footprints 18,000 ft up on the Men-lung Glacier.

The marks were made by a flat-footed creature with five toes, one much bigger than the rest. The prints measured 13 in long and 8 in across, indicating a creature no less than 8 ft tall.

The photographs and Shipton's impeccable knowledge - he was an expert on footprints - just had to be believed. And the search for the Abominable Snowman attracted new interest.

Then, in 1952, the mighty Everest mountain was finally conquered by New Zealander Edmund Hillary and Sherpa Tensing Norgay. Although Hillary found giant prints too, he remained sceptical about the existence of the Yeti. But he was later to mount an expedition investigating the existence of the creature and how man adapted to life in extremely high altitudes. The expedition ended with Sir Edmund returning clutching a Snowman scalp which he had come across at the Khumjung monastery. Zoologists classified it as a goat antelope.

In 1957 Texas oilman Thomas Slick took up the trail. He and his party found tracks that Nepalese villagers said had been made by Yetis which had killed five people in that area. But no sign of the creatures was spotted on this expedition.

British mountaineer Don Whillans spent a day in 1970 photographing strange footmarks 13,000 ft up in the mountains of Nepal. That night, he said, the light of the moon allowed him to see clearly an ape-like creature bounding on all fours along a nearby ridge.

In 1978, Sir John (now Lord) Hunt, who had led the original Hillary-Tensing assault on Everest, returned to Nepal with Lady Hunt to commemorate the twenty-fifth anniversary of the 1953 ascent. They saw and photographed large tracks in the snow right outside their huts. Lord Hunt also related a story told him by the abbot of Thangboche monastery about his encounter with a Yeti.

When the monks blew on conch shells and horns, the intruding Yeti ambled quietly away

---

This beast, loping along sometimes on his hind legs and sometimes on all fours, stood about five feet high and was covered with grey hair. The Yeti stopped to scratch, picked up some snow, played with it and made a few grunts. Instructions were given to ward off the unwelcome visitor. Conch shells were blown and the long, traditional horns sounded. The Yeti ambled away...

Further clues to the Abominable Snowman can certainly be found in remote monasteries of Tibet. But following a Communist takeover, Tibet has become inaccessible to foreigners.

BIGFOOT

More accessible however - although in many ways even more mysterious - are the forests and mountains making up the wilderness that covers the entire west coast of North America. Throughout that wild terrain lurk creatures of no known species. Yet over the years they have become widely known, and been given the familiar name of Bigfoot.

In 1851 the first recorded newspaper report of such a creature was published. Strangely, it was not a report from the West Coast, where most Bigfoot sightings have since been made, but in Greene County, Arkansas. This 'animal bearing the unmistakable likeness of humanity' was thought to be a 'survivor of the earthquake which devastated the area in 1811'. The creature was seen chasing a herd of cattle.

The Arkansas Bigfoot was observed chasing cattle - the Himalayan Yeti is said to be a menace to yak herds

---

No less an eminence than President Theodore Roosevelt recounted another early Bigfoot sighting. In 1903 the president, a keen hunter, retold the story of two trappers in the Salmon River district of Idaho who were attacked by a mysterious creature.

In 1924 came the most dramatic encounter with a Bigfoot so far recounted. Albert Ostman, also a lumberman, from Langley, British Columbia, said he had been camping opposite Vancouver Island when he was snatched by a giant Bigfoot. Ostman said the beast picked him up, still in his sleeping bag, and carried him 'like a sack of potatoes' for approximately three hours to its lair.

As dawn broke, Ostman realized that he was being held by four Bigfeet - male and female adults, and a pair of male and female children. He still had his rifle with him, but was reluctant to use it since the ape-like family had done him no harm. He also still had a few cans of food and other provisions that were buried in his sleeping bag. These he consumed while in captivity. The Bigfoot family, meanwhile, collected spruce tips, sweet grass and roots for their meals.

The lumberman was given reasonable freedom of the valley in which he was held, although always followed by at least two of the creatures. But eventually, fearing that he had been kidnapped as a possible husband for the female child, he took the opportunity to escape. He fed the largest (8 ft tall) Bigfoot some snuff and, while the creature rushed to bury his face in a stream, Ostman fled.

Reports of man-like beasts on the North American continent go back as far as the early 1800s. Indians told settlers stories about the wild, hairy creatures of the forests. They described them as being about 8 ft tall, with a broad chest and shoulders but virtually no neck.

But it was not until the early years of the nineteenth century that the first European, explorer David Thomas, discovered evidence of the strange animal - in the shape of footprints at least 14 in long, near Jasper, Alberta.

Above: *An expedition's tent on a glacier beneath the peak of Everest. One of the mountain's challengers was the first European to see a Yeti, in 1921.*

Above: *Edmund Hillary and Sherpa Tenzing, the conquerors of Everest, photographed returning in triumph in July 1953. Hillary found footprints but remained sceptical about the yeti.*

He had been held captive for an entire week but, fearing ridicule, did not tell his story for some time. And when he did, it seemed incredible...except for the many later pieces of evidence which backed his descriptions of the Bigfeet.

Lumberman Albert Ostman was carried by a giant male Bigfoot for over three hours until it reached its lair

---

At Mica Mountain, British Columbia in 1955 occurred one of the clearest sightings so far of a Bigfoot. It was made by William Roe, who was cunningly hidden in a bush when a female Bigfoot, standing about 6 ft tall, approached.

The massive creature, weighing around 300 lb, was unaware that she was being watched. When she got to within 20 feet of Roe she actually squatted by the bush in which he was hiding. This enabled Roe to make a thorough study.

He noted the shape of her head, what kind of face and hair she had, a description of her body and the way she walked. So extraordinary was the Bigfoot that Roe fleetingly wondered whether he had unwittingly stepped on to a film set.

His report of the encounter continued:

Finally, the wild thing must have got my scent, for it looked directly at me through an opening in the bush. A look of amazement crossed its face. It looked so comical at that moment I had to grin. Still in a crouched position, it backed up three or four short steps, then straightened up to its full height and started to walk rapidly back the way it had come. For a moment it watched me over its shoulders as it went, not exactly afraid, but as though it wanted no contact with anything strange.

Roe admitted that at the time he considered shooting this unique creature as proof of its existence. He even got to the point of raising his rifle and aiming. But Roe could not fire. 'Although I have called the creature "it", I feel now that it was a human being. And I knew I would never forgive myself if I killed it.'

BREAKTHROUGH

The big breakthrough in the hunt for Bigfoot came on 20 October 1967. Roger Patterson, a former rodeo cowboy and rancher, was tracking the forests around Bluff Creek with an Indian friend, Bob Gimlin. They emerged into a clearing and, beside a creek, saw what they judged to be a female Bigfoot ambling along the bank. Patterson grabbed his 16mm movie camera and shot an amazing 29 feet of colour film as she loped across his field of vision. The pair also took casts of footprints left by the beast.

The shaky film was shown worldwide and most experts believed it to be genuine. But one copy was given to Bigfoot investigator Dr Napier, who believed that a hoax had been perpetrated. He wrote in his report: 'The upper part of the body bears some resemblance to an ape and the lower half is typically human. It is almost impossible to conceive that such structural hybrids could exist in nature. One half of the animal must be artificial.'

This leading expert on Bigfoot does have the final, convincing word on the mystery, however. He wrote: 'North American Bigfoot or Sasquatch has a lot going for it. Too many claim to have seen it, or at least to have seen footprints, to dismiss its reality out of hand.'